Markets and Medicine

Markets and Medicine

The Politics of Health Care
Reform in Britain, Germany,
and the United States

Susan Giaimo

Ann Arbor

THE UNIVERSITY OF MICHIGAN PRESS

2005   2004   2003   2002   4   3   2   1

A CIP catalog record for this book is available from the British Library.

Library of Congress Cataloging-in-Publication Data

Giaimo, Susan.
    Markets and medicine : the politics of health care reform in
Britain, Germany, and the United States / Susan Giaimo.
        p.   cm.
    Includes bibliographical references and index.
    ISBN 0-472-11271-6 (cloth : alk. paper)
    1. Medical policy—United States.   2. Health care
reform—United States.   3. Medical policy—Germany.   4. Health
care reform—Germany.   5. Medical policy—Great Britain.   6.
Health care reform—Great Britain.
    [DNLM: 1. Health Care Reform—economics—Germany.   2. Health
Care Reform—economics—Great Britain.   3. Health Care
Reform—economics—United States.   4. Health
policy—economics—Germany.   5. Health Policy—economics—Great
Britain.   6. Health Policy—economics—United States.   WA 540 FA1
G429m   2002]   I. Title.
RA394 .G52   2002
362.1—dc21   2001008275

for Henry

Table of Contents

Tables

Acknowledgments

This book, which has its origins in a dissertation, would not have been possible without the assistance and support of a number of individuals and institutions. Financing for field research on the dissertation in 1991–92 came from two sources. The Fulbright Commission awarded me a travel grant to Germany and arranged for institutional affiliation with the Johann-Wolfgang-Goethe Universität in Frankfurt am Main. The Steuben-Schurz-Gesellschaft provided financial support through the Berlin Air-Lift Scholarship (Luftbrückenstipendium). In addition, a Wisconsin Alumni Research Foundation Fellowship from the University of Wisconsin–Madison gave me the much-needed time and financial support to write up the dissertation results.

A number of sources provided financial and institutional support that allowed me to complete my research and writing on the book. The Robert Wood Johnson Foundation awarded me a generous postdoctoral fellowship through its Scholars in Health Policy Research Program at the University of California at Berkeley and the University of California at San Francisco from 1994 through 1996. This fellowship also financed conference and research trips to Germany and Britain in 1995. I wish to thank all those associated with the this postdoctoral program, especially Eileen Connor, Alan Cohen, Hal Luft, Richard Scheffler, and Franci Duitch. A Robert Bosch Foundation Scholars Program in Comparative Public Policy and Comparative Institutions fellowship allowed me research time at the American Institute for Contemporary German Studies (AICGS) at Johns Hopkins University in the fall of 1997. I thank Carl Lankowski, the AICGS director at that time. The Minda de Gunzburg Center for European Studies at Harvard University provided me with a short-term opportunity grant that financed a research trip to Germany in January 1998. Abby Collins of the Center provided helpful encouragement and assistance. The Massachusetts Institute of Technology provided me with financial and institutional support to conduct research on my book. The German-American Academic Council and the Social Science Research Council granted financial support to undertake collaborative research on health policy with Dr. Philip Manow in 1997.

I am also grateful to a number of individuals and institutions who provided me with invaluable advice and assistance in my research over the years. Dr. Albrecht Magen, president of the Steuben-Schurz-Gesellschaft, provided contacts for me to interview for my dissertation research. Klaus Scheunemann of the Steuben-Schurz-Gesellschaft also came to my aid and arranged several important interview contacts for me during the dissertation research. Even more valuable was the hospitality he and his family provided me, which made for an enjoyable year in Germany. Dr. Hans Ulrich-Deppe and his colleagues at the Institut für Medizinische Soziologie at the Johann-Wolfgang-Goethe Universität discussed my work with me. Dr. Deppe also allowed me the use of his institute library. Professor Josef Esser of the Johann-Wolfgang-Goethe Universität provided helpful advice during my stay at the university in 1991–92, as did the students in his graduate research seminar. Mathias Wismar and Marian Döhler also provided insightful comments and advice. Researchers at the King's Fund Institute in London offered feedback on my research and granted me access to the institute library. Guy Howland, policy director of the Institute of Health Services Management in London, also met with me to discuss my work in 1995. Donald Light suggested a number of contacts for me to interview in Britain in 1995. Many thanks to Rudolf Klein, who engaged me in illuminating discussions of British health policy during my research visits to Britain in 1992 and 1995. Christopher Ham also discussed the NHS reforms with me during my first visit. I am also grateful to Rainer Müller of the Center for Social Policy Research at the University of Bremen for inviting me to a conference that he organized on comparative health policy in May 1995 and to his colleagues for providing me with accommodations during my stay. Wolfgang Streeck, Fritz Scharpf, and Renate Mayntz, the directors of the Max Planck Institute for the Study of Societies in Cologne, Germany, kindly permitted me to be a visiting scholar there in 1995 and 1998. Researchers at the Max Planck Institute also discussed my research with me, and Jürgen Feick and his colleagues granted me access to his newspaper archive of German health policy and politics. The Institute of Economics, Economy Policy Research Institute at the University of Hanover, Germany, provided institutional support in January 1998 and an opportunity to discuss my work with researchers there. I also thank Peter Lutz for answering my questions on German health insurance.

A number of people read my work and provided me with helpful guidance on my research over the years. My thanks begin with those at the University of Wisconsin–Madison, particularly my dissertation committee: Leon Lindberg, Graham Wilson, Odin Anderson, John Witte, and Karl Kronebusch. Wolfgang Streeck also gave useful advice and ideas and made penetrating comments on the dissertation chapters. Rockwell Schulz provided me invaluable direction in the early stages of my research. I also thank Jonah Levy, who read an earlier draft of the book manuscript, and the anonymous reviewers whose comments on the manuscript greatly improved the book. Paul Pierson's comments on a related chapter and article served me well in refining and sharpening my argument for the book. Harry West read a draft of the introduction. Cathie Jo Martin provided helpful suggestions, as did David Kirp and my colleagues in the Robert Wood Johnson postdoctoral program, especially Kelly Devers, Ruth Given, John Wilkerson, and Jon Oberlander. I want to give a special thanks to John Zysman, who was a true mentor in every sense of the word.

The book could not have been completed without invaluable assistance from a number of persons. Hanna Albert did careful translations of German interviews and transcriptions of these and British interviews. Chavi Nana also transcribed interviews. Andrew Sung initially set up my newspaper data base on health policy. Steve Lamola and Maisha Gray contributed thorough and careful research assistance on the data base, and Joelle Rogers completed it. Linda Howe provided copyediting suggestions for several draft chapters. I am greatly indebted to the editors and production staff at the University of Michigan Press, especially Rebecca McDermott, who believed the book was worth publishing and initially secured the contract; Ellen McCarthy, for subsequently shepherding it through the production process with patience, professionalism, and good humor; and Marcia LaBrenz for her patient assistance at the copyediting stage.

I must also thank friends and colleagues for their moral and intellectual support. I am profoundly indebted to Philip Manow. Through our collaboration on research and countless discussions, I have learned an enormous amount not only about German health care policy but also German social policy and politics more generally. But even more important have been the friendship and hospitality that he, Christiane Borgwardt, and their children—Nick, Meike, and Tilman—have provided over the years. Thanks also to Ulrike Schneider for arranging interview contacts and institutional support at Hanover in 1998, for extending me her hospitality during my visit, and for enhancing my understanding of German health care through many discussions and our collaboration at the AICGS. Elizabeth Jones and Caroline Pare kindly gave me shelter (and a Rolling Stones ticket) during my 1995 visit to London. Thanks also to Maribeth Kazmierczak for her friend-

ship and invaluable advice on interviewing, Ralf and Barbara Henneking for
their hospitality in Bonn, and Andreas Etges for computer support at a critical time and for his ongoing friendship. I am also grateful to Stuart White,
Dan Kryder, and Ann Raffin for their friendship and advice. Thanks also to
Helen Ray and Pam Clemens.

In addition to these friends, others have helped me keep things in
proper perspective and have provided much-needed respite from the toil of
research and writing. Among them are Wendy Larson, Tim Gallagher,
Courtney Hayes and her family, Hal and Carol Hansen, Dan Schneider and
Donna Fabiani, Andrea Bailey, Paula Mohan, Kathleen Stemper, Rhonda
Plotkin, and the rest of the Milwaukee crowd. Kelly Devers and Kristin Car-
man have provided friendship and advice over the years and hospitality
during my research in Washington, D.C.

My biggest thanks go to my family for their love and encouragement
throughout this project, especially my mom, Marilyn Giaimo; my siblings,
Mary, Kathy, and Mark; my brother-in-law, Gary; the Wends (David,
Alice, El, Chris, Tammy); and my dad, Sam, who lived life to the fullest and
in so doing showed me what really matters. Finally, my appreciation and
love go to my husband, Henry Wend, and my son, Sam Wend, not merely
for bearing with me on this project, but for sharing their lives with me.
Their presence served as a gentle reminder of what is most important in
life. Were it not for Henry's reading of numerous drafts of the chapters, and
his untiring encouragement, love, and coparenting, this book would still be
unfinished. So I dedicate it to him.

Common Abbreviations Used in the Text

AAHP	American Association of Health Plans
AALL	American Association of Labor Legislation
AFL	American Federation of Labor
AMA	American Medical Association
ARM	Annual Representative Meeting of the BMA
ASI	Adam Smith Institute
BÄK	Bundesärztekammer (Federal Chamber of Physicians)
BMA	British Medical Association
BMAS	Bundesministerium für Arbeit und Sozialordnung (Federal Ministry of Labor and Social Affairs)
BMG	Bundesministerium für Gesundheit (Federal Ministry of Health)
BMJ	*British Medical Journal*
BPI	Bundesverband der pharmazeutischen Industrie (Federal Association of the Pharmaceutical Industry)
CBO	Congressional Budget Office
CCHMS/ CCSC	Central Committee for Hospital Medical Services (renamed the Central Consultants and Specialists Committee)
CDU	Christian Democratic Union (Germany)
CHC	Community health council
CHI	Commission for Health Improvement
CMA	California Medical Association
CPS	Centre for Policy Studies

CSU	Christian Social Union (Germany)
DGB	Deutsche Gewerkschaftsbund (German Federation of Trade Unions)
DHA	District Health Authority
DHHS	Department of Health and Human Services (U.S.)
DHSS	Department of Health and Social Security (U.K.)
DMU	Directly managed unit
DoH	Department of Health (U.K.)
DRG	Diagnosis related group
ERISA	Employee Retirement and Income Security Act
FDP	Free Democratic Party (Germany)
FHSA	Family Health Services Authority
FPC	Family Practitioner Committee
GMSC	General Medical Services Committee
GP	General practitioner
GRG	Gesundheitsreformgesetz (Health Care Reform Act), 1988
GSG	Gesundheitsstrukturgesetz (Health Care Structural Reform Act), 1992
HB	Hartmannbund
HIP	Health Improvement Program
HMO	Health maintenance organization
IEA	Institute of Economic Affairs
IHSM	Institute of Health Services Management
JCC	Joint Consultants Committee
KAG	Konzertierte Aktion im Gesundheitswesen (Concerted Action in Health Care)
KBV	Kassenärztliche Bundesvereinigung (Federal Association of Sickness Fund Physicians)
KV	Kassenärztliche Vereinigung (Association of Sickness Fund Physicians)

LMC	Local Medical Committee
MCO	Managed care organization
ME	NHS Management Executive
MSA	Medical savings account
NFIB	National Federation of Independent Business
NHI	National health insurance
NHS	National Health Service
NICE	National Institute of Clinical Excellence
NOGs	Neuordnungsgesetze (Health Care Reorganization Acts), 1997
PCG	Primary Care Group
PPO	Preferred provider organization
PSO	Physician-sponsored organization
PSRO	Professional standards review organization
RB	Representative Body of the BMA
RHA	Regional Health Authority
RVO	Reichsversicherungsordnung (Imperial Insurance Code; later known as the SGB V, or Sozialgesetzbuch 5, the Fifth Book of the Social Law)
SME	Social market economy (*soziale Marktwirtschaft*)
SPD	Social Democratic Party (Germany)
SRM	Special Representative Meeting of the BMA

Introduction

Cost Containment and the Governance
of Health Care

In all advanced industrial societies, the political settlements around social protection that have underpinned postwar capitalism are facing enormous pressures. With the onset of slower economic growth in the mid-1970s, these systems of social protection—whether statutory welfare states or private arrangements—have come under growing fiscal strain. In addition, major socioeconomic and demographic changes have created new social risks alongside older ones. All of these conditions place growing demands on systems of social provision to meet these needs. Furthermore, the costs of social spending have increasingly become bound up with broader concerns over economic competitiveness and efforts at economic adjustment. In short, systems of social protection are up for reform and renegotiation.

The struggles over the new terms of these bargains have provided high drama. In western Europe, welfare state reform was the flash point for electoral battles, strikes, and demonstrations in the 1990s. In the United States, efforts to slash spending on statutory health care programs provoked political brinkmanship from Democrats and Republicans alike, culminating in two high-profile government shutdowns in 1995 and 1996. But such conflicts were not confined to statutory welfare states. President Clinton's ill-fated effort to transform the private fringe-benefit health care system into a national insurance program transformed the political landscape with the Democrats' subsequent loss of Congress, and it opened up a broader debate over the parameters of social provision and the role of government and private actors. Even where efforts to reform systems of social protection have been less dramatic, the consequences have been no less important. This is because such restructuring involves similar questions about the proper role of the state, the market, societal interests, and the individual in protecting against the hardships of economic insecurity, illness, and old age.

But exactly how are the social bargains underpinning capitalism changing? Public debates and the scholarly literature on welfare state reform provide us with only partial answers. Public debates all too often take the form of simple arguments pitting proponents of market solutions against those advocating an active state role in social provision. But conducting the debate in these terms ignores the reality that markets in practice have required vigorous state action to create or maintain them. The debate also fails to acknowledge that there are alternative arrangements to the market and the state in financing, providing, and administering social programs.

Much of the academic literature on the nature of welfare state reform in the contemporary period also suffers from a narrow focus. The scholarly literature thus far has tended to focus on the question of retrenchment and has overwhelmingly confined its analysis to statutory welfare state programs. But efforts to rewrite the political bargains underpinning capitalism not only concern questions of coverage or levels of generosity of social programs. They also involve fundamental political questions of governance whereby policymakers seek to control sectoral actors—especially providers of services—in order to realize cost-containment objectives. Such challenges to providers are occurring in both private and public systems of social protection.

This book explores how advanced industrial countries have sought to recast the governance arrangements underlying their capitalist bargains in health care since the late 1980s, and the extent to which such efforts involve the use of markets or other instruments to control sectoral actors. Health care reform provides an excellent window through which to investigate such transformations. First, health care comprises a major share of social provision in all advanced industrial societies and consumes a significant portion of gross domestic product in most of these nations. Thus, the costs of health care spending have been a cause for concern. In addition, health care systems provide a substantial share of employment, so that cost-containment efforts have important repercussions on the broader economy.[1] Furthermore, because health care can involve basic questions of life and death, efforts to alter health care systems arouse considerable public anxiety. Finally, efforts to reform the capitalist settlements in health care have not only involved questions of access or financing or levels of coverage but also governance. This is because health care systems have crystallized political bargains with doctors that accorded them important roles in policymaking and administration and that accommodated their professional autonomy. In the 1990s, governments and private payers hoping to control health care outlays challenged the terms of these bargains and provoked bitter conflicts with the medical profession.

Britain, Germany, and the United States serve as case studies to explore how cost-containment reforms have sought to alter health care governance. In each country, the medical profession exerted enormous influence and autonomy in policy-making and health care system administration, and policymakers in all three countries sought to curb medical power and autonomy in an effort to rein in health care costs. Moreover, markets were a feature in each country's reform project. But the case selection conforms to the "most different systems" approach of comparative analysis (Marmor, Bridges, and Hoffman 1983), which allows us to explore whether or how different health care or political institutions produced similar or distinctive responses to the common pressure for cost containment.

First, each country had a distinctive health care system with specific governance arrangements involving doctors, payers, and the state. In Britain's National Health Service (NHS), the central state financed and provided health care and governed the health sector through a hierarchical administrative apparatus. But alongside this state hierarchy, corporatist arrangements granted the medical profession an official role in policy-making and administration. In Germany, the federal government played a less direct role in the health care system. Its primary responsibility lay in setting the basic parameters of statutory national insurance, and it delegated to associations of doctors and insurers the public authority to implement policy and administer the health care system on its behalf. In the United States, the government's presence in the health sector was even further circumscribed. Public insurance programs only covered specific groups of the population, while a private, voluntary, fringe-benefit system provided health care for most Americans. Though this meant that employers and private insurers were prominent actors in deciding questions of health care coverage, power in running the health care system lay primarily with the medical profession. But rather than possessing an official role in policy-making, doctors exerted their power and autonomy largely at the level of the individual practitioner.

Second, even though each country sought to curb doctors in the quest for cost containment, their reform approaches showed considerable variation in terms of the mixtures of governance instruments and their effects on medical power. And even though markets were part of their reform projects, their markets differed in terms of the actors who introduced them, their goals, their targets, and the permissible scope and degree of competition. In Britain, Margaret Thatcher sought to smash the corporatist bases of medical power through the discipline of market competition. Yet Britain ended up with a new governance regime that strengthened central state control, limited competition, and circumscribed but did not destroy corporatism. In Germany, the Christian-Liberal government of Helmut Kohl followed an even more eclectic approach that combined markets, corporatism, and direct state intervention in health care administration. But rather than seeking to destroy corporatism and substitute it with the market, Kohl sought to save it by repairing its defects. Moreover, he continued to work through corporatism to discipline doctors. The market experiment was in fact a cautious affair targeted at insurers that left the corporatist position of the medical profession intact. In the United States, Bill Clinton attempted a bold program of government-led market reform and national insurance. His plan would not only have placed new controls on medical power, it would also have enhanced government authority at the expense of employers and private insurers. Though Clinton did not realize his ambitions, reform nonetheless continued. But it was a market reform led by private payers in a largely unregulated fashion, and the market they unleashed transformed governance arrangements with physicians in profound ways.

The reasons for these different reform outcomes lay in the specific constellation of actors and institutions in the political and health care systems of each country that underpinned the capitalist settlement in health care. Together, they created distinct reform politics in each nation that produced different mixtures of governance instruments and that proved more or less amenable to market solutions. Formal institutions and the balance of political forces in the political arena either granted or denied health care stakeholders entry to the policy process to shape reform and thus affected the capacity of governments to formulate and enact a radical market program.

However, the political arena tells only part of the story of health care reform. A full explanation requires that we look also at the health sector itself and its interplay with the political arena. Thus, existing policies and institutional arrangements in the health sector both created and reinforced certain expectations on the part of the public and stakeholders as to the appropriateness of state intervention in the health sector. The statutory, universal systems of Britain and Germany created public expectations of state intervention to safeguard solidarity and prevent market-driven inequities. By contrast, key stakeholders in private system of health care provision in the United States viewed such state intervention as illegitimate. In addition, the governance arrangements in the health care systems of Britain and Germany provided policymakers with the institutional capacity to control the behavior of sectoral actors and thus control the scope and pace of market reform. In the United States, Clinton's health plan would have provided the government with the institutional wherewithal to regulate the market behavior of sectoral actors. But the legislative demise of the president's proposal deprived government actors of the necessary institutional linkages through which to control and shape the process of market reform in the private health care system.

The rest of this chapter further develops the argument. The first section addresses the shortcomings in much of the welfare state literature, namely, its focus on statutory social programs and its insufficient attention to governance aspects of reform efforts. The second section discusses how the capitalist settlements in health care institutionalized particular governance arrangements with doctors in each country. The third section traces the growing fiscal pressures on health care systems and explains both why governments and private actors assigned much of the blame for health care inflation on the medical profession and also why they saw markets as the solution to the cost problem. The final section presents each nation's reform response and explains their particular reform approach in greater detail.

The Limited Scope of Welfare State Studies

The Diversity of Welfare Capitalism

Postwar capitalism in the advanced industrial societies has been undergirded by political settlements that accepted the market mechanism to allocate resources but demanded some level of social protection against its devastating economic inequalities and insecurities. Social protection arrangements that limit the market have been essential to its survival, ensuring the reproduction of the work force and preventing or ameliorating social misery (Polanyi 1944). And though the welfare state is usually associated with the task of social protection, it is also embedded in markets and critical to the efficiency of the economy (Esping-Andersen 1994; Titmuss 1987a).

The phrase *Keynesian welfare state* is the shorthand for these postwar settlements, but this designation belies the diversity of institutional arrangements and division of labor among state, private-market, and societal actors in social protection. Esping-Andersen (1990), for example, has identified three ideal-type welfare state regimes: the social democratic, conservative corporatist, and liberal. In the social democratic welfare state, the state plays a prominent role in financing and providing services. In the corporatist welfare state, associations representing labor, employers, or other functional groups finance and administer compulsory and universal social insurance programs. In the liberal welfare state, public welfare programs are residual and targeted to specific groups outside the labor market, leaving most individuals to rely on the market for social provision.

The health care systems examined in this book are also critical parts of social protection and roughly correspond to these welfare state regimes. Germany's national health insurance scheme, with its payroll financing and administration by quasi-public groups representing labor, employers, and professional interests, is one of the main pillars of the corporatist welfare state. In the United States, the prominence of employer-provided fringe benefits alongside limited public health insurance programs conforms to the liberal welfare state regime. Britain does not fit easily into Esping-Andersen's schema. Britain's Beveridge welfare state combines liberal and social democratic elements. However, with its state administration and ownership, tax financing, and universalistic coverage, the NHS is closer to the social democratic pole.

Despite this rich institutional diversity in social provision, most studies of the welfare state have confined their analysis to statutory programs. This strict demarcation of the welfare state is warranted in order to avoid diluting the concept to include all manner of actors and policy domains, which would render it useless as an analytical tool.[2] But an exclusive focus on statutory programs overlooks the importance of private, occupational fringe-benefit systems that may complement, substitute, or compensate for limited public provision. It is encouraging to note the development of studies of private welfare arrangements that preserve the analytical distinction between these and statutory welfare states and that explore their interaction with public programs (see Rein 1996; Shalev 1996; Stevens 1988).

An exclusive focus on the statutory welfare state also overlooks other actors who play important roles in social protection. For instance, families—and especially women—have played critical roles in caring for children and elders. But with some notable exceptions (Esping-Andersen 1999; Gordon 1990; Orloff 1993; Sainsbury 1994), most of the welfare state literature has downplayed or ignored the caring contribution of women to the household and broader economy largely because it has gone uncompensated.[3] Other actors play important roles in social protection. In Germany's corporatist welfare state, for example, churches and associations representing the professions have legally recognized roles in administering welfare state programs and as "parapublic institutions" (Katzenstein 1987) occupy a space somewhere in between public and private. The United States relies on the nonprofit sector to provide social welfare services (Salamon 1992; Smith and Lipsky 1993).

In short, efforts to reform systems of social protection may target these nonstate actors and institutions and may have as much an impact on society as reform of statutory programs. In the United States, where employer-provided fringe benefits cover the bulk of the population, changes in the coverage or rules governing these programs arguably affect more people than do reforms in public social insurance programs. The erosion of private arrangements for social welfare, either through the family or employer-provided fringe benefits, may generate new demands for public policy interventions. To ignore such changes because they fall outside the public welfare state would miss an important part of the transformation of the capitalist bargain in those countries that rely on nonstate arrangements.

Moreover, to the extent that governments in countries with more generous statutory welfare states are encouraging citizens to rely more on private provision (as in pensions) or considering doing so, there is all the more reason to study reforms in these occupationally based or private forms of social protection. Private actors may have greater freedom of action to determine benefits and eligibility and may operate under different rules than governments or quasi-public authorities of statutory welfare states. Governments may find it more difficult to control the behavior of private financiers and providers of social services. In addition, the character of social rights may differ in critical respects between private arrangements and statutory, universal ones. Identifying and understanding the implications of these differences for social provision warrant a comparison of public and private systems of social protection.

For all these reasons, I use the term *systems of social protection,* rather than relying on an overly broad conception of the welfare state. *Systems of social protection* acknowledges the range of institutional variation in the settlements underpinning capitalism. It also allows for a comparison of the statutory, universal health care systems of Britain and Germany with the private, employer-provided fringe-benefit system of health insurance in the United States. But the term recognizes that there may be important differences in state capacity to govern public and private arrangements, in notions of social citizenship, and in the distribution of benefits and burdens that may make private systems insufficient substitutes for statutory welfare states. Moreover, it allows for an examination of the interrelationships between public and private arrangements.

The Nature of Reform in Systems of Social Protection

A further shortcoming in the literature on the welfare state is its restrictive conception of policy change that ignores transformations of governance arrangements. First, many welfare state studies are concerned with measuring "welfare state effort" (Wilensky 1975) or retrenchment in social programs, and they use macrolevel quantitative indicators such as levels of public spending or proportion of gross domestic product to social spending (ibid.; Stephens, Huber, and Ray 1999). Others measure changes to the welfare state in terms of the size of public sector employment (Clayton and Pontusson 1998). Pierson (1994), however, employs more nuanced measures of welfare state retrenchment. He distinguishes programmatic retrenchment, which involves lower benefit levels and tighter eligibility rules in specific programs, from systemic retrenchment, in which modifications in the broader policy environment, such as ballooning public deficits or public discourses that denigrate "big government," erode support for social spending in the future. In short, he considers structural and political causes of retrenchment. Using the mix between public and private financing as a measure of retrenchment, he has concluded that Western welfare states changed very little up through the 1980s (Pierson 1994, 1995).

These studies are valuable because they measure broad trends in social spending across and within nations over time. Because they show that the basic contours of the welfare state and its component programs have largely remained in place, they suggest that predictions of the welfare state's imminent demise are premature. But they do not tell the entire story of policy change in systems of social protection. Quantitative measures of macrolevel shifts in spending often fail to capture qualitative changes occurring in the delivery of social services or in governance arrangements at the microlevel. These qualitative changes are not trivial. Transformations in delivery systems or in the power relations among state and sectoral actors may have considerable bearing on the costs, quality, and accessibility of welfare services. Furthermore, conceiving of welfare state change in terms of retrenchment can lead us into a cul-de-sac. Some reforms—such as deep spending cuts—may simply be exercises in retrenchment. But some may be serious efforts to restructure welfare states and make them responsive to new demands, not to dismember them.

Furthermore, some of the biggest changes taking place in systems of social protection involve efforts to rewrite the underlying governance arrangements between the state and sectoral actors and to redefine the power relationships among these actors themselves. Studies that explore whether retrenchment is occurring, and that focus on spending levels or eligibility rules, cannot capture reform efforts that target the power and prerogatives of sectoral actors.

Modes of Governance in Health Care

Governance refers to the ways that policymakers try to manage, coordinate, or control the activities of sectoral actors (Lindberg, Campbell, and Hollingsworth 1991). Different governance arrangements guide the behavior of sectoral actors in different ways. Streeck and Schmitter (1985) have identified four ideal-type governance regimes.[4] Thus, in a community, principles of spontaneous solidarity guide families. In the market, dispersed competition guides firms. Under statism, public officials coordinate societal actors through a hierarchical chain of command. Finally, under associationalism (better known as corporatism), the state delegates authority to a limited number of functional interest groups or sectoral or professional associations to implement policy on its behalf (ibid., 128, 134).

These and other modes of governance may be present in a health care system. But in the health sector, a critical question confronting policymakers has been the proper reach of medical power. The health care systems in Britain, Germany, and the United States crystallized political settlements with doctors that accorded them substantial influence in policy-making and health care administration as well as accommodating their professional autonomy, but in distinctive ways. In Britain and Germany, corporatist bargains with doctors granted the medical profession an official and privileged place in sectoral governance and a measure of autonomy, but at the same time attempted to set boundaries to medical influence. In the United States, a professional model of sectoral governance did not accord the medical profession similar public status in policy-making and governance. Nor did it provide state actors with many controls over medical power. Indeed, the distinguishing feature of the bargain in the United States was the enormous freedom of action it permitted individual doctors. But before discussing how these particular bargains operated in the health care system, it is useful to describe corporatism's potential as a governance instrument that privileges yet sets limits to the power of organized interests.

Corporatism as a Tool of Governance

Under corporatism, the state confers upon groups representing major economic or functional interests an officially recognized role, or "public status," in policy-making and administration (or what Offe has termed "political status"), whereby they share in the "state's authority to make and enforce binding decisions" on policy (Streeck and Schmitter 1985, 131).[5] The state accords these associations a privileged place in negotiating policy, which often implies more than mere consultation, and delegates authority to them to implement public policy on its behalf. These organizations are also accorded considerable latitude to determine how to implement policies and to run the sector (Schmitter 1989; Streeck and Schmitter 1985, 127–29; see also Cawson 1986, chap. 2; Eckstein 1960, 22–25).

This privileged inclusion in policy-making and administration is a source of power and prestige for organized interests. At the same time, corporatism sets limits to their power in a variety of ways. Thus, in exchange for their public status, the state expects associations to control their members so that they comply with agreements reached with the state or with other negotiating partners and so that the pursuit of their collective self-interest is compatible with the aims of broader public policy (Streeck and Schmitter 1985, 127–29).[6] The state may provide associations the means to discipline the rank and file through such weapons as compulsory membership or an official monopoly of representation (Schmitter 1979). Under some variants of corporatism, state actors try to construct a system of countervailing power by requiring opposing interests to comanage the sector and to check each other (Lehmbruch 1984; Stone 1980, chap. 1). The state may also use direct measures (along a continuum of intervention) to ensure that sectoral actors implement policy. Thus, the state may mandate policies that associations must observe and implement. If they fail to do so or to ensure that their members are in compliance, state actors may then threaten more direct intervention in sectoral administration. Usually, such threats are sufficient to convince these groups to comply. But if they are not, then state actors may resort to direct administration by decree until these associations find a way to implement the laws (Streeck and Schmitter 1985, 131, 134–35). Ultimately, state actors must possess the authority and the means to decide fundamental questions about the basic parameters of their exclusive domain within the sector (procedural regulation), even as they allow associations considerable latitude to determine the details of implementation and administration (substantive regulation).[7] Of course, the state may choose to include associations in negotiations on such fundamental questions. But the authority to declare such questions its exclusive domain implies that the state must have a measure of autonomy from sectoral interests.[8] If the state lacks the means to set boundaries to the power of sectoral actors, then corporatism is vulnerable to "capture," whereby an association may come to dominate policymakers or other associations in the relationship and exploit its privileged position in governance to its advantage (ibid.; Schmitter 1985).

In practice, however, such controls and autonomy may be difficult to achieve. In ceding officially recognized roles in governance to associations, the state may become dependent on them to implement its policies and lack administrative alternatives to do so itself. In addition, their role in sectoral administration may lead associations to claim for themselves a right to negotiate policies, which state actors may find difficult to deny. Political factors may also limit state autonomy. The political system may grant sectoral actors entry to the policy process through a number of channels—and these actors may be important constituencies of the governing parties that policymakers may find difficult to ignore.

The foregoing describes a strong version of corporatism, but corporatism displays some variation. For instance, weaker forms involving less compulsion on the part of the state or associations exist.[9] Corporatism can also exist at different levels of the economy or society, in a variety of policy domains, and may involve a broad or narrow range of sectoral interests.[10] State actors can play a range of roles in corporatism, from negotiating policies directly with sectoral interests, to facilitating agreement among sectoral actors by offering concessions to grease the wheels of exchange, to enforcing agreements. The British and German variants of corporatism in the health sector have differed on these dimensions, with different consequences for their effectiveness as a governance instrument.

Professionalism is an alternative form of associational governance that differs from corporatism in important respects. Whereas under corporatism, the state accords organized interests an official role in policy-making and administration, it does not do so under the professional model. Indeed, professional associations usually resist state sponsorship or state efforts to give them responsibility for public policy as an affront to their collective freedom. In addition, the controls over individual practitioners are usually much weaker under professionalism than under corporatism. To be sure, professional associations will set ethical and educational standards and norms for the profession. They will also license practitioners to ensure that they meet these standards and to limit entry to safeguard their monopoly. But the hallmark of professionalism is the elevation and defense of individual freedom from both lay intrusion and peer review. Professional associations will not only resist state controls over their members, they will also be reluctant to discipline their own except for egregious departures from professional norms, for collective forms of organization that threaten individual practice.

In short, professionalism is quite limited in its effectiveness as an instrument of sectoral governance. Because the state does not sponsor interest organizations or delegate policy-making roles to them, it has limited authority to dictate their behavior. Rather than controlling the behavior of individual practitioners, the state and professional associations accommodate it.

Professional Autonomy and Governance

Professional autonomy has been a central concern for doctors.[11] Indeed, the political settlements between the state and physicians not only set out their respective jurisdictions in sectoral administration and policy-making but also institutionalized certain understandings of professional freedom. Doctors place a premium on autonomy because it defines them as a profession and sets them apart from other occupations. A profession is "an occupation which has assumed a dominant position in the division of labor, so that it gains control over the determination of the substance of its own work. Unlike most occupations, it is autonomous and self-directing" (Freidson 1970, xvii).

Autonomy, however, is a multidimensional concept (Schulz and Harrison 1986; Tolliday 1978). Schulz and Harrison (1986) have disaggregated autonomy into its social, economic, and clinical components. Social and economic autonomy, for example, consist of doctors' power over their choice of specialty and location of practice, their earnings, and the nature and volume of medical tasks. Clinical freedom allows doctors to accept or reject patients at will; to control diagnosis, treatment, and evaluation of patient care; and to direct the activities of other health care professionals. In addition, autonomy not only consists of several components but also varies cross-nationally as doctors have tolerated limits to their freedom in certain areas in order to preserve it in others (Döhler 1989; Schulz and Harrison 1986). Tables 1 and 2 illustrate cross-national differences in economic autonomy as measured by levels of physician remuneration.

Autonomy can also operate at individual and collective levels (Garpenby 1989; Stone 1980). For example, individual practitioners exercise clinical freedom when their treatment decisions are not subject to review by their peers or by laypersons. But medical associations also possess clinical autonomy when they have exclusive jurisdiction to review the treatment decisions of individual practitioners, to decide the content of medical education, and to set clinical standards. Medical associations may also enjoy collective autonomy in running the health sector and, to protect it from lay intrusion, may curb the freedom of individual doctors.

But for all its variation, the core of medical autonomy is clinical freedom. As Freidson notes, "so long as a profession is free of the technical evaluation and control of other occupations in the division of labor its lack of ultimate freedom from the state, and even its lack of control over the socioeconomic terms of work do not significantly change its essential character as a profession" (Freidson 1970, 25).[12] Yet it, too, is subject to limits and to exchange. Any surrender of clinical autonomy is bound to be con-

TABLE 1. Physicians' Earnings Relative to Other Occupations in the United Kingdom, Germany, and the United States, 1965–92 (ratio of physician average income to average employee compensation)

Year*	United Kingdom	Germany	United States
1965	n.a.	6.74	4.53
1971	n.a.	7.58	4.86
1977	2.19	6.36	4.11
1983	2.35	5.38	4.45
1986	2.34	5.24	4.54
1989	2.33	4.89	5.21
1992	n.a.	4.95	5.09

Source: OECD Health Data 1998.
*Years selected due to availability of comparable data for two or more countries.

TABLE 2. Physicians' Mean Gross Income in the United Kingdom, Germany, and the United States, 1965–92 ($/exchange rate)

Year*	United Kingdom	Germany	United States
1965	n.a.	15,728	28,960
1971	n.a.	33,446	45,300
1977	14,532	68,653	60,400
1983	28,320	70,428	104,100
1989	47,213	104,282	156,000
1992	n.a.	138,929	177,000

Source: OECD Health Data 1998.
*Years selected due to availability of comparable data for two or more countries.

troversial among doctors, since it cuts to the heart of their professional identity. But they are more likely to accept settlements that place outer boundaries on its exercise, such as global budgeting, rather than detailed scrutiny of their treatment decisions by lay authorities. They are also more likely to accept such monitoring when it is done by their own, rather than by outsiders.

Political Settlements between Doctors and the State in Britain, Germany, and the United States

The institutional arrangements in the health care system in each of these countries granted doctors a privileged position in health care governance and accommodated their professional autonomy in distinctive ways. They also varied in the extent to which they constrained medical influence and power.

In the British NHS, governance consisted of a hybrid of corporatism and state hierarchy (Giaimo 1995). Alongside hierarchical tiers of state managers, the British Medical Association (BMA) enjoyed a privileged, close relationship with the health ministry in negotiating policy and legally sanctioned roles in NHS administration, exemplifying what Cawson has termed *bipartite corporatism* (1982, 1986). In exchange for this official status in governance, the medical profession accepted limits to its economic and social freedom, for example, in remuneration arrangements and employment status. Yet the bargain also accommodated considerable clinical freedom that served the interests of both doctors and the state. Under the terms of an "implicit concordat," individual doctors enjoyed substantial clinical freedom as long as they respected global budgets set by the state and rationed scarce resources on its behalf (Klein 1983; 1995, 177).

However, this governance hybrid was far from symmetrical. Instead, doctors dominated the relationship, and managers largely deferred to medical judgment (Harrison 1988). At the same time, the BMA proved itself an unreliable corporatist partner with the state, incapable of controlling individual doctors and delivering them to agreements reached with the health ministry. And except in the most egregious cases, there was little scrutiny or sanction by professional bodies of poor medical decisions.

In Germany, the political settlement underpinning national health insurance was also corporatist, but of a variety that involved medical associations and insurers in a "private interest government" (Streeck and Schmitter 1985). Under this arrangement, the state usually confined itself to setting out broad policy aims in framework legislation and then delegated the task of implementation to associations of doctors and insurers, granting them legally recognized latitude to do so. The medical profession and insurers also enjoyed an official place in formulating policy with the government. In exchange for official status in governance, the state expected medical associations to curb the autonomy of their members. In contrast to the BMA, these associations had greater capacity to do so.

Yet corporatism did not always serve as an effective instrument of control. Insurers lacked the ability to act as a counterweight to medical power, and medical associations sometimes failed to discipline their own. Even so policymakers believed that corporatism's reach was too limited and that it needed to be extended to other parts of the health care system.

In the professional model of governance in the United States, the American Medical Association (AMA) and its state and local counterparts were powerful actors in policy formulation and in sectoral administration. But that power did not derive from an officially sanctioned insider status in negotiating policy. Rather, the AMA's influence in the political arena lay in its ability to marshal its considerable resources to engage in classic pressure group tactics, such as lobbying lawmakers, financing campaigns, and forging strategic alliances with other health care stakeholders to defeat legislation that threatened its vision of professional autonomy. That vision was the autonomy of the self-employed solo practitioner. Governments, private insurers, employers, and hospitals accommodated the freedom of the solo practitioner in the health care system, allowing doctors to set their own fees and treat patients as they saw fit.

The professional model was therefore even less effective in controlling the profession than corporatism was. It was also very poor at controlling health care costs. By not incorporating the AMA into policy-making, governments also had little leverage over the association or its members. And in championing the vision of solo practice, the AMA refused to set limits to the incomes or clinical freedom of its members.

Over time, governments and payers in each country grew disenchanted with these settlements. Though there were a number of reasons for the cost crisis in health care that became apparent from the mid-1970s onward, policymakers held the bargains with physicians responsible and sought to alter the terms of these arrangements. Before turning to their efforts to recast the settlements with doctors, we need to understand the sources of health care inflation and why policymakers viewed the bargains with doctors as responsible for it.

The Health Care Cost Explosion

The initial cause for alarm was the steep rise in health care outlays that coincided with the recessions of the mid-1970s. Not only was health care consuming an ever-greater share of gross domestic product, but the rate of medical inflation was accelerating and outpacing that of the general economy in many Western countries. However, our three countries did not fare identically, as tables 3 and 4 show. The United States was first in the world in health spending, while Britain was among the lowest spenders of the industrialized countries. But despite the differences, health care expenditures had become a political problem in all three countries.

A number of factors have been responsible for health care inflation, some of them common to all advanced industrial societies. Demographic developments have been a big driver of health care costs. The populations of Western countries have been aging, and older persons disproportionately suffer from both acute illnesses requiring high-tech interventions and chronic conditions entailing long-term care. Neither type of care comes cheap. At the same time, birthrates have failed to keep pace with increasing longevity, which means fewer working-age persons in the future to shoulder the growing cost of caring for their elders (OECD 1996a).[13] The health sector has also been fertile ground for costly technological innovations that save lives. Coupled with universal health care programs or widespread third-party payment by private insurers, it has been difficult to dampen demand for such treatments (Weisbrod 1985). In addition, as advanced industrial societies transition to a postindustrial economy, many of the service sector jobs replacing manufacturing employment tend to have lower productivity and wages, making it difficult to find adequate resources to finance social programs (see below) (Iversen and Wren 1998).

But health care inflation also lies in the specific design of health care systems themselves. Health care systems with a multitude of private insurers tend to have higher administrative costs than single-payer systems (Heidenheimer, Heclo, and Adams 1990, chap. 3). Health care systems that lack a way to cap spending or tie it to the economy have trouble enforcing cost discipline; instead they experience rampant cost-shifting among payers and subsectors. Those systems that do little to control supply—such as technology, medical personnel, and hospitals—and that allow patients unrestricted access to them also have higher costs than those systems with strong controls.

The political settlements with doctors have also been responsible for health care inflation. Health care systems with open-ended fee-for-service remuneration arrangements reward doctors for providing care rather than withholding it. They also have more trouble controlling the volume of services than do fixed prospective arrangements like capitation (which encourages fewer services) or salary (which decouples volume of services from physician income). Fee-for-service arrangements may also tempt doctors to use their superior medical knowledge to generate their own

TABLE 3. Health Care Spending as a Percentage of Gross Domestic Product in the United Kingdom, Germany, and the United States, 1960–97

Year	United Kingdom	Germany	United States
1960	3.9	4.8	5.2
1965	4.1	4.6	5.9
1970	4.5	6.3	7.3
1975	5.5	8.8	8.2
1980	5.6	8.8	9.1
1985	5.9	9.3	10.6
1990	6.0	8.7	12.6
1991	6.5	9.4	13.4
1992	6.9	9.9	13.9
1993	6.9	10.0	14.1
1994	6.9	10.0	14.1
1995	6.9	10.4	14.1
1996	6.9	10.5	14.0
1997	6.7	10.4	14.0

Source: OECD Health Data 1998.

TABLE 4. Per Capita Health Care Spending in the United Kingdom, Germany, and the United States, 1960–97

Year	United Kingdom	Germany	United States
1960	54	48	149
1965	76	78	212
1970	99	149	357
1975	229	467	605
1980	537	913	1,086
1985	472	743	1,798
1990	1,024	1,650	2,799
1991	1,129	2,018	3,035
1992	1,252	2,433	3,276
1993	1,112	2,350	3,468
1994	1,213	2,533	3,628
1995	1,313	3,080	3,767
1996	1,358	3,017	3,898
1997	1,457	2,677	4,090

Source: OECD Health Data 1998.

demand and incomes by providing patients with treatments they may not need (Cromwell and Mitchell 1986). In the Western health care systems in the postwar period, the supremacy of the "biomedical model" privileged curative care and the use of expensive surgical and high-technology procedures in hospitals over preventive and primary care in less expensive outpatient settings (Estes, Wallace, and Binney 1989). This model also legitimated and institutionalized the structural dominance of the medical profession in the health care system, its control over allied health professionals, and the deference on the part of lay authorities to medical expertise.

Policymakers, payers, and health policy analysts increasingly held doctors responsible for much of the cost spiral in the health care system. Some faulted their privileged role in policy-making and administration as giving doctors a toehold from which to deflect or block policies that threatened their interests. In some countries, physicians' high incomes were an issue; in others, doctors' freedom to enter lucrative specialties and the concomitant devaluation of primary care were cause for concern.

Most important, clinical freedom increasingly came under fire. By virtue of their (near) monopoly on prescribing, performing surgery, hospitalizing patients, and providing many other kinds of medical treatments, physicians were the pivotal actors who determined how health care resources were used. The sum total of their treatment decisions in large part determined the total volume of health care services, hence, the total costs of the health care system (Anderson 1985; Wilsford 1991).[14] Also problematic was evidence showing enormous variation in rates of surgery for the same diagnosis that could not be explained by the condition of the patients or other scientific criteria (Wennberg 1984; Yates 1987). This suggested that doctors were making treatment decisions with little regard to their clinical effectiveness. Nor did they consider whether the treatments they provided were the most cost-effective or whether a less expensive treatment could yield the same medical outcome. And the profession had done little to address these concerns. Except for egregious violations of clinical standards, peer review mechanisms did not exist, or if they did, they lacked measures to assess the clinical and cost effectiveness of treatments and imposed only the lightest of sanctions.[15] Because of these weaknesses, the reviews served as a tool to shelter doctors from rigorous scrutiny by their peers as well as to keep lay authorities at arm's length.

By the 1990s, health care costs also became enmeshed in broader debates over the costs of social protection and economic competitiveness. Much of the debate has focused on economic globalization—that is, the growing integration of the world economy—and the effects of intensified competition on the welfare state, though there is also concern over the welfare state's impact on economic performance (Garrett 1997; Pfaller, Gough, and Therborn 1991; Pierson 2001). In addition, some arguments focus on economic changes other than globalization.

Let us begin with the arguments around globalization. Economic globalization is said to exert three pressures on systems of social protection. The first is intensified trade competition, whether from newly industrializing countries, former communist bloc countries, or other industrialized nations (Martin 1997). Welfare states that rely on payroll-based financing seem especially vulnerable to this kind of competition, as employers and some policymakers contend that their social insurance contributions or fringe benefits have driven up nonwage labor costs to ruinously uncompetitive levels. The solutions are to set up operations in countries with lower labor costs, rationalize production and shed unneeded workers, and cut their social outlays or find new sources of funding for these benefits from general revenues or individual private provision.

The second aspect of globalization lies in the integration of capital markets and financial market deregulation, which have unfettered financial capital since the 1980s. Welfare states that depend on general revenues for their financing seem especially vulnerable to the threat of footloose financial capital. If tax revenues are insufficient and large budget deficits instead finance the welfare state, financial markets are likely to inflict punishment through capital flight and runs on the currency.

Third, globalization is said to create mass unemployment, which affects both state-financed welfare states and statutory payroll-based social insurance systems. As low-skill jobs have shifted to newly industrializing countries, long-term unemployment among unskilled workers in Western countries places a dual and conflicting burden on Western welfare states. As the numbers outside the labor force grow and become more dependent on welfare state transfers, a shrinking base of those in work must shoulder the financial burden of social expenditures. They not only pay for more spending on unemployment benefits or retraining programs but must also continue to finance the growing commitments of universal pensions and health care programs. In welfare states financed from general revenues, the disjuncture between welfare state beneficiaries and contributors may translate into budget deficits. In employment-based welfare states, it may take the form of rising nonwage labor costs, which are alleged to hinder competitiveness and discourage job creation.

Other analysts agree that economic conditions have changed but believe that such changes are rooted in the shift to postindustrial society rather than globalization (Iversen 2001; Iversen and Cusack 1998; Pierson 2001). Postindustrial society is characterized by the expansion of the service sector and the decline of manufacturing. The shift to postindustrial society has important consequences for the welfare state. To the extent that the service sector has lower productivity than the manufacturing sector, slower economic growth and lower revenues to finance welfare state outlays will follow. In some countries, manufacturing companies in the exposed sector have made ample use of the welfare state to ease the transition out of employment of older, less productive workers through the use of generous early retirement pensions and disability schemes. Where such schemes are financed out of payroll taxes, the end result has been "welfare without work" (Esping-Andersen 1996b), with growing numbers of persons dependent on the welfare state and shrinking numbers of workers to finance such schemes. This situation not only places a severe financial burden on the welfare state but also drives up nonwage labor costs, which, in turn, inhibit job creation in both the export sector and the sheltered service sector (Hemerijck and Manow 1998; Manow 1997a; OECD 1996b; Scharpf 1997; Visser and Hemerijck 1997).

Still others point to regional economic integration, such as the European Union (EU) or the North American Free Trade Agreement (NAFTA), as a threat to systems of social protection. But they maintain that integration is the result of political decisions rather than inexorable economic forces. In their view, the stringent requirements for participation in a common European currency will not only curtail member governments' ability to pursue an independent (reflationary) monetary policy. The provision for a budget deficit ceiling of 3 percent of gross domestic product will also limit their ability to use deficit spending to pay for social programs to deal with unemployment arising from economic integration (Pochet and Vanhercke 1998). The EU's internal market and currency union founded on a restrictive fiscal and monetary regime will also result in "regime shopping" and a "race to the bottom" in social provision, forcing governments to slash their welfare state outlays in order to attract or retain firms to operate within their borders (Streeck 1995, 1997; Streeck and Schmitter 1991).

For this analysis, the significant point is that economic changes, whether the result of globalization, of the advance of postindustrialism, or of political choices surrounding regional economic integration, share similar diagnoses when it comes to systems of social protection, including health care arrangements. In brief, changes in the economy have produced growing numbers of people dependent on the welfare state and a shrinking base from which to finance social provision. This has triggered a fiscal crisis of the welfare state and other forms of social protection. At the same time, rising social spending in payroll-based systems of social protection feeds back into higher social insurance charges or fringe benefits, placing firms at a competitive disadvantage with respect to rivals with lower labor costs and discouraging job creation in both sheltered and export sectors. Countries with welfare states financed from general revenues may be able to avoid burdening firms with high labor costs, but their governments face unpalatable choices of raising taxes, ballooning budget deficits, or cuts in social provision. Voluntary fringe-benefits systems may grant employers opt-out solutions such as curtailing or not providing social benefits to their workers.

Policymakers, employers, and even the public increasingly recognize the economic pressures on systems of social protection, but there is no agreement on what can or should be done (see Iversen and Wren 1998). Market liberals, for example, argue that governments in both employment-based and general-revenue-based welfare states must scale back social provision or else face the discipline of the market in lower competitiveness, continued unemployment, or welfare state bankruptcy. Much of the popular discussion of globalization assumes that governments have much narrower room to maneuver and can do little but engage in welfare state retrenchment. Some of the gloomier scenarios predict that European welfare states will eventually converge around Anglo-American welfare institutions or "policy dualism," in which middle classes opt out of public programs and seek private insurance cover, leaving the poor and those outside the labor market dependent on residual social assistance that is woefully inadequate in both political support and levels of financing (Baldwin 1994, 52–54; Rhodes 1995). Others, however, point to more hopeful solutions that reconcile economic competitiveness, welfare state solvency, and equity (Scharpf 1999; Visser and Hemerijck 1997). The cases of health care reform in this book can lend empirical evidence to allow more reasoned judgments on the possible futures for different systems of social protection.

The Allure of the Market

The calls for reform of capitalist bargains in the 1980s and 1990s coincided with a resurgence of market remedies in the debates over reform. For many, the market was an appropriate response to the failure of Keynesian economic management to deal with stagflation in the 1970s. Yet market prescriptions were not limited to macroeconomic policy but were also proposed for the welfare state. In addition, proponents of the market were not confined to one political ideology or party; on the contrary, those sympathetic to market solutions ranged across the political spectrum. And the particular market proposals showed variation in their specifics, their justifications, and in the role of the state.

The New Right—a loose term that encompassed market liberals and social conservatives—viewed postwar capitalist settlements and their associated social programs as harmful to the capitalist economy and liberal democracy. Neoliberals argued that the welfare state siphoned off funds into consumption that could have gone into productive investment, thereby stunting economic growth (Gamble 1994, esp. chap. 2). Social conservatives believed that welfare programs created disincentives to work and encouraged dependency (Mead 1986; Murray 1984). The New Right also held the postwar capitalist settlement responsible for a plethora of political ills. The welfare state and mixed economy had created a crisis of "ungovernability" that manifested itself in electoral politics: as politicians bid for votes by making exorbitant promises of generous social spending, they fueled excessive public expectations that government could not possibly meet, precipitating a crisis of legitimacy (Beer 1982b; Birch 1984; King 1976). The governability crisis was also apparent in economic management, as the Keynesian welfare state had made governments too dependent on powerful producer and provider groups in economic and social policy. These groups not only produced economic rigidities but, because they often worked with policymakers behind closed doors, they challenged democratic decision making by elected legislatures. For the right, the solution was to restrict the reach of the state to core activities and to let the market return as the guiding force on economic and social actors. New Right arguments were strongest in countries with liberal institutions and traditions, like the United States and Britain, and found adherents among leaders of conservative parties, such as Margaret Thatcher, Ronald Reagan, and Newt Gingrich.[16]

However, critiques of postwar capitalist settlements calling for greater latitude for the market were not confined to the right. Forces on the center-left, such as Bill Clinton and the Democratic Leadership Council within the Democratic party in the United States, and later, Tony Blair and his "modernizing" wing of the Labour Party in Britain, agreed with the New Right that social programs too often punished individual initiative and created dependency and that markets could substitute for heavy-handed state controls and direct state provision. But they believed that systems of social protection could be reformed in ways that advanced efficiency and equity, and that government had a critical role to play in this project. They hoped to harness the market to social ends by forging partnerships between public and private forces in economic and social provision that advanced efficiency and equity (Blair 1996, esp. chaps. 14 and 34; Giddens 1998; Weir 1998, 71; White 1998).

Market proposals thus reflected the variety of perspectives of their proponents. But to simplify analysis, I make a few broad distinctions. One set of market prescriptions called for deep retrenchment of social programs and much greater reliance on private market arrangements and actors in financing and provision. This could entail tighter eligibility rules for benefits, greater cost sharing by beneficiaries, spending cuts, and in extreme cases, complete privatization of statutory social programs. An alternative set of market prescriptions called for the importation of competition into systems of social protection, not to destroy them but to assure their survival. The idea was that competition would promote efficiency and obviate the need for choosing between politically unpalatable retrenchment or higher contributions or taxes. Yet it also required vigorous monitoring of the market by state actors to protect equity.

The second set of market remedies became particularly prominent in health care reform debates in the 1980s and 1990s. Its leading exponent was Stanford health economist Alain Enthoven and his theory of managed competition (1987, 1993). He argued that health care delivery systems could be much more efficient if providers and insurers were subjected to competitive forces. But he warned that unrestricted market forces would destroy the solidarity of risk-pooling in insurance, and he therefore argued that the state had to set limits to competition in certain areas and to anchor the market in a statutory guarantee of universal health care. Though much of Enthoven's work was directed at the United States, his ideas also captured the imagination of neoliberal research institutes and policymakers overseas. Indeed, in an ironic twist, Enthoven found himself a prophet rejected by his own land.

Efforts to contain social spending and to rewrite the bargains in systems of social protection thus can encompass broad changes in financing, provision, and governance arrangements in these systems. This book, however, explores the narrower question of how cost-containment projects in Britain, Germany, and the United States since the late 1980s attempted to reconfigure governance arrangements in the health sector and, in particular, the political settlement with physicians. It investigates the extent to which these reform projects used market competition or other governance instruments to curb medical power. Though all three countries faced a common imperative to contain health care costs and sought to curb physician prerogatives, their reform paths were quite distinctive. Their particular reform approaches, ways of controlling physicians, and the boundaries to the market were the products of different reform politics in each country. Mapping the politics that produced these distinctive reform responses is the task of the next section.

Three Reform Paths, Three Ways of Using Markets

Policymakers in all three countries deemed health care costs excessive and responded with reforms that sought to alter the terms of sectoral governance with the medical profession. Yet their market reforms varied in their goals, targets, and the scope of competition permitted, and in some cases they were combined with other governance instruments. In Britain, Margaret Thatcher set out to shatter the old statist-corporatist edifice that had accorded the medical profession a dominant position in NHS governance. Through competitive forces, she hoped to boost the efficiency of health care delivery and make hospital doctors more accountable for their use of resources. She also hoped that market incentives would make managers demand more cost-effective care from doctors, and she granted them the tools to hold the medical profession to account. But she and her successors ended up creating a new governance hybrid that sharply circumscribed competition, enhanced central state control, and placed corporatism under new limits while falling short of destroying it.

Germany's reform approach was a distinctive combination of corporatism, state intervention, and market. But rather than seeking to destroy corporatism, Helmut Kohl largely worked through it to tame medical power, even while seeking to repair its defects so that insurers might become a more effective counterweight to physicians. In addition, Kohl's reforms contained a strong dose of state intervention in sectoral administration of doctors and insurers. The government also grafted a cautious market experiment onto the larger corporatist trunk, but it stopped well short of threatening the medical profession's place in corporatism. Moreover, the market was directed at long-standing inequities among insurers and was also seen as an alternative to repeated state forays into sectoral administration.

In the United States, the Clinton administration attempted government-led market reform within a national health insurance scheme. Had its effort succeeded, it would have greatly expanded government authority in the private health care system. Though Clinton failed at the legislative stage, health care reform nevertheless continued. But it was a market reform led by private employers in a chaotic process of "unmanaged competition" that has proceeded in the absence of an effective or coherent framework of government regulation. Targeting the autonomy of individual medical practitioners, this kind of market reform has profoundly transformed health care delivery and governance arrangements.

What explains each country's particular mix of policy instruments in its efforts to reform health care governance arrangements? More specifically, why were the market experiments limited in Britain and Germany, but so unrestrained in the United States? And why did physicians fare differently under each country's reform project? The answers to these questions lie in the specific politics of reform in each country, which created particular reform policies. The politics of reform, in turn, were the product of the interplay between actors and institutions in the political and sectoral arenas. Together, these set limits to or encouraged the use of unrestrained market forces as a reform tool.

Formal political institutions and the balance of forces in the political arena either provided or foreclosed opportunities for health care stakeholders to shape the content of reforms (and even block them) at the stage of formation and enactment. The presence or absence of stakeholders affected government capacity to realize a radical market reform program at these stages of the policy process. But the reform process also continued in the health care system itself. Existing policies and institutions in the health sector created and reinforced different solidarities and expectations about the legitimacy of government intervention to set the parameters of the health care system. In addition, existing governance arrangements either provided or denied state actors the requisite leverage to control the behavior of sectoral actors and to shape the process of market reform. Let us consider the interplay between the political and sectoral arenas in greater detail.

The Political Arena

Many explanations of policy outcomes point to the primacy of state structures (Evans, Rueschemeyer, and Skocpol 1985; Immergut 1992; Steinmo and Watts 1995). Formal political institutions establish rules of the game that may make legislation easier or harder to enact. Where political authority and decision making are centralized, as in unitary and Westminster parliamentary systems, enactment of controversial legislation tends to be easier than in federal or presidential systems where dispersed decision-making structures provide opponents with multiple "veto points" (Immergut 1992). Electoral systems also shape politics and policy outcomes. Proportional representation arrangements tend to produce multiparty systems and coalition governments, requiring compromise and negotiation among governing parties. Conversely, simple plurality systems tend to inflate electoral majorities so that one-party rule is the norm, making it easier to enact legislation unscathed. Political structures thus provide state actors with more or less autonomy from societal interests (whether expressed as interest groups or through political parties) to formulate and enact their agendas (Nordlinger 1981).

In contrast to state-centered theories, which emphasize political-system structures in explaining policy outcomes, interest-group theories highlight the organizational characteristics of associations. These studies have found that fragmented interests are far better at exerting negative power and vetoing policy initiatives than at taking positive policy action. Likewise, state actors can more easily discount the views of interests that are divided into competing organizations than of those that are unified under one association (Wilsford 1991). But policy initiatives may fail not only because of government action or inaction, but because critical stakeholders may be too divided to deliver their support or that of their members. Other writers look less at interest-group organization than at coalitions across classes or their segments to explain policy outcomes (Gourevitch 1985; Pontusson and Swenson 1996).

Explanations of group or class power not only look at the organizational characteristics of associations but also their links to governing parties. The best-known example is the "power resources" school, which highlights the linkages between union movements and social democratic parties to explain certain economic and welfare state policies (Esping-Andersen 1985; Korpi 1983; Stephens 1979). Maioni (1998) combines party-system structures and power-resources explanations to show that the presence of a social democratic party was critical to the emergence of national health insurance in Canada. Although these theorists focus on social democratic parties and unions, their analysis of party and interest-group linkages can be used to study other political alliances, such as those between employers and conservative parties, and their policy outcomes, not just left-wing ones.

My explanation of health care reform acknowledges the importance of the political arena in shaping the reform outcomes at the stages of formulation and enactment. But it understands that politics and policies reflect a complex interplay between political institutions, party balances, and interest groups. Each country's political structures and party constellations were more or less porous to health care interests. This had a bearing on the content of reforms and whether or not they would be enacted.

The Sector

But the sector also influences the course of policy development. First, policy developments within a sector have "feedback" effects (Pierson 1993) that affect subsequent initiatives in the political arena. Sectoral actors, for example, may block the implementation of legislation, prompting subsequent reform initiatives. In addition, governments often confront "policy legacies"—that is, existing policies or supporting constituencies that have grown up around such policies—within a sector that influence their reform choices (Pierson 1993, 1994; Weir and Skocpol 1985). The British, German, and U.S. governments, for example, defined the current cost problems in health care partly in terms of yesterday's political bargains with the medical profession and tailored their solutions to address what they perceived to be the shortcomings in those arrangements. Finally, sectoral actors may undertake the task of sectoral reform themselves if governments fail to do so.

Each nation's health care system also institutionalizes and reinforces different expectations about the proper place of the state, the market, or interest groups in health care provision and governance. These expectations will view state efforts to set the parameters of the health care system as legitimate or not, and will set boundaries to the market in health care. Statutory universal programs that grant all citizens the right to health services according to need rather than ability to pay, and that pool the risk of becoming ill through universal schemes, create broad solidarities based on reciprocity (Baldwin 1990; Stone 1993). Bound together in a common health care scheme, both the middle classes and the poor share an interest in preserving universal access to quality care. The public expects the state to intervene when necessary to safeguard solidarity and to limit market forces that may introduce distinctions based on health or wealth.

Private health care systems, by contrast, foster much narrower notions of equity, and key stakeholders cherish their freedom to determine coverage and benefits as a way to control their own health care costs or maximize their profits. Thus, commercial insurers follow a narrow definition of fairness that relates premiums to health risk (Stone 1993). Many insurers and employers will also regard government intervention aimed at broadening solidarity through national insurance as an illegitimate intrusion into their autonomy.

Finally, the health sector may provide or deny governments the leverage to control sectoral actors and the pace and scope of market reform. Statutory systems grant governments greater legitimacy and legal authority to set the parameters of health care than do private systems. Just as important, existing governance arrangements in the health sector may provide or deny policymakers the institutional linkages to sectoral actors and hence the capacity to curb their behavior.[17]

Linking the Political and the Sectoral Arenas

The particular reform paths and the specific ways of using the market in each country were the product of the interplay of political and sectoral actors and institutions. In Britain, the political arena granted Margaret Thatcher enormous capacity to formulate and enact a radical market-reform program. The market reforms were the product of a centralized and secretive review process that excluded the usual health care stakeholders. She enjoyed the advantages of single-party government, a large and disciplined parliamentary majority, and a unitary political system, all of which made it relatively easy to enact her reforms over the vocal opposition of most health care interests. Furthermore, the hierarchical administrative apparatus in the NHS granted policymakers the institutional leverage to impose the market from above. But for all these advantages, the market turned out to be quite limited in practice, state centralization became more pronounced, and corporatism survived (albeit with new restrictions). Though some of the reasons for such market restraint were technical, most were political. In particular, the universalism of the NHS reflected a broad notion of solidarity shared by the public and the major political parties, who expected the government to protect that solidarity from the market's advance. Finally, the governance arrangements in the NHS—its centralized state administration and financing—meant that government ministers could not escape responsibility for health service performance. As a result, they deemed it necessary to constrain the market in order to prevent a political backlash.

In Germany, sectoral governance arrangements and a porous political system made it difficult for Kohl to engage in radical experimentation with a market in health care. Corporatism in the health sector granted doctors, insurers, employers, and unions a voice in policy reform debates in the political arena. A political system characterized by coalition governments, federalism, and shifting partisan balances reflecting state and national election results also meant that the political influence of these and other stakeholders varied over time. The reform laws thus were the product of compromise and negotiation blending corporatist governance, emergency state intervention in sectoral administration, and a cautious market experiment among insurers. Indeed, the market was limited to address solidarity concerns of a number of stakeholders and to appease the medical profession and its allies in the governing coalition. Lastly, corporatist arrangements in the health sector granted policymakers the legal and institutional leverage to limit the market behavior of insurers.

In the United States, Clinton sought to use the government to construct and control a market and embed it in a framework of national health insurance. But the political system's separation of powers, independent congressional parties, and a legislative process porous to interest groups required negotiation and compromise if the president was to realize his ambition. The Clinton administration's strategy to devise and enact this ambitious agenda was ill-suited to this difficult political terrain. His task was made that much harder by the division and inaction of key potential allies of reform—employers in particular—who proved unable to deliver their members to support the president.

The health sector also contributed to the demise of Clinton's attempt at a managed market and the resultant chaotic market-reform process that followed. The private fringe-benefit system created the expectations toward government intervention opposite those in Britain and Germany. Many employers and insurers viewed Clinton's effort to enhance government capacity in the health sector as an encroachment on their freedom to decide coverage and control their costs. Subsequent efforts by the U.S. government to control the market were stymied by regulatory federalism, which erected institutional barriers to effective and coordinated regulation by state and federal actors over the actions of private insurers and employers.

Plan of the Book

The rest of the book proceeds along the following lines. Chapter 1 sketches the institutionalization of corporatist-statist governance in the British NHS up to the Thatcher reforms of 1989 and discusses the problems with this arrangement. Then chapter 2 describes Thatcher's effort to introduce a new governance regime in the NHS and explains why the internal market experiment turned out to be so limited in practice. Chapter 3 provides an overview of the development of corporatist governance and its problems in Germany; chapter 4 tells how Kohl sought to repair corporatism and explains his government's caution with the market. The professional governance model in the United States and its problems as a governance and cost-control instrument are presented in chapter 5. Chapter 6 analyzes Clinton's failed effort at government-led market reform and describes how private actors have unleashed the market to radically recast governance arrangements. The conclusion considers the implications of markets for health care governance and derives broader lessons about policy change in systems of social protection.

CHAPTER 1

Health Care Governance in the British NHS to 1989

A Hybrid of Corporatism and State Hierarchy

The governance arrangements underpinning the National Health Service since its establishment combined corporatism and state hierarchy. But the relationship was not symmetrical: doctors were the dominant actors, and managers played supporting roles. At the same time that NHS administrative arrangements failed to provide the state sufficient capacity to govern the health sector, corporatism offered no substitute because medical associations failed to police their own members.

This chapter provides a brief sketch of NHS governance up to the Thatcher government's reforms of 1989. It begins by tracing the origins of the corporatist-statist hybrid. The chapter then describes the roles played by the medical profession, managers, and politicians in this hybrid. Finally, it identifies the limitations of this governance arrangement.

Origins of the Corporatist-Statist Settlement

The corporatist settlement with the British Medical Association (BMA), much older than the NHS itself, dates from the creation of national health insurance (NHI) for manual workers in 1911.[1] In order to induce general practitioners (GPs) to participate in the NHI scheme, the government of David Lloyd George acceded to the BMA's demand that general practitioners have a formal role in health policy-making and administration. The government created a decentralized administrative structure of Insurance Committees, which included representatives of the medical profession as well as payers, to oversee the medical benefits portion of NHI. These committees replaced working-class mutual bodies, friendly societies, and medical aid associations with which the BMA had previously locked horns over terms and conditions of service (Anderson 1989, chap. 3; Day and Klein

31

1992; Eckstein 1958, 22–27; Little 1932, 328–32).[2] In addition, the medical profession won exclusive jurisdiction over both clinical practice and economic remuneration through the creation of local medical committees (LMCs). Composed entirely of the medical profession and dominated by the BMA, the LMCs had the power to conduct limited peer review of doctors and to decide the method of physician remuneration (Little 1932, 328). Doctors also advanced their professional autonomy by securing the principle and practice of free choice of physician and eliminating closed panel practice (Day and Klein 1992, 466). These arrangements thus removed the counterweight to medical power that the friendly societies had provided prior to 1911. Finally, the BMA won state recognition as the official representative of the medical profession with the right to negotiate policy matters affecting physicians with officials at the highest levels of government, but only after the threat of a boycott prompted Lloyd George to enter into negotiations with the association on questions concerning implementation of the National Health Insurance Act (ibid., 465–67; Little 1932, 329–30, 332).[3]

The health sector underwent a second major transformation in structure and governance in 1948.[4] World War II exposed the shortcomings of the national health insurance scheme even as the public became accustomed to state planning and coordination in the health sector. The biggest problems were that NHI excluded substantial segments of the population and many services.[5] In addition, decentralized administration allowed wide variations in the provision of services, while the existence of voluntary and public hospitals fostered duplication. Equally important, the war made apparent the precarious financial condition of voluntary hospitals and their dependence on public funding for survival (Anderson 1989, chap. 3; Eckstein 1958, 26–29, and chaps. 3 and 4). The accumulation of problems in the health sector, public tolerance of state planning, and cross-class solidarity bred by the war effort all provided fertile ground for the emergence of the National Health Service.

The creation of the universal National Health Service under the Labour government of Clement Attlee ushered in a hybrid arrangement of statist and corporatist governance. Under the NHS, the central state claimed for itself an enduring presence in health care governance and assumed responsibility for guaranteeing universal health care, financing it through general revenues, and determining the total amount of health care spending to be taken from the national budget. The government nationalized hospitals, placed hospital doctors under salaried employment, and created a hierarchical administrative apparatus to run the health care system. The administrative apparatus in place before the Thatcher reforms of 1989 comprised the Department of Health (DoH) at the center; Regional Health Authorities (RHAs) responsible for regional planning, special services, and oversight of District Health Authorities (DHAs); DHAs providing hospital care and engaging in health planning for the local population; and local general practitioner services, which fell under the separate purview of Family Practitioner Committees (renamed Family Health Services Authorities, or FHSAs, after 1989).[6]

The introduction of a state bureaucracy in the health sector, however, did not displace corporatist arrangements. Rather, the NHS accommodated both forms of governance. Thus, alongside the various tiers of health authorities there existed a parallel administrative structure composed entirely of representatives of the medical profession. Through its medical advisory machinery (medical committees that advised RHAs or DHAs and their management), the BMA and its constituent bodies provided advice and sent representatives to serve on the administrative bodies of the NHS (see Garpenby 1989, 182–88, 192–94; Ham 1985, esp. 153–56). The role of the medical profession in health care governance was strengthened by administrative reforms of 1974, which brought doctors directly into the NHS bureaucracy and further cemented its corporatist arrangements. The reorganization created management teams at local, district, and regional levels, consisting of a doctor, a nurse, and lay managers (Garpenby 1989, 194), and introduced consensus management, which effectively gave doctors a veto over administrative decisions (Harrison 1988, 24).

As well as conceding a role in health care administration to the medical profession, the Attlee government and its successors continued to accord the BMA a privileged position in formulating health policy, thereby acknowledging the association's claim to be the main (if not exclusive) voice of the medical profession. The health ministry and the BMA found themselves enmeshed in a web of formal and informal contacts, which ranged from representation on royal commissions to talks with the secretary of state for health and the prime minister. It was the informal contacts at the national level, rather than formal channels, that constituted the more effective means of influence (Garpenby 1989, 136–41). Thus, the NHS constituted a form of "bipartite corporatism" between the government and an organized interest group (Cawson 1982, 1986): the state negotiated policy with the BMA while relying on the organized medical profession to implement this policy on its behalf.

As with the National Health Insurance Act in 1911, the medical profession had little influence on the legislation that created the NHS in 1946. The BMA did not oppose a national health service per se, having itself proposed something similar a few years earlier, but it was eager to assure a role in health care governance for itself and its members and to preserve the clinical freedom of physicians. Physician opposition to these areas of the law prompted Bevan to resume negotiations with the BMA, which culminated in amending legislation in 1948 that incorporated concessions.[7]

This political settlement acceded to the BMA's demand to preserve areas it deemed critical to professional autonomy. First, the Attlee government dropped its plans for a full-time, salaried service through local health centers and instead retained capitation as the primary basis of remuneration, thereby preserving the independent-contractor status of general practitioners. Second, the Labour health minister, Aneuran Bevan, secured the participation of senior hospital specialists (or, consultants) by agreeing to supplement their salaried employment with private practice and private beds in NHS hospitals, and by introducing an award system of bonus payments whose recipients were to be determined by the medical profession alone (Eckstein 1958, 1960; Grey-Turner and Sutherland 1982, chap. 3; Day and Klein 1992). Doctors also carved out substantial areas of clinical and social autonomy at the microlevel: managers refrained from questioning doctors' treatment decisions and the ways in which they structured their work, and except for the most egregious transgressions, medical organizations undertook no peer review of their members' clinical decisions (Harrison 1988, 22–24; Pollitt 1993, 3).

Yet the political bargain between the state and physicians embodied in the NHS worked both ways. Even as the state granted significant influence in policy formulation and implementation to the organized medical profession and substantial clinical autonomy to individual practitioners, it sought to harness that clinical freedom in the service of broader public policy aims. Under an "implicit concordat," which remained an informal understanding rather than a formal agreement, the government did not question clinical decisions, as long as doctors did not challenge the state's authority to set the global budget for the NHS and rationed scarce resources on its behalf (Day and Klein 1992, 471; Klein 1989, 235). Doctors also sometimes disguised such rationing decisions in clinical terms.[8] Until the 1980s, policymakers, managers, and the medical profession respected the concordat's division of labor. NHS managers acted as "diplomats" who smoothed internal conflicts in hospitals, facilitated the work of doctors, and did not question their clinical decisions (Harrison 1988, 51–55).

Doctors also found that their role in negotiating health policy and running the health service had limits. The state sometimes excluded them from negotiations over fundamental questions about the structure of the health care system, as it had in 1911 and 1946 (Day and Klein 1992; Eckstein 1960, chap. 4). While reserving these constitutional matters for itself, however, the state subsequently brought the BMA in to negotiate the specifics of implementation and granted it a crucial collective role in administering the new health care system. On these latter matters, the association won the right to "argue its case rather than merely to present it" (Eckstein 1960, 101), and policymakers tended to seek agreement with the BMA rather than merely to take its views into consideration (ibid., 101–2; see also Day and Klein 1992).[9]

This corporatist-statist hybrid had its shortcomings and provided the Thatcher government with grounds to embark on a quest to reform the NHS in the late 1980s. The medical profession's own organizational characteristics rendered it a weak and unreliable corporatist partner with government. Yet state administrative arrangements also put government ministers in the awkward position of taking the heat for health system performance failures while denying them the means to prevent or ameliorate such policy disasters. Neither corporatism nor state hierarchy granted policymakers the leverage over doctors or managers necessary to govern the NHS effectively.

Shortcomings in NHS Governance

Weak Corporatism

If corporatism is to be an effective form of governance, the leadership of an interest group must be able to control the behavior of its members and deliver their compliance to agreements reached with the government (or with other interest associations). These leaders must also have sufficient authority to enter into negotiations and to conclude agreements with the state or other interest groups. In addition, the group should have the status of the exclusive, official representative of the profession or economic group in question.[10] The BMA possessed none of these attributes.

Although the government has recognized the BMA as the trade union for the medical profession since 1911 (Day and Klein 1992; Little 1932, 329–30), in the political arena it is far from the exclusive representative of physicians. Instead, it has had to contend with other associations claiming the allegiance of the profession, even though nearly 75 percent of practicing doctors are BMA members.[11] The Royal Colleges, which represent various medical specialties in primarily scientific and educational matters and claim as members the cream of the medical profession, have been allies, but also rivals, of the BMA. The status of the Royal Colleges since 1967 as charity organizations precludes their taking any explicit political role (Garpenby 1989), though they have occasionally become embroiled in health politics. But the ban on explicit political activity has led to a de facto and de jure division of labor with the BMA. Still, the BMA considers the support of the Royal Colleges important in any major conflict with the state (Garpenby 1989, 119). Cooperation was institutionalized in the Joint Consultants Committee (JCC), composed of representatives of the BMA and the Royal Colleges, which acts as a voice for hospital specialists on medical matters (though not on terms and conditions of service) (ibid., 116–21; BMA n.d.; Grey-Turner and Sutherland 1982, 67–68, and chap. 5). Normally, the relations between the BMA and Royal Colleges are cordial, but sometimes temporary estrangements occur, and the Colleges have been known to undercut the BMA's position with government by taking a more moderate policy stance, as they did during the creation of the NHS (Grey-Turner and Sutherland 1982, 60–74, 314–16).[12]

At the same time, the BMA's political effectiveness has been undermined by divisions among its members, which serve to render a unified course of action difficult. A major imbalance exists between office-based general practitioners and senior hospital doctors (or consultants), with the major share of power accruing to the latter. Because of strict demarcation between ambulatory and hospital care, consultants rather than GPs decide whether or not to admit a patient to the hospital and thus have an exclusive say over the patient's course of hospital treatment. Consultants have also controlled a given number of hospital beds and used them according to their own determination (Freidson 1970, 35–39; Harrison 1988, 22–24, 37–38; Pollitt 1993). The creation of the NHS institutionalized practices that further favored consultants at the expense of general practitioners. Thus, the salaried remuneration of hospital doctors freed them from their reliance on GP referrals for their livelihood, which had been the procedure in the NHI system (Glennerster, Matsaganis, and Owens 1992, 9). Consultants also enjoyed the benefits of a lucrative distinction award system, and their private practice, also accommodated by the NHS, further emancipated them from any dependence on GPs for their income.

The BMA's internal structure replicates the demarcation between hospital and office-based doctors, making it difficult for the profession to forge a common policy line. Separate craft committees within the BMA represent different sections of the profession in negotiations with the state, for example, the General Medical Services Committee (GMSC) for general practitioners and the Central Consultants and Specialists Committee (CCSC) for senior hospital doctors. (Indeed, the BMA's creation of the CCSC in 1948 to counter the claims of the Royal Colleges to be the sole voice of hospital doctors is an overt reflection of the continuing rivalry between general practitioners and specialists.) Until 1975, the status of these craft committees was independent of the BMA leadership and its assembly, the Representative Body.[13] Since then, however, the craft committees have become subject to the delegated authority of the Representative Body (Grey-Turner and Sutherland 1982, chap. 9). Still the GMSC and CCSC possess considerable freedom of action, because their officers continue to be elected by regional and local committees of GPs and consultants that remain outside of the formal BMA structure (Garpenby 1989, 116–19). Furthermore, the GMSC and CCSC are answerable to the assembly, which limits direct control of the BMA executive over their actions.

The BMA's internal democracy has at times inhibited decisive political action and hamstrung its leaders in their negotiations with the state. The BMA's constitution grants the rank and file, through the Representative Body, substantial influence over both the content of policy and the actions of the Council (the executive of the BMA) and the craft committees. Indeed, for much of the twentieth century, the BMA was plagued by an internal power struggle between the Representative Body and the Council: both bodies are separately elected and thus have independent power bases, but the Representative Body refuses to delegate adequate authority to the Council.[14] The Council, for example, must return to the Representative Body if it alters the latter's motions in negotiations with government. The Council must also secure the Representative Body's approval of its actions; the executive cannot simply make an agreement with the government and then report back to the membership at the next annual meeting (Chambers 1972). It is not unknown for the BMA membership to reject agreements forged by the BMA's leadership (be it the Council or the craft committee leaders) with the Department of Health. The Representative Body's detailed control over the actions of the Council and its refusal to delegate authority to it thus violate one of the key tenets of corporatist bargaining, which is the ability of an organization's leaders to deliver the membership to agreements they reach with the state or other bargaining partners.

In turn, the BMA leadership lacks effective sanctions over its own members (much less physicians outside the organization), which weakens its ability to enter into and keep agreements made with the state or to maintain solidarity in the event of industrial action. The expulsion of a doctor from the BMA is a rare occurrence. Ostracism, which the BMA has wielded against those physicians who refuse to follow its policy line, has been ruled libelous and illegal by the courts, whose decisions reflect the liberal principle of the right to freely practice one's profession. Thus, the BMA Council is effectively limited to offering advice and issuing warnings on certain employment arrangements for doctors and exercising moral suasion (Grey-Turner and Sutherland 1982, 114, 123–27, 189–90, 295–305, 326–29, chap. 9; Little 1932, 89–90, 264–66, 294–5, 329–30). Furthermore, as a voluntary association, the BMA cannot coerce its rank and file to submit to agreements it has reached with government; it must contend with the possibility that dissatisfied members can leave or ignore association policy. Further undercutting the BMA's authority is the fact that nonmembers have a voice in the medical advisory machinery in NHS administration.[15] These provisions have at times rendered the BMA Council overly cautious in its negotiations with the government, for fear of offending nonmember doctors or losing members to other organizations. In addition, the absence of any systematic peer review by either the BMA or Royal Colleges until the 1990s, meant that the medical profession had few instruments with which to monitor or discipline its members' behavior in the area of medical practice. Any review that did exist was voluntary and irregular (Pollitt 1993, 4).

Finally, the BMA's reluctance to embrace an explicit trade union role has weakened its position in relation to the state. The BMA membership has long harbored an ambivalence toward such a role, a situation reflected in the association's dual legal status as a corporation and a union (Chambers 1972, 49–50). Many physicians believe that trade union issues conflict with professional norms, and so they eschew the strike weapon as unprofessional behavior that would only harm patients. In other instances, doctors have feared that industrial action against the government would be undermined by those physicians who choose not to honor it (Grey-Turner and Sutherland 1982).[16] Although a closed shop would enhance control over the rank and file, the association has rejected such a course as a violation of the right of freedom of association.

Central Accountability but Weak Central Controls

If policymakers could not rely on the BMA to hold up its side of the corporatist bargain and control individual practitioners, they might have been expected to rely on the NHS administrative apparatus and its cadre of managers. Hierarchical administration should have provided governments with the means to control NHS performance, but for reasons discussed below, it did not. All the same, statism accorded the central state such a prominent role in NHS administration and financing that government ministers in London found it difficult to avoid blame for NHS performance failures.

NHS managers were not the counterweight to physician power that they might have been. In dealing with doctors, managers essentially conceived of their role as one of facilitating consultant autonomy; they avoided intruding on consultants' prerogatives in running the hospitals (Garpenby 1989, 194; Harrison 1988, 24). The organizational reforms of 1974 further weakened management's leverage over doctors, since physicians now had a veto over administrative decisions, while retaining their own advisory machinery independent of managerial control.

Central policymakers also lacked critical monitoring tools. One glaring problem was a lack of information on what lower levels of the NHS were doing with their money. The Department of Health, for instance, did not know what medical procedures cost and had little information on how hospitals spent their budgets. This was not accidental; under a system with global annual budgets, in which hospitals were owned by health authorities, there seemed to be little need to know how much procedures cost so long as hospitals remained within their allocations. Besides, until the 1980s, there was no central system to evaluate the performance of individual managers. Paralleling the dearth of information at the center, managers at lower levels lacked measurement indicators to monitor the actions of the physicians in their hospitals (Griffiths 1983; Klein 1989, chap. 7; Pollitt 1993). Both the government and managers had only quantitative indicators that measured inputs (like the amount of money devoted to health care or the number of hospital beds) and outputs (like the number of operations performed). But they did not have qualitative indicators to evaluate whether a particular treatment was effective (Klein 1989, chap. 7).

Poorly defined relationships and the expectations of actors at different levels also made it difficult for the central government to demand accountability from administrators and clinicians. From its inception, the NHS manifested a tension between the center and the periphery that was never fully resolved. According to the doctrines of ministerial responsibility and parliamentary accountability, government ministers were answerable to the legislature for their own performance and that of the civil servants in their departments (Day and Klein 1987, 26–27, 33–35; Norton, 1984, 376). In the NHS, this implied that accountability should have started at the lower levels and moved upward to the secretary of state for health, who, in turn, was responsible to Parliament. Aneuran Bevan stated the relationship in characteristically succinct and vivid terms: "When a bedpan is dropped on a hospital floor, its noise should resound in the Palace of Westminster" (quoted in Day and Klein 1987, 76). At the same time, however, the central government expected the lower tiers of the NHS to possess some measure of discretion in implementing central policy directives and in using resources to fit local circumstances; its job was to set priorities and overall budgets (Day and Klein 1987, 77; Ham 1985, 1988, esp. 408). The government in London thus set the overall NHS budget and relied on the Department of Health and health authorities to allocate this global budget to hospitals and GPs at the local level.

Global budgeting proved highly effective in keeping the lid on overall health care expenditures while relieving the center of the tasks of detailed micromanagement, but it was basically a blunt instrument unable to guarantee efficient practices at the level of the individual doctor or manager. Global budgeting also deprived policymakers of both knowledge about and control over the activities of local units. In addition, the formula for allocating budgets actually penalized those facilities that performed more surgical procedures and treated more patients.[17]

If accountability to elected officials was uncertain, democratic responsiveness to health care consumers and local communities was equally problematic. Although the NHS administrative machinery provided for community representation on community health councils (CHCs) and in health authorities, in both of these bodies community interests were much weaker than those of providers and managers. Through their treatment decisions in hospitals in their role as providers of health care, and in their involvement in various advisory committees and NHS administrative bodies, senior hospital doctors constituted the dominant voice in decisions about resource use at local levels (see Ham 1988, 398–400, 408). The administrative reorganization of 1974 further blurred the lines of accountability. The management teams dispersed responsibility among a number of decision makers on any one committee, and as a result, no single person could be held accountable for the performance failures—or the successes—of a particular unit.

These different types of accountability, with correspondingly different norms, only made it harder for the central government to control the NHS. Although political accountability would seem to imply that managers and doctors must be sensitive to elected officials and voters either at the national or the local level, this type of accountability sometimes clashed with managerial accountability to efficiency, effectiveness, and fiscal regularity (Day and Klein 1987, 26–27, 33–35). Likewise, doctors' clinical accountability to provide the best possible treatment for the patient, regardless of cost, often conflicted with political and managerial accountability.

This state of affairs prompted Prime Minister Thatcher to commission an investigation in 1983, to be carried out by Sir Roy Griffiths. Griffiths, who became one of Thatcher's close advisers, introduced the ideas and methods of private sector management into the public sector. His report on the NHS was highly critical of consensus management precisely because of the dearth of personal accountability and its tendency to foster "lowest common denominator decisions." As the report tartly observed, "if Florence Nightingale were carrying her lamp through the corridors of the NHS today she would almost certainly be searching for the people in charge" (Griffiths 1983, 12).[18] Griffiths recommended the introduction of general managers in place of the management teams at all levels of the NHS. General managers alone would bear responsibility for their own unit's performance. Griffiths also advised extending performance reviews of managers to all levels of the NHS to strengthen hierarchical oversight. At the same time, he pushed in the opposite direction by proposing a system of devolved management that would grant each manager a fixed budget for his or her unit. Similarly, he proposed that consultants be made responsible for departmental hospital budgets in order to prevent managers from running roughshod over doctors and to coopt the medical profession in the task of managing the NHS. Finally, the Griffiths Report advised that the government separate strategic and day-to-day administrative decisions by creating a supervisory board for the former and a management board for the latter.[19] The government implemented the report's recommendations in 1985.

In the end, the thorn of political accountability provided the most compelling reason for Thatcher to seek changes in NHS governance. Because statism accorded the central government the primary voice in decisions about provision and financing, voters and Parliament held it responsible for NHS performance, good or bad. Furthermore, they also held the government of the day responsible for safeguarding universal access to care. Voters could ostensibly use the ballot box to call the government to account for its stewardship for the NHS, though this was a blunt instrument wielded infrequently. Parliamentary accountability filled the gap, as government ministers had to face regular questioning from members of Parliament (MPs) for any breakdowns in the NHS, even if they lacked the control mechanisms to prevent them (Harrison 1988, 92–97).

For Margaret Thatcher, such flaws in NHS governance were all too apparent. The government was blamed for NHS performance failures, yet it could not control the doctors or managers who made the operational decisions on the use of resources at lower levels. Deeming this situation politically intolerable, she concluded that the settlement surrounding NHS governance had to change.

CHAPTER 2

The British Reforms

Markets, Managers, and the Challenge to Corporatism

On January 25, 1988, Prime Minister Margaret Thatcher abruptly announced a thoroughgoing review of the National Health Service on the television news program *Panorama*. The announcement took most of her cabinet colleagues by surprise: Thatcher made her decision and aired it publicly without prior consultation of the cabinet or advance notice to Parliament (Delamothe 1989a). The outcome of the review was the publication in January 1989 of the white paper *Working for Patients*, which heralded sweeping changes in NHS governance.

With this document, Thatcher gave notice of her intention to shatter the corporatist bargain with the medical profession by means of a radical market reform. At the same time, the white paper proposed sweeping powers for lay managers over individual doctors. Not surprisingly, the reforms sparked one of the most venomous and heated conflicts between physicians and government in decades.

But for all her market rhetoric, the NHS reforms fell short of Thatcher's radical vision. The NHS got an internal market, but one that was heavily managed from the center. A decade after *Working for Patients*, a new governance hybrid was emerging in the NHS that blended greater state centralization, market forces, and diminished corporatism. The new settlement was a partial victory for the medical profession, preserving physician influence in some areas but also setting limits on it in others.

To account for this reform outcome, I explore the interplay between actors and institutions in the health sector and political arena. Thatcher's neoliberal predilections predisposed her to market solutions to the NHS's ills, and the political system granted her considerable capacity to define and enact a radical reform agenda. Policymakers also possessed the institutional linkages to the NHS to impose the market from above. But these same linkages also set limits to the kind of market that was politically feasible. Powerful political constraints required Thatcher's successor, John Major, to control the pace and scope of marketization and to continue to accord doctors a role in health care governance, albeit under new terms defined by the government.

This chapter explores Conservative governments' attempts to radically transform the governance of the NHS in the 1990s and, with it, the political settlement with physicians. We have already seen how the corporatist-statist hybrid contained serious defects as a governance instrument. This chapter begins by sketching the more immediate pressures and the lines of debate that led up to Thatcher's review of the NHS and her internal market reforms. Following that is an account of the policy-making process behind the publication of the white paper and of the medical profession's bitter and confused reaction to the reforms. The chapter then assesses the extent of the changes to NHS governance and provides an explanation for the reform path. It concludes with a brief discussion of the continuities and changes in health care governance under the Labour government of Tony Blair.

The 1980s: The Health Care Debate Heats Up

The trigger behind Thatcher's attempt to transform health care governance was a political crisis over NHS funding. By the late 1980s, the NHS had become a battleground between two camps, with the main lines of conflict centered on government funding policies versus perceived inefficiencies in NHS service delivery. The first camp consisted of health care professionals, many in the media, the Labour party, and even some Conservative members of Parliament. This side argued that the government's failure to provide adequate financial resources to the NHS was the root cause of its poor performance. As evidence, they pointed out that NHS spending under Thatcher had fallen short of meeting the health ministry's own estimates, which calculated that the NHS needed to grow at an annual rate of 2 percent per year to meet the demand posed by the rising number of elderly persons, technological advances, and government policy goals (Ham, Robinson, and Benzeval 1990, 12–14; Klein 1989, 229–30). Table 5 indicates that while real resources for the NHS rose in the 1980s, they did so more slowly than in the 1970s.

The underfunding camp also argued that Thatcher's austerity programs hit the hospital sector especially hard. For instance, the government's efficiency savings program, begun in 1981, reduced health authority budgets to correspond to centrally calculated "efficiency savings." But because the government did not specify how or where such savings were to be made, there was no way of knowing whether savings actually resulted from efficiency improvements, reduced quality of care, or layoffs of needed staff (Harrison 1988, 56–57). In addition, the government halted the older system of soft budgeting, which had allowed current cost overruns to be covered by adjustments in the following year's hospital budget, and substituted them with a hard budget regime.[1] This meant that health authorities and hospitals had to absorb any deficits they incurred and could no longer expect the government to bail them out next year. The financial situation for many hospitals usually worsened in the autumn and winter as they approached the end of the fiscal year, and many health authorities and hospitals overshot their budgets and responded with layoffs of staff and closures of beds and wards (Chantler 1988, 6; Ham, Robinson, and Benzeval 1990, chap. 1; Klein 1989, chap. 7; Vallance-Owen interview, March 13, 1992).

The more alarmist version of the underfunding argument contended that Thatcher intended to privatize the NHS by various stealth measures. Thus, "contracting-out" of catering and laundry in NHS hospitals were the entering wedge for full-scale privatization, as were policies encouraging private provision and insurance. Ultimately, government's underfunding policies would fuel dissatisfaction with poor service and facilities, encourage people to "go private," and eventually erode public support for the NHS to such a degree that privatization would be feasible (Klein 1989, 215–17). Given proposals earlier in the decade to privatize the NHS, the underfunding critics had reason to be worried.[2]

The other camp in the NHS debate, the inefficiency camp, included the government and its allies. They pointed out that the NHS had received

TABLE 5.   Real Resources to NHS
Hospital and Community Health
Services, 1974–89 (expenditure
adjusted for NHS pay and price
increases; 1974–75 = 100)

Year	Index
1974–75	100
1977–78	105
1980–81	110
1983–84	113.5
1986–87	114
1988–89	116

Source: Adapted from U.K House of Commons Health Committee 1991, 3, 5.

more money than in the past (though they did not differentiate between nominal increases and those adjusted for inflation) and that the health service was treating more patients than ever before. Thus, any responsibility for poor performance lay with inefficient managers, hospital workers, and doctors, not government funding policies (Klein 1989, chap. 7). In addition, the method of funding health authorities and hospitals was flawed because it punished "efficient" hospitals that treated patients outside their area (the cross-boundary flow problem) (see Enthoven 1985).[3]

But it was the issue of waiting lists that crystallized and epitomized the debates over the NHS. For the underfunding camp, waiting lists for elective surgery were the most damning evidence of the government's failure to commit enough resources to the health service. For the inefficiency camp, the lists represented poor resource management by health authorities and hospitals. In addition, waiting lists focused attention on the problems of governance, especially where it concerned the medical profession. Some analysts blamed doctors for long waiting lists, arguing that allowing consultants to practice private medicine on the side inevitably created a conflict of interest: if they could encourage NHS patients to go private, they would reap a handsome fee and the patient would be able to "jump the queue" for elective surgery (Yates 1987). Others added that scheduling operations by waiting lists, whereby patients were not contacted until a week prior to their surgery once they had reached the top of the list, caused cancellations of operations and operating rooms to go unused. Critics suggested that consultants adopt a diary system instead, so that patients and surgeons would schedule a fixed appointment in advance for elective operations (Enthoven 1985). But managers proved unwilling to challenge consultants' "quasi-ownership" of pay beds or their method of scheduling operations (Harrison, Hunter, and Pollitt 1990; Pollitt 1993).

Whatever the reasons for the burgeoning waiting lists, the queues had become a highly visible sign of NHS failure and a political liability for the Thatcher government. The lists were a cause of public concern because they appeared to violate the principle of equity underpinning the NHS, which held that access to care was to be based on medical necessity, not ability to pay. Yet, evidence showed that the poor and elderly were on the lists in disproportionate numbers. Some argued that this was because these were the segments of the population that were the sickest and thus most likely to use the health service, and that waiting lists were a fair way to allocate scarce resources to the neediest cases. But critics responded that it only demonstrated the inequity of the NHS, since the most vulnerable groups in the population bore a disproportionate burden of waiting for treatment (up to a year or more) while those who could afford to jump the queue with private insurance did so. Moreover, the operations for which people waited were usually not those involving experimental technology but were instead fairly common procedures like hip replacements.[4] Such delays for mundane treatments seemed to indicate that consultants were only interested in treating complex and clinically interesting cases (Yates 1987). Opinion polls indicated growing dissatisfaction with Thatcher government austerity policies and cited long waits for elective surgeries and for appointments to consultants as the two biggest complaints (Blendon and Donelan 1989; Harrison 1988, 87–90).

Indeed, the number of persons on the waiting lists had worsened over time. Those waiting for elective surgery had increased from 500,000 in 1948 to approximately 750,000 in the years between 1973 and 1982 (Yates 1987, 2–3), even if those waiting longest were for relatively minor procedures. Table 6 provides waiting list data for the 1976–86 period.[5] Though the more recent numbers showed a decline, they remained well above those in 1948.

What finally forced the government's hand was the public nature of the debate over the NHS, which came to a head in the autumn of 1987. Throughout the year, there had been widespread media coverage of burgeoning waiting lists, ward closures, and staff layoffs. And on December 7, 1987, the presidents of the three most prestigious Royal Colleges (Physicians, Surgeons, and Obstetrics and Gynecology) made a rare public foray

TABLE 6.   NHS Hospital Inpatient Waiting Lists, 1976–86 (number of patients on lists)

Year	Waiting List
1976	588,264
1977	591,096
1978	628,361
1979	695,726
1980	635,881
1981	619,393
1982	725,865
1983	703,755
1984	682,599
1985	661,249
1986	681,901

Source: British Medical Journal 1988, 1414.

into politics by issuing a joint declaration that the NHS faced imminent disaster unless adequate funding were found (Hoffenberg, Todd, and Pinker 1987; Ham, Robinson, and Benzeval 1990, chap. 1; Klein 1989, chap. 7; 1995, 177–78). Along with the BMA's commissioning of a survey of hospital consultants on the extent of underfunding (Central Committee for Hospital Medical Services 1988; Klein 1989, chap. 7; 1995, 182), doctors had moved from a policy of quiet pleading with the government to one of open confrontation. Even the president of the Institute of Health Service Management, which represented NHS administrators, called for a radical review of the NHS (Klein 1989, chap. 7). Finally, the case of a baby in Birmingham who had died after repeated cancellations of a needed heart operation for lack of nursing staff generated widespread media coverage and scathing parliamentary criticism of government policy in the NHS (Ham et al. 1990, chap. 1; Scrutator 1987).

With the BMA and the normally reticent Royal Colleges airing their concerns in public, the medical profession seemed to have violated the terms of the "implicit concordat" with the government. Doctors were questioning the government's claim to budgetary autonomy and their responsibility for rationing in what they perceived as intolerable conditions of scarcity (Day and Klein 1989, 27; Klein 1989, 235).[6] Facing mounting pressure from all sides, Thatcher promised to commit more money to the NHS in the upcoming year and announced her plans for an NHS review.

Working for Patients

The Political Context of Thatcherism

The NHS review reflected a broader sea change in political thinking and policy-making in Britain. The ascendancy of Thatcherism challenged the postwar consensus on the welfare state and mixed economy, and entailed a fundamental reassessment of the role of the state and interest groups in these domains.[7] Thatcherism offered an alternative to the consensus, blending a neoliberal restoration of the market alongside a traditional Tory reassertion of state authority. Both strands of thought left their imprint on the NHS review and its policy recommendations.

As an ideology, Thatcherism celebrated the free market and individualism. Its vision of society was that of a collection of individuals whose relationship to government was through elected representatives or political parties rather than through organized interests. Similarly, the economy was one of individuals or firms guided by the market, not by the state or groups (whether trade unions, professions, or large business associations).

The flip side of this championing of the market was Thatcherism's disdain of both corporatist negotiation—or "collectivism"—and "excessive" state intervention in the economy and society, both of which had been a major part of the postwar consensus (Beer 1982b). Under the terms of the postwar consensus, both the Conservative and Labour parties accepted a role for the state in the economy and social provision. In concrete terms, this meant some nationalization, Keynesian economic policies to ensure steady economic growth and full employment, and a Beveridge welfare state that assured the population a basic social minimum through universal, flat-rate pensions and health care, both provided by the state.[8] The consensus also extended to recognizing the legitimacy of interest groups in the policy process under corporatist arrangements.[9]

Thatcher, however, set out to destroy that consensus. According to Thatcherite doctrine, corporatism was both undemocratic and inefficient: it stifled and overruled the voice of the individual voter in the political arena, and it caused economic rigidities. Collectivism was also responsible for Britain's "ungovernability" in the 1970s, that is, policy paralysis and deadlock as a result of producer groups and voters "capturing" and making excessive demands on the state.[10]

Thatcherism's conception of the state was less straightforward, however. On the one hand, Thatcherism shared the neoliberal abhorrence of excessive state interference in the economy and social provision on the grounds that it produced economic rigidities, siphoned off resources to the welfare state and consumption, and crowded out private investment in more productive uses. Thus, policies like privatization and monetarism fit the vision of a state scaling back its responsibilities for economic performance.

On the other hand, Thatcherism asserted the need for a strong state. But *strong* in this sense meant a state with a requisite degree of autonomy from society to be able to make authoritative decisions and govern. Vigorous government action thus was critical to restoring the authority of the central state (Bulpitt 1986). Further, advancing the neoliberal project of resuscitating the market required that the central government marshal its power and authority to create market institutions, curb the economic and political power of collective organizations, and overcome opponents of the neoliberal agenda (like unions, churches, and local governments) (ibid.;

Crewe and Searing 1988; Gamble 1994; Kavanagh 1987, 1990; Richardson 1994). Even though Thatcher hated a big state, she was ready to use state power to advance her economic agenda.

Thatcherism was not only a doctrine or set of preferred policies but also a distinct policy style that rejected the negotiation and inclusion, whether of cabinet members or producer groups in the economy, that had been a regular feature of the postwar consensus. Thus, Thatcher abandoned tripartite negotiations with the peak associations representing capital and labor, and she eschewed royal commissions whose hallmarks were broad consultations and consensual policy recommendations. She also rejected the advice of traditional Westminster civil servants and Establishment politicians and instead relied on outside advisors and neoliberal research institutes like the Adam Smith Institute (ASI), the Institute of Economic Affairs (IEA), and the Centre for Policy Studies (CPS). Indeed, Thatcher actively appointed top civil servants and even set up her own Policy Unit as a source of policy ideas distinct from the civil service (Wilson 1992). The prime minister also centralized decision making in cabinet committees. Ultimately, she completed her takeover of the party by purging the "wets"—those sympathetic to the mixed economy, state social provision, and corporatist consultation—from her cabinet in 1981 and installing neoliberals in their place (Kavanagh 1987, chaps. 3 and 4, and pp. 65–91, 95–96, 256–65).

In short, Thatcher further centralized decision making in what was already a highly centralized political system. In the Westminster model of parliamentary government, the cabinet rather than the legislature is the locus of decision making: parliament cannot amend and rarely rejects legislation, and its committee system has limited authority and serves mostly as watchdog and critic of government (Harrison 1988, 92–93).[11] Party discipline also tends to be quite strong, while the simple-plurality electoral system tends to inflate majorities. Indeed, Thatcher enjoyed huge majorities after the 1983 and 1987 elections and faced a divided opposition.

Thus, Britain's political institutions granted the prime minister a number of advantages in formulating, enacting, and introducing a radical reform program into the NHS. In addition, the state's prominence in financing, providing, and managing the NHS granted Thatcher the institutional wherewithal and legal authority to introduce a market agenda into the health sector. Even so, there were political and technical limits to how far she or her successor, John Major, could go in transforming the governance of the NHS.

The Genesis of the Internal Market: The NHS Review

The policy-making process surrounding the NHS review was centralized and secretive; it typified Thatcher's style of non-negotiation and her disdain for consensus politics. Rejecting her predecessors' usual format of a Royal Commission, Thatcher instead opted for the creation of a ministerial group chaired by herself and involving a few trusted advisers. The review team excluded the organized medical profession and other health care interest groups from participation, and did not consult widely (Vallance-Owen interview, March 13, 1992; Klein 1989). It was learned that the review team instead relied on the input of a few doctors who were favorably inclined toward market incentives and who had pioneered experiments in peer review and in involving consultants in the management of hospitals.[12] The secretary of state for health, Kenneth Clarke, justified such secrecy:

> The BMA, the Royal Colleges, never recovered from the feeling that they had not been consulted. They were deeply shocked that we weren't going down the traditional path. . . . We would have found the whole thing easier had we consulted. On the other hand, experience I think would show, had we consulted we'd have taken two, three years over the process, and the input from the interest groups, as well as from the rest of the political world, would largely have been in favor of the status quo, slightly amended with more money, and we would never have come up with any reforms at all. (Clarke, quoted in Day and Klein 1992, 472)

If the usual health policy interests did not contribute substantially to shaping the reforms, some neoliberal think tanks did. The IEA, CPS, and ASI all prepared proposals for the review and advocated some type of market in health care, though the CPS and ASI had more influence on the review than did the IEA.[13]

The review began as a response to the widespread perception of a crisis of funding, but for political and economic reasons left the financing of health care untouched.[14] The most radical financing proposals came from the IEA, which advocated vouchers for those who wished to opt out of the NHS and purchase private insurance. But the review team believed that the public would not tolerate the IEA's proposals to scrap the tax-financed basis of the NHS for an insurance-based system (whether compulsory national insurance or private insurance). Employment-based insurance would also have likely provoked the opposition of business and undercut Thatcher's efforts to reduce labor costs in order to make Britain an attractive place to do business and invest. Further, the instrument of central budgeting made the NHS quite effective in controlling costs; any type of insurance system would have only cost more (Klein 1989, 237–38). Similar calculations of political acceptability also guided the government's decision to not introduce patient copayments for hospital stays (Butler interview, March 19, 1992).

Having decided that privatization was off the table, the review team instead shifted its focus to reform of the delivery system. With this shift in emphasis, ideas for the internal market came to the fore. This idea owed much to the model of the American health maintenance organization (HMO) and to the work of Alain Enthoven, a Stanford health economist and the guru of the theory of managed competition, even if the review team never consulted him. Indeed, the Thatcher government had studied American HMOs earlier in the decade (Glennerster, Matsaganis, and Owens 1992, 8), and both the CPS and ASI recommended adapting the HMO model and some type of provider competition to fit within the context of a publicly financed health care system.[15] Enthoven had originally floated the idea of an internal market in the NHS in 1985, and his proposal subsequently influenced the research institutes that advised the review team. Elements of his 1985 proposal also found their way into Working for Patients.[16] The different proposals envisioned district health authorities or other organizations headed by managers as taking the lead role in purchasing health care services. Kenneth Clarke, however, wanted to give GPs a direct role in commissioning hospital care for their patients and championed recommendations to that effect.[17]

The white paper that emerged from the review offered a blueprint for NHS reform that was compatible with Thatcher's predilection toward market solutions to public policy problems more generally. By prodding NHS actors to be more efficient, competition promised to address the government's underfunding critics without having to resort to a politically perilous transformation of existing financing mechanisms. Greater efficiency could also avoid further infusions of cash into an unreconstructed health care system (see Lawson 1993, 614). At the same time, however, the document incorporated strategies to strengthen NHS administration that had originated with the 1983 Griffiths managerial reforms. As we shall see, both market competition and stronger managerialism challenged the political bargain with the medical profession in fundamental ways.

The Internal Market

The internal market lay at the heart of the government's white paper, *Working for Patients*. It was designed to prod doctors and managers toward greater efficiency (DoH et al. 1989b, 6–8). The market transformed existing health care actors into separate purchasers and providers. Prior to this, each DHA had directly managed the hospitals in its area and thereby provided care directly to the local population. Under the internal market, however, DHAs became purchasers of health care for their populations and won the freedom to buy services from either NHS or private hospitals if they could provide services more cheaply and quickly (DoH et al. 1989b, esp. chaps. 4 and 6). Since "money would follow patients," patients could bypass the long waiting lists in their districts, while hospitals that could provide treatment in a more timely fashion would be rewarded financially.

General practitioners could also secure a role in purchasing in the internal market if they enlisted in the fundholding scheme. Fundholding was voluntary and initially restricted to large GP practices (those with at least 11,000 patients). Fundholders were initially limited to purchasing outpatient diagnostic and treatment services, certain inpatient and day surgery cases—especially elective surgeries for which there were long waiting lists—and diagnostic lab and X-ray tests performed by hospitals on direct referral from GPs. Over time, however, policymakers allowed practices with as few as 3,000 patients to be eligible for fundholder status and expanded the range of services they could purchase (see NHS Executive 1995a, 1995c, 1995d). Like DHAs, GP fundholders were free to contract with NHS hospitals within or outside their districts or with private sector facilities in order to obtain faster or less expensive treatment (DoH et al. 1989b, esp. chap. 6).

The other side of the purchaser-provider divide concerned hospitals. Hospitals could now become freestanding Trusts independent of DHA control. The white paper granted Trusts a range of powers: they could employ their own staff directly, set pay to local market conditions instead of abiding by national pay scales, enter into contracts with other providers, dispose of their assets as they saw fit, retain surpluses and build up reserves for improving services or financing investments, and borrow from the government or the private sector (DoH et al. 1989b, chap. 3).

Stronger Management

Working for Patients also sought to strengthen the position of managers at all levels of the NHS. Managers were to be the government's allies who would implement the internal market reforms. They would be responsible for developing and monitoring contracts. They would also act as a counterweight to medical power, exerting stronger oversight over doctors to ensure that they provided cost-effective care.

Hence, the white paper proposed new statutory powers for managers in their relations with consultants. The first area of change applied to the employment of consultants. Consultants would no longer be employed by a distant Regional Health Authority but would instead be employed directly by the Trust hospitals in which they worked. Trust managers would specify the contracts, monitor compliance, and theoretically could fire a consultant if local market conditions dictated such a move. In addition, managers would draw up detailed job plans for consultants specifying the services provided and the time that doctors were expected to devote to the NHS. These changes would abolish lifetime tenure and nationally determined pay scales for consultants. In their place would be a flexible, decentralized labor market. Administrators also gained a statutory voice in the appointment of new consultants to hospital posts (see DoH et al. 1989b, chap. 5).

The reforms also proposed that managers have some influence in distinction awards. These were financial payments for consultants as determined solely by their peers in the medical profession and on the basis of clinical criteria. The 1989 white paper granted senior health authority managers a voice in nominating consultants for distinction awards and mandated that such awards supplement clinical criteria with evidence that the doctor in question had contributed to the management and development of the NHS (DoH et al. 1989b, chap. 5).

Finally, the reforms required all consultants to participate in medical audit, or peer review, to encourage clinical "best practice." While doctors alone would conduct such peer reviews, DHA managers were expected to ensure that medical audit was in place and have access to the results generally. Local managers could initiate an independent professional audit if not satisfied with the quality or cost-effectiveness of services (DoH et al. 1989b, chap. 5).

Managerial scrutiny of general practice would be nearly as extensive as that for hospital care. Administrators were directed to work with general practitioners to set up and oversee a system of medical audit for all GPs. In addition, in an effort to control the amount of NHS expenditure on prescription drugs, which the government deemed too high, Family Health Services Authorities would monitor the prescribing patterns of general practitioners through indicative drug budgets (DoH et al. 1989b, chap. 6).

In addition to granting managers new authority over the medical profession, the white paper built upon precedents laid out under the Griffiths reforms designed to enhance the capacity of the central state to monitor the behavior of NHS actors in the internal market. *Working for Patients* called for "an effective chain of management command running from Districts through Regions to the Chief Executive and from there to the Secretary of State" (DoH et al. 1989b, 13). Thus, the government reorganized the Regional and District Health Authorities along managerial lines prevailing in the private sector. Health authority boards became smaller and saw the appointment of executive and nonexecutive members with managerial and business skills. In addition, the secretary of state designated the chairs of the RHAs and DHAs and the nonexecutive members of the RHAs, while local authorities, trade unions, and health care professions were deprived of their right to appoint representatives to health authority boards (DoH et al. 1989b, chap. 8). In addition, responsibility for the performance of each health authority, FHSA, and Trust hospital was vested in the person of a general manager. FHSAs, moreover, lost the administrative autonomy they had enjoyed since the inception of the NHS and now came under the guidance of the NHS Executive (DoH et al. 1989b, 23, 60–62; NHS Management Executive 1990, 5–7). These structural changes not only gave a preference to persons with a business background, but in practice the appointments made by the secretary of state were often individuals whose loyalties and sentiments matched the government's.

Finally, the government sought to separate politics from management to prevent excessive political interference in day-to-day administration. *Working for Patients* specified a Policy Board to set strategic priorities and a separate Executive to handle operational affairs and to ensure that policies set by the Policy Board were implemented in the NHS (NHS Management Executive 1991; DoH et al. 1989b, chap. 2).

But even as the central government strengthened its administrative capacities in the NHS, it also expected managers at local levels to implement policies with considerable discretion and autonomy.[18] As we shall see, however, the government encountered difficulties in its effort to devolve authority and enhance upward accountability at the same time. Similarly, separating politics from administration was no easy task in a publicly financed and administered health service. But we must first account for the reaction of the medical profession, since doctors were a primary target of the reforms.

The Medical Profession Fights Back

The BMA's Critique

As might be expected, the BMA was appalled by *Working for Patients*. The association took issue with much of the content of the white paper as well as its unaccustomed exclusion from formulating the reforms. The BMA's critical stance toward the NHS reforms and its analysis of the sources of the difficulties in the health service had changed relatively little since 1989.[19] But for tactical reasons discussed below, the BMA found it necessary to soften its more militant opposition to the internal market reforms. A consistent criticism was that the problems of the NHS stemmed from government policies of underfunding. While noting that the government's emphasis on preventive and community care was admirable, the BMA maintained that it diverted money from the acute hospital sector.[20]

The BMA also harbored serious reservations toward the internal market. The association worried that the purchaser-provider split and competition in the health service would produce inequality in services available to patients, threaten the comprehensiveness of the NHS, and put cost containment and profit considerations ahead of patient care and choice. Even though the white paper barred this, the BMA feared that Trust hospitals would eliminate unprofitable core services, such as emergency care or certain elective procedures. Cutthroat competition might also encourage hospitals to turn away unprofitable patients. A two-tiered NHS would be the result, with patients in deprived areas lacking access to certain services. Trusts and competing hospitals also threatened the survival of district general hospitals, which offered a comprehensive range of services for the district population.

In addition, the BMA took issue with the rapid pace of implementation and the high costs associated with constructing the internal market. It deplored the lack of pilot studies and argued that health authorities, fundholders, and hospitals did not have the computer systems and costing information needed for contracting. The BMA also highlighted the high transaction costs and the swelling of managerial ranks associated with creating the internal market, and contended that these new administrative costs diverted scarce funds away from patient care.

Doctors also feared encroachment on their professional autonomy from newly empowered managers concerned only with the costs of treatment in a competitive environment. Medical audit, for example, might become "value for money" reviews rather than an exercise to improve clinical standards.[21] Giving managers a say in specifying consultant contracts and Trust hospitals the power to hire and fire consultants at will would certainly alter the social autonomy of doctors to decide the form and pace of their work. The BMA also charged that allowing Trust managers to set pay and conditions of service locally would undermine the even distribution of hospital doctors throughout the country by luring them to high-salary areas. But the profession also worried that patient care could be harmed by managers more interested in cutting costs than in clinical criteria.

Naturally, the medical profession took affront to the changes in the corporatist bargain that the reforms implied, though it couched its criticisms in terms of democratic accountability. Thus, the BMA publicly complained that appointing business people to Trust and health authority boards and barring consumer and professional representatives undermined the accountability of the health service to patients. Privately, however, the profession lamented its loss of corporatist representation in administration and its lack of input in the reforms. According to the GPs' craft committee:

> The imposition of the new [GP] contract and the implementation of the NHS Review changes have changed fundamentally the arrangements for GPs to be represented in the NHS administrative/management structure. Put simply, what was previously regarded as a partnership between the profession and NHS administration, embodying a consensual style of management, has been changed to a managerial system which is ostensibly confrontational and in which professional representatives are required to fulfill a "trade union" role in relation to local FHSA or Health Board management. . . . Whatever further changes may be applied to the NHS, it is improbable that general practice can ever regain its special "Partnership" relationship with FHSAs. (General Medical Services Committee 1991, 18)

But the most difficult issue for the BMA was GP fundholding. Officially, the BMA opposed fundholding on the grounds that a multitude of small purchasers would fragment the NHS and render population-based planning of health services by health authorities impossible. In addition, to the extent that fundholders contracted only with certain hospitals or consultants, the scheme would reduce patients' choice of provider. But the BMA also feared that giving GPs financial responsibility for purchasing would create conflicts of interest, with doctors putting cost considerations before patient needs in making referrals for hospital care. In addition, the

BMA publicly fretted that the scheme would reinforce inequities among GPs by granting fundholders (who tended to be larger practices with the means to take on the administrative burdens of fundholding) numerous advantages over non-fundholders (who tended to be smaller, poorer practices in inner cities).[22] And although this was not the official policy line, BMA leaders and many of the rank and file were concerned that fundholding had generated damaging divisions within the profession and had empowered certain groups of doctors at the expense of others (see below).

The BMA offered its own alternatives to *Working for Patients*. Like its criticisms, its positions were fairly consistent over the years, though over time, some of its recommendations softened to accommodate the reality of the internal market and purchaser-provider split. Thus, the BMA consistently called for more money for the NHS, particularly for the hospital sector. The amount varied, but in the past the association had proposed a formula whereby health care expenditures would rise with the growth of gross domestic product (*British Medical Journal* 1988, 1415, 1418). The BMA also argued for pilot studies to test the internal market. In addition, national pay scales should be retained to ensure a fair distribution of medical personnel. Naturally, the organized medical profession should be fully involved in consultations and negotiations on further policy developments.[23] Since GP fundholding was the most divisive issue for the BMA, the association had trouble devising a clear alternative. BMA leaders expended substantial energy to try to find alternatives to fundholding that would close the fissures within the profession.

Tactical Disarray within the BMA

With its exclusion from the NHS review, the BMA found itself in an unaccustomed "outsider" position. Even though Kenneth Clarke consulted BMA leaders at meetings in 1989 and 1990, relations between the association and the government were highly strained.[24] The meetings bore little fruit, as the BMA proved unable to deter the government from its course of action. In response, the BMA embarked upon a very public campaign of opposition consistent with its newfound outsider position. This included a virulent media campaign in spring 1989 to "educate" the public about the likely dangers of the *Working for Patients* reforms. The BMA took out newspaper advertisements critical of Clarke and the reforms, did interviews, and held press conferences and public meetings to discuss the NHS changes. The media blitz and public meetings matched the government's high-profile campaign to promote the reforms.[25] At its special representative meeting in May 1989, the BMA advised doctors not to cooperate with GP fundholding schemes or hospital Trusts and demanded immediate negotiations with the government (*British Medical Journal* 1989; Lowry 1989).

Being forced into an outsider position meant that the BMA also had to focus its energies on actors outside the executive branch, which was the normal and more effective channel of influence in policy-making in the British political system. Thus, the association lobbied members of Parliament, gave evidence to the House of Commons Social Services Committee and the Health Committee in their inquiries on the reforms, met with opposition politicians, and held fringe meetings at the main party conferences. The BMA also helped local GPs organize opposition to Trust hospitals. But none of these efforts succeeded. The government enacted the reforms into law as the NHS and Community Care Act in June 1990 and approved the first wave of hospitals that applied to become Trusts.[26]

A number of events induced the BMA to search for a new strategy toward the government. One was the passage of the NHS Act in 1990. The strategy of outright opposition made sense when the reforms were still at the proposal stage, but seemed futile now that the white paper had become law. But a second change was the election of a new chairman of the BMA Council, Dr. Jeremy Lee-Potter, in the summer of 1990. Lee-Potter was decidedly more moderate in his approach to the NHS reforms than his predecessor, Dr. John Marks, who had led the public campaign against *Working for Patients*. Lee-Potter believed that the policy of noncooperation was no longer an option and that the BMA would get further by means of private, informal talks and direct access to the government rather than by pressing its case through the media (Delamothe 1990; Vallance-Owen interview, March 13, 1992). Only by regaining insider status could the BMA press its case effectively to the government and thereby shape and slow down the implementation of the reforms. Another event was Thatcher's ouster and the installment of John Major as prime minister in the autumn of 1990. Both Major and his new head of the DoH, William Waldegrave, seemed more conciliatory toward the BMA than their predecessors.

Lee-Potter's moderate stance bore some fruit in the form of high-level meetings with the secretary of state, informal communication with DoH officials, and a few informal meetings with Major (BMA 1991a, 3; 1992a, 5; Vallance-Owen interview, March 13, 1992). However, the BMA's reading of the new political situation and its hope of reasserting its influence appeared too optimistic. Despite the BMA leadership's protestations in private meetings with DoH officials and ministers, the government continued to press ahead with its implementation of the reforms, approving more hospitals' applications for Trust status in 1991 and 1992 and encouraging more GPs to become fundholders by reducing the minimum practice size (Glennerster, Matsaganis, and Owens 1992, 10; Mihill 1992a; Jones 1991; Timmins and Jones 1991).[27]

At the same time, however, the Major government noticeably slowed the pace of implementation. Under its "steady state" policy, the government exerted tight central control over the implementation process, allowing only larger hospitals to become Trusts and granting GPs generous start-up payments to aid the transition to fundholding. Its decision, however, was not a conversion to the BMA's point of view but was rather the product of careful political calculation: Major knew all too well that the NHS was popular with voters and did not want to risk losing the 1992 election by ramming through the reforms in reckless fashion (Brindle 1991b).

The Conservatives' surprise victory at the polls in April 1992 dashed any hopes the BMA might have harbored of halting the Conservative government's reform program. The NHS was a high-profile issue during the election campaign, and opinion polls revealed widespread public dissatisfaction with the NHS reforms and seemingly registered little support for the Conservative party. But Major won the election on economic and taxation issues, albeit with a vastly reduced parliamentary majority. Major then pressed on with implementation of the NHS reforms under a new secretary of state, Virginia Bottomley.[28] Rather than pointing the BMA in the direction of reconciliation with the government and acceptance of the NHS reforms, the election results only exacerbated and brought out into the open long-standing divisions within the BMA over its future policy direction.

Dilemmas of Representation for the BMA

The divisions among the BMA's members toward the NHS reforms severely undercut its political effectiveness in its dealings with the government. But the BMA's inability to settle on a strategy toward the government or a position toward the reforms was not simply an argument pitting the leadership against the rank and file. Instead, such questions pierced the organization at all levels, splitting the Council as well as the membership. Nowhere was the dissension starker than with GP fundholding.

General practitioner fundholding opened up two lines of division within the association. The first line of cleavage was that dividing general practitioners and consultants. Many GPs found fundholding attractive because it provided them a new voice in hospital care. But this influence came at the expense of consultants' freedom to decide which patients to treat and when in the hospitals. Some consultants feared encroachment on their turf by budget-wielding GPs who might threaten to send their patients to different hospitals that could promise faster or cheaper service (see Glennerster, Matsaganis, and Owens 1992, 26–27).

Fundholding also created fissures within the ranks of general practitioners. Most GPs initially resisted the idea of fundholding.[29] But their opposition gradually eroded as more of them saw the potential benefits of the scheme. As it turned out, fundholding proved to be quite popular with many general practitioners. By 1994, over 2,000 of the 9,100 GP practices in England (or nearly 22 percent of GPs) had joined the scheme (National Audit Office 1994, 7); by 1996, more than 40 percent of the population of England was projected to be covered under fundholding (NHS Executive 1995d, 1). The number of fundholders was expected to grow as the government reduced the minimum practice size (NHS Executive 1994b, 1995a).

Non-fundholding GPs, however, felt differently. They feared that the internal market would constrain their freedom to make referrals to the hospitals and consultants of their choice. Unlike fundholders, who were free to contract with whichever providers they chose, non-fundholding GPs had to depend on DHA purchasers to take account of their preferences when developing contracts with hospitals (DoH et al. 1989b). As a result, non-fundholders feared that the internal market would leave them behind, and they resented the powers of GP fundholders (Beecham 1992f, 1992g). Non-fundholding GPs also wanted to be involved in purchasing hospital and other health services.

But as more and more GPs signed up for fundholding, the association had to find some way to soften its opposition to the scheme if it hoped to keep these doctors within its ranks. Yet it also had to appease non-fundholding GPs and hospital consultants. The BMA leadership pursued a number of strategies to deal with this dilemma. One was for the BMA to fudge its position in an effort to bridge its internal schisms. On the one hand, its official policy by 1993 acknowledged the reality of fundholding. The BMA had little choice here, since continued resistance undermined its claim to represent all GPs, and the government had steadfastly refused to meet with the GMSC on fundholding issues until the association withdrew its opposition. The BMA also feared that continued opposition would provoke fundholders' exodus to a new rival, the National Association of Fundholding Practices.[30] On the other hand, delegates to BMA meetings continued to voice their criticism of fundholding, passed motions deploring the effects of the market, and called upon the government to rethink the purchaser-provider split.[31] Thus, far from signaling a wholehearted conversion to the benefits of fundholding, the BMA's acceptance of fundholding was a tactical move to prevent a fatal split within its ranks and to remain relevant in health policy-making, while its continued criticism of the scheme sought to appease non-fundholders and consultants.

The other strategy that BMA leaders pursued sought to forge a new consensus among the membership and recover the association's leading role in health policy and within the NHS itself. Toward that end, the leadership issued a number of discussion papers, the most important of which were *Leading for Health,* issued in 1991, and *Future Models for the NHS* in 1995. While medical leaders and the documents declined to endorse a specific model, BMA officials leaned toward either of two alternatives. One would have retained the purchaser-provider split but abolished fundholders and substituted them with larger GP-led health authority purchasers. The other would have scrapped the internal market and purchaser-provider split altogether, instead empowering health authorities, with the involvement of both GPs and hospital doctors, to plan for services (Beecham 1992g; BMA 1991b, 1995).[32]

Still, members were divided on the wisdom of Lee-Potter's moderate policy line, as registered by BMA membership meetings between 1991 and 1993. At the 1991 annual meeting, for example, delegates instructed the Council to "seek constructive dialogue with the Government rather than confrontation" (Beecham et al. 1991, 128), thereby endorsing Lee-Potter's approach. At the same time, however, delegates directed the BMA to "monitor the effects of the reforms[,] publicise the flaws [and] increase its criticisms of those reforms" and reiterated the association's view that the reforms did not solve the basic problem of NHS underfunding (ibid.).[33]

Continued polarization over policy direction made effective leadership of the profession all but impossible. Rather than having a mandate for a clear and agreed-upon course of action, Lee-Potter had to expend an inordinate amount of energy trying to convince the membership that his "constructive dialogue" approach was correct. Until these internal divisions were resolved, the BMA chairman had little hope of influencing government policy.

Structural factors constrained Lee-Potter and weakened his effectiveness in his dealings with the government. Some of these were internal to the BMA, while some were external. First, internal democratic structures within the BMA exacerbated the Council's leadership problems. Because the BMA's constitution grants the Representative Body significant voice in determining association policy, the Council lacks the freedom to set policy independently of the rank and file.[34] Second, because the BMA is a voluntary membership association, doctors are free to exit the association if they are unhappy with the leadership or its policies. Thus, Lee-Potter and the Council were limited in the extent to which they could disregard the members' opinions or force them to accept a particular policy line. Since the BMA claimed to represent all doctors, it had to somehow accommodate the opinions of both fundholders and non-fundholders, and both consultants who supported and those who opposed Trusts, in such a way as not to lose members. Moreover, since the Council possessed little or no sanction power over rebel members, its main weapon consisted of moral suasion (Grey-Turner and Sutherland 1982, 326–27 and chap. 9). For all these reasons, Lee-Potter could do no more than gently prod the profession toward a policy of "constructive dialogue" over a period of years.

External constraints also limited the BMA Council's maneuvering room. The economic dependence of most physicians on the NHS, especially general practitioners who were not allowed to engage in private practice, meant that a BMA call for a strike, boycott, or other form of noncooperation with the government's health service reforms was not a realistic option. Most members would not have tolerated the financial loss entailed by such action. In addition, the BMA also had to contend with other medical organizations that challenged its claim to represent the medical profession in the political arena. This meant not only heading off the new National Association of Fundholding Practices but also seeking the support of the Royal Colleges. Otherwise, the government would be able to vanquish the medical profession through a divide-and-conquer strategy.[35]

In fact, the Royal Colleges and the BMA did not act as one, though the divergence was more on tactics and strategy than on views toward the substance of the reforms.[36] The Colleges found the BMA's early militancy too negative and preferred instead a dialogue with the government (Macpherson interview, April 8, 1992). This moderation in part stemmed from the fact that the Colleges were legally barred from taking on an explicit trade union role or getting enmeshed in questions concerning pay and conditions of service for doctors. But if the Royal Colleges refused to engage in open warfare with the government, that did not mean that they stood completely above the fray. After all, public criticism of Thatcher's funding policies by the presidents of the three most prestigious Royal Colleges had precipitated the NHS review in the first place. The Colleges had also engaged in behind-the-scenes activity during the review in an effort to influence the government. On the whole, however, the Colleges engaged in more muted activity than the BMA, using traditional avenues of access, such as attending meetings with and submitting position papers to the government and DoH.

Lee-Potter's inability to bridge the internal divide afflicting the membership or to devise a clear policy line ultimately led to his forced departure in 1993. On the heels of the annual meeting's grudging acceptance of fundholding, the Council broke with tradition and refused to support the reelection bid of its chairman and instead chose Alexander Macara.[37] The new chairman followed a two-pronged approach. On the one hand, he took a tough public line, using strong language to point out the shortcomings of the reforms to the BMA membership and to the media. In this way, he boosted the morale of the BMA rank and file in ways that Lee-Potter's more moderate tone had been unable to do. On the other hand, Macara continued to follow his predecessor's strategy of negotiating with the government and taking a more reasonable line than his public comments suggested (interview with medical journalist, July 21, 1995).[38] Following Lee-Potter's path, Macara also tried to forge a consensus among different doctors' organizations to restore the profession's former position in the NHS. Thus, the BMA, Royal Colleges, and other medical bodies organized a conference in November 1994 entitled "Core Values for the Medical Profession in the Twenty-first Century." The conference report noted that doctors were demoralized and confused by the rapid changes in the NHS in recent years, and that the reforms challenged their traditional roles, values, and responsibilities. But it also admitted that the profession was slowly coming around to the new health care environment even while it sought to find its place in it (BMA et al. 1994).

How effective was BMA strategy? It was clear that while the BMA's initially militant stance had won the hearts and minds of the public, it had nonetheless failed in its larger aims. After all, the association proved unable to dissuade Thatcher from enacting the internal market or Major from implementing it. Nevertheless, Macara's strategy to regain an insider position for the BMA in order to influence subsequent policy developments bore some fruit. As we shall see, the BMA may have lost the war to defeat the internal market, but it still won some important skirmishes, not just with Major but especially with his successor Tony Blair.

Assessing the Reforms

For all the rhetoric of markets and competition in *Working for Patients,* the reforms in practice fell far short of a free market in health care. Rather, the Major government took care to limit the play of competition even as it strengthened its capacity to intervene centrally. Thus, NHS governance was transformed from a hybrid of corporatism and state hierarchy to a new combination of market, state centralization, and curtailed corporatism. Under this new regime, doctors managed to hold on to many of their prerogatives, but also saw changes to the corporatist bargain. This new hybrid also had implications for the balance between equity and cost containment in health care.

The Political Bargain with Physicians: Corporatism Curtailed but Preserved

With *Working for Patients,* Thatcher had declared war on corporatism and had sought to deploy market competition and managerial controls to destroy doctors' collective power and to curb the freedoms of individual clinicians. Initial events suggested that the government had succeeded in breaking the power of the medical profession: the BMA's exclusion from the NHS review and its subsequent outsider campaign appeared to signal the demise of corporatist consultation, while the purchaser-provider split and the powers granted managers seemed set to destroy the freedoms of doctors at the microlevel.

But the decade since the publication of the white paper provides evidence of both change and continuity. Policymakers did not destroy corporatism completely; on the contrary, the BMA saw a partial restoration of its position in negotiating health policy even as it lost much of its corporatist representation in NHS administration. Some physicians did quite well under the internal market, while others lost ground. As described above, the BMA struggled to adapt to this new terrain even as it fought to preserve its past prominence.

In the matter of negotiating health policy, the BMA managed to preserve its relevance at the national level. But it had to accept that there were limits to the scope of negotiations. The corporatist bargain had accorded the BMA the status of negotiating partner with government on most areas of health policy. But this had never implied that the medical profession had an automatic right to negotiate or veto all aspects of health policy. The history of health politics in the twentieth century showed that the state excluded the BMA from negotiating on the basic structures of the health care system, as in 1911 and 1946. Both pieces of legislation passed over the opposition of doctors. But in both cases, the BMA's virulent opposition to being shut out of the talks, as well as its objections to certain substantive points of the legislation, subsequently persuaded government officials to resume negotiations with it in order to secure the cooperation and participation of doctors in the new health care systems. In negotiating the details of implementation, the BMA scored important victories protecting vital areas of physician autonomy while ensuring a legally recognized role for itself in administering the new health care systems. Thus, between these rare ruptures in the usual policy pattern, the BMA enjoyed a close, privileged relationship with the health ministry and negotiated as a matter of course policies that affected its members (Day and Klein 1992; Eckstein 1960, chap. 4).

The policy-making process surrounding *Working for Patients* in many respects conformed to this pattern. As had happened in the past, the medical profession was again reminded that its status as a negotiating partner with government rested on custom, not on legal right, and that what it could negotiate did not extend to decisions on the fundamental contours of the health care system.[39] Thatcher's ramming through the white paper without the BMA's input, combined with Major's consolidation of her reforms over the BMA's protests, made this point painfully clear to doctors.

But as in 1911 and 1948, the BMA found that policymakers were willing to accord it a place in negotiating the details of implementation, particularly on the terms and conditions of service for doctors. Discussions, both formal and informal, resumed at all levels: "As in all good marriages, we went through a period of separation, but the divorce proceedings are off the agenda right now. In fact, we're back on reconciliation" (Roxan interview, July 18, 1995).

Major's willingness to restart talks allowed the BMA to preserve much of its influence at the national level. One example was the BMA's victory on the question of devolving decisions on consultants' pay. *Working for Patients* had announced the government's intention to scrap the central pay-bargaining machinery and instead have Trust managers decide pay and conditions of service of all NHS personnel.[40] These changes would have effectively ended consultants' lifetime tenure and the BMA's national-level input on their terms and conditions of service. But by 1995, Major had retreated. While Trusts rather than RHAs now held consultant contracts, these contracts largely followed nationally determined agreements on pay scales and terms of service (interview with DoH official, July 19, 1995; Sturges interview, July 19, 1995), thereby safeguarding consultants' tenure and the BMA's national presence. Hedging its bets, the BMA also enhanced its presence at the hospital level by establishing bargaining units and training union negotiators in Trusts (Beecham 1992d; Hart 1992b).

Still, even though talks had resumed at the central level, things were not quite what they had been before. The internal market created a number of new actors with important positions in the NHS. As a consequence, the health policy network became more crowded, and the association found it was no longer the only voice that the government had to consult or heed. Nor was it the only actor whose goodwill the government had to depend on for its policies to succeed. Now, the BMA had to share the political space with a greater number of health care actors and to make its voice heard above such organizations as the National Association of Fundholding Practices, a rival organization representing GP fundholders, and the National Association of Health Authorities and Trusts, which represented managerial interests, as well as perennially contending with the Royal Colleges.

In spite of improved relations with Major, BMA leaders believed they had lost ground in the political arena:

What that means for the BMA is a swing back toward the position where the BMA is beginning to exert a little more authority than it practiced three or four years ago. I would still say, though, that we're not anywhere near the position of power and authority that we had eight or nine years ago when doctors were very much in the driving seat. I think we're in the passenger seat now, giving directions. Whether we take up driving again or whether we want to take up driving is a matter of debate. Or whether it makes sense for there to be more than one driver in the future. And I think we're working toward that last scenario. . . . And we get back to the stage where, when the BMA gives a view on an issue, that's listened to—I'm not saying always followed, because we don't always get it right, but certainly that the BMA has an authority in the society which should be listened to. (Roxan interview, July 18, 1995)

In the domain of health care administration, the changes to the corporatist bargain were even more substantial. The medical profession found itself barred from collective representation on health authorities and boards of directors of Trusts, even though local medical committees remained in place.[41] The managerial revolution meant that doctors now had to share power with more assertive administrators in running the NHS. The BMA also had to contend with managers as potentially new allies of government.

The new power-sharing between doctors and managers had consequences for professional autonomy, particularly for hospital consultants. But again, there were both continuities and changes to professional freedom as a result of compromises struck between doctors and the Major government. In the area of distinction awards, managers indeed made some inroads: Trust managers were now represented on the award committees, and the criteria for awards included consultants' contribution to efficiency and to the management of the NHS as well as clinical excellence. Moreover, outsiders—managers, Trusts, health authorities, and MPs—now had access to the names of the recipients of such awards (see NHS Management Executive 1994c, 1995b, 1995f; Sturges interview, July 19, 1995). Yet, the changes to distinction awards did not go as far as originally proposed but instead represented a face-saving compromise for both the government and the BMA. The Major government had originally intended to introduce performance-related pay for consultants (Beecham 1992e; Hart 1992b). But after consultants protested that this threatened their prerogative to set their own professional standards, a government working party came to a compromise agreement that left much of the previous system unchanged.[42] Still, a precedent had been set. No longer were distinction awards the exclusive purview of clinicians; now, doctors had to include lay officials in the decision process.

Managers' authority to hold consultants accountable for their performance also constituted new inroads by laypersons in physicians' professional autonomy. For example, in specifying the number of hours consultants were expected to devote to NHS service, job plans were a potentially powerful tool for managers to control doctors' activities. In addition, managers not only had the statutory means to hold consultants to account, but also the incentive to do so. Because managers were subject to review from above, and their pay and job security were tied to the financial performance of their hospitals, they had an interest in ensuring that hospital resources were used in the most cost-effective way. Even so, administrators generally refrained from using job plans as a stick with which to beat consultants, and in any case, clinicians generally did far more for their NHS hospitals than their contracts required (interview with DoH official, July 19, 1995).

Thus, the legal authority accruing to managers did not necessarily entail a definitive shift in the balance of power between them and clinicians. The degree to which managers have gained and consultants have lost is difficult to determine since no national studies are available. Anecdotal evidence suggested that relations between managers and clinicians varied by hospital, but that the relationships tended to be more collaborative than confrontational, as clinicians and managers recognized their interdependence and common stake in the good performance of their hospitals (Klein 1995, 244). If managers were perhaps no longer the deferential diplomats they had once been, neither had they become the overlords of the medical profession.

The subject of medical audit was perhaps the most controversial aspect of the reforms, since it went to the heart of individual practitioners' clinical freedom and the profession's collective claim to set its own standards of practice. Again, the effects of the reforms in these areas have been mixed. *Working for Patients* required all consultants to participate in medical audit and authorized managers to review their results. But the government was careful to avoid an outright clash with the medical profession on its most cherished aspect of autonomy. Thus, medical audit as it evolved in practice was a compromise. The medical profession was now required to police its own members' treatment decisions for clinical effectiveness. Managers were to have access to the results of the reviews and could order an independent audit if they suspected that quality or cost-effectiveness had been compromised. This implied that doctors would now have to take into account criteria other than just clinical standards. Still, the medical profession alone was to determine the standards of medical audit and undertake the reviews; managers were to remain more at arm's length in the process.

How effective, then, was medical audit in influencing clinical practice? On the one hand, medical audit seemed to be a potent way for the government to get the profession to follow "best practice" by adhering to clinical standards, though whether it was also effective in persuading doctors to explicitly consider the costs of their treatment decisions was unclear. The medical profession claimed that it had come around to accept the legitimacy of peer review based on medical standards, if not economic or efficiency criteria (BMA et al. 1994; Conference of Medical Royal Colleges 1989). This suggested that the profession appeared to recognize that monitoring the clinical freedom of individual practitioners was the price to be paid to preserve its collective autonomy. In addition, to the extent that physicians were willing to impose sanctions on doctors whose practice patterns varied widely from their peers, medical audit held out the potential to deliver the same results from doctors that direct involvement by laypersons would. On the other hand, the effectiveness of peer review in changing physician behavior depended on whether doctors were willing to sanction their own and whether managers would push them to do so by reviewing the results of the audits themselves or threatening outside reviews if dissatisfied with the results. Early evidence, however, was not encouraging. The peer-review process remained poorly developed, many doctors regarded it as a marginal activity, standards were set locally by clinicians (thus allowing for wide variation) rather than using nationally agreed measures of performance, and education rather than sanctioning of physicians remained the goal of such exercises (Pollitt 1993).

General practitioners, like consultants, also found themselves subject to medical audit and managerial scrutiny of the results. But again, the BMA succeeded in staving off more stringent controls over GPs' clinical freedom. The clearest example of this involved indicative drug budgets, which would have amounted to a global budget for each GP's prescribing, and the levying of financial penalties for those who exceeded their budgets. Following negotiations between the DoH and BMA, however, the Major government agreed to keep budgets as advisory tools rather than as hard budgets, dropped the financial sanctions, and allowed members of the medical profession rather than lay managers to monitor doctors' prescribing patterns (Beecham 1990c).

The biggest impact of the reforms was GP fundholding's alteration of the balance of power within the medical profession. As fundholding granted GPs a greater voice in hospital care, it forced consultants to change their practice patterns and their clinical and social autonomy. Fundholding thus restored some of the power that primary care doctors had lost in 1948 (Glennerster, Matsaganis, and Owens 1992, 9).[43] Consultants now had to be more responsive to GPs or risk losing patients to other clinicians or hospitals.

Consultants and general practitioners were quite aware of this shift in the balance of power. A meeting of hospital managers, consultants, and local fundholders over contracts illustrated this new power reality. At the meeting, the consultants reproached the managers for agreeing to the contracts. One GP fundholder retorted to the consultants, "'It's all about your power. You can't bear the thought that you are not top dogs any more. That's what it's all about'" (Glennerster, Matsaganis, and Owens 1992, 26). However, most GP fundholders in the survey by Glennerster and his colleagues recognized an interdependence between themselves and their local hospitals and consultants. Declared one fundholder, "Our interests and theirs are the same. We can't afford for them to close" (ibid.).

Fundholding also extended the range of social and clinical autonomy of GPs in their own practices. A survey of first-wave fundholders indicated that they took up fundholding because they wanted to improve patient care and reduce waiting times for hospital treatment, develop office-based diagnostic and minor surgery capacity, change office staff and improve office premises out of their own budgets without having to get approval from their Family Health Services Authority, and gain more control over their professional lives. Others chose fundholding because they wanted to preserve their freedom to refer patients where they wished and not cede this power to DHA purchasers (Glennerster, Matsaganis, and Owens 1992, 13).[44]

For non-fundholding GPs, the results were more mixed. Some DHAs consulted them in their purchasing decisions or delegated the task of purchasing to consortia of non-fundholding GPs. In these examples, nonfundholding general practitioners benefited from fundholding indirectly (Klein 1995, 241–42). But there was also evidence that fundholders and their patients sometimes received faster access to elective surgeries than did non-fundholding GPs and their patients (Whitehead 1993), suggesting that fundholding's benefits accrued primarily to those who participated in the scheme.

On balance, then, the NHS reforms curbed medical power in some areas but granted doctors opportunities for influence in other areas of health policy and administration. GP fundholders were the clearest beneficiaries of the internal market. But consultants, too, had new capacities to influence administrative decisions in their hospitals if they were willing to assume some managerial duties themselves, such as taking responsibility for their own departmental hospital budgets. Even if reforms did not go as far as Thatcher perhaps had initially envisioned, the changes still signaled that physician power and autonomy would no longer go unquestioned. More than in the past, doctors had to share power with managers in the running of the NHS, even in areas considered the domain of medical professional autonomy. Still, the medical profession did not lose all of its professional prerogatives, and it still had a role in determining the details of health policy, even though it was one voice among several.

This assessment begs the question of why the Thatcher government's reform program, which was aimed at abolishing the medical profession's privileges, pulled its punches in implementation. One reason boiled down to pure political calculus. The Major government realized that it could not run the NHS without doctors or with a profession whose morale was completely shattered. The NHS, after all, was popular with voters, and continued rancor between the government and the medical profession would have undermined public confidence in the reforms and invited electoral disaster. Hence, Major pursued the "steady state" policy, restarted talks with the BMA, and conceded some points of autonomy to the profession. The question then is, Why did the government leave clinical freedom in the hands of the profession, if curbing it seemed so critical to improving accountability and cost-effectiveness in the NHS? Klein (1998) has quite plausibly suggested that policymakers still valued the rationing that the medical profession did on their behalf under the implicit concordat. If the government wanted to continue to offload the difficult job of rationing scarce resources onto the medical profession, then it had to continue with its side of the bargain, which meant leaving clinical decisions in the hands of doctors.

But the medical profession also escaped the full brunt of the reforms because market competition was never given free rein. Had the internal market been a highly competitive one, some expensive or inefficient hospitals would have surely gone bankrupt. Managers wishing to avoid such outcomes might very well have increased pressure on clinicians and challenged their treatment decisions. But the reality turned out to be quite different. The reform program did create an internal market of separate purchasers and providers, but that market was one in which the central state tightly managed its workings and constrained competitive forces. As a result, medical power was not annihilated by the tide of market forces, but merely curtailed in a new governance regime.

The Limits of Liberalization in a Universal Health Care System

With *Working for Patients,* policymakers attempted to graft together two very different governance regimes in the NHS. On the one hand, the government asserted that market competition and devolved decision making would prod deferential managers and unaccountable clinicians to search for more efficient ways to provide services. The market would also roll back the state, or at least transform the nature of its intervention. Detailed command-and-control would become a thing of the past. Instead, the central government would confine itself to setting out a strategic vision for the health service, specify performance targets, and then rely on the NHS Executive to ensure that the goals were translated into practice throughout the health service. The Executive would not become entangled in the day-to-day operational decisions of the health service; these would be left to local managers, purchasers, and providers. In addition, political meddling would largely be abandoned; politics would be separated from management.[45]

In fact, the managerial reforms worked in the opposite direction of devolution to strengthen both the legal authority and institutional capacity of policymakers for centralized intervention in the NHS. As noted above, the secretary of state of the DoH now had the authority to appoint chief executives of health authorities and hospitals, while local governments and the health professions lost their representation at local levels. But the Major government took centralization even further, subsequently streamlining the NHS bureaucracy by eliminating the regional tier of health authorities and incorporating its functions directly into the central NHS Executive (DoH 1993, n.d.; NHS Executive 1994a). A senior official in the Department of Health candidly admitted that the structural reforms had enhanced central state capacity and acknowledged the tension between the government's devolution intentions and the reforms in practice:

> I think what we're doing is we are putting into place a system which can either run as a decentralized system or can run as a very tight command and control. I honestly think . . . it's going to do both. The presumption is now one of decentralizing, empowering, devolving, but the fact of the matter is—and I think this is again where I think this is the same in any business—there comes a point where you take control because something's got to the level where it needs, the top of the organization feel that they need to intervene for whatever sets of reasons. At that point, you need a command structure. . . . The government is a centralizing government. It preaches devolution, but in fact it's centralist. (Interview with senior official in DoH, July 20, 1995)

The Major government also sought to isolate politics from administration by moving the NHS Executive to Leeds and leaving behind in Whitehall the civil servants and politicians responsible for setting health policy. The move reinforced in physical terms the intellectual gulf between bureaucratic and managerial cultures (interview with a senior official in DoH, July 20, 1995). However, even a geographical separation of personnel and buildings was not enough to overcome the intertwining of politics and management. The task of setting targets and measuring managers' adherence to them often subjected administrative performance to short-term political considerations that had little to do with the clinical needs of patients. One example of this was the Major government's *Patient's Charter* issued in 1991 (DoH 1991b). The document listed a number of consumer rights for patients, most of which centered on specified waiting times for appointments to consultants, for elective surgery, even for the arrival of an ambulance. But some of the charter's directives served political aims. A clear example was the directive on waiting lists, which ordered lower-level managers to clear from their hospital waiting lists all persons waiting more than two years for an operation, regardless of medical need. Predictably, the numbers of patients with more serious conditions on the lists grew while those with minor ailments obtained earlier treatment.[46] But since waiting lists were a highly charged political issue and a focal point of the 1992 election campaign, the DoH was under heavy pressure from government ministers to carry out the order.

The NHS Executive confessed that the boundary between politics and administration was not clear-cut and acknowledged that its work also consisted of providing support to ministers in their dealings with Parliament and with health authorities: "There will be a few occasions where a more hands-on approach is needed, either for political or managerial reasons and this has to be understood by all concerned" (NHS Management Executive 1991, 7). This sort of intrusion was to be infrequent and of a short-term nature, such as providing damage control for the government on politically sensitive matters such as controversial hospital closures or in cases of severe operational failures of the NHS (ibid., 21). But interference from the center turned out to be more enduring in practice, as the streamlining of health authority structures indicated. Further indications were the frequency and detail of central directives to lower levels in the reformed NHS (see NHS Executive 1995e).

Explaining the New Governance Regime

What sort of explanation exists for this seemingly paradoxical reform strategy of more market *and* more state in the NHS? To make sense of this reform outcome, we must look at the interplay between sectoral and political actors and institutions. First, we need to explain why Thatcher settled on the solution she did. The shortcomings in the existing governance arrangements within the NHS influenced her definition of the health care problem and fed into her neoliberal critique of the welfare state and the professions and her preference for market solutions. Because NHS governance placed the state and medical profession in high relief, they were easy targets for neoliberal charges of a "big state" and "unaccountable collectivism," or corporatism. Indeed, to neoliberals, the NHS epitomized all of the worst elements of statism and collectivism that afflicted the wider British economy and that were allegedly responsible for Britain's economic decline in the postwar period. Both forms of governance caused rigidities, while corporatism allowed a powerful interest to rule the welfare state with impunity. The BMA's inability to control its members demonstrated to Thatcher that the medical profession was undisciplined, irresponsible, and incapable of carrying out public policy functions that corporatism expected. Thatcher thus sought to use competition to atomize physicians, break up their collective bases of power, and force them to be more cost-effective in their treatment decisions and their scheduling of work. Stronger managers, too, would complement market forces by holding practitioners accountable for their use of NHS resources.

But the internal market was anything but laissez-faire. Instead of stepping aside and letting competitive forces take over, the state figured prominently in the NHS internal market. How do we account for this implementation pattern? One reason is that the Thatcher government recognized that it had to marshal the central state's authority and bureaucratic machinery to impose the market on recalcitrant doctors. Vigorous state action included excluding the BMA from negotiations, ramming through the reform legislation without detailed discussion or consensus building, mandating new obligations on the medical profession (like medical audit), and relying on NHS managers to implement new controls on physicians.

Also important was that state actors possessed the capacity to intervene in the NHS and impose the market from above. The hierarchical chain of command in the NHS, from the Executive down through the tiers of health authorities, served as the conduit through which the government could create and shape the market in the health sector. Moreover, the NHS's statutory guarantee of universal access to health care gave government officials the legal authority to set rules for the behavior of purchasers and providers in the internal market.

But the structural changes in NHS administration provided clear evidence that centralized state control was to be an enduring fixture in the NHS landscape and not simply a temporary intrusion into doctors' and managers' decision making in order to create a market or vanquish intransigent physicians. Similarly, the Major government's actions suggest that it recognized that the effort to separate politics from management was futile and therefore made the Executive responsible for both the development of policy and assuring its implementation. So we need to account for this enduring state presence in the NHS market, and the inseparability of politics from management.

One reason lay with the formidable technical problems associated with creating a market from scratch. Such problems provided a rationale for vigorous state intervention and guidance from the center. Among these difficulties were the lack of computers and information on prices and costs of services, as well as the dearth of managerial know-how to engage in contracting. All of these deficiencies prompted detailed support and intervention from the NHS Executive to help purchasers and providers take on their new roles.

But political considerations were the most important factor behind the central state's continued presence in the market and its control over the scope of competition. The universal citizenship rights that the NHS embodied crystallized a broad solidarity and commitment to equity among the public. More than any other branch of the British welfare state, the NHS has epitomized—or at least aspired to epitomize—a comprehensive notion of community based on Marshall's (1963) idea of social citizenship, and it has expressed this solidarity as the right of all to a comprehensive level of care, (nearly) free of charge, on the basis of clinical need rather than ability to pay (Klein 1989, 1995; Ministry of Health n.d.; Speller 1948; Titmuss 1974, 1987b). Moreover, the public has continued to expect the state to act as the guarantor of this right.

This attachment to the solidarity and egalitarianism underpinning the NHS has been persistent, deep, and broad, and not just among the Labour party (which, after all, had created the health service). Opinion polls have consistently shown the public to be firmly committed to the principles of tax-financed, universalistic, publicly provided health care based on need rather than ability to pay and willing to shoulder higher taxes for the NHS (Klein 1995, 135–36; Taylor-Gooby 1991, chap. 5). A further indication of the broad support for the NHS is the relatively small role that the private sector has played. Private insurance covered only 11.5 percent of the population in 1990, a proportion similar to that in other OECD countries (Klein 1995, 155; Timmins 1995, 507).[47] Moreover, private coverage has served more as a safety valve to absorb excess demand for elective surgery, rather than providing the middle class a path of permanent exit from the public system. Those with private insurance still receive most of their care from the NHS as public patients because private policies tend to be limited to profitable elective procedures or amenities like private hospital rooms or choice of specialist (Klein 1995, 156–57).

Public support for state-provided, universal health care extended beyond the public and the Labour party. The Tory wing of the Conservative party, always sympathetic to state intervention in the economy and social welfare, accepted the universalism of the NHS. Having been cowed under Thatcher's tenure, the Tory wing regained some of its lost influence under Major and increasingly challenged the neoliberal wing of the party.

NHS managers, too, remained attached to the "public service ethos" of providing care based on medical need. While many administrators embraced the "culture of purchasing" (Klein 1998), this did not necessarily mean that they had adopted market or commercial values. Indeed, the then chief executive of the NHS, Duncan Nichol, argued that the health service was a "social market," which provided a public service and which therefore had to be run differently from a private market. Since the NHS was a public welfare service and health care continued to be viewed by many as more than just a mere commodity, managers had to balance efficiency and profit concerns with the requirement that the population have access to a decent standard of health care.[48] Though some managers chafed at the degree of central interference in their freedom to manage, many more opted for a cooperative strategy of joint purchasing or "commissioning" of services rather than adversarial, cutthroat competition with providers or other purchasers (Light n.d., 1997).

Finally, the particular intertwining of the NHS with the political system made it hard for the government to let go once the market was in place. Because the central government provided and guaranteed universal care and decided the NHS budget, it had a direct stake in how that money was spent. Government ministers had to deal with both the Treasury's perennial concerns over "value for money" and Parliament's concern for the level of the quality of services. As long as politicians refused to part with centralized state financing for other kinds of financial arrangements—such as privatization, compulsory national insurance, or devolving financing responsibility to local governments—then the government in London would continue to be held directly accountable by voters and by Parliament (especially through the highly visible question time period, which gave MPs the opportunity to grill government ministers on a regular basis) for perceived or actual shortcomings in performance of the health service and in the level of resources allocated to it. Such accountability made it impractical to separate operational from political decisions or to completely devolve decision making to lower-level managers or freewheeling market forces. To do so would have meant that politicians would have been held hostage to the performance of the NHS and responsible for its disasters while being denied the means to minimize or prevent such failures. As one DoH official admitted:

> As politicians they can't avoid, much as they would like to, though, I suspect, getting involved in some of the nitty gritty *and are expected through the systems of public accountability to say things about a particular . . . incident in a particular hospital.* And that's how they choose to interpret their responsibilities and that's what's expected and that's fine. That's actually awfully heavy on staff. Finding out what happened, packaging it into a form that's presentable, the press releases, the defensive parts of the parliamentary questions. Actually, once the center starts getting involved in that, it starts to try to manage the process out there, so it starts disempowering the Trusts' chief executives, because it's saying, "Well, we didn't like what you've done there, so you'd better change it, the ministers won't like it, they get nervous." In

fact, ministers might not be too worried at all, but who knows until you've asked them. But usually one can anticipate their reactions to things. (Interview with senior official in the Department of Health, July 20, 1995; emphasis added)[49]

The broad public support for the universalism of the NHS not only made radical privatization schemes appear politically suicidal, but also required that Thatcher and Major carefully craft and constrain the workings of the internal market to avert the most egregious inequities and chaos that unbridled competition would have unleashed. To avoid political embarrassment, the government could not permit competition to choose winners and losers; indeed, no Trust or GP fundholder could be allowed to fail. These political calculations explain Major's decision to pursue a "steady state" policy that amounted to a centrally controlled, cautious introduction of the internal market up to and after the 1992 election.[50] Controlling the pace of liberalization sometimes involved preempting market forces altogether, as with Major's decision to pursue a state-directed rationalization of London hospitals. Rather than allow market forces to decide which hospitals would survive or die, the government chose to carefully orchestrate the process from the center in accordance with the recommendations of a special inquiry set up to study the question (James 1995).[51] Both Thatcher and Major also set the rules of the market in such a way as to minimize the risk of insolvency on the part of Trusts and GP fundholders as well as to discourage them from neglecting the most vulnerable patients. Thus, fundholders incurred only limited financial liability for treating the sickest patients, while the scope of hospital services they could purchase was also restricted.[52] The government also restricted fundholders' and hospitals' ability to dispense with their "profits": any surpluses in their budgets had to be plowed back into improvements in patient care. All hospitals, moreover, were legally required to provide a full array of services—even unprofitable treatments like emergency room care—to prevent them from dumping difficult patients onto other institutions. Finally, the DoH moved toward a capitation-based system to allocate budgets to purchasers that would adjust for inequities based on the health status of patients (Maynard 1991; DoH et al. 1989b).

In sum, one cannot make sense of this seemingly contradictory mixture of "market and state" unless one looks at both the sectoral and political arenas and the interactions between them. Britain's political institutions, which centralize power in the cabinet, promote party discipline, and inflate electoral majorities, facilitated Thatcher's aggressive pursuit of her radical market agenda and permitted her to enact her reforms with relative ease. Yet, formal political institutions and parliamentary majorities do not in themselves explain the content of Thatcher's policy choices, nor do they account for the leaching out of the more radical aspects of the market reforms during the course of their implementation. Even with a large parliamentary majority, Thatcher discovered that there were limits to how far she could push her neoliberal vision in the health care system. Although she and her neoliberal compatriots abhorred the idea of a big state, the fact remained that the state's overwhelming presence as payer and provider in the NHS made other alternatives like privatization or a national insurance system politically and financially costly. Both she and Major decided that unleashing a laissez-faire market into a health service built upon the principles of universalism, solidarity, and public financing would have entailed prohibitive political costs, and therefore they sought to mold and tame the market with state power.

The Market and Other Health Policy Goals

Aside from their effects on governance, what effect did the Conservatives' market reforms have on other health policy goals? Did the reforms help policymakers balance the public expectation to guarantee equity with their own desire for cost containment? On the question of equity, the record is mixed. The reforms did not yield sufficient efficiency gains to make a noticeable dent in waiting lists for elective hospital treatments: waiting lists rose from 700,000 in 1992 to nearly 1.3 million by 1998 (*Economist* 1998). Waiting lists in and of themselves do not offend equity if they are based on medical need. But the political settlement surrounding the creation of the NHS, which permitted consultants to engage in private practice and treat patients with private insurance in NHS facilities, has allowed those with the financial means to jump the queue for elective surgery for those conditions or procedures for which there is a long wait. Queue jumping thus violates the principle of access to care according to medical need. Still, its extent remains limited. As noted above, the proportion of the population with private coverage has always been a small minority, and private policies are normally confined to profitable elective procedures or amenities like private hospital rooms or choice of specialist (Klein 1995, 155–57; Timmins 1995, 507).[53] Even so, the question for public policy is whether the rationing of elective treatments imposes undue suffering upon those on the lists. In answering this question, the duration of the wait and the severity of the medical condition, rather than the absolute numbers on the waiting lists, are the more appropriate indicators. However, much of the political debate has concentrated on the numbers of those on the lists.

Another criticism is that the internal market introduced a new kind of inequity among NHS patients themselves. According to critics of fundholding, the wait for elective surgery was no longer exclusively a matter of medical need but now also the ability of one's purchaser to pay. Though the evidence was not definitive, it suggested that larger fundholding practices used their market savvy and budgets to secure faster services for their patients than did non-fundholding practices.[54] On balance, however, the NHS weathered the changes of the internal market to retain its universalism, and the Conservative reforms were a quite limited challenge to solidarity. Universal access to medically necessary care remains a statutorily guaranteed right of social citizenship; policymakers designed the market to prevent the most egregious inequities and cream-skimming.

Did the market deliver its hoped-for cost discipline? Britain has maintained its record of being one of the low health care spenders in the OECD, but this was less a result of market competition than other policy instruments. Indeed, there was rather little competition in many areas because past policies had limited the supply of hospitals and specialists, though areas with sufficient supply gave purchasers real choices (Klein 1995). If anything, the internal market helped fuel health care costs with its enormous expansion of administrative personnel to write and monitor contracts and generous financial inducements for GPs to take up fundholding.[55] However, the government's largesse proved fleeting, as Major subsequently resorted to a policy of austerity that kept NHS spending increases well below the rate of inflation.[56] In short, the cost discipline in the NHS owed less to market competition—which was quite limited—than to the vise of tight global budgets and the public's tolerance of waiting lists.

Epilogue: The Restoration of Hierarchy and Corporatism and the Retreat of Competition under Blair

The New NHS

If anyone wondered which mode of governance would prevail in the NHS once the Conservatives had been turned out of office, they did not have to wait long.[57] Within a year of taking office, the Labour government of Tony Blair issued its plans for the NHS in its 1997 white paper *The New NHS:*

Modern, Dependable, which served as the basis of the 1999 Health Act. Blair broke with some of his predecessor's policies, but also consolidated and extended developments begun under Major. The emergent governance regime reasserted the hybrid of corporatism and state hierarchy, with competition in retreat.

The Blair government preserved the purchaser-provider split, but its internal market would be one that accommodated a heavy dose of planning and stable, long-term collaboration among purchasers and providers rather than cutthroat competition and short-term encounters. Thus, *The New NHS* required that each health authority, in consultation with all general practitioners in the locality as well as hospital consultants, draw up a Health Improvement Program (HIP) to guide GPs and hospitals in purchasing and providing care for the population in their locale. Purchasers and providers were also required to sign three- to five-year contracts instead of annual agreements.

The Blair government broke with the Conservatives by abolishing GP fundholding. Its reasoning was that fundholders were too numerous and too small to be able to plan for the health and community services of the local population. Fundholding had also introduced inequities in access to hospital services that had put their patients ahead of those of non-fundholders. Still, Blair sought to retain the benefits of a health service led by primary care that Thatcher and Major had championed. So instead of fundholders, Primary Care Groups (PCGs), representing all GPs as well as community nurses in a locality, were created to purchase services on behalf of health authorities. The PCGs, which were much larger than GP fundholders, were expected to counteract the tendencies toward fragmentation that fundholding had encouraged.

The white paper also sought to reverse the democratic deficit that had been a hallmark of the Conservatives' hierarchical reforms. Trusts now had to include community representatives on their boards, open their board meetings to the public, and publish annual reports of their performance.

The New NHS also went some way in repairing the damaged relationship between the BMA and the state. Indeed, Blair's NHS in many ways mirrored the BMA's vision for the health service. This was not accidental, since Labour had consulted the BMA when devising its plans in opposition.[58] The white paper was also a lifeline to help the BMA deal with its debilitating internal splits. Abolishing GP fundholding would help the BMA overcome the fault line that had divided fundholders and non-fundholding GPs, and requiring Trusts to involve clinicians in contract negotiations with PCGs restored some of the influence consultants had lost to GP fundholders. Finally, the government reassured the BMA that the medical profession would have important, legally recognized roles to play in NHS governance through the PCGs and HIPs, even though it stopped short of restoring corporatist representation on the boards of health authorities or Trusts. In many respects, then, the white paper signaled a return to the consensus management and corporatism that had existed between 1974 and 1985.

However, this did not imply a return to unquestioned medical dominance. Rather, doctors had to accept new constraints on clinical freedom in exchange for the recovery of their corporatist status. Not only did Blair retain his predecessors' requirement that the profession police its members through peer review (or medical audit), but he went further in rewriting the terms of the political settlement with doctors. With the creation of two new national bodies, the National Institute of Clinical Excellence (NICE) and the Commission for Health Improvement (CHI), the government put doctors on notice that determining the clinical content of their work would no longer be their exclusive domain. Instead, the profession would have to share this with laypersons. Thus, NICE had the mandate to develop and disseminate guidelines for clinical and cost-effective practice and for peer-review procedures. The CHI was to ensure that systems of peer review and quality assurance were in place locally. The membership of both bodies not only included doctors but also representatives of other health professions, patients, and academics. Moreover, by including health economists on the membership of NICE and requiring cost-effectiveness as a criterion for guidelines, the government expected doctors to explicitly consider the costs of their treatment decisions and to balance clinical with economic imperatives.[59]

The NHS Plan

If *The New NHS* represented interim measures to correct what it perceived as the flaws of the Conservatives' internal market, the Blair government presented its own sweeping, long-term vision for the health service with *The NHS Plan*, issued in 2000.[60] Many commentators focused on the white paper's provisions for the problem of underfunding and the burgeoning waiting lists that are its most visible indicator. Blair's pledge to devote £20 billion ($31 million) to the NHS over four years, an increase of 6.1 percent, will bring British health care spending closer to the European Union average.[61] Much of it will go for additional doctors, nurses, and hospitals (DoH 2000, 11, and chaps. 2–6).[62] Blair also pledged not to depart from tax financing and centrally determined budgets for the NHS (ibid., chap. 3). At the same time, however, the government indicated that it would encourage the NHS to purchase private sector services for patients where there were long waiting lists and insufficient supply in the public sector (ibid., chap. 11). Though this was a departure from past Labour party hostility toward private medicine, it shared similarities with the two previous Conservative governments to encourage the NHS to make greater use of the private sector.

And just as Thatcher did not want to "throw more money" at an unreformed and inefficient health service, so Blair sought to "modernize" its governance arrangements. But instead of doing so through the market, Blair hoped to harness hierarchy and corporatism while trying to give managers and doctors some room for flexible innovation in fulfilling centrally determined goals. Moreover, rather than pursuing his vision through imposition and exclusion, Blair undertook a genuine renegotiation of the political settlement with a range of health care stakeholders. Thus, Modernization Action Teams, consisting of NHS staff, patient representatives, doctors, and managers, consulted the public and NHS staff and worked with the government to prepare the white paper (ibid., 3, 14, Annex 2). In addition, the white paper mandated changes in NHS governance structures to institutionalize the inclusive approach in policy implementation. Alongside the Primary Care Group purchasers and the existing administrative machinery, there would now be modernization boards at national and local levels—tripartite bodies consisting of NHS managers, doctors and other health care professionals, and local governments or patients—charged with monitoring the implementation of the white paper's reforms (ibid., chaps. 6, 10). Blair's strategy of inclusion won broad support for the reforms, with virtually all the major health care stakeholders signing on to the document (ibid., preface).

If *The New NHS* was further proof of the government's determination to include doctors in policy-making and implementation, policymakers nonetheless required further concessions from them. Continuing in the vein of the Conservatives, the Labour government sought to rein in the amount of time that consultants devoted to private practice by means of job plans and annual reviews, bonus payments or distinction awards for more service to the NHS, and banning private practice by new consultants in their first seven years of NHS employment. But in contrast to Thatcher, who dictated similar policies from above, Blair secured the BMA's approval for these changes (ibid., chap. 8).

The government also attempted to address the perennial tension between center and periphery. Hoping to depoliticize and devolve administrative decisions, it curtailed the powers of the secretary of the state of the DoH. The appointment of directors of Trusts and health authorities would pass from the secretary to a separate appointments commission; instead of the secretary deciding major administrative reorganizations, an independent panel would be responsible for recommending changes; and consultants who appealed their dismissals would do so locally rather than to the secretary (ibid., 67–68). In addition, local NHS providers and health authorities that met standards of good performance (set by the center) would be subject to less central oversight and would receive greater autonomy and additional money to implement policies. The government also promised to reduce the barrage of directives from the central Executive (ibid., chap. 6, esp. 63–66). Still, politicians and bureaucrats at the center retained important powers. The NHS Executive, the CHI, and NICE would continue to set national standards and targets of performance for local NHS managers and providers to follow. Local-level managers and providers would be monitored by and accountable to higher tiers, and the secretary of state and NHS Executive retained reserve powers to intervene to correct or take over failing organizations at lower levels (ibid., chap. 6, esp. 57–69).

It remains to be seen whether the central state will be able to confine itself to setting out broad targets, national standards, and strategic priorities and then allow local actors some measure of freedom to determine how to implement them. The Blair government has gone some way to reinvigorate local participation and accountability and to reward local purchasers and providers for their initiative. But though NICE could be construed as a sign of the government's commitment to do no more than to promulgate national targets, the fact remains that such standards are to be developed by a *national* body, not by local peer-review committees. Similarly, with the creation of the CHI, the central state has taken upon itself the responsibility for ensuring that medical audit is in place locally rather than delegating the job to district managers as the Thatcher reforms had. Moreover, the secretary of state, the NHS Executive, and the CHI retain broad reserve powers to intervene directly into the activities of local actors should they fail to execute their responsibilities (DoH 1997, 49, 59; 2000, chap. 6).

In short, the Blair government will confront the same dilemmas of control and devolution that have dogged its predecessors since 1948. As long as health care continues to be centrally financed and budgeted, Blair will likely be held responsible for NHS performance. If anything, his government may be held to even tougher account than previous governments because of its commitment to devise better performance measures and to publish them nationally. This will make performance failures that much more visible to the public and to Parliament and may encourage policymakers to redouble their efforts to control the NHS periphery. Until local governments are given the power to raise their own taxes for health care and some voice in determining services locally, efforts at devolution face a hard road.

It also remains to be seen whether Labour will truly maintain the separation of purchasers and providers, or whether the official encouragement of collaboration will revert to the cozy relationships that preceded the advent of the internal market. Granting consultants a voice in devising HIPs might help the BMA, but could reverse Conservative efforts to enhance primary care. Likewise, by involving GPs and consultants, HIPs are likely to blur the boundaries between purchasers and providers.

If Thatcher's revolution failed to leave the NHS with a competitive market, it nevertheless bequeathed a new health politics. The corporatist restoration is not to be a return to the days before 1989. The BMA still has a place in negotiating the terms and conditions of service for physicians, but is no longer the dominant or exclusive voice in health policy. Moreover, corporatism's survival is now more than ever contingent on the medical profession accepting the duty to monitor the clinical decisions of its members, to weigh clinical criteria against cost-effectiveness, and to share with laypersons the authority to govern the health sector, even to define what constitutes good medical practice. This is the new NHS with which the BMA must contend.

CHAPTER 3

The Corporatist Settlement in German National Health Insurance

Germany's statutory national health insurance system is underpinned by a corporatist arrangement that grants groups representing major societal interests important responsibilities in health care financing and administration. The core of corporatist governance, however, is more narrowly defined to include only the medical profession and insurers in policy-making and implementation. While corporatism has allowed the state to govern the health care sector, it has also granted the medical profession considerable institutional power at the expense of insurers. These imbalances, along with corporatism's incomplete reach over the health sector, have been responsible for some of the problems in German health care.

This chapter traces the corporatist settlement in German health care prior to the Kohl government's reforms of the late 1980s and 1990s. The first section identifies the main actors and institutions in German health insurance. The next focuses on the corporatist arrangement between doctors and insurers. It briefly sketches the historical development of corporatism and then delineates the main responsibilities of physicians and insurers in sectoral governance arrangements in the postwar period. The third section discusses the cost and equity problems arising from the institutional arrangements in the German health care system, and with corporatism in particular. The fourth section describes how governments responded to these problems in the 1970s and 1980s by working within the corporatist framework and seeking to rectify its deficiencies.

Institutions and Actors in the National Health Insurance System

Germany's national health insurance program, compulsory for those below a specified income, covers 90 percent of the population.[1] In 1990, over

1,100 sickness funds (*Krankenkassen*) provided statutory national health insurance to the population (see table 7); by the decade's end, less than 500 funds remained. From its inception, national health insurance has institutionalized class and status differences. The basic divide has been between the primary and the substitute funds. The primary funds have provided compulsory coverage primarily to blue-collar workers and to specific occupational or sectoral groups. These include company funds (*Betriebskrankenkassen*) set up by firms to insure their own work force; professional or guild funds (*Innungskrankenkassen*) that insure specific professions or trades; funds for agricultural workers (*landwirtschaftliche Krankenkassen*); and funds for workers in specific industries, such as the See-Krankenkasse for maritime workers and the Bundesknappschaft for miners. Local funds (*Ortskrankenkassen*) have served as insurers of last resort for employees who could not gain entry into the other types of funds. The substitute funds (*Ersatzkassen*) historically were reserved for salaried white-collar employees. This organizational variation belies the trend toward standardized benefits over time, as the federal government has required all funds to provide a minimum benefits package covering all medically necessary services. Still, important institutional differences among the funds have persisted well into the 1990s and have been a source of some of the cost and equity problems in German health insurance.

National health insurance is financed from payroll contributions divided equally between employers and employees. Financing follows the solidarity principle (*Solidaritätsprinzip*) so that the contribution rate of a fund is set at a percentage of the gross wages of its members rather than on the basis of each member's health risk. The principle also implies that the contribution rate is the same regardless of household size so that dependents are covered without additional fees (Cassel and Henke n.d.; OECD 1997, 82).[2] Thus,

TABLE 7. The Sickness Funds in the German Health Insurance System, 1990

Number	Type of Fund
268	Local funds (*Ortskrankenkassen*)
694	Company funds (*Betriebskrankenkassen*)
153	Professional/guild funds (*Innungskrankenkassen*)
19	Funds for agricultural employees (*landwirtschaftliche Krankenkassen*)
7	Substitute funds for salaried employees (*Ersatzkassen für Angestellte*)
8	Substitute funds for wage-earners (*Ersatzkassen für Arbeiter*)
1	Seamen's fund (*See-Krankenkasse*)
1	Miners' fund (*Bundesknappschaft*)

Source: Federal Republic of Germany, *Bundesministerium für Arbeit und Sozialordnung* (Federal Ministry of Labor), 1991, 75.

while substantial redistribution occurs by income, age, gender, family size, and health status, it is confined to the membership of a fund rather than taking place across the entire population, as redistribution in Britain's NHS does. Contribution rates are supposed to cover the costs incurred by a fund, which include the cost of health care received by members as well as administrative costs. This self-financing requirement for national insurance means that funds are limited in their ability to run deficits from year to year.

The German medical profession is organized into different associations. The most important are the Associations of Sickness Fund Physicians (Kassenärztliche Vereinigungen, or KVs), compulsory membership bodies that provide ambulatory care to the insured population, negotiate fees on behalf of member doctors, and along with insurers, run much of the health care system under state auspices. The Federal Association of Sickness Fund Physicians, or Kassenärztliche Bundesvereinigung (KBV) represents the KVs in the national political arena. In addition, all doctors must belong to Land- (state-) level chambers (Ärztekammern), which are responsible for scientific and educational matters. The Federal Chamber of Physicians (Bundesärztekammer) brings together the state chambers and also has some influence in national-level policy debates. In addition, a number of voluntary membership associations represent physicians in the political arena, the most important of which is the Hartmannbund. But because the voluntary associations do not have the official status in policy-making and administration that the KVs do, they are correspondingly less influential with the government.[3]

Compared to Britain's centralized and state-administered National Health Service, the German federal government plays a more indirect and circumscribed role in the health care system. Federal arrangements require the national government to share jurisdiction over the hospital sector with the states (Länder) (Altenstetter 1987; Schneider 1991; Schulenburg 1992). Rather than being under direct control of the national government, most hospitals are either nonprofits run by religious orders or else public institutions run by municipal governments. Moreover, corporatism accords a range of societal actors roles in health insurance administration. Doctors and insurers also have substantial freedom to administer the health insurance system. Corresponding to their shares in health care financing, employers and unions enjoy parity representation on the elective and administrative bodies of the sickness funds.[4]

But even though it does not directly finance or provide health care services, the federal government remains a critical player in the health care system, setting the parameters of national insurance and ensuring that the population has access to care, largely by mandating requirements on sectoral actors. Thus, the federal government sets the income threshold below which insurance is compulsory, requires sickness funds to offer medically necessary benefits to all insured persons and health care providers to supply such care, and mandates employers to provide insurance to their employees and to share in its financing. The federal government also sets the terms of the corporatist relationship among doctors and insurers, which is the subject of the next section.

The Corporatist Core: Doctors, Sickness Funds, and the State

Origins of the Corporatist Settlement

The corporatist settlement in health care came out of intense class and group conflicts associated with Germany's industrialization. State actors constructed corporatist arrangements to resolve such conflicts in the health sector. But the terms of that settlement empowered doctors and employers at the expense of insurers and workers.

Statutory national insurance was enacted in 1883 as part of Chancellor Bismarck's landmark social insurance legislation designed to coopt the burgeoning industrial working class.[5] Bismarck hoped that social insurance would buy the allegiance of workers to the state and wean them away from the trade unions and the Social Democratic party (SPD) and their voluntary insurance schemes, but his plan backfired. Because workers financed two-thirds of insurance and enjoyed similar proportional representation on the boards and assemblies of the sickness funds, the trade unions and the SPD essentially colonized the administrative posts of the funds with their own personnel (Leibfried and Tennstedt 1986).

In addition to being vehicles for working-class participation in social insurance administration, the sickness funds wielded substantial power over an atomized medical profession. Through the weapon of closed panel practice, funds could choose or exclude which physicians would be able to treat their members. Contracts were concluded with individual doctors, and remuneration was by capitation or salary. Chafing at these constraints on their incomes, doctors formed a union in 1900, the Leipziger Verband (later known as the Hartmannbund), which led the way in industrial action. Its aims were to protect private practice from the encroachment of national insurance and to ban selective contracting by the funds and secure fee-for-service remuneration (Kirkman-Liff 1990, 73–75; Leichter 1979, 129; Stone 1980, 51). Between 1900 and 1911, doctors averaged 200 strikes per year and won roughly 90 percent of them (Kirkman-Liff 1990, 74; Stone 1980, 47).

In 1911, the government sought to bring order to the health care system by rationalizing the number and organization of funds, codifying different laws under the Imperial Insurance Code (Reichsversicherungsordnung, or RVO), and proposing legal measures to regulate doctors and insurers. Unhappy with the government's actions, the medical profession called for a general strike in 1913. The government responded with the Berlin Treaty, which established regular mechanisms between doctors and insurers to resolve conflicts. It established committees composed of equal numbers of doctors and insurers to select physicians for insurance practice and to regulate contracts between the two parties. The funds continued to negotiate contracts with individual physicians, and reimbursement arrangements remained at the discretion of each agreement. But with the treaty, doctors had made important inroads on deciding their terms and conditions of service. The treaty was in force for ten years, but with its expiration, conflict between doctors and insurers resumed (Kirkman-Liff 1990, 73–75; Leichter 1979, 128–33; Stone 1980, 51–52).

Weimar governments intervened in the escalating industrial strife with a series of emergency decrees issued between 1923 and 1931 that comprised the origins of the current corporatist model (Stone 1980, 53). During the waning years of the republic, the Brüning government issued interim agreements that led to the creation of the Associations of Sickness Fund Physicians (Kassenärztliche Vereinigungen, or KVs) in 1933 (Kirkman-Liff 1990, 76; Webber 1992a, 212–13). Along with the sickness funds, these were regional-level corporatist bodies organized under the public law (Körperschaften öffentlichen Rechts). Membership in the KVs was compulsory for all physicians wishing to treat national insurance patients. The KVs secured from the state a monopoly to provide ambulatory care to the insured population and to negotiate binding agreements with the sickness funds on the terms of physician service. Policymakers also agreed to open up access to national insurance patients to more doctors (Stone 1980, 27, 52–53; Webber 1992a, 212–13).[6]

Stone (1980, 52) argues that this corporatist model was premised on the notion of countervailing power, but the practical effects of government policies were to strengthen the medical profession, particularly as a collective actor, at the expense of insurers. To be sure, the state granted the funds new leverage over the profession by mandating that physicians be paid from a fixed capitation budget and by granting insurers the authority to monitor physician practices for "excessive" services (ibid., 53). Yet the profession scored even bigger victories. In exchange for doctors' cooperation in stabilizing the national insurance system during the Great Depression, the Brünung government acceded to the demands of the voluntary associations (the Hartmannbund in particular) to create the KVs (Webber 1992a, 212–13). This meant that the funds lost much of their power to dictate the terms of physician service: they could no longer engage in selective contracting but instead had to negotiate with the KVs, not individual doctors, and had to accept the medical services of all KV doctors.

Subsequent state modifications of the national insurance system weakened insurers and the working class even further and correspondingly strengthened the hand of doctors and employers. The Nazi dictatorship introduced parity financing and representation between employers and employees on the sickness funds and thereby destroyed working-class dominance of social insurance administration. The regime also gutted self-governance by purging Social Democrats and union members from fund administration (Katzenstein 1987, 173; Leibfried and Tennstedt 1986; Rosenberg 1986), and it banned salaried employment of physicians in outpatient clinics run by the funds (Leibfried and Tennstedt 1986).

The health care system of the Federal Republic (FRG) cemented the dominance of physicians at the expense of insurers and workers. Under the postwar health care system, the regional associations of doctors and insurers recovered the rights of self-administration and collective bargaining that had existed before the Nazi takeover. But the bans on selective contracting and salaried employment of doctors by the funds remained.[7] Workers, too, failed to recover their former dominance in social insurance administration because the Federal Republic retained parity financing and representation on the funds. For other reasons, the funds were poorly positioned to act as effective counterweights to the medical profession and lost much of their ability to articulate the interests of the working class: internal democracy on the funds was anemic, with candidates for office often running unopposed (Katzenstein 1987, 68–69), and as decisions on benefits shifted to the legislative arena, the funds lost much of their discretion and self-governance in these areas (Rosenberg 1986, 122).

Corporatist Governance

The KVs and sickness funds form the core of corporatism in the health sector. Together, they approximate a "private-interest government" (Streeck and Schmitter 1985). Through this variant of corporatism, the state regulates, or governs, the health sector indirectly by setting out the broad goals of health policy in framework legislation and then delegating tasks of implementation to the KVs and sickness funds. Policymakers generally give doctors and insurers wide latitude to determine the details of policy implementation through collective bargaining. These rights of self-administration, or self-governance (*Selbstverwaltung*), have the backing of law. Under corporatist governance, the KVs and sickness funds conclude collective agreements covering the terms of service and remuneration of office-based physicians. The medical associations and insurers also determine and periodically update the list of medically necessary services covered by national health insurance. And they review physician practice patterns to detect and sanction doctors who exceed the norms of their peers.

In addition to their prominent role in health care system administration, the KVs and sickness funds also enjoy official status in policy formulation. Through legally prescribed remiss procedures, government officials must consult the peak associations of relevant health care interests on major policy proposals (Stone 1980, 30). This means regular consultation of the KBV, which represents the KVs in the national political arena, as well as the umbrella associations of the sickness funds. The policy-making role of the KBV and insurers' associations often goes beyond formal consultation to negotiations with the health ministry and elected politicians.

But even as corporatism confers upon doctors and insurers substantial authority in matters of health care governance, it also provides the state with considerable leverage over their actions. As corporate bodies organized under public law, the KVs and sickness funds are legally obliged to implement federal health policies (Stone 1980, 27) as mandated in legislation. Moreover, unlike private associations, these public-law bodies are also subject to state regulation of their internal affairs, including state specification of their rules of membership and internal governance procedures (BMAS 1991, chap. 22).

In addition, the state can indirectly control the behavior of individual physicians through the substantial authority it has granted the KV leadership to control the rank and file (see Stone 1980; Webber 1991, 52).[8] These control instruments have allowed the medical leadership to curb the economic, social, and clinical autonomy of individual practitioners. First, individual doctors have surrendered their economic autonomy to the KVs, which are the exclusive bargaining agents for office-based physicians under national insurance. Individual doctors cannot charge what they like for their services but must abide by the fee agreements concluded between the

KVs and sickness funds. Membership in the KVs is also compulsory for ambulatory physicians who wish to treat national insurance patients, so doctors who are dissatisfied with their medical association have few options. If they choose to leave the KV and insurance practice, then they would forgo a substantial part of their income, since 90 percent of the population is covered under the national insurance system. Second, the KVs set limits on the social autonomy of individual doctors with their authority to set the terms of and license physicians for national insurance practice. Finally, the medical associations possess the authority to monitor and sanction the clinical decisions of individual practitioners under economic monitoring reviews (*Wirtschaftlichkeitsprüfungen*).

Corporatism thus grants the medical profession considerable collective autonomy, as expressed in the self-administration rights of the KVs, in exchange for setting and enforcing boundaries on the exercise of autonomy by individual physicians. But these control mechanisms do not always guarantee the medical profession's compliance. As discussed below, they are sometimes more potential than actual levers of control. Still, they tend to enhance the reliability of the KVs as corporatist partners able to stick to agreements struck with insurers and state actors.

As a fail-safe device in the event that doctors and insurers fail to fulfill their legal obligations to implement government policy, corporatism also allows the state to resort to stronger measures of control. The state can suspend the rights of self-administration of both the KVs and insurers and substitute these with direct rule by decree. Such encroachment is usually temporary, however, lasting only until these associations assume their public obligations to implement the law. It is also rare, as the threat of direct intervention normally suffices to keep the associations and their members in line (Streeck and Schmitter 1985, 131, 134–35; Webber 1992a). Rarer still (though not unheard of) is the state's decision to exclude doctors and insurers from deliberations concerning fundamental matters of the health care system and reserving these as its exclusive domain.

Cost and Equity Problems in the German Health Care System

Despite these advantages as an instrument of governance, corporatism has not been able to solve all the serious policy problems in the German health care system. In fact, the corporatist bargain contained a number of defects that contributed to the rising costs in the health care system that became apparent in the 1970s. In addition, the organizational characteristics of the sickness funds not only tolerated health system inefficiencies but also gave rise to glaring inequities. Yet for all the problems with corporatist arrangements in the ambulatory sector, other areas of the health care system fared even worse. The absence of alternative governance instruments to control these sectoral actors was also a factor behind escalating health care costs.

Fragmented Insurers Facing Monopoly Providers

Corporatism is premised on a strategy of countervailing power, which, in turn, requires that doctors and sickness funds be in roughly equal balance (Stone 1980, 18). But this condition has seldom held in the German health sector. Instead, imbalances in the corporatist relationship have given advantages to doctors at the expense of insurers. As discussed above, past policy decisions in the state's construction of corporatism favored doctors over insurers. In the contemporary period, imbalances have largely stemmed from the organizational fragmentation among the sickness funds in the face of monopolistic KVs.

First, rivalries between primary and substitute funds have encouraged a game of "ruinous competition" that has fueled health care inflation (Bernardi-Schenkluhn 1991, 685). Well into the postwar period, the substitute funds had a superior public image approximating private insurance because they offered more generous packages than the primary funds (Safran 1967, 134; Stone 1980, 81). Federal legislation has since made benefits packages more uniform between the statutory funds, but the public has still perceived the Ersatzkassen as offering more generous benefits than the primary funds (interview with BMG official, December 6, 1991). Despite a lack of evidence, the substitute funds have also enjoyed an image of providing better care for their members (Schulenburg 1983, cited in Files and Murray 1995, 303). To be sure, the substitute funds tend to have a healthier membership than the local funds. But this has less to do with the quality of care that their members receive than to the effects of mandatorily assigning different occupational groups to different funds, as will be discussed below.

Separate collective bargaining procedures between primary and substitute funds also stoked medical inflation. The substitute funds historically have remunerated doctors more handsomely than the primary funds, further contributing to their image as being one step below private insurance (ibid., 303; Stone 1980). They could afford to do so because their members tended to be healthier and wealthier than those of the primary funds. And the collective bargaining system allowed the substitute funds to be generous. Germany falls short of an all-payer system that would require insurers to present a unified front in the face of the monopolistic KVs and perhaps encourage them to work together to bid down doctors' incomes. Instead, the substitute funds have concluded fee agreements with the KVs separately at the national level, while the primary funds have worked in concert to negotiate collective agreements with the KVs at the Land level. The contracts concluded by the substitute funds, in turn, have served as a benchmark that the primary funds have felt compelled to follow in order to prevent their healthier and wealthier members from defecting to their more generous rivals (Bernardi-Schenkluhn 1992, 685; Hoffmann 1991; interview with BMG official, December 6, 1991; Stone 1980, 79–81, 149–51). The KVs have exploited the separate bargaining rounds to bid up their fees with the primary funds. In short, competition among funds has not reduced health care costs but actually fueled them because such competition has occurred on the basis of image and generosity of remuneration.

Information Asymmetries between Doctors and Insurers

The power imbalance between doctors and insurers is also present in the critical area of information. It has operated in the area of physician reimbursement as a result of how doctors are paid and by whom under German national health insurance. Doctors are paid fee-for-service from a capitated budget negotiated between KVs and funds at the state level. But rather than billing the funds directly for services provided to their patients, physicians submit their lists of treatments provided to their own KV, which then reimburses them. All the funds do is negotiate with the KV the Land-level budget.

Economic monitoring procedures (*Wirtschaftlichkeitsprüfungen*) are supposed to offset this information imbalance to some extent. Since 1931, sickness funds have had the authority to compel review and sanction the clinical decisions of KV doctors that are deemed excessive or fraudulent. In the course of such reviews, the KVs submit to insurers information on physician practice patterns. The funds themselves monitor drug prescribing (Stone 1980, 53, 93–95, 113, chap. 7; Webber 1992a, 227–28).

But the review process has been marred by power and information asymmetries. Until 1977, the KV doctors usually enjoyed exclusive or majority representation on the economic monitoring committees. Even if funds sent representatives, they often did not have voting rights. This situation changed in 1977, when the funds secured parity representation and voting rights with physicians on the committees. Still, the reviews tended to reinforce the status quo in medicine because they relied on economic averages of a doctor's peer group rather than scientific standards of quality or treatment outcomes. Moreover, only doctors whose prescribing patterns were far above the norm were reviewed, and the sanctions were generally weak—consisting mainly of counseling or warnings rather than financial penalties (Döhler 1987; Stone 1980, chap. 7, esp. 114–22). In addition, the dearth of standards that would scientifically measure outcomes of treatments meant that insurers lacked a way to independently determine whether the treatments that doctors provide are appropriate. Lacking such scientific expertise, lay members on the review committees tended to defer to the judgment of the reviewer (*Prüfarzt*), who was a doctor and whose sympathies were usually closer to the physician in question rather than to the sickness funds (Döhler 1987).[9] Moreover, the reviews did not measure the cost-effectiveness of treatments, which would have compared whether a less expensive treatment could provide the same medical outcome. Finally, doctors have sometimes fought efforts by insurers to obtain clinical data as an encroachment on their clinical and economic freedom (Webber 1992a, 227–28).[10] In sum, economic monitoring has sometimes been as much a way for the KVs to shield the clinical autonomy of individual practitioners as to curb it.

Imbalances in Political Influence

Doctors have also tended to wield greater influence over policy in the political arena than have the sickness funds. This is in large part due to the proportional representation electoral system and the specifics of German history, which have produced center-right coalition governments for much of the postwar period that have been sympathetic to physician interests. Specifically, the Free Democratic Party (FDP), which has been a partner in nearly every postwar coalition government, considers the medical profession one of its core clienteles and has championed its interests in health policy matters. In addition, politicians fear that the medical profession, which has traditionally enjoyed public prestige, might sway public opinion against government health policies. So they have sometimes accommodated the medical profession in order to avert electoral disaster. Finally, the KBV has been quite effective in exerting influence on policy through its lobbying of the Bundestag parties and the chancellory (Webber 1992a, 241–43).

The sickness funds, by contrast, have not exerted comparable influence over government leaders. The local funds, with a primarily working-class membership, have enjoyed close relations with the Social Democratic party

(SPD). But the SPD has been in government for far fewer years than the Christian Democratic Union (CDU), and even during its longest tenure in office (1969–82), the SPD governed with the FDP, thus requiring a balance of medical interests against those of the funds.

Yet the political system still provides the sickness funds with some avenues of influence. As a heterogeneous catchall party (Kirchheimer 1966), the CDU—along with its sister party in Bavaria, the Christian Social Union (CSU)—contains both a trade union wing and a business wing, with internal party committees institutionalizing their voice in internal party politics. The trade union wing has claimed primary jurisdiction over the party's business wing on matters of social policy and has aligned itself with the blue-collar local funds (see Döhler 1991, 255, 272; Webber 1991, 84). Within the federal bureaucracy, the labor ministry, which was responsible for health policy up to 1991, has been sympathetic to the CDU's labor wing (Webber 1992a, 241). Indeed, during periods of Christian Democratic rule, the ministers of labor (and again in 1992, the head of the health ministry) have been drawn from the trade union wing of the CDU or CSU. However, CDU leaders must reconcile both wings of the party when devising policies, and developments outside the health care system—such as economic concerns of employers—may sometimes outweigh those of the labor wing and its sickness fund constituency. In addition, the divisions among the funds also dilute their political effectiveness vis-à-vis the KBV and KVs. The substitute funds look to the FDP to advance their interests, while the SPD and CDU labor wing are the allies of the local funds (ibid., 243).

But health policy is more than just a battle between doctors and insurers and their party allies. Rather, policy outcomes often reflect complex compromises with a range of different stakeholders that may accommodate or challenge the interests of doctors or insurers. In addition to representation within the main political parties discussed above, labor unions and employers can claim a legitimate voice in health policy debates because they finance health insurance and occupy administrative roles within the sickness funds.

German federalism, moreover, provides an important entry point for the Länder and for the opposition parties, to the extent that the latter are in power at the state level. The parliament's upper chamber, the Bundesrat, is composed of delegations of the Länder governments, which in turn, have a veto over federal laws that directly affect their interests. Between 1972 and 1982, as well as from 1991 to 1998, the SPD held a majority in this chamber even though it was in opposition in the lower house (Bundestag). Still, divided government does not guarantee the SPD (or, for that matter, any opposition party) a positive say in federal health policy, if the federal government narrows the scope of its legislative proposals to bypass the Bundesrat. Furthermore, while the Bundesrat delegations reflect the partisan composition of the Land governments, they are not mere appendages of the national parties. When the interests of the states are at odds with those of the national government or of the national parties, the Bundesrat delegations may break ranks with their Bundestag colleagues even when they are of the same party.[11]

Ideological affinity between the moderate wings of the CDU and SPD on social policy questions has facilitated cross-party cooperation in health policy even during periods of divided government.[12] Both parties have accepted the central tenets of the social market economy (*soziale Marktwirtschaft*) in the postwar era. This doctrine accepts the market economy for allocation of goods but not for distribution of income, and it requires that the state guarantee a generous welfare safety net for those who lose out in the market. This does not, however, imply that the state provide social welfare services directly. Instead, consistent with the principles of subsidiarity and self-governance, the state relies on associations representing major societal interests, such as churches, medical associations, insurance funds, unions, and employers, to do so by granting them an official status in welfare provision under public law (Cassel and Henke n.d.; Katzenstein 1987, chaps. 1 and 4; van Kersbergen 1995; Rimlinger 1971, 138–48). For health policy, the consensus on the social market economy has two consequences. First, it means that politicians of the two main parties accept that a range of interests have a legitimate voice in health policy-making. Second, the cross-party cooperation among the moderate wings of the CDU and SPD sometimes yields policies that advance the interests of the sickness funds at the expense of the medical profession.

Medical Politics and Uncertain Compliance

Some of the problems with corporatist governance are also rooted in the organizational characteristics of the medical profession. Corporatism accords the KV leaders substantial legal controls over their membership. Unlike the British Medical Association, the decision-making procedures within the KVs themselves have insulated the leaders from the rank and file and granted them the latitude to strike deals with insurers and the state. The executive committees of the KVs enjoy wide latitude in negotiations on fees with the sickness funds, with the KV assemblies tending to ratify such contracts. Since the KVs assemblies meet only twice a year (compared to the executive boards' monthly meetings), they can do little more than exert a control function. The KVs have often successfully excluded dissenters from internal policy-making processes, and their chairmen have withheld information from the rank and file (Webber 1992a, 245–47; Safran 1967, 104–5).

But even with this array of controls, the KVs cannot always guarantee that they will be dependable corporatist partners with insurers or the government. This is because the Janus-faced identity of the KVs and KBV creates tensions with the membership that sometimes make it difficult for the leaders to fulfill their corporatist obligations (Webber 1992a, 214). As public-law bodies, the KVs must orient their behavior to the common good (*gemeinwohlorientierte*), which normally means that they must implement government policies and ensure that their members are in compliance. Yet the KVs are also supposed to represent the interests of the medical profession (ibid.; Stone 1980, 52). Sometimes, this dual-representation mandate works to insulate the KV leaders from disgruntled members and to persuade doctors that their public obligations require them to accept a policy that they may find abhorrent. At other times, the strain of dual representation sparks internal revolts, especially when members believe that the leadership's acceptance of government mandates has betrayed their interests. KV leaders may then side with the rank and file and threaten to withdraw their cooperation with the state and payers (Webber 1992a, 255–67).

In addition, rivalries between the KVs and voluntary associations sometimes make the public-law bodies uncertain allies of policymakers. The relationship between the KVs and Hartmannbund ranges from a de facto division of labor to outright competition.[13] Normally, the KBV pursues a more moderate policy line and leaves it to the Hartmannbund to mobilize doctors against an unfavorable government policy (interview with BMG official, June 5, 1992). Lacking the legal mandate to implement government policies, the Hartmannbund can afford to be more militant than the KVs. But sometimes the relationship is not so cooperative, and the Hartmannbund sees its role as that of watchdog over the KBV to ensure that the latter does not concede too much to the sickness funds or the state (Bosch interview, June 1, 1992). When facing harsh criticism from the voluntary organizations that resonates with their own members, the leaders of the public-law associations may take a tougher policy stance than they would otherwise like.

Inequities and Inefficiencies among Insurers

The organizational differentiation of sickness funds along class and status lines has also produced serious inequities among the insured population.

Whereas white-collar employees could choose their own fund, blue-collar workers were assigned to one of the primary funds according to their particular sector or occupation, or, if no other fund was open to them, to a local fund. This mandatory assignment of wage earners to certain funds gave rise to adverse selection and uneven burdens in financing health insurance, especially for the local funds. Substitute funds, which insured salaried employees, enjoyed a healthier and wealthier membership and could levy correspondingly lower contribution rates. Manual workers, by contrast, are on average sicker and earn less than white-collar workers. But while company and professional funds could avoid the more disadvantaged members of society by closing their doors to those outside their employment or their professions (Hoffman 1991), local funds had no such luxury. As insurers of last resort, they covered a disproportionate share of sicker and poorer segments of the population as well as the unemployed in the declining sectors of the economy and blue-collar workers.[14] As a result of this adverse selection, they had to levy much higher contribution rates on a smaller income base to cover their health care outlays than the company, professional, or substitute funds (Bernardi-Schenkluhn 1992, 661–62; Files and Murray 1995; Stone 1980, 80–81). Thus, while the average contribution rate for health insurance in 1990 was 12.5 percent of income, in some local funds it ran as high as 15.6 percent (KAG 1992, 206–7).

Mandatory assignment of workers to certain funds was also deemed responsible for some of the inefficiencies in the health care system. With a captive membership, the primary funds had little reason to be responsive to patients in the areas of service, price, or quality of care. If they faced a budget shortfall, the sickness funds merely raised their contributions to cover it, and members could do little but accept the increases. A captive membership also gave the funds little reason to demand more efficient (or higher quality) care from the KVs. Their passivity toward the medical profession, in turn, further undermined the countervailing power strategy upon which effective corporatism depended.

Corporatism's Limited Reach

Given this litany of the flaws with corporatism among the KVs and insurers, one might think that policymakers would be eager to dispense with it. But this was not the case. In fact, other areas of the health care system that lay outside corporatism's purview—namely, the pharmaceutical and hospital sectors—fared even worse than the ambulatory sector and were responsible for a large portion of health care inflation and expenditure (see table 8).[15] Instead of public-law, corporatist bodies with the obligation to implement federal policies and with the authority to conclude collective agreements binding on their members, hospitals and drug companies were represented by voluntary associations with weak sanction powers. Alternative governance mechanisms in these subsectors were either weak or nonexistent or else worked in ways to deprive federal officials of the means to pursue a comprehensive and coherent cost-containment strategy for the entire health care system.

This was especially apparent in the hospital area, where federalism divided jurisdiction between national and state authorities. Rather than cooperating, the Länder often resisted any federal actions that they considered encroachments on their turf (Altenstetter 1987). The Bundesrat afforded them a veto over various federal efforts to bring cost discipline to the hospital sector. In addition, hospital financing arrangements, which divided responsibility between corporatist actors and the states, made a coordinated cost-containment strategy difficult to realize. Though capital budgets of the hospitals were the responsibility of the Länder, the sickness funds financed their daily operating costs—on a per diem basis that encouraged long stays. The funds also concluded agreements separately with each hospital rather than with a provincial or national umbrella association.

In addition, the structure of the federal bureaucracy has limited the governance capacity of national policymakers in the health system. Germany's "cooperative federalism" has bound the federal and state governments in shared policy tasks. Institutionally, it translates into a small federal health ministry that has lacked the administrative capacity to implement its own policies. Instead, the national health ministry relies on the Land bureaucracies to supervise many areas of federal health policy, such as contracts between doctors and insurers, or on the corporatist associations of doctors and insurers to implement federal laws and directives (Katzenstein 1987, 19–22, 45–46).

In short, for all its flaws, corporatism offered national governments better leverage over sectoral actors than the arrangements that existed in other parts of the health sector. Hence, national policymakers seeking to enforce cost discipline on the rest of the health care system looked to corporatism as their model.

Policy Responses in the 1970s and 1980s: Working through Corporatism

By the mid-1970s, the health care system was hit with a cost explosion that could not be ignored. Economic growth had begun to slow, while health care outlays and contribution rates escalated sharply. From 1970 to 1975, health spending grew at an average annual rate of 19.4 percent, far in excess of the 10 percent annual rate between 1960 and 1970 (Stone 1980, 141–43). Policy experts worried that rising health care expenditures, coupled with an aging population and declining birthrate, threatened the long-term fiscal viability of the social security system. Public support to rein in doctors' incomes was also growing. The popular perception that physician incomes were excessive was not unfounded; in the previous decade, the KVs had won open-ended fee-for-service reimbursement, and doctors' incomes remained well above those of other occupations (ibid., 93–95, 141–51, 155–57).

But policymakers responded to the perceived cost crisis by working within the corporatist framework and attempting to address its shortcomings rather than searching for an alternative governance regime. Working with the corporatist grain comprised a two-pronged approach of concertation and corporatization, which was first formalized in the 1977 Health Care Cost Containment Act (Gesundheitskostendämpfungsgesetz) and pursued subsequently in the 1980s.

With concertation, state actors brought together the major health care stakeholders and exhorted them to "coordinate their behavior according to general systemic needs" (Döhler 1991, 250).[16] The 1977 law created a national-level roundtable, the Concerted Action in Health Care (Konzertierte Aktion im Gesundheitswesen, or KAG), composed of peak associations of health care providers, sickness funds, trade unions, employers, and federal, Land, and local government officials (100 Begriffe aus dem Gesundheitswesen 1991, 24–25). The roundtable's task was to recommend annual increases in health care spending, based upon broader economic indicators, that providers and payers were expected to follow when negotiating collective agreements. Thus, the law explicitly sought to link health spending to broader economic performance.

In 1985, the Kohl government attempted to bolster the moral suasion and authority of the Concerted Action by adding a standing Council of Experts to its membership. Composed of doctors, social policy experts, and health economists, this seven-member council serves as an independent advisory board to the Concerted Action and produces reports on specific problems in the health care system.[17] These reports were expected to bring additional pressure to bear on sectoral actors to eliminate inefficient practices (Alber 1989, 26–27; 1991).

Corporatization (Döhler and Manow-Borgwardt 1991, 1992) constituted the second prong of the state's cost-containment strategy. Under this approach, state actors mandated new joint tasks in the area of cost-containment to the corporatist bodies of doctors and insurers. These tasks extended the reach of self-governance of KVs and insurers to decision areas that had been outside their purview. Corporatization also aimed to correct the imbalance in the relationship between doctors and insurers by placing new limits to the exercise of physician power and by granting the funds new authority in sectoral administration.

The Health Care Cost Containment Act and subsequent state actions illustrate the corporatization approach in practice. First, to strengthen insurers in the task of cost containment, the 1977 law removed economic monitoring from doctors' exclusive purview and granted sickness funds parity representation on the review committees (see Stone 1980, 98–103, chaps. 7 and 9). Second, the legislation required all funds to use a common relative value scale when negotiating collective agreements on fees with the KVs (prior to this the substitute funds used a different scale than the primary funds). In 1987, the Kohl government continued in this direction by mandating that KVs and insurers update the relative value scale to reward consultative services and reduce the value of high-tech diagnostic tests. Policymakers hoped that these provisions would grant the funds the financial wherewithal to influence medical practice in ways consistent with cost containment (Brenner and Rublee 1991; Stone 1980, 153). A common national scale also might help reduce some of the rivalry between primary and substitute funds that had worked to bid up physician incomes in the past.[18] (The mechanism for calculating doctors' fees is discussed below.)

Third, the Kohl government breathed new life into the Federal Committee of Physicians and Sickness Funds (Bundesausschuß der Ärzte und Krankenkassen), in existence since 1955, by significantly expanding its range of tasks. Since 1985, the committee has developed guidelines for decisions on the siting of new medical equipment in physician offices and for the regional distribution of doctors, regulated contracts between doctors and insurers, developed a voluntary prescription-drug price list to guide insurers, and decided which new treatments and therapies should be covered under statutory national insurance (Döhler 1991, 275–77; Döhler and Manow-Borgwardt 1991, 17–18; 1992).

Finally, the government required that budgeting mechanisms regulate collective bargaining between funds and doctors in order to contain costs.[19] The 1977 law reintroduced fixed global budgets for physician reimbursement and required similar budgets for dentists and prescription drugs. However, the government refrained from setting these budgets itself but instead relied on the Concerted Action, KVs, and insurers to do so.

This process of fee-for-service within a budget worked as follows. First, the Concerted Action based its recommended increases in health care spending on the development of wages and salaries in the broader economy, which the KVs and funds were supposed to observe in their own bargaining (Stone 1980, 153–54, 158). At the national level, the federal associations of sickness funds and physicians set a point value for each service listed in the relative value scale. Then, at the Land or regional level, the KVs and funds negotiated a budget from which to pay for physician services. They also negotiated a monetary conversion factor to translate the point values in the relative value scale into deutschemarks. The KVs paid their member doctors fee-for-service, but overall physician reimbursement stayed within the boundaries of the budget by means of the following procedure.[20] The national relative value scale assigned a fixed point value for each service, but the monetary conversion factor floated within a given range to keep total physician reimbursement within the Land-level budget. Thus, while overall physician reimbursement was stable, the system caused considerable uncertainty for individual physicians: it was not uncommon for doctors to see lower reimbursements during or at the end of the year to stay within the budget.

Containing costs by working within corporatism yielded mixed results. The rate of increase in health care spending slowed until the early 1980s, but then began to escalate again. There were limits to concertation's effectiveness in enforcing cost discipline on sectoral actors. The roundtable could not assure that providers and insurers would abide by their recommendations since its directives were voluntary and lacked the backing of law or other sanctions (Hartmannbund n.d.; Reinhardt 1990; Ryll 1990; Schneider 1991; Schulenburg 1983, 1992; Stone 1980, 154–55, and chap. 9; Webber 1992a). Moreover, the 1977 law permitted the funds and KVs to veto the roundtable's recommendation and conduct private negotiations.[21]

Consistent with corporatism's incentive structure, however, physicians adjusted their behavior and observed a policy of voluntary fee restraint in the 1980s in an effort to fend off threatened state encroachments in their self-governance (Webber 1992a). Still, each time the KVs departed from their voluntary incomes policy (as they did in 1983 and 1984), physician incomes rose rapidly (Döhler 1991, 53–54; Webber 1989, 269, 284). However, the cost performance of subsectors where corporatist constraints were not present fared even worse than the ambulatory sector (see table 8).

TABLE 8. Expenditure Trends in German National Health Insurance, 1980–88 (percentage change from previous year)

Year	Ambulatory Care	Drugs	Hospital Care	Total Spending
1980	+8.7	+10.6	+9.5	+11.0
1981	+7.4	+8.4	+7.3	+7.3
1982	+2.6	+1.1	+8.3	+0.5
1983	+5.0	+4.9	+4.6	+3.5
1984	+6.5	+7.6	+7.3	+8.0
1985	+3.9	+6.8	+5.5	+5.0
1986	+3.2	+6.2	+7.0	+4.9
1987	+3.3	+7.2	+4.6	+4.3
1988	+3.3	+8.2	+3.7	+7.7

Source: KBV 1994, table G13.

Conclusion

The corporatist bargain in German health insurance therefore held both promise and problems for policymakers. It provided the state with important direct and indirect leverage over doctors and insurers. But it also contained several defects that made it hard to contain medical power and that needed to be addressed if corporatism was to increase its effectiveness as an approach to containing health care costs. Yet, despite its shortcomings, the cost-containment tools of corporatism—compulsory membership organizations with the authority to conclude collective agreements that were binding on their members—were better than the absence of governance instruments that prevailed in other parts of the health care system. After all, the costs in the hospital and pharmaceutical fields were escalating sharply and placing a heavy financial burden on the national insurance system. But the stakeholders in these areas were subject to even less discipline than office-based doctors and sickness funds. Thus, the incomplete reach of corporatism posed a further problem for federal policymakers intent on controlling health care costs.

For Helmut Kohl, the question in the late 1980s was whether to continue with past policies that worked within corporatism while attempting to repair its flaws, or whether to strike out in a radically different direction and scrap corporatism for a new governance regime, such as market competition or statism. How he answered this question is the subject of the next chapter.

CHAPTER 4

The German Reforms

Grafting the Market onto Corporatism

On June 2, 1992, health minister Horst Seehofer emerged from a closed-door retreat to announce a blueprint for a new health care reform. In the autumn of that year, the legislature enacted his blueprint as the Health Care Structural Reform Act, or Gesundheitsstrukturgesetz (GSG). In both style and content, the GSG departed from politics as usual. Doctors and other health care providers were conspicuous in their lack of influence over the policy-making process. The KVs and insurers, moreover, had to submit to a rare state intrusion in their realm of self-governance. At the same time, the government embarked in a new direction with a market experiment in the health care system. These measures were the government's response to the apparent failure of corporatist governance to deal with cost control under previous reform legislation enacted in 1988. Less than five years after the passage of the GSG, however, the Kohl government introduced yet another set of reforms, which brought the medical profession back to the bargaining table, and restored and even extended corporatist self-governance of doctors and insurers. Even so, the government sought to deepen market forces in the health care system.

This seemingly schizophrenic reform pattern followed a political logic. In 1992, the government took the unusual step of suspending self-governance and administering the health care system by decree. But this did not amount to a replacement of corporatism with an enduring state hierarchy. Rather, state encroachment was intended as a short-term emergency measure until corporatist actors took up their policy obligations. Moreover, Kohl continued to delegate responsibility for cost containment to the public-law associations of doctors and insurers and even extended their responsibility to cover other parts of the health care system. So while the Kohl government experimented with market forces, the market was meant to supplement corporatism, not destroy it. Indeed, a striking feature of the market was how little competition was permitted. This caution reflected political realities, with the government under considerable pressure from both Left and Right to limit the scope of competition. In short, the particular mix of governance instruments in German health care reforms reflected a dynamic political process involving compromises with different health care stakeholders and their allies in the political system at different points in time.

This chapter provides an account of the Kohl government's particular reform strategy that combined state intervention, a limited market, and corporatism. It tells the story of health care reform in three stages. The first is the 1988 legislation, which conformed to the corporatist model of policymaking and governance. Next is the 1992 law that was the government's drastic response to the failure of corporatism-as-usual as a tool of cost containment. The third stage, the 1997 legislation, was an attempt to both restore corporatism and simultaneously deepen the market. The chapter then assesses the effects of the reforms on doctors and insurers, and it explains the government's reform strategy in terms of the political forces underpinning the capitalist bargain in health care.

Much Ado about Nothing: The 1988 Health Care Reform Act

Contents of the Law

The costs of the German health care system had become a perennial concern for policymakers since the mid-1970s. By 1986, rising health care costs had become a political problem too difficult for the Kohl government to ignore, especially with federal elections looming in the following year. Health insurance contributions exceeded 12 percent of wages, a threshold that the Kohl government deemed politically unacceptable (Webber 1989, 269). Escalating insurance contributions threatened to alienate employers, a core CDU constituency, by saddling them with higher labor costs, and voters by reducing the paychecks of employees. The government responded with the 1988 Health Care Reform Act (Gesundheitsreformgesetz, or GRG), which was the handiwork of the minister of labor, Norbert Blüm. Stabilizing contribution rates (*Beitragssatzstabilität*) was the government's overriding priority, and with the GRG, policymakers for the first time wrote this principle into law and mandated it as a condition for all contracts between providers and payers (Schneider 1991, 91).

Notwithstanding Kohl's inflated rhetoric that the GRG was "the achievement of the century" and a "sweeping structural reform of the health care system" (*Der Spiegel* 1992a, 115), the law was in reality a continuation of the prior strategy of cost containment through corporatism while addressing the shortcomings in the corporatist framework that appeared to be driving health care inflation.

Continued corporatization. First, the GRG extended the scope of collective bargaining by the KVs and insurers to areas of the health care system outside their traditional domain or where cost-control mechanisms were lacking. Thus, the law introduced a price-setting system (*Festbeträge*) for prescription drugs. The pharmaceutical industry was notably absent from participating in this scheme. Instead, the government required the Federal Committee of Physicians and Sickness Funds to designate drugs into different categories, and the peak associations of insurers for setting reference prices based on cheaper generic equivalents (Döhler 1991, 279; Iglehart 1991b, 1754–55; Schneider 1991, 95–96).

Second, the GRG mandated new joint tasks between KVs and insurers to give the funds greater leverage over doctors and to force practitioners to be more cost-conscious in their treatment decisions. Thus the KBV, KVs, and insurers were required to develop guidelines to monitor the volume of drugs and physical therapy that doctors prescribed. Physicians who transgressed these guidelines would be subject to economic monitoring reviews and stronger financial sanctions. Moreover, the reviews would assess doctors' treatment decisions on the basis of efficiency as well as quality of care. The state also became more exacting in its mandates on sectoral actors, for example, stipulating that the KVs and funds review a random sample of 2 percent of KV doctors each quarter (Bernardi-Schenkluhn 1992, 658–59; Hartmannbund 1989, 15–16; Iglehart 1991b, 1754; Webber 1991, 73–74). To combat fraud and encourage cost-effective care, the law directed the KVs to provide funds with better information on the services that doctors provided.

Hospital reforms. The government also attempted to grant the sickness funds the wherewithal to implement its cost-containment policies in the hospital sector. But progress was limited, due to opposition from the Länder and the KVs. For example, the GRG granted the sickness funds the authority to refuse to sign contracts with hospitals that they deemed to be inefficient or superfluous, but they had to obtain the consent of the Land governments before doing so. The GRG also authorized insurers and KVs to set rules with the hospital associations to permit hospitals to provide limited pre- and post-inpatient care that had long been the exclusive domain of ambulatory providers, and to develop price lists for hospital services that doctors were to use to refer patients to less expensive facilities (Hartmannbund 1989, 27). However, the effectiveness of these lists as a cost-containment instrument was questionable, since doctors were not compelled to use them when making referrals (Webber 1991, 62–64).

Patient cost-sharing. The law departed from the corporatist approach to cost containment by introducing patient copayments for pharmaceuticals, hospital inpatient stays, physical therapy, and spa cures.[1] However, the copayments were minor, averaging DM 3 per prescription, and hardship clauses exempted disadvantaged segments of the population.

The Politics of the GRG

The GRG reflected a politics of inclusion that yielded multiple concessions to well-placed sectoral interests. A long and tortuous process of negotiation with major health care interests in 1987 and 1988 forced policymakers to dilute or abandon some of their more radical plans. In addition, a special committee intended to help the social policy experts of the governing parties in the Bundestag and the Ministry of Labor resolve their differences in drafting the bill had the opposite effect. Disagreements between the ministry and the party experts required higher-level meetings, which only created additional points of entry to health care interests, who used these openings to win concessions in the legislation (Giaimo and Manow 1997, 189; Webber 1989, 1991). For instance, while the GRG required doctors to share power with the sickness funds on matters of clinical practice, the KBV, along with the FDP's social policy expert on the coalition committee, succeeded in diluting those provisions that the medical profession found most odious—such as the required volume of random sampling (Bosch interview, December 4, 1991; Brenner interview, December 5, 1991; Hartmannbund 1989; Webber 1991, 70–72, 74, 86).

Other stakeholders fared less well than the doctors. The reference pricing system, which excluded drug companies from its deliberations, was a major defeat for the pharmaceutical industry. But the defeat was self-inflicted, since the industry proved itself unable to follow a policy of voluntary price restraint. The peak association of the pharmaceutical sector, the Federal Association of the Pharmaceutical Industry (Bundesverband der pharmazeutischen Industrie, or BPI), was a voluntary body that did not have the authority to compel its members to comply with price agreements, and its members refused to grant it a mandate to negotiate on their behalf with the government (Webber 1991, 65–70).[2] In other words, because the government could not count on the BPI to play the role of corporatist partner, it delegated the task to the KVs.

Coalition politics also yielded mixed results for patients. The FDP's promotion of "individual responsibility" (*Selbstbeteiligung*) dovetailed with the CDU's desire to address employers' perennial concerns over higher contributions and labor costs. Patient cost-sharing through copayments thus appealed to these interests. Still, patients had allies in the labor wing of the CDU and in Minister Blüm, who came from its ranks and secured the hardship clauses in exchange for the introduction of copayments (Döhler 1991, 254–55, 272, 278–79; Webber 1991, 85–86).[3]

If the GRG's politics of inclusion dashed Blüm's hopes for significant health care reform, so did the process of implementation in the health care system itself. Three years after the law's passage, many of its key provisions had yet to be implemented. Sickness funds and KVs remained deadlocked in their negotiations on practice guidelines and the implementation of the random sample review procedures, while half of the pharmaceutical market remained without fixed reference prices. Part of the delay lay in the technical difficulty in developing guidelines and in predicting the volume of drugs that physicians would be likely to prescribe. Drug companies also packaged medications in larger sizes to escape the price-setting scheme.

But the basic difficulty was due to the way that doctors used their position in corporatist administration to thwart the government's intentions. The GRG contained consent clauses that required the agreement of both doctors and insurers on the practice guidelines, which the KVs exploited to refuse to come to terms with the sickness funds (Bernardi-Schenkluhn 1992, 658–61; Brenner interview, December 5, 1991). The KVs' intransigence reflected their concern that the guidelines and monitoring requirements would create an intrusive bureaucracy that would interfere with doctors' freedom to prescribe and that would impose costly financial sanctions on offenders (Brenner interview, June 1, 1992). Having to negotiate such guidelines with insurers also challenged the medical profession's understanding of its collective and individual clinical freedom. Finally, if knowledge is power, then having to share patient data with insurers threatened to undermine the power advantage of the KVs. The funds might find it easier to monitor and punish individual doctors for fraudulent billings. The information might also enhance the position of insurers in collective bargaining with the KVs (Webber 1992a, 227–28, 230–31).

Lastly, Kohl's lack of enthusiasm to implement the GRG contributed to its failure. Facing a string of Land elections, the chancellor wanted to avoid a messy fight with his coalition's key health care constituencies. So he deserted his hapless health minister, Gerda Hasselfeldt, who had been appointed to head the newly created Ministry of Health (Bundesministerium für Gesundheit, or BMG) in January 1991 (Kurbjuweit 1992; *Der Spiegel* 1992a). Hasselfeldt lasted little more than a year in the job.

Embedding the Market within Corporatism: The Health Care Structural Reform Act

New Pressures for Reform

Despite the problems with its implementation, the GRG initially seemed to meet its expectations as contribution rates declined in 1990. But the cost discipline proved short-lived. Average contribution rates climbed from 12.2 percent at the beginning of 1991 to over 13 percent at the end of 1992, while expenditures in all areas of the health care system continued to rise rapidly (*Frankfurter Rundschau* 1991b, 1992a; KBV 1993, 7; *Der Spiegel* 1992a). The sickness funds' surplus in 1990 became a DM 10 billion shortfall by 1992, prompting insurers to raise their contribution rates (BMG 1993a, 7; BMG 1993b, 13–14).

The health care system's financial troubles became enmeshed with broader economic and political concerns for the coalition and fears of a voter backlash. The social insurance system was financing a considerable share of the economic and social costs of German unification; rising health insurance contribution rates in part subsidized the health care costs of the eastern Länder (Giaimo and Manow 1999, 977; Hinrichs 1995, 662–63). The health insurance hikes came on top of an income tax surcharge that violated the government's pledge to not raise taxes to finance unification. In addition, the government's recent pension reform changed the formula for calculating pension amounts from gross to net income. This meant that rising social insurance contributions or taxes would reduce pensions and potentially alienate retirees, a core CDU constituency (interview with BMG official, June 5, 1992). Another CDU constituency, the business community, was also growing restive. Employers argued that rising social insurance contributions were driving up labor costs to uncompetitive levels (KBV 1993 7; *Der Spiegel* 1992a, 114; *Der Spiegel* 1992b). Finally, media coverage of the GRG interpreted rising health expenditures and contribution rates as an indication that patients had done their part in bearing the load of cost containment but providers had not.[4]

Finally, with fourteen elections at local, Land, and European levels scheduled for 1994 and a national parliamentary election later that year, the coalition reasoned that it courted disaster at the polls unless it could deliver economic improvements and bring social spending under control. A new health care reform that inflicted the pain of adjustment on the voters early enough in the electoral cycle seemed to be the solution (interview with BMG official, June 5, 1992). If the reform lessened the pain on patients and made providers ante up, it would demonstrate to voters that the government cared about an equitable distribution of the burden of cost containment.

A new political resolve to force health care providers to do more for cost control thus began to solidify among Kohl and members of his governing coalition. One sign was the coalition partners' agreement in January 1991 to introduce major structural reforms in hospital financing and in the organization of the sickness funds in the next law, which they had declined to do with the GRG.[5] The second was the appointment of the CSU's Horst Seehofer to replace Gerda Hasselfeldt in the spring of 1992. Seehofer's background suggested that he would be a formidable adversary against the "health care lobby": he came from the CSU's trade union wing, his sympathies lay with the sickness funds, and his experience in drafting parts of the GRG fueled his disgust with providers' intransigence (Kurbjuweit 1992; *Der Spiegel* 1992b). Before accepting the post as health minister, Seehofer insisted on two conditions: a free hand to embark on a project of sweeping reform and the chancellor's backing for such an enterprise. He got both (*Der Spiegel* 1992a; 1992b, 161).

A Break with the Politics of Inclusion

The 1992 "reform of the reform" signaled a sharp break with past policymaking patterns. The GSG was the product of an extraordinarily rapid and secretive policy process in which health care provider groups found themselves thoroughly marginalized. In the first round of talks, which took place in May 1992, the governing coalition hammered out the basic reform concept in the course of only three weeks (*Der Gelbe Dienst* 1992; *Der Spiegel* 1992a). The talks were conducted behind closed doors and in a secluded setting away from the glare of the media. The participants at these meetings involved only a coalition commission consisting of the social policy experts of the CDU/CSU and FDP, plus an expert on national health insurance from the Ministry of Health who provided technical support to the politicians (*Der Gelbe Dienst* 1992; interview with BMG official, June 5, 1992). According to Manfred Zipperer, a senior official in the health ministry, the government consulted the major interest groups representing physicians, as well as those for the hospitals and sickness funds. But the doctors' representatives presented contradictory reform proposals from one week to the next. Unable to reach a consensus with providers, the coalition decided on the basic outlines of a reform plan on its own (Zipperer interview, July 5, 1995).

Seehofer then embarked on a second round of talks. Because his reform plans included the hospital sector, he needed the support of the Länder and the opposition Social Democratic Party, since it held a majority in the Bundesrat. He thus included the SPD and the Länder in talks with the governing coalition (*Der Spiegel* 1992b, 160–61). These talks bore fruit with the so-called Lahnstein compromise (named for the town in which the agreement was hammered out) in September 1992 (ibid., 161; Peel 1992b). Zipperer described the two stages of talks:

> In May, the government developed its concept, but realized then that it could not pass the plan without the Länder or the opposition. So in October, they [the coalition] met in Lahnstein with the Länder and the opposition and bargained with them. Representatives of the Länder, the government and the opposition sat in one room and worked out this idea. [This was] a very exceptional procedure; I have only heard of a similar cooperation like this in 1989–90 when we reformed the pensions. This was done because it was a major social problem; in that instance as well, a consensus was sought with the opposition. (Zipperer interview, July 5, 1995)

The success of these talks, then, was due to Kohl's willingness to cut a deal with the Social Democrats and especially to Seehofer's skill in turning the usual obstacles of coalition politics and divided government to his advantage. Kohl telephoned the Social Democrats' party chairman and promised real talks, while Seehofer found common ground with the SPD's social policy experts (*Der Spiegel* 1992b, 161). He also played the FDP and SPD off one another in a skillful game of bargaining and isolated the Liberals by striking a cross-party deal between the CDU/CSU and the SPD.

To minimize the chances of veto by interest groups, the health minister limited the number of participants to the talks (ibid., 160–61). Indeed, with the Lahnstein agreement, doctors and other health care providers wielded even less influence than in May. The Lahnstein compromise was essentially a deal between the governing coalition, the Social Democrats, and the Länder. As Zipperer observed, "In October, the interest groups played no role in the dealings. The politicians made their decisions among themselves" (Zipperer interview, July 5, 1995).

Also unusual was the speed with which the reforms were enacted. In contrast to the GRG, which had been the product of two years of party and interest-group wrangling, Seehofer allowed only a brief consultation period between the initial coalition agreement in May and the final passage of the bill into law. Once the cross-party agreement had been secured, the draft bill sailed through parliament later that autumn and took effect on January 1, 1993. All told, a mere seven months had elapsed from the talks in May to the law's effective date (*Der Spiegel* 1992b, 160; Peel 1992a).

Contents of the GSG

Many of the contents of the GSG were as radical as the policy process that produced them. The law was a particular mix of state intervention, market innovation, and continued corporatist self-governance. In a forceful response to the KVs' apparent foot-dragging on the GRG, the state resorted to its reserve powers to administer the health sector by decree. Even so, the state's extraordinary intervention in sectoral administration was consistent with corporatist governance, since it was designed as a temporary show of force to convince doctors and insurers to fulfill the provisions of the law on their own. At the same time, the government continued to rely on corporatism by delegating new cost-containment responsibilities to the KVs and insurers and by attempting to bolster the authority of the funds. Finally, the government introduced market forces on the insurers' side, but with the aim to enhance solidarity, not undermine it.

State intrusion in sectoral self-governance. As an emergency cost-containment device, the law set global budgets for most areas of the health care system—ranging from physician reimbursement, hospitals, prescribing of drugs and other therapies, to the administrative costs of the funds—for three years. Since the law required that the budgets could not exceed the revenues of the sickness funds, it explicitly tied health spending to the development of wages and salaries, and it did so more directly and forcefully than the GRG's admonition that the principle of contribution-rate stability guide sectoral actors in their collective bargaining. For pharmaceuticals, the GSG imposed a two-year price cut ("solidarity contribution") of 5 percent for drugs without reference prices and a 2 percent reduction for over-the-counter medicines (KBV 1993, 33; *Der Spiegel* 1993e, 182).

The GSG made a further inroad in collective bargaining between the

KVs and sickness funds by mandating that the fee schedule for KV doctors be revalued to raise the value of primary care services and reduce that of technical services. The BMG was to devise the new schedule subject to the approval of the Federal Chamber (*Der Spiegel* 1993e, 182).

The legally imposed budgets, and the encroachment on sectoral self-governance they represented, were the "sticks" in the government's approach toward the KVs and insurers and were consistent with its role as enforcer under corporatism. At the same time, the government proffered a number of "carrots": if doctors and insurers agreed to fulfill their obligations to implement government policies, then policymakers would restore to them their self-governance rights. The clearest example was in the budgeting policy: the GSG specified that state-set budgets would last only three years (two years for the drug price freeze) (GAO 1993, 41; *Der Gelbe Dienst* 1992). This limited duration indicated that state actors intended such interventions as a short-term measure and expected to retreat from detailed health care administration once the corporatist actors negotiated the mandated cost-containment provisions in their collective agreements. A similar process was at work in other areas of the health sector as described below.

Controlling drug costs. Alarmed at the escalating cost of drugs and the lack of progress between the KVs and sickness funds in negotiating prescribing guidelines and reference prices, the government took vigorous action. It imposed a price freeze on the pharmaceutical industry, suspended self-governance of insurers and doctors in the area of negotiating guidelines, and put doctors financially at risk for the cost of prescription drugs. Thus, the GSG empowered the health ministry to set a global budget for prescription drugs for each KV and to hold all members of a KV financially liable for cost overruns.[6] But again, the government offered a carrot. If the KVs agreed to negotiate prescribing guidelines with the sickness funds and to monitor member doctors as the law specified, the ministry would no longer set prescribing budgets. If they refused, however, then budgeting by decree would continue. Similar provisions applied for the area of physical therapy (KBV 1993, esp. 38–39).[7]

Extending joint tasks under corporatism. Even as it suspended sectoral self-governance in some areas, the government continued to rely on KVs and insurers to jointly implement other parts of the law. Thus, the GSG directed the Federal Committee of Physicians and Sickness Funds to extend the system of reference pricing to all drugs and to decide on the siting of new high-tech equipment in hospitals (GAO 1993, 48; KBV 1993, 16–17; *Der Spiegel* 1993b). The state also empowered insurers and KVs to jointly limit the number of new KV doctors to address a physician surplus, by allowing them to declare certain geographical areas and specialties closed to new practitioners and by extending the duration of physician training (GAO 1993, 10–11, 41–45; KBV, 1993, 19–28; *Der Spiegel* 1993c). The law also repeated the GRG's directives that the KVs share more patient billing information with insurers.

Lastly, in an effort to make insurers a more potent countervailing force to the medical profession, the GSG required substitute funds to follow the same regulations as the primary funds when negotiating reimbursement agreements with the KVs (KBV 1993, 55–58). By forcing uniform procedures on all classes of funds, the government hoped to approximate an all-payer system and to thereby put a stop to the substitute funds' practice of setting a higher benchmark through their separate collective agreements with the KVs.

Hospital reform. The GSG also signaled the government's effort to mandate effective cost-control mechanisms in the hospital sector. First, the law mandated new reimbursement arrangements for hospitals, abolishing the per diem payment for hospital operating costs and directing that a prospective budgeting system replace it. The new system, akin to DRGs in the United States (see chap. 3), would pay hospitals a set payment for a specified operation or for treatment of a specified illness and was to be compulsory for all hospitals by 1996 (OECD 1997, 93–94). Second, the government sought to delegate responsibility for implementing the new payment system to the collective bargaining partners in the hospital sector. Thus, the law directed that sickness funds and hospital associations would eventually negotiate the new payment system through collective agreements, much as the KVs and insurers did in the ambulatory sector. But until the hospitals had the new payment system in place, the health ministry would set the hospital budgets by decree (GAO 1993, 11, 45; KBV 1993, 49–50).[8]

Market mechanisms to enhance solidarity and efficiency. The most innovative and potentially far-reaching changes in the GSG involved the introduction of market forces into the sickness funds to rectify long-standing disparities between blue- and white-collar workers. First, the law granted blue-collar workers the right to choose their insurer beginning in 1996, though within some limits: substitute funds would have to open their doors to anyone who wished to join, while company and professional funds could choose but were not compelled to do so (GAO 1993, 14; KBV 1993, 57; *Der Spiegel* 1993c, 69). Thus, a company fund could confine membership to a firm's employees and retirees, but if it chose to open its doors to wider membership, then it had to accept all applicants. Second, to level the playing field among different types of funds competing for patients and to prevent them from competing on the basis of better health status and incomes of patients, the GSG introduced a financial risk-adjustment scheme (*Risikostrukturausgleich*) prior to free choice of fund. Funds with healthier and wealthier members would now have to make financial transfers to those with sicker and poorer members, to erase the unfair advantages of the substitute funds and help the local funds (Bernardi-Schenkluhn 1992, 661–62; GAO 1993, 13–14; KBV 1993, 56–57).[9] While the primary aim of these measures was to enhance solidarity and equity of health insurance, the government also hoped that free choice of insurer would make the funds more responsive to consumers and more willing to compete for members on the basis of lower contribution rates and better customer service (*Der Spiegel* 1993c, 69).[10]

More patient cost-sharing. Finally, the government continued to rely on patient cost-sharing, but the copayment hikes under the GSG were moderate. As before, the law exempted certain groups of the population from copayments as hardship cases (BMG 1993b).[11]

With the GSG, then, the government targeted providers and sought to force them to assume greater responsibility for implementing its cost-containment policy. Indeed, the coalition calculated that the new law would save the sickness funds DM 10 billion in health care spending in 1993. Out of that amount, patients would bear only DM 1.73 billion in higher copayments, with providers shouldering the rest (KBV 1993, 11).

Doctors' Response to the GSG

Medical Militants

The medical profession's response to the Health Care Structural Reform Act was decidedly negative. The public-law bodies in particular were appalled at their effective lockout from meaningful negotiations on the new health care reforms and their failure to budge the coalition partners from their reform course. The best the KBV could claim were concessions on some minor details of the legislation, such as a liability ceiling for KV doctors for the first year of the drug budget (*Der Spiegel* 1992b, 160; 1993a, 203; KBV 1993, 4, 9). Like the KBV, the Federal Chamber of Physicians had no influence on shaping the basic principles of the reform.[12]

Medical associations were equally dismayed over the substantive contents of the new law. First, they argued that subjecting health spending, physician remuneration, and prescribing decisions to economic indicators like national income was flawed, and that the proper benchmarks were demographic changes and the medical needs of an aging population (Brenner interview, December 5, 1991; Kloiber interview, June 4, 1992; Peel 1992c). Second, doctors realized all too well that the health ministry's stringent budget-setting and its placing the KVs financially at risk for "excessive" prescribing would certainly squeeze their incomes (KBV 1993, 31). Third, doctors feared that prescribing guidelines and drug budgets threatened their clinical freedom. Finally, the KVs and KBV viewed the GSG's legal decrees, specifications, and timetables as state encroachments upon their role in sectoral administration and free collective bargaining (see KBV 1993, 33). The KBV chairman, Winfried Schorre, summed up doctors' fears. As reported in *Der Spiegel*, he asserted that the Seehofer reforms were a "'dead-end policy of a planned economy in health care'" and urged doctors to fight for the "'recovery of medical freedom,' and above all, 'a fair income. It is a question of each mark!'" (1993c, 65).

Different medical associations responded to the draft bill and the GSG with a variety of opposition tactics. The Hartmannbund resorted to its usual inflammatory rhetoric and embarked upon a virulent public campaign.[13] But it had no obligation to pursue moderation, since it was an outsider to the policy process and did not operate under the constraints that the public-law bodies did. Instead, the Hartmannbund was fulfilling its role as champion of doctors' private interests and acting as a safety valve for physicians who were disaffected with the KVs.

What was unusual was the militancy of the KBV and the Federal Chamber of Physicians before and after the GSG had become law. The KBV prefers, and has usually enjoyed, closed-door discussions with the state. It tends to avoid overt displays of militancy, even though it may voice opposition to government legislation in muted tones, in order to not jeopardize its privileged access. Once a law is enacted, legal associations—the KVs and Chamber—then discuss ways of implementing the legislation because they are legally bound to do so (Brenner interview, June 1, 1992).

But their unaccustomed position as outsiders to the policy process and the substantive losses they incurred in the GSG led the KBV and the Federal Chamber to open hostility toward the government. The head of the Federal Chamber, Karsten Vilmar, threatened a doctors' strike to protest the law (Parkes 1992a, 1). The KBV initially tried a path of moderation, calling for renewed talks while the legislation was being considered in the hope that it would exert some influence (*Die Tageszeitung* 1992). When moderation failed, the KBV shifted tactics and sought to mobilize the rank and file by circulating to KV doctors a publication that lambasted the GSG and prophesied dire consequences for office-based physicians.[14] It also tried to turn public opinion against the reforms by providing physicians with posters and information sheets for their office waiting rooms, which alerted patients to the law's constraints on physician prescribing (KBV 1993, esp. 59–61).

However, such militancy turned out to be a public relations disaster, sowing confusion and fear among doctors and patients alike early in the law's implementation. The KBV's leader at the time, Ulrich Oesingmann, found it necessary to publicly reassure patients that they would continue to receive medically necessary medications (*Der Spiegel* 1993a, 1993b). In addition, the medical profession came under scathing criticism from the media. The popular press ridiculed the medical profession's claims that the reforms were turning its members into paupers and noted the high incomes of physicians (*Der Spiegel* 1993c; see also 1993a, 203; 1993b). Finally, the doctors' public campaigns and strike threats in the summer and fall of 1992 alienated chancellor Kohl and hardened his support for his health minister. "They have gone too far," Kohl declared to Seehofer (*Der Spiegel* 1992b, 161).

Seehofer, by contrast, received extensive media praise for his resolve to take on the "health care lobby" in order to save the health care system (*Der Spiegel* 1992a; 1993d, 181; 1993e). Both his coalition partners and the opposition SPD praised his intellectual and political skills, his blending of toughness with a public image of reasonableness and moderation (*Der Spiegel* 1992b, 160). And Seehofer did not hesitate to remind KV doctors of their obligations as public-law bodies by announcing that those who took part in a strike would lose their permit to treat national health insurance patients for six years on the grounds of dereliction of duty. Following this statement, doctors dropped their talk of strikes and grudgingly began the task of complying with the law (*Der Spiegel* 1993c, 58; 1993d, 181).

A Divided Profession

Much like their counterparts in Britain did in protesting the process and content of the Thatcher government's reforms, the GSG generated much sound and fury on the part of medical leaders in Germany. In a similar fashion, the GSG precipitated severe internal stresses within the KVs that set the members against their leaders and sowed dissension among different groups of doctors.

First, the GSG brought to the fore the tensions inherent in the dual mandate that constrained the corporatist bodies. The KVs are supposed to simultaneously represent the interests of doctors and fulfill the broader public interest by implementing laws on behalf of government. But many doctors rebelled against this dual mandate and, with the GSG, sensed a sell-out on the part of their leaders. The *Medical Tribune* vilified the chairman of the KBV, Ulrich Oesingmann, as a "double-agent" who had betrayed the KV doctors, since he had attended the secret talks with the government but had failed to avert the new burdens that the law placed on the medical profession (*Der Spiegel* 1993a, 203). KV doctors repudiated his leadership later in 1993 and replaced him with Winfried Schorre, whom they saw as someone who would fight for their interests and their incomes (*Der Spiegel* 1993c, 65). Schorre's task was no easier than his predecessor's, however, since he faced the challenge of leading a divided and demoralized medical profession. He had to restore the rank and file's confidence in its leaders and address their trepidation over the effects of the GSG on their incomes and freedom. This dilemma helped to account for the KBV's continued militancy, at least in its rhetoric (ibid.).

Aside from opening up a yawning chasm between the leaders and the rank and file, the GSG cut deep fault lines between different groups of doctors. First, the law's tight caps on physician incomes, coupled with a growing doctor glut, worsened existing distributional conflicts among KV doctors. To make matters worse, the GSG permitted specialists from university clinics and specialty hospitals to enter into ambulatory care before restrictions on such practice went into effect, thereby precipitating a mass influx of new doctors into the KVs (*Der Spiegel* 1993b, 201) (see table 9). But because their reimbursements had to stay within the cap, most doctors would experience declining incomes as a greater number of physicians chased a fixed pot of deutsche marks (Jost 1998, 700–701). To the extent that some practitioners provided unnecessary services or billed fraudu-

TABLE 9.   Trends in the Number of KV Doctors, 1980–93 (western Länder)

Year	Number of New KV Doctors (net)	New KV Doctors (net, in percentages)	Number of New KV Doctors (gross)	New KV Doctors, (gross, in percentages)
1980	800	1.4	3,030	5.5
1982	1,290	2.3	3,230	n.a.
1984	2,050	3.4	4,020	n.a.
1986	1,910	3.0	3,950	6.2
1988	1,460	2.2	3,670	5.5
1990	1,850	2.6	3,970	5.7
1992	3,210	4.2	4,950	6.4
1993	8,490	11.0	9,850	12.7

Source: KBV 1994, from figs. A15, A16.

lently in an effort to maintain their own incomes, all doctors would suffer because their reimbursements would be adjusted downward to remain within the budget.

In addition, the GSG's other cost-containment measures deepened divisions between primary care doctors and specialists. Changes to the fee schedule promised income losses for specialists who did high-tech procedures and income gains to primary care practitioners who did more talking to patients. The drug budget provisions were especially problematic in this regard. Holding KV doctors collectively liable for overruns in the drug budget meant that those doctors who prescribed relatively few drugs and therapies would have to bear the cost of those who ordered far more (GAO 1993, 47; KBV 1993, 36–46). As the KBV's Brenner explained, general practitioners and internists tend to prescribe the majority of prescriptions, while radiologists prescribed relatively few (Brenner interview, July 13, 1995). Many specialists would therefore have to cross-subsidize the activities of their primary care colleagues.

The consequences for physician incomes were predictably harsh. With the influx of new doctors and the fee schedule changes, there was a corresponding surge in the volume of physician services, particularly among specialists trying to maintain their incomes, and a sharp decline in the conversion factor. Doctors' incomes fell sharply as a result (Jost 1998, 700–701).

These distributional conflicts threatened to undermine the KV leadership's ability to represent the profession. They also created internal stresses that threatened an implosion of the medical associations and thus a destabilization of corporatist governance. Doctors' unhappiness was not lost on Kohl, and his next reform effort sought to address these grievances.

The Health Care Reorganization Acts

Background: The Welfare State and the Standort Debate

Following the GSG's introduction, health care expenditures followed a similar pattern as they did with the previous law. Costs initially stabilized, giving the government hope that the GSG reforms had succeeded. Contribution rates remained stable, averaging 13.5 percent of wages in 1996, and the budget for pharmaceuticals remained in the black (see table 10).

But budgeting by decree did not produce lasting cost discipline or address the underlying structural problems of the health sector. Doctors subsequently had trouble staying within their drug budgets and were slated to make substantial refunds to insurers in 1997. But for political reasons, the health ministry chose not to enforce the sanctions. As the KBV's Brenner noted, the budget overruns were so large in some KVs that it would have required them to demand reimbursements in the range of DM 20,000 per physician (Brenner interview, January 14, 1998). Holding physicians collectively liable for overruns of individual doctors would have provoked a bitter fight with the medical profession. Moreover, the ministry lacked the technical capacity to calculate the monetary value of prescriptions written by individual physicians (OECD 1997, 98–99).

Germany's hospital and pharmaceutical prices also accelerated sharply in the 1990s, when compared to either the previous two decades or to other OECD countries (OECD 1997, 74–75). Indeed, inpatient costs rose 20.4 percent between 1992 and 1995 (ibid., 90). Much of the increase was due to higher employment costs in hospitals, but some Länder were also responsible because they passed legislation that put the provision of health care ahead of budgetary discipline (ibid., 92–93). Germany also had the dubious honor of ranking second in health spending in the OECD, even after

TABLE 10. Social Insurance Contributions in Germany, 1950–96 (as percentage of gross wages; western Länder)

Year	Total	Health*
1950	20.0	6.0
1955	20.2	6.2
1960	24.4	8.4
1965	25.2	9.9
1970	26.5	8.2
1975	30.5	10.5
1980	32.4	11.4
1985	35.1	11.8
1990	35.6	12.6
1991	36.7	12.2
1992	36.8	12.8
1993	37.4	13.4
1994	38.9	13.2
1995	39.3	13.2
1996	41.0	13.6

Source: Manow 1997a, table 6, 40 (Bundeministerium für Arbeit, 1997 figures).

*Average contribution rate to all funds; except 1950–69, average contribution rate to blue-collar workers' funds only.

excluding for the costs associated with unification (ibid., 68). In 1996, the deficit in the health care system stood at DM 6.3 billion (Manow 1997b). With wages growing more slowly than GDP, sickness funds once again found themselves contemplating a contribution hike.[15]

Containing the health care system's appetite for resources seemed all the more pressing in the context of the highly charged debate over the welfare state and its effect on economic competitiveness. A deep recession in the early 1990s, along with the collapse of East German industry shortly thereafter, created record levels of joblessness. The welfare state was a critical safety valve for coping with the rising numbers of unemployed, especially in the eastern Länder, accounting for approximately 18 percent of the financial transfers from western to eastern Germany (Heilemann and Rappen 1997, 15). Most of these transfers financed early retirement pensions and unemployment insurance (ibid., 13). In addition, whether the result of globalization or the drive toward economic and monetary union in Europe, German firms were under intense pressure to remain competitive in the new world economy. Many employers, academics, and politicians across the political spectrum thus came to view rising nonwage labor costs with alarm. They maintained that Germany's generous payroll-based welfare state, along with rigid labor market regulations and high wages, diminished the country's attractiveness as a site to do business and invest (the so-called Standort debate). They also argued that high labor costs also erected barriers to job creation—particularly in lower-productivity services—which then created more unemployment and inactivity and led to a crisis in financing the welfare state (Esping-Andersen 1996, chap. 3; Hemerijck and Manow 1998; Hinrichs 1995, 660–61; OECD 1997, esp. chap. 3; Scharpf 1997). The worries were not groundless, as social insurance contributions accounted for nearly 41 percent of wages in 1996, putting German labor costs among the highest in the OECD (OECD 1996, 76).

Businesses thus clamored for relief from their social insurance contribution share. But with unemployment rising in the western and especially the eastern Länder, it was politically difficult to make a case for slashing unemployment insurance or early retirement pensions. Both programs were essential to managing the costs of unification, and many firms and unions in the west relied on various early retirement schemes to shed unneeded labor by externalizing the costs onto the welfare state in this fashion (Manow 1997a).

But decisions on European integration meant that employers could not count on the government to assume much more of the burden of German unification or to bail out the social insurance system. At Germany's urging, member states in the European Union seeking to meet the Maastricht Treaty's provisions for a single currency also agreed to stringent budgetary constraints as a condition of entry. The Stability and Growth Pact of 1996 stipulated a maximum budget deficit of 3 percent of gross domestic product. Already deeply in the red, Germany was in danger of missing the entry criteria for the single currency. Under these circumstances, the Kohl government had no enthusiasm to assume a larger share of welfare state financing through deficit spending. Nor could it seriously contemplate further tax hikes given that the chancellor had already violated his earlier election pledge that German unification would not require new taxes.

Where, then, could economies be made in the welfare state, if employers, unions, and politicians were unwilling to gut early retirement pensions or unemployment insurance? The health sector provided an opportunity. Unlike early retirement pensions and unemployment schemes, health insurance was not central to firms' labor rationalization strategy, nor was it so visibly central to underwriting the costs of unification. Furthermore, because the GSG's legal budgets were set to expire in 1996, the government needed to find some other way to control health care costs. Another reform effort thus was in the offing.

Contents of the Neuordnungsgesetze

The Kohl government's effort produced the Health Care Reorganization Acts (Neuordnungsgesetze, or NOGs 1 and 2), both of which went into effect in 1997. The immediate goal of the legislation, as before, was to keep a lid on contribution rates and health care costs, especially the share paid by employers, even if this meant burdening patients more. Policymakers also restored and extended corporatist governance of the health sector, but placed the immediate task of cost containment on the sickness funds rather than the medical profession. At the same time, they sought to use market forces rather than state decrees to guide the pricing decisions of insurers. This new emphasis on the market as simply a cost-containment tool rather than as a means to reconcile efficiency and equity, and the new burdens placed on insurers and patients rather than doctors and employers, reflected a new balance of political forces in German health policy.

Restoring corporatist self-governance. NOG 2 lifted state-set budgeting for doctors' services and transferred it back to the domain of free collective bargaining. Each KV was to negotiate a regional-level budget with the sickness funds as before. But now the KVs were to develop and enforce a budget for each doctor, based on physician specialty, that set a fixed conversion factor up to a certain volume (*Regelleistungsvolumen*). Fees for services above the volume limits would be subject to a floating conversion factor to stay within the doctor's individual budget cap. With these measures, the government hoped to bring an element of certainty to doctors' incomes and to address their dissatisfaction with state encroachment in collective bargaining and their self-governance rights (*Dienst für Gesellschaftspolitik* 1997a; Jost 1998, 703–4; Wasem interview, January 10, 1998).

NOG 2 also permitted the KVs and sickness funds to negotiate target budgets (*Richtgrößen*) to monitor the prescribing patterns of individual doctors instead of negotiating a global budget for each KV (*Dienst* 1997a; Wasem interview, January 10, 1998). This measure simply reiterated the government's intentions with the two previous reform laws.

Corporatization of other subsectors. The NOGs extended the scope of corporatist bargaining to cover physical therapy, home care, spa cures, and rehabilitation services. The health ministry would no longer set budgets for these services by decree, as it had under the GSG. Instead, peak associations of the sickness funds and relevant providers would negotiate binding collective agreements covering reimbursement. In addition, the law authorized the Federal Committee of Physicians and Sickness Funds to develop prescribing and practice guidelines (*Richtlinien*) for such care (*Dienst* 1997a).

Tightening the vise of the market. With state-set budgets rescinded, Kohl needed to find another mechanism to prevent a renewed cost surge in the health sector. His solution was to intensify market forces by expanding choice of insurer and at the same time bring the state into sickness funds' decisions on contribution rates. Hence, NOG 1 stipulated that if a sickness fund hiked its contribution rate, it would also have to raise copayments on its members by a corresponding percentage. Furthermore, the law relaxed the waiting period on choice of insurer and permitted members to immediately switch to a different fund in the event of a contribution increase. Funds contemplating a rate hike would presumably think twice about doing so or else face these painful consequences. This scheme, then, was a unique mix of market discipline and state interference in the self-governance of the funds.[16]

Greater patient cost-sharing. The government expected patients far more than before to pick up the tab for rising health care costs. Patients would pay more out of pocket not only as a result of the scheme that automatically tied copayment increases to contribution rate hikes, but also because NOG 1 raised copayments across the board by DM 5. In addition, the government planned to dynamize copayments, that is, index them to the development of wages and salaries, starting in 1999 (*Dienst* 1997a; 1997b, 6–7, 9–10; Manow 1997b). Copayments would have likely increased at a greater rate under this scheme than if they were linked to the rate of inflation in the economy (which tended to be very low) or the result of discrete government actions. In the latter case, politicians might be cautious and avoid hefty copayment hikes if they feared a backlash from voters. As a result of these changes, copayments were estimated to increase from DM 9 billion to DM 14 billion, or about 20 percent of all drug costs; if expected contribution hikes were included, then the share of patient cost-sharing would be even higher (Manow 1997b; OECD 1997, 103).

Since greater patient cost-sharing measures were bound to be unpopular, politicians sought ways to deflect blame for these measures and to avoid the most glaring violations of equity. Thus, the copayment-contribution linkage scheme presumably would hold profligate sickness funds, rather than health ministry decrees or government legislation, responsible for greater patient cost-sharing. It was also an automatic-pilot approach that would not need repeated government actions for enforcement. Dynamizing copayments would work in a similar fashion, as broader economic developments, rather than discrete, visible legislative decisions, would be the basis to calculate copayment levels. But, to limit political damage, the government continued to protect the most vulnerable groups in society by broadening the scope of the population eligible for hardship exemptions.[17]

Extending market experiment. The NOGs permitted the statutory funds, to a limited degree, to compete for members by differentiating their products. In doing so, the statutory funds could adopt some of the practices of private insurers. They could now offer marginal services to their members as extras at a correspondingly higher contribution rate. They could also experiment with novel reimbursement arrangements, such as deductible plans (*Selbstbehalt*), reimbursement of members for health care costs rather than direct payment of providers, and contribution rebates for lower-than-expected use of health services. These measures would ostensibly encourage individuals to assume greater personal responsibility for their health care. But they were controversial because they could potentially reward those with better health or higher incomes that accrued from luck or inheritance rather than from individual behavior, and that might be subtle forms of cream-skimming.

NOG 2 also permitted funds to experiment with selective contracting with subgroups of doctors on new forms of health care delivery, though such agreements were subject to KV approval. If extended further, this change had the potential to encourage competition among physicians.

Party Politics and the NOGs

The politics underlying the NOGs were quite different from those that produced the GSG. The balance of power among sectoral actors had shifted, as had the strength of parties in the political arena. These shifts shaped the debates and outcomes surrounding the 1997 reforms, yielding laws that were far less favorable to patients and sickness funds and far more generous to the medical profession.

First, the NOG legislation was a second-best solution to Seehofer's ambitious agenda to enact major structural reforms that would have included the hospital sector. Seehofer's wish list was ambitious and would have addressed inefficiencies that had long plagued the hospitals. Proposals included single-source financing to replace dual financing by sickness funds and the Länder, a single budget for all hospitals in each Land instead of individual hospital budgets, a return to self-administration and a pullback of the state in pricing hospital services, better coordination of ambulatory and hospital sectors, and corporatization of the hospital sector (interview with health expert of the FDP, January 23, 1998; Rath 1996). However, the ideas drew opposition from a range of actors—but primarily the hospitals and the Länder—and initial legislation was rejected by the Bundesrat (Jost 1998, 701–2; OECD 1997, 93–94; Rath 1996).

The cost problems in the hospital sector stemmed from a number of structural characteristics described earlier. But the Kohl government believed that part of the problem lay with its inability to regulate the hospital sector and saw corporatism as the answer. Indeed, policymakers initially discussed extending corporatist governance to the hospitals during the development of the 1992 GSG law. However, the proposal, which was pushed by the SPD, never made it into a draft law because the FDP opposed it as too statist and inflexible (Griesewell interview, January 19, 1998; interview with health expert of the FDP, January 23, 1998; Rath 1996). The idea was to transform the federal hospital association from a voluntary body into a corporatist, public-law organization with compulsory membership and the authority to negotiate with sickness funds binding agreements on its member hospitals.

Unable to marshal the necessary political forces for radical hospital reform, the government settled for a more modest agenda. The legislation that did pass withdrew the health ministry from setting prospective payments (the per-case and special payments) as it had under the GSG and delegated this task to associations of sickness funds and the federal hospital association (Göpffarth 1997; Wasem interview, January 10, 1998). However, the health ministry continued to set interim global budgets for individual hospitals according to the development of public-sector pay (OECD 1997, 93–94). While these modest reforms marked a clear defeat for Seehofer and the hospital association remained a voluntary body, the new law nevertheless moved the sector closer to de facto if not de jure corporatism. This was because the prospective payment system to be negotiated by the sickness funds and the hospital association would be binding on member hospitals. Furthermore, the payment system would also apply to nonmember hospitals through the contracts they concluded individually with the sickness funds (Wasem interview, January 10, 1998; and e-mail correspondence, August 12, 1998).

Second, the greater influence of employers with the NOGs marked a pronounced shift in the balance of health sector forces. Employers already could claim a legitimate voice in health policy matters owing to their role in financing and administering the health insurance system. But mass unemployment arising from recession and unification, and the burden it placed on nonwage labor costs amplified their voice in the health care reform debate. Employers found a channel of political influence within the CDU itself. The economic woes magnified the influence of the party's business wing (*Wirtschaftsflügel*) over health policy, even as the labor wing's clout diminished. This was a marked reversal of the usual internal party politics of the CDU, in which the business wing deferred to the union wing on matters of social policy.[18]

This power shift left its imprint on the contents of the NOGs. In an effort to appease employers' demands for contribution-rate relief, the Kohl government enacted the linkage mechanism and copayment hikes that would have shifted the task of cost containment—or the penalty of higher costs—onto insurers and patients: insurers would face severe pressure not to raise contributions to retain members. But in the event that funds raised contributions and copayments, patients would bear a disproportionate cost. Hence, the linkage scheme threatened the long-standing principle of parity financing underpinning German health insurance, since employees would now be responsible for their half of the insurance contribution as well as bearing additional costs through rising copayments (Manow 1997b; *Frankfurter Rundschau* 1996b, 3). The best that the CDU's labor wing could claim was the widening of scope of hardship exemptions to cover a greater portion of the population.

Third, the relative power of the political parties had changed in ways that not only advantaged employers but also physicians. The Christian-Liberal coalition survived the 1994 national parliamentary election, but its position was more precarious than before, having a razor-thin majority of ten seats in the Bundestag. This new electoral reality resuscitated the nearly moribund FDP. Still smarting from their defeat over the GSG, the Liberals dug in their heels during coalition talks on the NOGs in 1995 and made it clear that they would not countenance "another Lahnstein" deal with the Social Democrats. Recognizing that he could not ignore the Liberals if he wanted his government to survive, Kohl directed Seehofer to enact a reform that would secure the assent of the FDP and that did not need the Bundesrat's approval.[19] Further invigorated by electoral successes at the state level in 1996, the Free Democrats then sought to distinguish themselves from their coalition partners by championing a neoliberal agenda. Thus, in the name of greater "individual responsibility," they supported the cost-sharing provisions on patients, as well as the stronger market mechanisms and private insurance–style measures on the sickness funds.

But the Liberals' support for market forces in health care went only so far. In a nod to their physician clients, the reforms safeguarded the position of the KVs by requiring their approval for any experiments with selective contracting with subgroups of doctors (Brenner interview, January 14, 1998; *Dienst* 1997b; OECD 1997, 105–6). The intercession of the FDP was the most important reason for doctors' easy treatment, though other aspects of the policy process also worked in their favor. Unlike the GSG, the NOGs were the product of broad consultation of health care stakeholders in the so-called Petersburg talks. These negotiations gave the KBV a point of entry through which to secure a number of concessions.[20]

The course of implementation was as much influenced by political considerations as was enactment of the reforms. With new Bundestag elections looming in 1998, the almost certain unpopularity of the cost-sharing measures was not lost on politicians. In addition, the plan to tie copayments to contribution rate increases posed a host of technical problems, raised issues of fairness, and contained a loophole for insurers, all of which made implementation a difficult proposition. Pharmacists predicted an administrative nightmare if forced to differentiate drug prices among a range of health plans. The health ministry harbored reservations about the equity of the scheme that would levy different copayments based on a person's membership to a particular fund, even though the illness or medication was the same as that of a person in another fund (Brenner interview, January 14, 1998). Finally, while the linkage mechanism had been enacted into law, it had not been deployed against any sickness funds. This was because the risk-adjustment scheme provided insurers an escape hatch through which to avoid the effects of the contribution-rate-copayment hike: if a fund could make a case that its financial transfers to other funds required by the risk-adjustment scheme forced it to hike its contribution rate, then it would be exempted from raising its copayments. As of 1998, no fund had been forced to raise its contribution rates, nor had the linkage mechanism been deployed against any of them (Zipperer interview, January 23, 1998; Wasem interview, January 10, 1998). Facing such a formidable array of political and technical obstacles, the Christian-Liberal coalition deferred implementing the linkage scheme and was turned out of office in 1998 before its plan to dynamize copayments could take effect.

Policy Immobility after Kohl: The Schröder Government

The first years of Gerhard Schröder's SPD-Green coalition suggested that marketlike provisions would continue to play a limited role in statutory health insurance for the time being and that what competition there was would be carefully monitored by the government. Shortly after taking office in 1998, Kohl's successor repealed most of the NOG's provisions that mimicked private insurance (such as contribution rebates and deductible schemes offered by the statutory funds that ostensibly rewarded low health care use but that also acted as subtle cream-skimming tactics). Schröder also reduced or abolished many copayment provisions and declined to implement Kohl's plan for dynamized copayments. Instead of implementing the NOG's coupling of contribution rate hikes with automatic copayment increases, the new chancellor reimposed sectoral budgets as the main cost-control device, while promising that the budgets were an emergency measure and that major structural reforms would be enacted in the year 2000 to succeed them (OECD 1999, 73; Schneider 1998). As of fall 2001, major structural reforms had yet to materialize, and any substantial health care overhaul was likely to be postponed until after the 2002 federal election. In fact, the Schröder government appeared to backtrack further from its early pledge for radical reform. In spring 2001, the health minister, Ulla Schmidt, decided to forgive the financial liability incurred by the KVs for exceeding the drug budgets for the prior two years and declared that the KVs would be free from future penalties. But since the government did not introduce an effective substitute for the drug budgets it had lifted, drug costs surged 13 percent (*Economist* 2001a). The government also took precautions with competition among insurers. As discussed in greater detail below, it carefully monitored the behavior of the sickness funds and intervened in market developments when it deemed this necessary.

Assessing the Reform Pattern

The zigzag reform path under Kohl masks an overall reform pattern that largely continued with corporatist governance even as it sought to repair its defects. Policymakers sought to work within the rules and processes of corporatism to address the cost problems of the health sector. Still, because corporatism did not always conform to policymakers' expectations as a cost-control device, they sometimes made direct forays into sectoral self-governance. The government also introduced market incentives to bring efficiency to the corporatist framework and to obviate the need for enduring state intervention, but stopped well short of unleashing all-out competition.

This section steps back from the individual laws to assess this broader reform pattern. First, it analyzes the effects of the reforms on corporatism and the extent to which they have altered the relationship and roles of doctors and insurers in health care governance. Second, it specifies how German policymakers deployed market mechanisms in the health sector, but in a cautious and circumscribed fashion. Finally, it looks to politics and institutions to explain why the Kohl government did not abandon corporatism or construct an alternative governance regime of either a full-fledged market or state hierarchy in its place. I argue that health care reform entailed a series of compromises with different stakeholders who had opportunities in both the political and sectoral arenas to shape the formulation, enactment, and implementation of the reform laws. The variations in the particular mix of market, statist, and corporatist elements reflected fluctuations in the electoral fortunes of the political parties and the influence of various health care stakeholders over time. But the constellation of actors and institutions surrounding corporatism in Germany's national health insurance program militated against a radical break with the existing governance regime. Though some actors desired such a transformation, their influence was limited. Most stakeholders, for different reasons, harbored no such desire for radical change.

Corporatism Revitalized or Imperiled?

The Kohl government's reform strategy largely worked within the corporatist framework, even if it involved some elements of state hierarchy and market incentives to influence the decisions of the KVs and sickness funds and to prod them to assume their cost-containment tasks. The GRG conformed to an inclusive politics of negotiation and a delegation of cost-containment tasks to the public-law associations that were typical of corporatist governance. And however unusual the process and substance of the GSG appeared, they were consistent with the state's authority to set the basic parameters of the health care system and the relationships among its constituent actors. Moreover, the subsequent retreat of the state from budgeting by decree under the NOGs signaled the government's intention to revert to sectoral self-governance. Likewise, while market forces were part of the government's reform strategy, they remained circumscribed and did not displace corporatism.

Still, the reform path exposed corporatism's shortcomings and placed new stresses upon it. Like any other form of governance, it was not immune to conflicts between the state and sectoral actors in determining the boundaries of their respective domains. The medical profession, for instance, chafed at what it saw as the state's violation of the normal procedures of consultation and negotiation and the encroachment in self-governance under the GSG.[21] But the situation was not as one-sided as the profession maintained, and the state could not always count on the cooperation or compliance of sectoral actors. Certainly, corporatism granted the state important leverage over them. But it also accorded interest groups substantial influence in policy-making and autonomy in sectoral administration, which they sometimes exploited to thwart state initiatives and to advance their own interests.

The Medical Profession and the Corporatist Bargain

This was especially true of doctors. While Kohl stuck by corporatism, he also sought to correct its imbalances and curb the power of the medical profession. Thus, the GSG made clear that doctors could not expect an automatic right to negotiate the terms of health policy, but that the state retained the authority to set the parameters of sectoral governance and to mandate policy tasks on their public-law associations. At the same time, however, the porousness of the German political system often made it difficult for state actors to assert such authority. Indeed, the GSG was remarkable not only for the state's assertiveness, but also because of its rarity. In contrast to a unitary political system and centralized policy-making process such as Britain's, which made it relatively easy for Thatcher to enact her reform program, Germany's federal arrangements, coalition politics, and heterogeneous parties provided sectoral actors—including doctors—a number of avenues to influence the political process. Moreover, their legally anchored rights in health care administration gave doctors additional opportunities to thwart government policy at the implementation stage. Thus the state's ability to set the fundamental contours of the health sector also required political skill and determination on the part of its officials to strike deals with different stakeholders in the political process, and to deploy the various sticks and carrots that corporatism afforded them when sectoral actors put up resistance at the implementation stage.

Though the medical profession retained its self-governance rights in sectoral administration, it found that such rights must operate under new constraints. The KVs must share power with the sickness funds through an expanding range of mandated joint tasks, and both sides must work within increasingly specific timetables set out in legislation. In addition, the medical profession's collective autonomy hinges on the ability and willingness of the KVs to circumscribe the economic and clinical freedom of individual practitioners through budgets and guidelines. Policymakers increasingly expect individual practitioners to be more directly accountable for their prescribing and practice decisions in the ambulatory sector.

But the laws did little to challenge the KVs' monopoly position in corporatist governance. Insurers won the right to experiment with new forms of care, but such arrangements still required the sanction of the KVs, which, presumably, would block changes that threatened their monopoly. Future governments might broaden the scope for selective contracting, but they would first have to overcome formidable legal obstacles, such as the constitution's equal protection clause, which requires the sickness funds to contract with any doctor who accepts their terms (Jost 1998, 707). Barring constitutional revision or reinterpretation, any moves to demolish their monopoly position may have to come from the KVs themselves. KV leaders might conceivably choose this route in response to pressure from their rank and file or if they believed it would solve growing internal distributional conflicts among their members. Alternatively, policymakers might succeed in abolishing the KV's monopoly through a strategy of confrontation with these associations, or through a reform coalition that excludes them. But these would mark a clear change in both policy style and content.

Even as the state placed new curbs on doctors, it also extended their authority to other areas of the health care system. Nowhere is this clearer than in the powers of the Federal Committee of Physicians and Sickness Funds to develop practice guidelines for nearly all areas of the health care system.[22] With these new mandates, policymakers indicated their intention that doctors should remain on the top rung of the ladder of health professions, even if they must share their new authority with insurers. The new joint tasks also indicated that the government had decided to continue with corporatism, rather than scrap it, as a cost-control instrument.

The Sickness Funds and Contemporary Corporatism

The other side of the corporatist equation concerns the position of the sickness funds. Kohl's reforms sought to strengthen insurers in relation to providers. The clearest example of this strategy was in the expanded administrative powers of the sickness funds—primarily through joint tasks with the KVs—in hospital reimbursements, pharmaceutical prices, and guidelines for doctors. The jointly developed practice guidelines have the potential to provide insurers with new information about physicians' clinical decisions and thereby help them better monitor doctors and question the clinical and cost effectiveness of their treatments. Similarly, the NOGs also permit sickness funds and groups of doctors to develop new forms of care, such as a gatekeeper primary care model (*Häusarzte*) like Britain's GPs. If this model becomes widespread, it could give insurers some power to limit access to specialists. However, since both contracting and guidelines are at an embryonic stage, they remain potential mechanisms to control doctors.

In addition, the market reforms—limited as they are—may give the sickness funds reason to become more assertive in their collective bargaining with the KVs. Free choice of fund may encourage insurers to compete for patients on the basis of price by offering stable contribution rates. At the same time, the risk-adjustment scheme has reduced the advantages of a healthier and wealthier membership that the substitute funds wielded over the local funds. Coupled with the GSG's provisions for free choice of fund, it may become more costly in the future for the Ersatzkassen to reward doctors with more generous reimbursement agreements that serve as the benchmark for other funds to follow.

Also, to the extent that free choice of fund encourages insurers to compete on the basis of lower contribution rates, then the market would indirectly affect physicians, presumably in a direction to limit their incomes. But it remains to be seen whether sickness funds can really act as assertive purchasers of health care in the market and enforce cost discipline on providers. On the one hand, some of the traditional fragmentation among the funds has diminished with the market reforms, as insurers engaged in a flurry of mergers in advance of the GSG's provision for free choice. Thus, the funds are more concentrated now, with only 498 funds in 1997 as compared to 1,221 in 1993 (Ministry of Health, cited in Giaimo and Manow 1999, 982);

in fact, many of the remaining funds are local branches of Land-level entities that negotiate collective agreements on their behalf with the KVs. But by sharply restricting the possibility of selective contracting (requiring such experimental contracts be approved by the KVs), the Kohl government preserved the KVs' monopoly and denied the funds an important lever of cost control. In addition, insurers still lack important information on clinical decisions and treatments that doctors provide to patients, because the KVs, not insurers, continue to pay doctors for discrete medical services.[23] Such information asymmetries further limit the ability of the funds to act as knowledgeable and assertive purchasers in relation to doctors.

More serious is Kohl's decision to extend the scope of corporatist bargaining by KVs and insurers to drug prices and guidelines for other practitioners, which has placed the corporatist framework under enormous strain. To be sure, corporatization has empowered KVs and insurers by expanding their authority over new areas of the health care system, but it also means that they are now responsible for costs that are not necessarily under their direct control. And it is not at all clear that physicians or insurers desire this expanded authority. One underlying rationale for this expansion—that doctors' treatment decisions determine the volume and thus overall costs of the health care system and that the KVs and insurers already possess the authority to set drug prices under the GRG—may make sense. But holding doctors financially liable for the costs of pharmaceuticals has created serious internal stresses on the KVs, carving deep fissures among groups of doctors and fueling the resentment of those who might have to accept lower fees as a way to cover the prescribing excesses of their peers.

The KVs may decide that, in the end, holding individual doctors financially responsible for their treatment and referral decisions through guidelines and physician-specific drug budgets may be far better than forcing all doctors to shoulder the burden. Should austerity continue, however, conflicts over declining incomes will surely worsen, and physicians may rebel against these new controls on their economic and clinical freedom. If such internal unrest continues or intensifies, it will be increasingly difficult for the KVs to represent the interests of the profession as a whole. The future of the KVs would then be in question.[24]

Corporatism's Limited Reach

If the ambulatory sector has unresolved cost problems that corporatism alone may not be able to solve, the hospital sector provides an even more troubled picture. There, corporatism's reach falls short, yet alternative cost-containment mechanisms are not well developed. German federalism permits the Länder a veto over hospital reforms that threaten to diminish their influence. Prospective budgeting of hospitals has potential as a cost-containment tool but is in its early stages. Thus, assigning greater cost-containment tasks to sickness funds and KVs in the ambulatory sector cannot compensate for the absence of effective cost controls or regulatory instruments in the hospital sector. National-level policymakers will have to accommodate the reality of German federalism and garner the support of the states and the hospitals if they hope to realize thoroughgoing health care reform in the future.

A "Socially Bounded Market" within Corporatism[25]

Kohl's market experiment not only left intact doctors' monopoly position in corporatist self-governance, but also stopped well short of releasing unfettered competition on the sickness funds' side. Such cautiousness was deliberate, as the government sought to structure the market in ways that safeguarded the solidarity of national health insurance and limited or otherwise redressed insurers' attempts to compete for patients on the basis of better health risks. First, compulsory national health insurance continued to require that insurers take all comers, and that they could not reject persons on the grounds of health status or income. Second, 85 percent of benefits remained legally mandated for all insurers to offer; to prevent or minimize cream-skimming, the law explicitly barred funds from offering less generous benefits packages (Giaimo and Manow 1999; OECD 1997, 85). However, they could offer marginal benefits as extras at a correspondingly higher contribution rate.[26] Third, even if some cream-skimming did occur, the risk-adjustment scheme would discourage or otherwise compensate for such results by requiring financial transfers from funds with better patient profiles to those with poorer and sicker members.

Moreover, some of the most controversial provisions for competition among insurers either were not implemented by Kohl or were repealed by his successor. Schröder also extended Kohl's risk-pooling strategy toward the eastern states by requiring sickness funds in the western Länder to make financial transfers to those in the east for an indefinite period. The latter funds have been plagued by higher deficits and contribution rates than their western counterparts as a result of higher unemployment and lower incomes of their members (OECD 1999, 73).

Policymakers hoped that a carefully designed market would actually advance the solidarity of statutory health insurance by reducing the disparities in choice and contribution rates between white- and blue-collar workers. And they had some early successes in this regard. The financial transfers under the risk-adjustment scheme equalized historic differences in financing by substantially narrowing the range in contribution rates among all types of funds. In 1993, for example, 64 percent of insured persons paid contribution rates up to 1 percent above or below the average, while 36 percent paid more than that. But in 1996, 86 percent of insured persons found their contribution rates within 1 percent of the average (OECD 1997, 107). The big winners under this scheme were the local funds, which received compensation for their poor health risks from the substitute and company funds. Indeed, one fund had to pay approximately half of its contribution revenues to the risk-adjustment fund (ibid.).

The government designed the market with the aim of advancing efficiency and equity simultaneously, rather than forcing a politically intolerable trade-off between the two. By giving patients greater freedom to choose their insurer, subject to the solidarity protections described above, policymakers hoped that sickness funds would be induced to compete on price by offering lower contribution rates and better customer service. Lower contribution rates were to result from the funds realizing greater efficiencies or negotiating tougher fee agreements with the KVs, rather than accruing from better health risks of members.

However, the precautions taken in constructing the market have not been sufficient to address all possible inequities, especially with regard to the risk-adjustment scheme.[27] In theory, the risk-adjustment scheme should eliminate disparities in contribution rates based on health risks by requiring funds with a healthier population to compensate funds with a sicker population. But in practice, it has failed to adequately do so, largely because the adjustment formula fails to capture morbidity factors. Free choice of insurer has exacerbated the problem of adverse selection for the local funds by triggering an exodus of mainly younger and healthier members to the company funds (or to private insurance, if their incomes are high enough to allow such a move) that can offer lower rates because of their better health risks. Indeed, the difference in contribution rates ranged from 15 percent of wages for a local fund to only 11 percent for a company fund (*Economist* 2001a).

Correcting these problems has fallen to the government of Gerhard Schröder. To staunch the flow of members out of the local funds and to correct the shortcomings in the risk-adjustment scheme, the government in 2001 enacted legislation to introduce morbidity criteria into the formula. Thus, the law requires all funds to participate in a risk pool for high-cost cases covering hospital care, drugs, and sick pay benefits above a given threshold per insured member starting in 2002. Also in that year, funds may begin to devise disease management programs to treat members with chronic illnesses. Insurers will receive transfers from other funds to cover a portion of their expenses for such chronic cases. The ultimate aim is the construction of a "morbidity-oriented risk-adjustment scheme" incorporating morbidity factors to be fully operational by 2007 (BMG 2001a, 2001b). An emergency measure announced in 2001 requiring all funds to levy a minimum "solidarity" contribution rate of 12.5 percent (BMG 2001a; *Economist* 2001a) was not carried over into the law.

When all is said and done, caution rather than recklessness has been the hallmark of the German approach to market reform. Funds can do little in the way of competing on the basis of different products or benefits packages. Despite its flaws, the risk-adjustment scheme has narrowed differences in contribution rates even if it has not entirely succeeded in eliminating price competition based on health risks. Funds can do little in the way of selective contracting with providers. Explaining this tight regulation of the market is the subject of the next section.

The Roads Not Taken: Neither a Free Market nor a State Hierarchy

The Kohl government's reforms varied from one law to the next in their particular balance between corporatization, detailed state intervention, and market competition as a result of the shifting balance of forces in the political arena. Still, the overall reform path was that of a circumscribed market, a continuation with corporatism, and a lack of enthusiasm for an enduring state presence in sectoral administration. This broader reform pattern was the product of the interactions among a range of different stakeholders in both the political and health care arenas.

Forces on the left and center of the political spectrum welcomed competition if it evened out disparities between white- and blue-collar workers, but also wanted to limit its scope to prevent cream-skimming. Labor unions, through their role in health care financing and sickness fund administration, acted as proxies for patient and employee interests. They found allies in the political arena in the SPD and in the CDU's trade union wing. Indeed, the CDU's trade union wing was a continuous force championing patients in all of the Kohl government's health care reforms, trying to limit patient cost-sharing or insisting on hardship protections as compensation. Along with Seehofer, who came out of the trade union wing of the CSU, the CDU's labor wing also found common cause with the SPD in advancing free choice of insurer for wage earners and the interfund risk-pooling scheme of the GSG.

In addition to party and interest group forces wanting to limit the market in the name of equity, policymakers also had to contend with broad electoral support for equality in social insurance. First, even if the federal government did not directly provide health care, it still had the overall responsibility to ensure that the population had access to all medically necessary health services. Second, while class- and occupation-based insurance originally differentiated benefits among different groups and tended to limit solidarity to a fund's membership, this lessened over time. With unions and the party forces described above championing the same rights and benefits for blue-collar workers as white-collar employees, and with the government increasingly mandating similar benefits packages among all funds, the guarantee of access to care took on strong connotations of equality. Furthermore, financing health care from parity contributions by employers and employees created a strong sense of entitlement to the same level of care among the German public.[28]

The redistributive character of national health insurance only strengthened a sense of solidarity. Indeed, statutory health insurance is far more redistributive than other areas of the welfare state, such as pensions or unemployment insurance, which tie benefit levels closely to the level of one's contributions. By contrast, the level of health care an individual can claim is based on medical need rather than on ability to pay or contribution history (Hinrichs 1995; Stone 1995).[29] Moreover, the solidarity principle that underpins health care financing implies that the healthier and wealthier members within a fund (and with the risk-adjustment scheme, across different funds and segments of the population) cross-subsidize the health care of poorer and sicker members. In short, German national health insurance has been grounded in multiple bases of legitimacy—from reciprocity and mutualism between classes or groups arising from the pooling of good and bad risks through social insurance (Baldwin 1990; Stone 1993), altruism, or just plain self-interest in preserving one's entitlements. Together, these different sources of legitimacy in this universal program have given voters a common stake in assuring that all should have access to the same level of comprehensive quality care. Kohl could ill afford to introduce a market in health care that threatened to undermine this standard of equity because of the risk of incurring the wrath of a broad swath of the electorate (see also Giaimo 2001, 341–43).

But a variety of forces on the center-right had their own reasons to limit the market and maintain corporatist governance in health care. Their preferences and actions reflected the strength of Germany's social market economy (*soziale Marktwirtschaft*, or SME) and the relative weakness of laissez-faire models of the market in the economy and in the welfare state.[30] The SME acknowledged the market as the appropriate instrument to allocate productive resources and to generate wealth, but did not trust it to distribute its gains on the grounds that it would create intolerable inequalities, popular unrest, and the shredding of the social fabric. This entailed that the state guarantee a comprehensive welfare state to protect or otherwise compensate the losers in the market. The SME also legitimated subsidiarity and corporatist governance in the economy and welfare state. Hence, to prevent excessive state power, natural social groupings, such as churches, unions or employers, or the family provided social welfare services, with the state according them substantial self-governance rights and official recognition under public law to do so. Only when these bodies encountered difficulties in assuming their public tasks would the state intervene directly, and then only temporarily and in ways that enabled them to resume their ability to do so (Katzenstein 1987; Rimlinger 1971, 137–48; van Kersbergen 1995).

The social market economy also legitimated a form of "organized capitalism," which differed from laissez-faire models of a market with numerous small firms engaging in brute competition with one another. Under organized capitalism, by contrast, large associations managed the economy and the welfare state on behalf of government through state-sanctioned collective bargaining and associational self-governance (Shonfield 1965, esp. chaps. 11 and 12; Lehmbruch 1992; Dyson 1992a–c). Highly ordered and regulated relations, rather than chaotic, unrestrained competition, were the hallmark features of this model.

The ideas and institutions of the social market economy appealed to a range of political and social forces. Its emphasis on subsidiarity and social welfare was based in the traditions of social Catholicism and German conservatism and found expression in the postwar Christian Democratic party (Manow 1999; van Kersbergen 1995). The SME also bridged the divide between the CDU and SPD by accommodating the latter's demands for industrial democracy and codetermination (Rimlinger 1971, 137–48). Indeed, much of Germany's postwar social policy was the fruit of cooperation between the two parties in formal or de facto grand coalitions. The public-law associations themselves also cherished their privileged role in economic and welfare state governance. Finally, many in the economics profession subscribed to organized capitalism as the natural model of the economy rather than laissez-faire models based on numerous small firms engaged in competition (Dyson 1992a–c; Lehmbruch 1992).

The health insurance system's corporatist arrangements conformed to the SME. The model of associational bargaining under state auspices has been the guiding principle of order for the civil servants in the labor and health ministries (Döhler 1995, 394–99, esp. 398). As chapter 3 showed, these bureaucrats took an active role in organizing the sector and its actors into corporatist associations (ibid., 397). Kohl's more recent market reforms did nothing to suggest a radical departure from this model. Policymakers and health ministry officials took the lead in constructing the market and delineating the permissible areas of competition, not just to safeguard equity but also to shield the monopoly position of the public-law medical associations. The BMG's Zipperer described the type of market competition that the government sought to construct. He noted that the sickness funds should compete with each other to offer the "best services at the best price," and to innovate. But, he explained,

> Under no circumstances should competition lead to sickness funds and doctors treating only the good risks, and excluding the bad risks. . . . It would be devastating if doctors, in order to make a better living, would pass off the problem patients to the hospital or not treat them. This has not happened yet, and it would be devastating if the hospitals were to drive away the problem patients—to the university clinics, or somewhere else. This kind of competition may not happen. We must do everything possible—it is a task for the lawmakers to set the framework conditions [*Rahmenbedingungen*], so that competition remains a *social* competition, socially connected competition. This is not a contradiction, but it is something different than free competition. As we have a social market economy in Germany . . . and not a free market economy such as . . . in the USA. In your country there is an absolutely free market economy, with all the advantages but also disadvantages. (Zipperer interview, January 23, 1998) (italics added)

This is not to say that no one advanced liberal solutions for the health sector, only that their political clout was limited. The Free Democrats called for greater privatization of health care costs onto patients under the banner of "individual responsibility" and supported greater competition among the sickness funds and free choice of insurer. But its generally small slice of electoral support (only 5 to 10 percent of the vote in state and federal elections) underscored the weakness of the liberal tradition in Germany and among the public at large. Moreover, the FDP's position on the market was contradictory. Its support of more market on the insurers' side and privatization of costs onto patients was consistent with its liberal heritage. But in supporting physicians as part of its broader advocacy of the free professions, the FDP could not bring itself to endorse competition that would threaten the monopoly position of the KVs.

Other actors advocated a greater role for market forces, but like the FDP, they made little or no headway with policymakers. Company and professional funds wanted greater scope for competition on benefits, while all types of funds generally chafed at the barriers to selective contracting. There were health economists, including some on the Advisory Council of the Concerted Action in Health Care, who argued that the health sector would be more efficient if greater competition and choice were permitted (see KAG 1995, 1997).[31] In his own writings, the Council's chairman, Klaus-Dirk Henke, advocated greater competition among insurers on benefits or contribution rates and an end to oligopolistic providers (Henke n.d.; 1997a, 8–11). But under Kohl, such proposals made little headway.

In any case, the Advisory Council and its chairman stopped short of championing a freewheeling market. Henke himself took care to argue for a "socially bounded market" and "orderly competition" in health care: "It will be clear by now that it is not a matter of introducing free competition to the GKV [national health insurance] system on principle, but of seeking a solution between state and market regulation" (Henke and Raschold 1997, 167). Elsewhere he wrote that "the limits to competition in the social health insurance system must lie where market forces undermine the politically defined social functions of the SHI [social health insurance] system" (Henke 1997a, 10). Such social functions include in-kind benefits, risk-adjustment and revenue sharing, the requirement that funds accept all who apply, prohibition of risk-related contributions, and free and universal access to medically necessary services (ibid., 10–11). Henke also stressed that the state had to set the rules of competition and monitor health care actors' compliance if solidarity was to be preserved.[32]

Those who wished to tear down the monopoly on the providers' side not only had to contend with the FDP, but also the CDU, though the latter's reasons were broader and more complicated than the Liberals' protection of a key clientele. According to the health ministry's Zipperer, the government had good reasons to stick with corporatism and not to replace it with unrestricted selective contracting. Corporatism had proven itself an effective cost-containment mechanism because all member doctors were bound to the budgets and fee agreements that their KVs negotiated with insurers. In addition, the weight of history figured into the government's calculations. When funds had negotiated with individual doctors, as they did in the early decades of the twentieth century, relations between the two sides had been highly acrimonious and strike prone. The Kohl government was not eager to resurrect this kind of unrest. The Kohl government also had no desire to infringe on the long-accustomed right of patients to freely choose their doctor; but selective contracting would give insurers the legal authority to choose physicians for patients. Finally, in a personal remark, Zipperer explained that selective contracting raised difficult issues of quality of care: insurers had an interest in contracting with less expensive physicians, but given the absence of well-developed measures of quality, it would be difficult to know whether a less expensive doctor was a good doctor or one who was merely skimping on quality (Zipperer interview, January 23, 1998).

And for all their obstinacy, the KVs remained a valuable instrument of governance through which the state could influence the behavior of the medical profession, both individually and collectively. Compulsory membership made it impossible for individual practitioners to quit their KV even if they were unhappy with its policy stance. The KVs' monopoly over the provision of ambulatory care under national insurance, and their status as exclusive negotiators for and paymasters of doctors, made it economically infeasible for doctors to quit and pursue solely private practice. Finally, their status as corporatist bodies under public law required the KVs to accept responsibility to implement policies mandated by the state and granted the state some formidable if seldom used weapons of control. As the GSG showed, physicians' threats of industrial action were met with the government's threat to suspend their license to treat NHI patients. Finally, abandoning corporatist regulation would have deprived policymakers of their ability to coordinate and control numerous individual doctors or groups of practitioners that the larger KVs permitted.

The government's market experiment was also carefully controlled because policymakers had the capacity to do so. The statutory nature of national health insurance granted the state the legal authority to intervene in the health sector in order to guarantee its solidarity, and the corporatist public-law bodies granted it the institutional means to do so. Thus, while mandating competition among insurers, the state also limited their ability to pursue competitive strategies that would have harmed the most vulnerable individuals. In short, while statutory national insurance placed obligations on the state to ensure universal access, corporatism also gave it the means to shape the course of health care reform, including the pace of marketization.

If a health care system based solely on market principles did not find much favor among policymakers, neither did a state-administered national health service, nor continuing sectoral budgeting by decree. As Seehofer remarked, "We want to adhere to self-governance solutions as up to now, as tedious as it is for us. To put the state in place of self-governance would be worse" (*Der Spiegel* 1993e, 183). Zipperer elaborated further:

> It is his [Seehofer's] understanding, we have a motto for the law— "Give right of way to self-administration"—that is, it is better that self-administration does things than the state determine them. . . . It is the general policy of the federal government to say, withdraw the state— deregulation—[and] let the participants and not the state regulate things. And the state may only intervene when it is about basic questions—the basic or framework conditions—or if the system no longer functions, then the state may help. This is a certain understanding of the state; this differentiates the governing coalition [of Kohl] from the opposition, particularly the SPD, but also from the Green Party, which wants to concede a greater responsibility and influence to the state. . . . The SPD places more on the state; the CDU and even more, the FDP, place more responsibility on the individual. This is not to say that the one is good or the other is bad, but rather, these are varying views of the same world. (Zipperer interview, January 23, 1998).

Indeed, there were a host of political problems in continuing with administration by state fiat. It would have focused blame for unpopular austerity decisions directly on the federal government. For all its tediousness—the slowness of decision making, the wrangling with providers and payers—corporatism allowed the government to offload unpleasant cost-containment tasks onto sectoral actors. In addition, a radical transformation to a statist system would have certainly invited a prolonged and bitter struggle with a range of actors who had a stake in existing governance arrangements. Not only would doctors and sickness funds have protested, but employers and unions, who also played a part in administering the health care system, would have almost certainly entered the fray. None of these actors wanted to see their influence over health policy diminished.

Finally, the federal government lacked the capacity to assume direct responsibility for health care administration. The federal government is, as Katzenstein (1987) notes, a "semi-sovereign state" by deliberate constitutional design. The federal bureaucracy is quite small and relies heavily on the Länder bureaucracies for field administration in a system of "cooperative federalism" or "interlocking politics" (*Politikverflechtung*) (ibid., 45–58; Smith 1986, 51). Thus, a move to a state-administered national health service would have entailed a substantial effort at institution-building that Kohl proved willing to undertake.

The Limits of Corporatism as a Strategy for Cost Containment

Kohl's health care reform record raises a number of unanswered questions. The first concerns corporatism's future. The expanded range of cost-containment tasks that the government has delegated to physicians and insurers, which goes well beyond the services directly provided by office-based physicians, has made it very hard for the KVs to reconcile their dual mandate to carry out public policy tasks and also represent the interests of doctors. It remains to be seen whether the KVs will be able to adapt to these new responsibilities, or whether they will implode under their weight.

The other limitation of the corporatization strategy is that because it confines itself to governance matters, it does not address all the difficult problems of health care financing. Like other countries, Germany's health care system faces growing demands from an aging population and advances in medical technologies. But in the context of slower economic growth, stagnant incomes, and a consensus that labor costs cannot rise much more without disastrous effects on competitiveness and employment, payroll-based financing is not a sufficient revenue base. Even if payroll taxes were permitted to rise, the resultant unemployment and inactivity could, in the end, lead to a financing crisis of the social insurance system.[33] In short, Kohl's cost-containment strategy that focused on health sector governance was an important but incomplete response to the health care system's problems.

The mid-1990s saw the beginning of a serious and likely long-running debate on the question of health care financing.[34] A number of proposals aimed at putting health care financing on a sounder and more equitable footing. These included raising the income ceiling for contributions, bringing civil servants and the self-employed into statutory health insurance, bringing nonwage income and assets under the contribution levy, and relying on general revenues to finance elements not related to insurance but that underwrote German unification.

However, under Kohl's tenure, these measures remained at the discussion stage. Policymakers deemed the proposal to tax nonwage income as too radical. The most extreme views saw this as a slippery slope toward a state-administered national health service. And at least in the medium term, transferring even part of the burden from wages and salaries to the federal budget would have either worsened the federal deficit and complicated Germany's participation in the European Union's single currency or else required the government to raise taxes even as it was proposing to cut them.

Other proposals would have merely shifted costs from employers to employees. One such proposal would have fixed employers' share of the contribution and let employees' side float, with the latter financing the difference.[35] A more radical option championed by the Free Democrats suggested the abolition of contribution-based insurance and its replacement with compulsory individual insurance, while compensating employees with a "wage subsidy." But unions, the SPD, and the CDU labor wing argued that such changes would have destroyed parity financing. Even employers balked at the wage subsidy option for fear of losing their role in health care administration and the leverage over labor costs it afforded them outside the collective bargaining arena (Giaimo 1998).

Hence, the immediate outcome was political paralysis. Lacking the will or ability to forge support for radical innovations in financing, Kohl instead tried to appease employers by shifting costs onto insurers and employees under the NOGs. But even these measures were deemed too controversial to implement.

A longer-term proposal on financing that also entered the debate would restrict the menu of statutory benefits to a basic universal package and allow individuals with the means and inclination to purchase supplementary coverage in the name of greater choice. But defining a basic benefits package promises to be a political exercise fraught with difficulty, unless policymakers succeed in offloading the task onto the corporatist actors such as the Federal Committee of Physicians and Sickness Funds. Likely criticisms of this solution are that permitting sickness funds to offer a greater differentiation of benefits based on individuals' ability to pay would import inequality into NHI and unravel the solidarity of statutory health insurance. (This charge of importing inequality into the statutory NHI resonates with criticism of Britain's GP fundholding scheme.) Supporters, however, might counter that the current trend toward relying on greater copayments—notwithstanding the hardship exemptions—is profoundly inequitable, since the sick rather than the healthy must still bear the financial burden; if the statutory menu of benefits remained universal and comprehensive (i.e., all medically necessary services covered), and safeguards for vulnerable groups were assured, then permitting people to purchase supplemental coverage might balance cost containment and equity in a socially acceptable way.[36] But this solution entailed considerable political and technical risks that the Kohl government was apparently unwilling to accept. Health care financing therefore remains a thorny issue for policymakers in the future to confront.[37]

Conclusion

Future German governments face difficult choices in continuing to ensure that all individuals have access to high quality care at an affordable cost. Thus far, however, the political and sectoral configurations underlying German health politics have impeded radical changes in governance or financing. The porousness of coalition governments and heterogeneous parties have accorded a wide range of societal interests a voice in health policy debates. Along with the consensus shared by politicians and health stakeholders around the social market economy and its corporatist form of governance, most stakeholders still want to maintain the status quo.

But the situation is dynamic, not set in stone. The power or preferences of political or sectoral actors could change in the future in ways that would countenance a bolder departure from corporatist governance or radical changes in financing. Such changes could either expand or undermine solidarity—or they might prompt a search to redefine it. Given the presence of powerful countervailing forces in the health sector and in the political arena, successful adjustment will likely hinge on forging a consensus with these stakeholders over a new conception of solidarity that continues to ensure broad provision, spreads the burden of adjustment fairly, and shelters the most vulnerable from harm.

CHAPTER 5

The Autonomy of the Solo Practitioner in a Liberal Health Care System

The United States

The health care settlement in the United States was one in which government actors largely played a supportive role to private actors. In contrast to Britain and Germany, the United States eschewed a universal statutory health care scheme for a system of private, employment-based financing and provision. This system not only granted employers and insurers wide latitude to determine coverage decisions, it also accorded doctors enormous professional autonomy, particularly at the level of the individual practitioner. In a further contrast with the universal systems of Britain and Germany, the U.S. health care settlement suffered from the twin problems of uncontrolled costs and inequitable access to care.

This chapter begins by sketching the main actors in the liberal health care system and providing a brief overview of its historical development. Employers, private insurers, and governments deferred to a professional model that safeguarded maximum freedom of action of individual doctors. The accommodation of solo practice sowed the seeds of health care inflation and prompted a series of government initiatives—most of them unsuccessful—to bring costs down in the 1970s and 1980s. Yet, as the last section shows, physicians were not solely to blame for the difficulties of the health care system; employers and insurers also bore considerable responsibility for the rising costs and gaps in access that had become more acute as the 1980s progressed.

The Liberal Health Care System

The Players

Reflecting the liberal welfare regime of which it is a part, the American health care system accords a preeminent place to private actors and voluntary arrangements in social protection (Esping-Andersen 1990; Ruggie 1996). Most Americans obtain health insurance through the workplace as a fringe benefit negotiated by labor unions or the result of an employer's voluntary decision to offer coverage. Those of working age who cannot obtain insurance through their place of employment must look to individual policies in the private market, unless they fit the eligibility requirements of public insurance programs. Employers and private insurers have exerted influence in health policy because of their preeminent role in financing and providing health insurance. In contrast to Britain and Germany, employers have usually paid the bulk of the premium. Unions were important in the initial development of the private system, but with declining membership starting in the 1970s, their influence in health policy has also waned.

Statutory insurance programs are limited to specific categories of the "truly needy" or "deserving" poor. Medicare, a federal insurance program, insures the elderly and the disabled; Medicaid, financed jointly by the federal and state governments, covers the most impoverished members of society; and there are also federal programs for the armed forces and their dependents. The federal and state government share of health care financing is considerable, accounting for 46.4 percent of health care expenditures in 1997 (U.S. Department of Health and Human Services 1999, 284).[1] Though the Medicare and Medicaid programs, created in 1965, represent the most visible government spending, public money has also underwritten hospital construction, medical education, and research.

Private providers are also dominant, though they may be either nonprofit or for-profit. Most doctors are in the private health sector. The majority of hospitals are owned by either nonprofit religious entities or local governments. Since the 1980s, however, for-profit hospitals (and insurers) have gained in prominence.

Origins of Private Employment-Based Health Insurance

The private system of employment-based insurance developed in lieu of statutory national coverage. But this does not suggest that national insurance was neither considered nor attempted. Indeed, the twentieth century is replete with numerous (but failed) initiatives to enact national insurance in the United States. Yet private actors joined forces with partisan allies in Congress to block these initiatives. Public policies also combined with private actors to institutionalize the private fringe-benefit system.[2]

The first effort at national insurance dates from 1915 with the efforts by the American Association of Labor Legislation (AALL), a coalition of social reformers and academics. Hoping to replicate their successful initiative for worker's compensation legislation in the states, the AALL sought a similar strategy for national health insurance. In 1916, the AALL devised a model national health insurance bill as a campaign for the states and, eventually, Congress to consider. But the initiative met defeat in Congress in 1918, and when the American Medical Association (AMA) declared its opposition to compulsory insurance in 1920, national insurance was a dead issue until the economic crisis of the 1930s.

For all of its policy expertise, the AALL displayed remarkable political naïveté. It failed to devise a political strategy to forge a supportive coalition with politicians or health care stakeholders, and its members apparently believed that their proposal would advance on the strength of the idea itself (Anderson 1985, 72, 84). But national insurance drew fire from a number of opponents. Their positions were not set in stone, however, and the battle lines were not what one might have expected. Organized labor, particularly the American Federation of Labor (AFL), proved to be one of the fiercest critics of national insurance. Its opposition arose from bitter experience with government support for employer lockouts and injunctions barring strikes. Labor leaders feared that government insurance would weaken the ties and loyalty of workers to their unions, many of which provided insurance schemes themselves. The medical profession, too, opposed national insurance, but its initial stance was one of uncertainty. Indeed, the AMA approved a study on national insurance in 1917, and prominent medical leaders had collaborated with members of the AALL on the issue. But faced with unrest from state medical societies, whose members equated the scheme with lower reimbursements, the association reversed its stance three years later. Like doctors, some employers' groups, such as the National Association of Manufacturers and the Chamber of Commerce, were initially receptive to national insurance. But the business community eventually opposed the scheme and argued for voluntary insurance instead as a way to cement the loyalty of their workers to the company. Private insurers at this time did not sell health insurance, yet they opposed the AALL bill because its provision for a funeral benefit would have threatened a lucrative share of their market. Drug companies, fearing the government as a monopoly provider, also resisted national insurance. Lastly, the AALL proposal became entangled in the broader context of World War I, with many opponents equating the scheme with the German enemy (ibid., chaps. 6 and 7; Starr 1982, 243–57).

The next reform initiative surfaced under Franklin Roosevelt's tenure during the Great Depression. The administration considered national health insurance as part of its Social Security proposals. But with the AMA stating its opposition to compulsory insurance, Roosevelt, fearing that the association would wreck his chances of enacting the pension and unemployment insurance programs, decided in 1935 to decouple the health care question from the Social Security Act and pursue it at a later date. However, the 1938 midterm elections, which ushered in the alliance of southern Democrats and northern Republicans committed to blocking further social insurance initiatives, put an end to the issue for the rest of the president's tenure (Starr 1982, 267–69, 277).

Harry Truman took up the cause of national insurance throughout his tenure in office. But employers and doctors joined forces to finance an effective campaign of opposition and found ready allies in Congress. The Republican congressional majority blocked Truman's effort between 1946 and 1948. Democrats subsequently regained their majority, but the conservative alliance between the party's southern wing and the Republicans reasserted itself to block social policy and civil rights initiatives, including national health insurance. Cold war politics also set the tone of the struggle. The AMA and congressional foes of "socialized medicine" linked their fight to the broader crusade against communism and successfully turned public opinion from its initially favorable stance to opposition (Marmor 2000, 6–10; Starr 1982, 280–89).

Repeatedly rebuffed by Congress, organized labor, which had become a champion of national insurance, turned its energies to an alternative arena, the labor market—and with good reason, since government policies had promoted the development of employment-based fringe benefits. During World War II, when wage and price controls were in effect, the federal government permitted employers to offer fringe benefits—including health insurance—instead of wage increases in order to attract and retain labor. With the Supreme Court's *Inland Steel* decision in 1948, unions won the legal right to include health insurance in the domain of collective bargaining. Unions responded by making health insurance a priority in collective bargaining, and workplace coverage expanded in the postwar period. Government tax policies also encouraged the development of private fringe benefits by granting employers a tax exemption on their insurance contributions (Stevens 1988).

Those who still sought a legislative solution to the problem of inadequate access to care scaled back their ambitions. Instead of trying for universal coverage, they sought public insurance for those who demonstrated obvious need, commanded public sympathy, and were deserving of government help. In the liberal political economy, this meant those who had good reason to be outside the labor market and who therefore did not have access to employment-based or private insurance. Senior citizens fit this description, and social security pensions already legitimated a government program for this group, not least because it was a contributory scheme (Marmor 2000, 11–17). The poorest members of society, especially the disabled and children of nonworking single mothers, also fit the criteria of support. Moreover, the grip of conservative southern agricultural elites was under attack both within and outside of Congress: the 1964 elections returned commanding Democratic majorities (including northeastern liberals), and the civil rights movement was gaining its momentum. This political environment yielded the Medicare and Medicaid insurance programs in 1965, the public insurance programs that sought to plug the gaps in coverage in the private, employment-based system.

But this patchwork system of private and public continued to leave certain groups outside the umbrella of insurance, particularly those outside the unionized sector and in contingent or casual employment. In response, the 1970s saw several national health insurance initiatives at federal level. But like their predecessors, they failed to be enacted. In 1970, Senator Edward Kennedy proposed a single-payer model of compulsory national insurance. The following year, President Nixon countered with a proposal for employer mandates and a public program for the working poor, and in 1974, he revised his plan to increase its scope and generosity. The initiative failed, but this time, organized labor and its progressive allies in Congress were to blame. Calculating that the 1974 elections would give them greater leverage to demand more, they held back. Following Nixon's resignation that year, however, the economic picture turned so bleak as to reduce the chances of enactment of reform initiatives for the rest of the decade. In 1978, Kennedy proposed national insurance again, this time based on competing private health insurers and fixed reimbursement of providers. President Carter countered with a proposal similar to Nixon's 1974 initiative. But with concerns over financing and the budgetary implications in a climate of stagflation, neither plan could muster the support of Congress (Starr 1982, 394–97, 404, 413–14).

Time and again, national insurance proposals fell victim to a combination of partisan forces and interest group alliances that found expression in political institutions. Separation of powers often placed Congress and presidents at loggerheads. Between 1938 and 1964, Congress (especially its committee system) entrenched a regional and partisan politics that proved poisonous to the chances for national insurance reform: the New Deal party system allied conservative southern Democrats, bent on preserving an economy that rested on nonunion labor and disenfranchised blacks, with a Republican party hostile to organized labor and sympathetic to business. This alliance worked to halt the advance of social legislation after the New Deal (Weir, Orloff, and Skocpol 1988, 21–25). In addition, health care stakeholders, particularly the organized medical profession and sections of the business community, forged a potent alliance against reform. Still, the balance of forces opposing national insurance was not constant. Sometimes, labor and progressive forces blocked reforms. The political system also reflected changes in the partisan balance and broader societal environment, both of which were sometimes amenable to expansions of insurance coverage, as in 1964.

The Nature of Medical Power in the Liberal Health Care System

The private health care system thus created a formidable array of stakeholders with access to a political process porous to organized interests. Yet, governance of the private health care system was more straightforward than the catalog of stakeholders would imply. Until the 1980s, public and private payers and health care system organizations and structures—even the organized medical profession itself—deferred to the archetype of maximum freedom of the solo practitioner in the professional mode of governance.

The Organized Medical Profession

Unlike its counterparts in Britain and Germany, the American medical profession has never been a corporatist actor. Rather, the nature of physician power and autonomy in the United States has been and remains much more fragmented, decentralized, and entrepreneurial. Medical associations have actively championed and protected the freedom of the solo practitioner from encroachment by lay authorities or by their peers.

The nature of medical power in the political arena is consistent with a liberal political economy. The AMA, the main representative of the profession, is not a corporatist actor charged with public policy duties but a private organization whose purpose is to safeguard the economic and political interests of doctors. Unlike their German or British counterparts, the AMA has no semiofficial status in policy-making: governments are not legally bound to consult it on health policy matters, nor does it act as an agent of the state implementing policy on its behalf. Still, the AMA was a powerful force in health politics for much of the twentieth century. But rather than enjoying official status as an insider negotiating terms of policy with the government, the AMA has exerted influence in the same ways as most other American interest groups: by exerting pressure on lawmakers from the outside through its lobbying activities, and by reaching into its considerable financial resources to make donations to political campaigns.

Still, the internal organizational characteristics of the AMA have undermined its power as a collective actor, especially its ability to take positive action in the political and health care systems, largely because it lacks the means to control individual doctors in and outside its organization. Because the AMA is a voluntary membership organization, doctors dissatisfied with it can leave or refuse to join in the first place. This freedom has made the AMA's claim to represent the medical profession more tenuous over time: in 1965, AMA membership stood at 65 percent of doctors, but this had dropped to 41 percent by the early 1990s (Skocpol 1996, 53, 198 n. 13).

In addition (and much like the British Medical Association), the AMA's internal democracy has hindered the leadership from taking decisive policy action.[3] Historically, internal power struggles between the executive (Board of Trustees), its assembly (House of Delegates), and its various councils and committees have roiled the association. By 1975, administrative rationalizations and an uneasy compromise requiring councils to be elected by the House but report "through" the Board appeared to have resolved many of these disputes (Campion 1984, 409–20). Still, because the AMA works on a parliamentary rather than executive model, the House of Delegates, not the Board of Trustees, is the main policy-making body (ibid., 77–78). As the final arbiter of AMA policy, its House can curtail the executive's ability to make policy independently and can withhold its cooperation.

The AMA's control over local medical organizations has also eroded over time. Through its hierarchical confederal structure, the AMA exerted a tight grip over state and county medical societies. Initially, the AMA was a confederation of state medical societies, which in turn were confederations of county medical societies. In many states in the early decades of the twentieth century, membership in these local bodies carried with it automatic membership in the AMA. Doctors also had a strong economic incentive to join local medical societies and the AMA, since the latter used its accreditation of hospital internship programs to force hospitals to grant admitting privileges only to local medical society members (Starr 1982, 168). However, since 1982, the AMA's grip over state and county bodies loosened considerably with its decision to permit direct or other forms of membership (Campion 1984, chap. 7, esp. 48).

Difficult relations with rival associations have also undercut the AMA's political authority. To keep them within its fold, the AMA has allowed medical specialties their own representation as distinct organizations in its House of Delegates since 1977. This is a novel form of representation, since the majority of AMA delegates represent state and local medical societies (Campion 1984, chap. 7). Despite this accommodation, the specialty societies have not hesitated to issue their own policy positions distinct from the AMA. In addition, some organizations that represent doctors on ideological or policy matters, such as the Physicians for a National Health Plan, have remained outside the AMA fold and thereby challenged the association's claim to represent the profession.

Member attitudes also hinder the AMA's political effectiveness. The AMA is both a scientific body and an organization protecting the economic interests of the profession. Yet many members have displayed ambivalence toward the association taking on a political role and have believed that it should confine itself to scientific matters and stay out of politics altogether (Campion 1984, 55). Historically, most members have disdained an explicit trade union role by the AMA as an affront to their professionalism.

The AMA's economic and political leverage over the profession is also weak because it does not control most aspects of physicians' terms of practice, though this was not always the case. During the first half of the twentieth century, the AMA and state and county medical societies set the terms of hospital privileges and of office-based practice. The AMA boycotted group practice, prepaid medicine, or salaried arrangements that rivaled solo practice, and it ostracized physicians who participated in such arrangements. In 1959, however, the Supreme Court ruled that such actions against contract medicine violated antitrust law, and the AMA was forced to abandon these sanctions (Starr 1982, 305, 327). In addition, federal antitrust policies, which have outlawed price-fixing by medical groups and blocked self-employed doctors from unionizing (Kuttner 1997), have denied the AMA an explicit trade union role with the authority to bargain fees on behalf of physicians. Instead, doctors have been free to set their own fees at the local level, subject to what insurers would pay. Finally, as discussed below, the AMA has done little to curb the clinical freedom of individual doctors.

But if the nature of medical power in the United States is decidedly not corporatist, this does not imply that American doctors are powerless. Rather, that power conforms to a liberal health care system and political economy. It is the power exercised at the individual level, with solo practitioners acting much like small businessmen and enjoying significant autonomy in all aspects of their work. Medical organizations historically placed few limits on this activity and, in fact, were quite effective in securing governments, and private insurers' recognition of it.

Institutionalizing the Autonomy of the Solo Practitioner

The postwar American health care system largely accommodated the AMA's vision of the solo practitioner. Neither the growth of private health insurance nor the introduction of government insurance programs encroached upon the freedom of individual physicians to set up practice where they pleased, charge fees for services as they saw fit, and decide the course of treatment.

First, private and public insurance institutionalized the economic autonomy of the solo practitioner.[4] As a way to keep third parties out of the economic transaction between doctor and patient, the AMA preferred indemnity insurance, in which patients paid the doctor and then sought reimbursement from their insurer, rather than direct insurance payments. But facing the threat of possible compulsory government insurance or voluntary prepaid plans controlled by consumers, the AMA made a strategic compromise to accept nonprofit insurance (known as Blue Shield plans) in the 1930s. Doctors accepted Blue Shield plans because they were often chartered and run by state medical societies and because they preserved fee-for-service remuneration (Starr 1982, 305–9).[5] In the postwar period, commercial, for-profit insurers entered the lucrative employment-based insurance market. They, too, did not challenge physician demands for fee-for-service and provided for indemnity arrangements or direct physician reimbursement (Bodenheimer and Grumbach 1994; Starr 1980, 331–34). Even the government insurance programs created in the 1960s accommodated the economic freedom of providers: under Medicare, doctors received fee-for-service payment without a fee schedule, and hospitals were reimbursed for their costs (Marmor 2000, 60–61; Starr 1982, 374–78). Medicaid also paid doctors on a fee-for-service basis though with some limits.[6] These private and public settlements would prove to have inflationary consequences.

Government also proved to be an ally of the profession in safeguarding the model of solo practice. Many states prohibited prepaid group practices, consumer-run cooperatives, and contract medicine, all of which threatened solo practice.[7] To assuage the AMA's fears of "socialized medicine," physician participation in both the Medicare and Medicaid programs was voluntary. Rather than direct government reimbursement, private insurers acted as intermediaries in processing physician billings in these programs (Starr 1982, 374–78).

Other health care institutions advanced the social autonomy of the medical profession. Hospitals opened their doors to both specialists and primary care physicians alike, leaving decisions on admitting privileges with their medical staffs (Starr 1982, 145–79). Outside of the limited scope of prepaid group practice, public and private insurers for the most part permitted free choice of doctor. Although the government subsidized medical education, determining the supply and mix of physician specialties remained the medical profession's domain through its control over medical education and hospital internship programs. Even so, medical organizations refused to interfere with individual doctors' decisions on where to locate their practices (Ruggie 1996, chap. 4; Starr 1982, 420–49).

Finally, clinical freedom of the individual physician thrived. Hospitals served as "doctors' workshops"[8] where physicians could hone their craft and specialize in high-tech procedures as they pleased. Hospitals rarely questioned physician treatments, and they benefited from long patient stays and the use of intensive and high-tech resources since they could recoup such costs from insurers. Insurers and employers declined to review physician treatment decisions and for the most part paid doctors for the services they billed. Medical organizations themselves resisted assuming responsibility for reviewing the treatment decisions of individual doctors.

In sum, by the 1960s, the health care system had institutionalized a particular political bargain of professional governance by doctors that enshrined the autonomy of the solo practitioner. Governments and private payers by and large refused to act as a countervailing force to challenge physicians. Outside of medical education, licensing, and setting the organizational terms of office-based practice, the AMA and state and county medical societies did little to control individual doctors. Indeed, much of their energy was spent on advancing the autonomy of solo practice. Thus, those who "governed" the health care system were individual practitioners making discrete, decentralized decisions. But this golden age of solo practice was not to last.

Cost and Access Problems in Health Care Governance

Inflationary Consequences of the Accommodation of Medical Autonomy

The introduction of Medicare and Medicaid, along with the continued expansion of employment-based coverage for working Americans, greatly expanded access to care. But public and private insurance was essentially grafted onto a governance regime that allowed doctors to treat patients as they saw fit and to charge what they pleased. This combination of open-ended reimbursement of costs, along with widened access to new populations, proved to be a highly combustible mix that ignited health care inflation. Coupled with slower economic growth in the 1970s, the health care system entered a prolonged cost crisis.

Governments initially responded with regulatory and planning initiatives. But these failed to control costs because they did not fundamentally transform existing health care system structures, methods of reimbursement, or physician prerogatives. In the 1980s, public and private sector cost-control efforts combined regulation of provider incomes and, more significantly, a competition strategy that foreshadowed the sweeping structural changes in health care delivery and reimbursement that were to come.[9]

The initial government response in the 1970s was to mandate legal limits to provider charges. State governments initiated hospital rate-setting and required hospitals to gain approval for capital projects under certificate-of-need programs. With the economy experiencing rapid inflation, President Nixon imposed statutory wage and price controls on the economy from 1971 to 1973 and extended them a year longer in the health sector. President Carter tried but failed to enact a hospital price-freeze. But these federal and state strategies proved to be of limited effect because they did not dispense with fee-for-service and cost-based reimbursement of doctors and hospitals (Starr 1982, 399–415).

A serious but short-lived effort at structural change involved the creation of planning machinery with the 1974 National Planning and Resources Development Act. The law required doctors to share power with consumers and local politicians in planning for community needs. But its effectiveness was limited: the agencies had little enforcement power, and Congress phased out the program in 1981 (Campion 1984, 344–48; Starr 1982, 402–3, 416).

The federal government also sought to control hospital costs through a peer-review program (professional standards review organizations, or PSROs) for Medicare.[10] This program sought to influence physician treatment decisions by mandating the development of explicit guidelines for hospital care (Starr 1982, 400–403). Yet PSROs stopped short of a direct challenge to clinical autonomy: Their mandate was the review of hospital lengths of stay rather than physician decisions as such, and their financial sanctions were directed at hospitals rather than doctors. Moreover, PSROs were composed exclusively of clinicians who were reluctant to discipline their own. As a result, these bodies were captured by the profession and never lived up to their potential as an instrument to influence physician treatment decisions (Stone 1980, 165–72). The Reagan administration's decision to dismantle the PSRO machinery effectively put an end to the government's challenge to physician governance, at least for the time being.

If the 1970s initiatives were mere shots across the bow, the 1980s efforts scored direct hits in the armor of professional autonomy. These may have been small hits in the opening salvo in the battle to curb professional freedom. But they were important not only because they reached their target but also because private payers as well as government joined the battle for cost containment. Furthermore, they set in motion more fundamental challenges to health care governance that would occur in the 1990s.

The first indication that the rules of the game were changing was the federal government's introduction of prospective payment in the Medicare program in 1983. Diagnosis related groups (DRGs) paid hospitals a fixed payment determined in advance for a particular diagnosis. DRGs were premised on the assumption that fixed prepayment would induce hospitals to eliminate unnecessary services. Though hospitals and their medical staffs found various ways to game the system, the idea of prospective budgeting had taken hold.[11]

The second sign of change was the federal government's modification of physician reimbursement under Medicare. Policymakers introduced a "resource-based relative value scale," which gave more weight and higher payment to primary care physician services while reducing payments for more technical, specialized, and costly services. The government also took cautious steps to limit the ability of doctors to charge patients over and above what Medicare allowed (Ruggie 1996, 162–65). But the measures only partly addressed the problem of physician costs: the scale preserved fee-for-service payment and failed to introduce any controls on volume, so it gave physicians the incentive to provide more services to maintain their incomes. The government also stopped short of banning extra billing outright. Still, the changes had made some inroads on doctors' freedom to charge as they liked.

The government's encouragement of health maintenance organizations (HMOs) proved to be the most far-reaching challenge to the postwar bargain with physicians, even if its full effects could not yet be discerned.[12] The 1973 Health Maintenance Organization Act ushered in a pro-competition strategy of cost containment in the private sector. The law required employers who provided insurance to their workers to offer a choice between traditional indemnity insurers and an HMO if one meeting federal qualifications existed in the area. The hope was that given a choice between a less expensive HMO and more expensive fee-for-service plans, employees would choose the HMO option. The government also provided start-up grants to HMOs to encourage their development.

HMOs held out the potential to curb health care costs by radically altering the incentives for providers and payers and curbing medical autonomy. HMOs track and authorize hospital stays in order to reduce the occurrence and duration of expensive hospital admissions. Closed-panel HMOs restrict patients' choice of provider to those on their roster and limit access to specialists and other expensive treatments through primary care gatekeepers or prior approval of referrals. Many HMOs also limit physician incomes through fixed, prospective capitation (a fixed monthly or annual fee for each patient that enrolls with a physician or medical group) or discounted fee-for-service. Capitation presumably reduces or eliminates frivolous care, since doctors cannot collect a fee for providing it but must absorb the cost of it themselves.

However, the government's policy moved in fits and starts in the 1980s, and so HMOs remained a potential cost-containment weapon. Indeed, government policies toward HMOs actually hindered their ability to compete with traditional insurers.[13] Consequently, HMOs expanded at a snail's pace and did not really take off until employers aggressively promoted them in their fringe benefits offerings to workers in the next decade.

Still, two private sector developments hinted at major changes in the offing. First, multistate, for-profit hospital chains and HMOs became more prevalent beginning in the 1980s. Answerable to shareholders concerned with the bottom line, they were poised to shake up the complacent relationships that had existed among physicians, nonprofit hospitals, and traditional commercial insurers. A second development was the awakening of formerly somnolent employers in the 1980s. After decades of extending insurance coverage and passively underwriting the open-ended reimbursement of providers, employers began to question the inflationary consequences of the settlement and to seek ways to rein in costs, even to contemplate a radical overhaul of health care governance.[14]

However, medical autonomy was not exclusively to blame for employers' woes. Employers and insurers also bore responsibility for problems of cost and access. These twin problems reinforced each other and dramatically worsened in the 1980s.

Free Riding and Cost Shifting in a Voluntary Health Care System

The problem of access lies primarily with incomplete coverage of private and public insurance, making health care unaffordable for those without insurance.[15] To be sure, most Americans were covered by group plans offered by their employer, while the elderly and poor largely outside the labor market had coverage under Medicare and Medicaid, respectively. However, this patchwork system of public and private insurance never approached universal coverage. Because the fringe-benefit system was voluntary, employers were free to not offer insurance, and many of them did not, particularly for contingent employment or in sectors where unions were weak. Workers in these types of jobs often had incomes too high to qualify for Medicaid yet too low to afford private insurance.

If voluntarism allowed employers to avoid providing coverage, private insurers also bore much of the responsibility for inadequate access. Pursuing profits and the "logic of actuarial fairness," commercial insurers sought out healthier, less costly people and segmented the market into ever-smaller risk pools (Stone 1993). They did so by using experience rating in their underwriting, whereby they set premiums at the expected or actual health care costs of enrollees and, in so doing, priced insurance beyond the reach of the low-paid, the sick, and their small-business employers (whose work forces were too small to adequately spread the risks of illness). Commercial insurers also excluded from coverage persons with preexisting medical conditions. Furthermore, they devised a range of cream-skimming tactics—some blatant, some more subtle—to attract healthier individuals and discourage sicker people from enrolling.[16] Actuarial practices spread throughout the employment-based market in the 1950s, since commercial insurers could offer employers with relatively healthy work forces attractive rates that were cheaper than those under community rating (which was a risk-pooling device that set the same premium for all subscribers in a given locality, used by Blue Cross and Blue Shield plans). To survive in the market, the Blues followed suit, and experience rating became the dominant pricing mechanism for insurance (Bodenheimer and Grumbach 1994; Starr 1982, 327–31).

However, problems of access also fueled health care costs. Though the uninsured could not afford care in a doctor's office, they had access to hospital care, since hospitals were legally bound to treat all who came through their doors. But this was costly from both economic and medical standpoints. Instead of obtaining less expensive primary care early on, the uninsured waited until their conditions worsened and required costly hospital treatment, or they used hospital emergency rooms for routine primary care, which was more expensive than that provided in a doctor's office or other outpatient setting.

This arrangement led to rampant cost-shifting as the costs of medical care for the uninsured were borne largely by employers who provided insurance. Hospitals and other providers who treated the uninsured (or who received low reimbursements from government programs) recouped their losses by charging higher fees to patients with private insurance. Private insurers, in turn, passed on the costs to employers through higher premiums (Reinhardt 1992). Thus, an elaborate but largely hidden cost-shifting game was being played, but with only some employers footing the bill.

This cost-shifting game did not arouse too much complaint from employers as long as the economy kept growing and American businesses were shielded from the effects of competition. But a number of factors converged in the 1980s to undermine firms' willingness to cross-subsidize the care of the uninsured. First, health care inflation began to rise rapidly in this decade, outstripping the general inflation rate. Employers experienced double-digit annual increases in insurance premiums; between 1987 and 1993, their insurance premiums rose 90 percent (Cooper and Schone 1997, 142).

Part of the reason for medical inflation lay with weak cost-containment mechanisms in the health care system. Doctors received open-ended reimbursement and had little incentive to use cost-effective alternative treatments, many patients had unlimited access to hospitals and specialists, and the diffusion of new medical technologies was difficult to control. Instead of instruments to relate health care outlays to broader economic performance or national budgets, rampant cost-shifting was the rule.

More tellingly, the spike in health care inflation and employer premiums coincided with broader changes in the American economy since the 1970s. Deindustrialization and the shift to a postindustrial economy brought with it the disappearance of unionized jobs in manufacturing that had come with generous fringe benefits. In their place arose service-sector jobs, subcontracted labor (in both manufacturing and services), and temporary positions. Such contingent employment was one of the chief ways that employers controlled their labor costs and remained competitive, since these jobs often paid low wages and did not come with fringe benefits (Freeman 1994).

The shifts in the economy, coupled with the voluntarism of employer-based fringe benefits, swelled the ranks of the uninsured. Employment-based insurance coverage began a secular decline, reversing the trend of public and private insurance expansion that had begun in the 1960s (Banks, Kunz, and Macdonald 1994, 19). In 1987, the peak year of employment-based coverage, 69.2 percent of Americans under age 65 (the eligible age for Medicare) had insurance through the workplace, and 14.8 percent, or 31.8 million, were uninsured (EBRI 1997). By 1998, the uninsured had risen to 18.4 percent of the nonelderly population (Fronstin 2000, 7). As the numbers of uninsured soared, the financial burden on those employers who still provided insurance became more onerous. As their insurance premiums rose, these employers complained that they were at a competitive disadvantage compared to their domestic rivals who did not provide insurance or to foreign competitors with lower labor costs.

By the early 1990s, employers who provided insurance became less willing to shoulder the access and cost deficiencies of the health care system. They argued that they could no longer afford to cross-subsidize the free riding of their competitors or accommodate the autonomy of health care providers. Some of them began to consider radical solutions. Large firms, particularly those represented by the Business Roundtable, formed a group to study the possibility of national health insurance and employer mandates (Martin 1995a). By requiring all employers to assume responsibility for the health care costs of their work force, national insurance would have solved the cross-subsidy burden and leveled the competitive playing field among firms. Some employers became increasingly attracted to the pro-competitive approach of HMOs to bring cost discipline to doctors and other providers. Employers' interest in reform found a sympathetic ally in President Bill Clinton, who wanted to control the costs of public and private insurance programs while at the same time addressing the problem of access.

Thus, the start of Bill Clinton's presidency in 1993 seemed propitious for a major reform effort. The alliance of business and the medical profession that had long opposed national insurance was beginning to unravel. Employers were indicating their readiness to challenge the postwar settlement with physicians. Even the medical profession's position was softening, with the AMA and other medical organizations proposing different versions of national insurance (see, e.g., Himmelstein, Woolhandler, and Writing Committee 1989; Skocpol 1996, 30–32).

Yet fundamental questions remained about how far to recast the settlement in health care. These centered on the proper role of government, private payers, and doctors in health care provision, financing, and governance and on whether to use markets or other instruments to control sectoral actors. How the Clinton administration and health care stakeholders answered these questions is the subject of the next chapter.

CHAPTER 6

Market Reform as "Unmanaged Competition"

The United States

On September 22, 1993, President Bill Clinton presented to Congress and the American public his vision for a sweeping transformation of the American health care system. With its guarantee of universal coverage through national health insurance, the president's Health Security Act would have marked a major expansion of the welfare state. And with its call for "managed competition," a unique blend of market forces and government regulation, the Clinton plan would have substantially extended the reach of government authority in the health care system.

Clinton's bold proposals initially met with public enthusiasm and a willingness among many members of Congress to work with the president. Less than a year later, however, the Clinton plan and alternative proposals for national health insurance were dead. But if Health Security's fate signaled the repudiation of health reform led by government, it did not mean that change was dead. Rather, private employers took it upon themselves to fundamentally transform the governance arrangements in the health care delivery system in a wrenching process of "unmanaged competition," which has radically reshaped the political bargain with physicians. This tortuous path of health care reform also had immediate implications for the partisan control of government and opened up a broader debate over the proper balance between state and society in providing for social protection.

This chapter explains how and why the United States ended up with this particular type of market reform. It chronicles Clinton's attempt to use government power to construct a health care market and to embed it in national insurance, and offers an explanation of why this endeavor failed. It then describes and explains the pattern of market reform by private actors that followed, concluding with a discussion of the consequences of this type of market reform for health care governance and for politics.

Reform, Stage One: Government-Led Reform through Markets and National Insurance

Contents of the Clinton Plan

With his plan for national health insurance and government-structured competition, Clinton sought to solve both the access and cost problems plaguing the American health care system simultaneously. First, to expand access, Health Security proposed compulsory, universal national health insurance through an employer mandate. The government would have also provided subsidies for insurance to small firms and individuals not attached to the labor market.[1]

Second, Health Security relied on competition among health plans and providers to control costs. At annual enrollment periods, employees would have a choice of health plan, though Health Security included financial incentives to encourage individuals to choose cheaper managed-care plans such as HMOs. More expensive insurers would either have had to reduce their costs in order to survive in the market or else attract enrollees by offering such extras as choice of provider or additional benefits, while levying a higher premium or imposing other forms of patient cost sharing (WHDPC 1993).[2] In addition, providers would have come under competitive pressure if they wanted to attract the patients of health plans, particularly the more restrictive HMOs that contracted with selected doctors and hospitals.

Third, government actors would have played a leading role in structuring competition to ensure universal access and to prevent insurers and providers from engaging in competitive practices that discriminated against the sicker and poorer. States were to establish quasi-public "health alliances" on a regional basis, to ensure that small businesses and individuals had access to affordable coverage, though large firms with more than 5,000 employees could constitute their own alliances (Martin 1995b). The alliances would have organized the market and "managed" the competition through extensive monitoring of insurers to be certain that price competition would not have been based on attracting the healthier and wealthier at the expense of the sicker and poorer (Starr 1994, 53, 102). Thus, Health Security would have banned insurers from excluding patients on the basis of preexisting medical conditions and required them to accept all enrollees. Plans would also have to charge alliance members community-rated premiums designed to pool financial risks across the entire alliance, and alliances would have adjusted premium payments among plans to compensate those insurers who enrolled patients with higher health risks and correspondingly higher health care costs.

Finally, the Clinton plan would have expanded substantially the federal government's authority over private employment-based insurance.[3] Thus, Health Security would have enacted a minimum comprehensive benefits package that all plans would have had to offer under national health insurance. In addition, a National Health Board, with members appointed by the president, would have possessed wide-ranging powers to regulate alliances and health plans. The National Health Board would have also had the authority to enforce a global budget cap by limiting insurers' premium increases to the rate of inflation (WHDPC 1993, chap. 5).

Health Security and Health Care Governance

Neither the Clinton plan nor the theory of "managed competition" on which it was based envisioned a laissez-faire market in health care. Rather, federal and state governments had to take the lead in structuring the market to prevent cream-skimming. This meant embedding the market within the confines of a statutory guarantee of national insurance and active, ongoing government regulation of insurers and providers. Otherwise, competitive pressures would tempt insurers and providers to avoid the sickest and least profitable patients and draw off the healthier and more profitable patients and thereby undermine the financial underpinnings of universal coverage (Enthoven 1988, 1993).

Health Security drew heavily from the theory of managed competition developed by Stanford health economist Alain Enthoven. Yet, the president's plan differed from Enthoven's theory in important respects. The administration believed that a budget cap at the national level was a necessary fail-safe device in case competition failed to deliver expected cost discipline, while Enthoven thought market forces would be sufficient. The Clinton plan in fact was designed as a compromise to appeal to both conservative and progressive forces in Congress and to key health care stakeholders (Hacker 1997).[4]

The Clinton plan was thus consistent with the broader political agenda and ideological outlook of the New Democrats. This conservative wing of the party, which became prominent under Bill Clinton, sought to move the Democrats away from the image of the party of big government and high taxes. It sought to devise new partnerships with government and the private sector, and to harness markets to public ends (see Weir 1998, chap. 1).

But for all its openness to market forces, and though it built on the familiar foundation of employment-based insurance, the Clinton plan was radical in its implications for health care system governance. National health insurance would have greatly expanded the authority of the states and the federal government to intervene in the health sector and regulate the behavior of private market actors, while the National Health Board and alliances would have granted them the institutional means to do so. But these measures would have challenged the freedom of employers and insurers to decide whether and to whom to offer insurance and how to design their benefit packages.

Health Security also would have fundamentally recast the terms of the postwar political settlement with physicians that had enshrined the autonomy of the solo practitioner. To be sure, many of the changes were already under way in the 1970s and 1980s with the growth of prepaid medicine, private investors, and government regulation of provider fees in the public insurance programs. But the Clinton plan would have hastened these developments. First, to the extent that HMOs displaced fee-for-service reimbursement with capitation arrangements, physicians' economic autonomy would have been sharply curtailed. In addition, a global budget for the health care system would have further squeezed provider reimbursements. Second, doctors would have seen a challenge to their clinical autonomy, since Health Security mandated *all* health plans participating in national health insurance, not just HMOs, to have utilization review mechanisms in place with which to monitor physician treatment and referral decisions (WHDPC 1993, 87). Third, the federal government would have encroached on physicians' social autonomy, particularly their freedom to decide on their medical specialty, by setting the mix of specialties and number of residencies in medical education (WHDPC 1993, chap. 17 and 140). Finally, HMOs' emphasis on primary care over specialty care—including the use of gatekeepers—would have created realignments within the medical profession. The losers would have been specialists, while primary care physicians would have seen gains in employment, income, and maybe even influence and prestige within professional organizations.

But even as the Clinton plan would have set limits on the freedom of individual practitioners, it would have also accorded the medical profession a legally recognized place in the determination and administration of health policy. Each regional alliance was to have a provider advisory board composed of doctors and other health care providers who practiced in participating health plans. Similarly, each participating health plan had to regularly consult a provider advisory board with members chosen by providers. The advisory board, moreover, would have had rights of access to plan information concerning the delivery of health care. But there were limits to medical influence in policy-making: because alliances were to represent employer and consumer interests, providers and owners of health plans were explicitly barred from membership on the boards of directors of regional alliances (WHDPC 1993, 61–62, 85–86).

If it would have hastened the demise of solo practice, Health Security also held out the potential for the medical profession to enhance its economic power through various forms of collective action. The Clinton plan would have relaxed antitrust rules to allow self-employed physicians to organize as unions or as networks that would bargain fees and conditions of services with HMOs or that would negotiate directly with employers (WHDPC 1993, chap. 23). These provisions would have given doctors a chance to recapture some of their economic and clinical autonomy lost to managed-care organizations.

In sum, the Clinton plan signaled nothing less than a new governance regime in health care with major implications for the power and position of sectoral stakeholders. It implied radical changes for the medical profession, though not uniformly in the direction of less influence. While it would have curbed the autonomy of individual doctors, the Clinton plan also promised the medical profession new avenues of influence in health policy-making and administration and new possibilities as collective economic actors. More significantly, the government would have encroached on the turf of employers and private insurers. Not surprisingly, then, Health Security encountered resistance from a number of stakeholders as well as party forces during the legislative stage. It is here that it foundered.

Explaining the Failure of the Clinton Plan[5]

Though the Clinton plan met with great fanfare when it was initially unveiled in the autumn of 1993, it never reached a floor debate in Congress. By the summer of 1994, the entire effort at national insurance was dead. How and why did this happen? Though I consider other explanations, my own interpretation stresses the interplay of sectoral and political actors and institutions. Actors and institutions in the political arena played a critical part in the story since the Clinton plan died at the legislative stage. But the health care system also influenced the reform outcome by designating as critical to any reform effort certain stakeholders whose voices politicians could ill afford to ignore. In addition, the policy preferences and political strategies of those stakeholders—employers especially—were not only affected by the political system and their own organizational capacity in the political arena but also by their position in the health care system itself.

In the postmortem, some have argued that the balance of political forces in Congress in 1993 did not support such an ambitious reform initiative. After all, Clinton had garnered only 43 percent of the popular vote in the 1992 election, which did not suggest an overwhelming mandate for anything. Even though the Democrats enjoyed majorities in both houses of Congress and occupied the White House, those majorities were not large enough to assure passage of major health care reform, since Senate Republicans had enough votes to mount a filibuster against Clinton's legislation. As Tuohy (1999) has argued, Clinton possessed the will but not the capacity to mobilize the authority needed to enact such an ambitious reform agenda.

But the political environment especially up to the 1992 election seemed more propitious for national health insurance than the foregoing would suggest. The old alliance of business and medicine that had long resisted national health insurance was coming unglued, and the position of its members was softening: many larger firms and their employee benefits managers were open to the idea of government reform, and some larger firms even went so far as to call publicly for national health insurance (Martin 1995, 1997). Even the AMA had proposed its own version of universal health insurance in 1990 (Skocpol 1996, 30). Opinion polls registered vast majorities of Americans unhappy with the health care system, and increasingly supportive of a radical overhaul (Hacker 1997, 18–19). Harris Wofford's startling election to the Senate in 1991 was due largely to voter support for his explicit call for national health insurance. Finally, Clinton made the issue a focal point of his own campaign in 1992. Thus, his election victory could have reasonably been interpreted as a signal to go forward with health care reform.

All the same, these positive signs masked a difficult institutional and political terrain that Clinton had to traverse. In general, American political institutions fragment authority and make radical policy change difficult and rare (Steinmo and Watts 1995; Weir, Orloff, and Skocpol 1988, esp. 21–24).[6] Unlike parliamentary systems, in which the fusion of executive and legislative personnel and common elections of both provide incentives for party discipline and for loyalty to the executive, the American system's separation of powers gives Congress the power to veto the president's proposals and initiate its own. Having separate elections for the president and Congress also permits parties substantial independence from the executive, and voters expect members of Congress to represent the district or the state as much as to display loyalty to the president even when he is of the same party (Mayhew 1974). Aside from these enduring features of constitutional design, transformations in Congress, parties, and interest groups in the 1970s made it even harder to build broad reform coalitions capable of taking positive political action on controversial issues. Changes in the rules governing primaries and campaign financing eroded the control of party leaders over candidate selection and rendered the two major parties little more than vehicles to funnel money—mostly from interest groups—to political candidates.[7] In the wake of Watergate, congressional decision making became more decentralized as the seniority system waned, subcommittees gained influence, and lawmakers became policy entrepreneurs (Deering and Smith 1985; Dodd and Oppenheimer 1985; Ornstein, Peabody, and Rohde 1985). That decade also marked the proliferation of single-issue interest groups (Schlozman and Tierney 1986). In short, decentralized decision making in Congress and a private system of campaign financing gave interest groups ample opportunities to influence legislative proposals.

While this institutional and political terrain poses formidable obstacles to major policy initiatives, it does not make them impossible. Rather, successful enactment requires that a president work with the terrain at hand and use these institutions strategically. The terrain also suggests that certain strategies may stand a better chance of success than others. Separation of powers suggests the need for negotiation and compromise between the president and Congress as an alternative to deadlock. If the president cannot always count on his party in Congress even when it controls both the executive and legislative branches, bipartisan cooperation offers an alternative path. Because the congressional committee system is so porous to interest groups, this suggests that striking deals with key stakeholders is critical for legislative success. Furthermore, balances of power among different actors are not frozen in time. Coalitions rise and fall; parties and interests may change personnel, ideological outlook, and policy preferences. We must keep in mind the dynamic nature of American politics and institutions in seeking explanations for the Clinton plan debacle.

Because Democratic majorities in Congress were slim, Clinton had to assiduously court his congressional colleagues or else include Republicans in a bipartisan strategy. But dissension in the Democratic ranks ruled out the first option. Some Democrats supported the president's plan, but others pushed for a more radical single-payer option, or advocated proposals that fell short of achieving universal coverage or cost containment, or threw up obstacles to Health Security while doing little or nothing to advance alternative reform ideas (Johnson and Broder 1997; Schick 1995; Skocpol 1996). The task of party unity was not made easier by the fact that a number of different committees and subcommittees had jurisdiction over health care legislation. The Democrats' disarray would seem to confirm the generalization that the undisciplined parties characteristic of American politics were culpable for wrecking the Clinton plan. But it cannot explain the Republicans, who displayed remarkable unity in opposing the Clinton plan. Indeed, the Republicans and their allies saw the defeat of the Clinton plan as critical to their strategy to win Congress in 1994 and to their broader ideological crusade to roll back the state (Johnson and Broder 1997, xiii–xiv; Skocpol 1996, 145–47). Their uncompromising position killed hopes for a bipartisan strategy. Had Democrats displayed the same unity in support of the Clinton plan as the Republicans did in opposing it, the legislative outcome might have been different.

The "policy legacies" (Pierson 1993; Weir and Skocpol 1985) of previous administrations and the existing health sector also made some options appear infeasible. The Reagan-era budget deficits Clinton inherited made it politically difficult to push for a state-administered system like Britain's or a single-payer option like Canada's and the higher taxes and government spending they would have entailed. A single-payer national health service would have most certainly alienated key stakeholders in the existing private, employment-based insurance system. Thus, Clinton's reform proposals sought to reassure employers (and larger private insurers) that their role in health care governance would not be displaced by a government-run program.

Indeed, employers were pivotal in deciding the fate of the Clinton plan. Their views were bound to carry weight in the health care reform debate in any case, since they financed health insurance for most Americans. But Clinton's decision to base national health insurance on employers' contributions only magnified their influence and put his plan hostage to the veto of business. Even so, Clinton's decision was not unreasonable. Many firms initially seemed amenable to national insurance. In the 1980s, new associations appeared on the Washington scene that provided a measure of centralization in aggregating business opinion on the need for health care reform (Martin 1995a). But business proved to be an erstwhile ally of the president. The sources of business inconstancy lay in both the health sector and the political arena. Employers enjoyed substantial freedom to control their labor costs and make decisions on health coverage in the voluntary fringe-benefit system, which made it difficult to forge a common line on health care reform. The business community also proved incapable of surmounting its organizational weaknesses in the political arena to rally around the Clinton plan.

Most businesses viewed the health care problem in terms of labor costs. But their position in the health care system shaped their attitude toward the Clinton plan and their calculations of whether it would serve their strategies of competitiveness. Many employers who already provided health insurance, blaming their high labor costs on the free riding of their colleagues who did not offer coverage, supported national insurance. The former believed that the answer to their labor-cost problem lay in the Clinton plan's employer mandate, which would have spread the cost of insurance to all firms and thereby leveled the competitive playing field among them. But many small businesses and service-sector enterprises viewed the voluntarism of employment-based insurance as vital to their economic survival, since the freedom to not provide insurance was what allowed them to keep their labor costs at competitive levels. Thus, many small enterprises vehemently opposed the Clinton plan on the grounds that it would saddle them with prohibitively high labor costs that would have driven them out of business (Judis 1995; Martin 1995b). But even among firms that provided insurance, there were those who rejected the Clinton plan because they feared that it would have increased rather than lowered their labor costs. In their view, either they would have been forced into regional alliances and subsidized insurance for small businesses or, if they were large enough to constitute their own alliances, they ran the risk that even larger state alliances would be able to negotiate better deals from insurers and leave them with higher premiums (Judis 1995; Martin 1995a, 1995b). For different reasons, then, these firms calculated that they could better control their own costs by going it alone, and the voluntarism of the American health insurance system permitted them to do so.

Aside from its effects on labor costs, the Clinton plan hit a nerve with many employers because it involved basic questions of corporate autonomy. Some employers—and not just small businesses—opposed Clinton's national insurance proposal as an illegitimate intrusion of the state into their domain of corporate governance. They correctly perceived that the employer mandate and a legislated minimum benefits package would have encroached upon their freedom to decide on insurance coverage for their employees. But some business executives were more alarmist, fearing that national insurance was an entering wedge for further government intrusion into other areas of corporate governance (Judis 1995).

Business leaders found it difficult to forge a common line on health care reform not only because the health care system granted them multiple ways to control their labor costs, but also because of their organizational fragmentation in the political arena. Unlike their British or German counterparts, who look to one or a few peak associations to represent them in politics, a number of different groups speak for American firms. These associations, moreover, are voluntary bodies and lack effective sanctions over recalcitrant members (Wilson 1985, chaps. 2–4; see also Katzenstein 1987, chap. 1; Martin 1995a, 2000). The organizational weakness of employers as political actors combined with their freedom of action in the health sector and made it that much harder for competing associations to build a unified front in support of the Clinton plan. Facing dissension in their ranks and defections of members to rival associations opposed to the Clinton plan, organizations representing large and medium-sized firms abdicated their initial support of national insurance and chose to remain on the sidelines. In doing so, they left the field open to the small-business federation, the National Federation of Independent Business (NFIB), to wage a virulent and effective campaign of opposition.[8]

In short, the varying views of firms toward the Clinton plan, coupled with organizational fragmentation in the political arena, made rallying support to the Clinton plan a difficult proposition for the leaders of the peak associations of business. Employers' disarray and display of negative power in this episode confirm Vogel's (1978) observation that American business people tend to identify with their own firm rather than their class as a whole and to resist government actions designed to shore up the capitalist system if they appear to threaten the survival of their own enterprise.

The partisan and interest-group terrain sketched above clearly made major health care reform a formidable task. But Clinton's reform strategy only worsened matters. That strategy was woefully unattuned to the political and institutional environment, which suggested the need to compromise and to forge a supporting coalition. The labyrinthine Health Security blueprint was the product of a secretive task force chaired by Hillary Clinton and an advisory group headed by Ira Magaziner. The task force was composed of top political officials in the administration and was supposed to handle the political side of health care reform, while the advisory group, composed of over 5,000 policy experts plus administration and congressional staffers, explicitly eschewed political considerations from their proposals and focused on policy questions instead (Hacker 1997, 122–23). However, this attempt to separate policy from politics proved fatal because it failed to take seriously the need for negotiation and compromise over the basic parameters of reform (ibid., 132–38). The task force and advisory group consulted congressional Democrats and an array of interest groups, but this was a far cry from genuine negotiations. As a result, the administration failed to build a supportive alliance among key congressional and health sector players.[9] To be sure, a strategy of inclusion carried risks of its own; efforts at negotiation and compromise might have diluted the president's ambitions or ended in deadlock. But early inclusion might have also given members of Congress and health care interest groups a stake in seeing the reform effort succeed and steeled their resolve to support it during what promised to be a difficult legislative road ahead.

The reform strategy appeared ill-suited to politics in other ways. Hillary Rodham Clinton's prominent role in the reform effort proved to be a political liability, since she lacked the legitimacy of a cabinet member approved by the Senate.[10] And instead of delegating to the secretary of the Department of Health and Human Services the day-to-day mission of advancing the reform effort, Bill Clinton chose to assume the burden himself. But as he discovered, presidents have other pressing policy concerns. As a result, the health care reform effort moved in fits and starts, plagued by delays that allowed opponents to step into the vacuum and define the terms of public debate (Clymer, Pear, and Toner 1994).

With the backing of the business community not forthcoming, Clinton might have sought to rally traditional Democratic constituencies, such as labor and the elderly, to his plan. Or he might have tried to mold public opinion to support Health Security to surmount the resistance of employers. His administration tried but failed on both counts. Traditional Democratic allies were either divided toward the president's plan or provided only lukewarm support (Skocpol 1996, 90–99).[11] Labor's political influence, moreover, had eroded in tandem with its loss of members over the years and its increasingly narrow and defensive posture (Weir 1998, 11–12).[12] In any case, Democratic allies proved no match for the well-organized, well-financed conservative organizations with grassroots support.

Indeed, opponents of Health Security waged a highly effective campaign to turn public opinion, which had been initially favorable, against it.[13] The NFIB admonished the public that the Clinton plan meant "big government" and a certain loss of jobs for those working for small enterprises. The Health Insurance Association of America (HIAA), which represented small and medium-sized insurers fearful of being devoured by managed-care organizations should the Clinton plan pass, ran negative ads targeted at lawmakers and opinion leaders in key cities. Even though the managed-care industry and large insurers favored the Clinton plan, they were not as effective in the public opinion war as the HIAA. Finally, conservative interest groups like the Christian Coalition mobilized their grass-roots base against the Clinton plan (Johnson and Broder 1997, 623; Schick 1995; Skocpol 1996, chap. 5, esp. 157–62).

The battle also was notable for the flurry of cross-lobbying between different interest groups and reverse-lobbying by congressional Republicans against potential supporters of Health Security. The Chamber of Commerce and the AMA came under heavy fire for their sympathetic stance toward the Clinton plan from congressional Republicans and the NFIB.[14] Such external pressure, combined with internal membership unease, compelled these potential allies of the president to withdraw their support.

It is striking how insignificant a role the medical profession played in the reform debate. But like labor, membership losses over the past three decades had weakened the AMA's political clout.[15] With a majority of doctors now outside the organization, its claim to represent the profession was less convincing to politicians than in the past. Nor did it have an inside position in developing Health Security, since it, like other interest groups, had been excluded from the deliberations of the task force.[16] More significant was that the profession was far from united on the question of health care reform. Rival medical associations took a line independent of the AMA, with some of them supporting the Clinton plan. The AMA's equivocation toward Health Security reflected both internal divisions and external pressures. Thus, in the summer of 1994, the AMA, along with organized labor and the American Association of Retired Persons (AARP), sponsored newspaper ads that publicly supported the key provisions of the Clinton plan, though without specifying the plan by name. But member doctors harbored serious reservations toward elements of Health Security, particularly its global budgeting and managed-care provisions, which they viewed as a threat to their incomes and professional freedom. The AMA also incurred severe criticism for its stance from the NFIB and the Republicans. In the face of external pressure and internal dissension, the AMA leadership muted its earlier public support of employer mandates and universal coverage (Skocpol 1996, 161–62, 205 n. 47).

Finally, some analysts argued that managed competition and alliances were too complex and unfamiliar for Americans to understand or support (Skocpol 1996, esp. 123–25). Admittedly, critics of Health Security seized on its technical complexity to attack it as a labyrinthine government bureaucracy. But complexity alone need not have spelled its defeat. As a counterexample, Republicans succeeded in enacting complex market-oriented reforms—some of which mirrored Clinton's proposals—for Medicare in 1996 and in the Balanced Budget Act of 1997. These changes passed, however, because they were largely invisible to the public, since they had not been published as a detailed legislative proposal in advance, and because the Republicans secured the support of key stakeholders, such as the AMA, through advance negotiations and concessions. Health Security, by contrast, was a complete blueprint released to the public with much fanfare and with little prior deliberation with health care stakeholders to get them on board. Thus, it was open for all to see—and to tear apart.[17]

More convincing is the contention that the quasi-public alliances—and the alternative to market and state forms of governance that they signified—were alien to the American liberal tradition and its strict delineation of public and private. This unfamiliarity not only confused the public but also policymakers and influential policy experts and advisers, such as the Congressional Budget Office (CBO), and provided Clinton's critics with potent ammunition that alliances constituted "big government."[18] Indeed, the costs of Health Security became a sticking point between Clinton and his foes in the battle for public opinion. The CBO's decision to classify corporate and regional alliances as part of government entailed higher burdens on the federal budget than the administration's calculations (CBO 1994, esp. 44–50). But the Clinton administration did not help its position by refusing to admit that its numbers might be too low and by insisting that premiums, not payroll taxes, would finance it (Hacker 1997, 124). Nor did it adequately justify to the public an expansion of government in the health care system and the higher taxes it might entail. But such reticence was consistent with New Democrat efforts to get beyond the party's traditional tax-and-spend image and with their commitment to "reinvent" or shrink government.

The Clinton plan's restricted choice of physicians and hospitals under HMOs also was undoubtedly alien to the experience of many Americans accustomed to free choice under fee-for-service medicine. Opponents of the plan highlighted these controversial features in their drive to turn public opinion against the Clinton plan, with great effect.

This analysis suggests that American political institutions were not solely responsible for the Clinton plan's failure. To be sure, separation of powers and decentralized decision making in Congress provided opponents entry to the policy process and ample opportunities to defeat the Clinton plan. But the preferences and strategies of political parties and organized interests crucial to the outcome also mattered. Had Democrats supported Clinton as much as Republicans opposed, him, and had large firms been able to unite around Health Security and marginalize small business, the outcome might have been different.

Reform, Stage Two: Employer-Led Market Reform

Employers Go It Alone

Though Clinton's attempt at government-led reform came to an inglorious end, this did not spell the end of health care reform. On the contrary, transformation of the health care system continued apace at breathtaking scope and speed. But rather than government actors leading the charge in reshaping the governance arrangements and institutions of the health care system, employers decided to go it alone and push the market forward themselves.[19] Under pressure from employers to hold the line on premiums, managed-care plans became increasingly aggressive with doctors and hospitals, forcing them to slash their costs by negotiating steep price discounts or accept capitation arrangements.[20] Many firms also prodded or required their employees to sign up with managed-care plans, either by offering them financial incentives to do so or limiting them to only one health plan. Indeed, by 1997, 85 percent of the work force was in some type of managed-care plan, up from slightly more than 28 percent in 1988 (Freudenheim 1994, 1998). Some employers even banded together in voluntary purchasing cooperatives, somewhat along the lines envisioned by the Clinton plan, to gain leverage over providers and insurers in the health care marketplace.

The go-it-alone approach, however, is a broad canopy that goes beyond promoting price competition among health plans and providers of care. It has also included employers shifting the costs of insurance onto their employees by forcing them to pay higher copayments or a greater portion of premiums, or by limiting the range of benefits offered by group health insurance plans. In addition, many employers have chosen to self-insure (see below) in order to confine their risks to their own work force and to avoid cooptation into states' risk pools for the uninsured. Other firms have taken the ultimate exit option by refusing to offer insurance at all.

This kind of reform is best characterized as a process of "unmanaged competition," whereby the application of market forces has proceeded in the absence of an effective regulatory framework that would prohibit or compensate for market failures. The relentless cost-cutting behavior of health plans and employers in a voluntary, private health insurance market has contributed to the numbers of uninsured, jeopardized their access to health services, and permitted managed-care plans to ration care without an adequate framework of accountability.

Government actors have taken a reactive stance that has largely responded to market developments. Where government action has occurred, it has often taken the form of incremental regulation of the insurance market to promote competition, as in overseeing mergers in the private insurance and provider markets (Given 1997), or inserting private market options into the public insurance programs of Medicaid and Medicare (Devers 1997; Moon, Gage, and Evans 1997; White 1995).[21] Government action of the market-hindering type, however, has been notably limited. Regulation of private insurance underwriting or of managed care's ways of delivering health services has been fragmentary and piecemeal. State consumer protections and enforcement have varied widely (Zelman and Berenson 1998, 163–64), while the federal government has largely been limited to "legislating by diagnosis."[22]

Likewise, federal government efforts to expand access to health insurance have also been quite modest. The Health Insurance Portability and Accountability Act of 1996 (better known as the Kassebaum-Kennedy Act) aimed to enhance labor mobility and preserve access to insurance by barring insurers from denying coverage to new employees with preexisting medical conditions. But because it made no provision that premiums would be affordable, and it contained waiting periods for some workers, the law has fallen short of achieving either goal. Moreover, because the legislation did not address those outside the labor market without insurance, it has not meant anything like universal coverage. Not surprisingly, however, Kassebaum-Kennedy was popular with businesses, since it contained no employer mandate to provide insurance, and it targeted the practices of insurers rather than firms.[23] Clinton and Congress also enacted the State Children's Health Insurance Program to cover children of the working poor whose incomes were too high to qualify for Medicaid. However, the program has fallen far short of enrolling all eligible children (EBRI 2000; Health Affairs 1997b; also see Thorpe 1997).[24]

Once the Clinton plan had died, many hoped that state governments would pick up the ball and enact universal coverage and consumer protections in the insurance market. After all, states often serve as laboratories of experimentation and innovation in social policy. But they have faced a range of obstacles in their efforts at universal coverage and comprehensive regulation of the insurance market (Grogan 1995).[25] One of the biggest barriers has been a federal pension law (discussed below) that has allowed businesses to evade state efforts to expand access and otherwise regulate health insurance. As a result, states have had to settle for incremental expansions of Medicaid and public insurance to the working poor, or consumer protections that do not extend to many employed Americans.

The government's limited leverage over private, employment-based insurance arises from a number of sources. In part, it reflects the arm's-length relationship between business and government and the sharply delineated boundary between public and private in a liberal political economy. This contrasts with Germany's corporatist political economy and public law that accord private interests public policy functions. In the United States, however, business executives vehemently opposed Clinton's proposals and subsequent efforts at regulation of the market as an illegitimate intrusion in their corporate decision making. However, the federal government has enjoyed greater legal and institutional capacity to set the parameters of public insurance programs. For instance, Clinton used executive orders to expand Medicaid without resorting to legislation and to mandate consumer protections for Medicare managed-care plans even as he repeatedly failed to win congressional assent for similar measures for the private sector (see Pear 1998i).

But a huge hindrance to effective regulation of employment-based insurance lies with regulatory federalism operating in the health sector, which has encouraged state and federal officials to work at cross-purposes in their efforts to control private actors. Though states ostensibly have jurisdiction over private insurance, a pension law, the Employee Retirement and Income Security Act (ERISA), has in fact denied them such authority over a broad swath of employer-provided insurance plans. This is because ERISA permits states to regulate the "business of insurance," but not employers' self-insured health plans, which cover 40 percent of the work force (Acs et al. 1996, 275).[26] At the same time, however, federal regulation of self-insured plans and employer-based health insurance more generally is notoriously weak.[27] The result is a dual system of government regulation that shields self-insured plans from the more stringent regulations that apply to other insurers.

Ironically, employer-led market reform has also meant in many instances fewer choices of providers *and* health plans by employees than under government-led market reform. While the Clinton plan would have reduced choice of providers by encouraging the growth of HMOs, it would have still required corporate and state alliances to offer individuals the choice of at least three health plans.[28] But under employer-led market reform, firms reserve their prerogative to determine the health insurance options they will offer as a fringe benefit, and many have opted to restrict the range of benefits. Most small firms have offered their workers only one plan, and even many large companies have limited employee options.[29] Many employers have herded their employees into managed-care plans that promise savings by limiting access to doctors and hospital care. Finally, cutthroat competition has unleashed an orgy of mergers in recent years, so that some cities find only one or two managed-care giants dominating the market.[30]

Backlash against Managed Care

This rapid advance of managed care in a market whose rules have yet to be defined has radically transformed the ways that many insured Americans receive health care.[31] The more restrictive managed-care plans (such as HMOs) limit patients' choice of providers and access to specialty care. Some patients may resent the novelty of restricted choice in and of itself. But the rapid advance of managed care has also raised broader concerns over quality of care and accountability of health plans for their rationing decisions. In an environment of cutthroat price competition, some managed-care plans may find it tempting to provide less care than is medically warranted in order to survive in the marketplace or to make a profit, and they may use mechanisms of control over patients and doctors to do so. An underdeveloped framework of rules over managed care may leave patients with inadequate means to prevent or punish plans for such behavior.

This is not to argue that managed care is necessarily dangerous to one's health. On the contrary, managed care offers great potential to improve quality of care even as it reduces costs in ways that fee-for-service solo practice did not. First, managed care differs from fee-for-service in how and what it pays providers. Fee-for-service paid providers for discrete treatments, thus financially rewarding doctors for providing care rather than for withholding it, and it often did not cover preventive care. But by paying providers a fixed amount in advance (capitation), HMOs theoretically discourage medically unnecessary or questionable care. Many HMOs also cover preventive care or health promotion programs (while traditional insurance often did not) on the grounds that this kind of care will yield cost savings over the long term. Second, managed-care plans scrutinize physician treatment decisions where fee-for-service did not. Such reviews, which may include advance approval of elective treatments or referrals, can be a powerful way to minimize medically unnecessary services. Third, the more restrictive HMOs contract only with certain doctors and hospitals, which can be a way to weed out unqualified practitioners. Fourth, these closed-panel HMOs also usually require patients to have a primary care doctor to act as a gatekeeper who coordinates their health care and makes the appropriate referrals to specialists. Fifth, some HMOs—especially those that contract with large group practices or employ their own doctors in a clinic setting, or health plans that integrate doctors and hospitals—can potentially coordinate care better than can largely unconnected solo practitioners. Such coordination across a range of providers and treatment settings can promote continuity of care. Lastly, some HMOs have been in the vanguard in developing and disseminating to their physicians scientifically based practice guidelines, which can help clinicians make better treatment decisions (see Zelman and Berenson 1998, esp. chaps. 4 and 5).

But these tools also serve as potent cost-containment weapons. In an environment of cutthroat competition, there are concerns that health plans may use these tools to put cost control ahead of quality in order to survive. Prospective payment may give providers incentive to skimp on care rather than to keep people healthy, especially if rationing expensive medical treatment is hard to detect. Review processes that empower managed-care plans to delay or refuse to authorize treatment may result in some patients being denied medically necessary treatment. Moreover, in deciding whether a proposed treatment will be covered, managed-care plan personnel may go beyond simply stating which benefits a policy covers to making determinations of medical necessity—in effect, practicing medicine.[32]

Nor has the for-profit status of many managed-care plans helped build public confidence in HMOs. The growing prominence of investor-owned plans in the 1990s, along with media reports of the million-dollar salaries and stock options earned by some of their chief executives, have helped fuel public cynicism with the rationing decisions of managed care.[33] Critics also cite evidence showing that investor-owned plans incur higher administrative costs and devote a smaller share of the premium to patient care.[34] Others argue that nonprofits tend to provide important community benefits, such as charity care for the uninsured and citizen participation in their governance, that for-profits do not. They fear that such community benefits will erode as investor-owned plans capture a larger share of the market and decline to provide such services themselves, or as nonprofits mimic their profit-making competitors—including converting themselves to for-profit entities—in order to survive. Critics fear that the short time-horizons arising from the schedule of quarterly dividend payments, combined with plans' accountability to shareholders interested in a good rate of return on their investment, may put some for-profits under enormous pressure to place cost containment and profitability ahead of patient care—even to the point of denying medically necessary treatments—and to ignore the needs of the broader community.[35]

In such a competitive free-for-all, the rationing decisions of managed-care plans have engendered public unease, not least because they take place in the absence of a framework of public accountability and in an incentive structure of prospective payment that rewards providers for doing less rather than more. This fear might seem paradoxical, given that surveys show majorities of HMO patients happy with their health care. Indeed, a Kaiser Family Foundation survey in 1997 found that most respondents were satisfied with the care they received from their own health plan (whether managed care or fee-for-service). Still, almost 60 percent said that people in managed-care plans might not get access to the care they need, and a slight majority favored government regulation of managed care.[36] Analysts of this survey and others conducted between 1995 and 1997 attributed the public's mistrust of managed care to difficult access and long waiting times that many patients experienced with such plans, as well as distressing media reports of cases of HMOs denying care inappropriately. Such cases were seen as fairly commonplace occurrences rather than as exceptions (Blendon et al. 1998, 83–84, 90–91).

However, managed care fares worse in terms of public image than it does in other assessments. Academic studies comparing managed care with fee-for-service have found that the quality of care is as good under HMOs as under fee-for-service plans (Miller and Luft 1994, 1997). While critics argue that the temptation to undertreat is built into the financial structure of managed care, there are ways to minimize such incentives. For instance, if a health plan capitates a medical group as a whole and distributes bonuses for good performance equally among all member physicians, the pressure on individual doctors to put cost before quality tends to be less severe than when capitation or bonuses are paid to each individual doctor. In practice, capitation of medical groups tends to predominate over that of individual practitioners (Zelman and Berenson 1998, 125). Finally, some health plans have well-developed peer-review mechanisms that provide physicians with substantial control over and autonomy from insurance personnel on treatment decisions and management of clinical practice.[37]

Still, even these efforts to safeguard quality or to devise objective assessments of managed care are not foolproof. Although HMOs generally have a good track record in providing good care for those who are younger and healthier, it is less certain that their incentive structures will ensure that patients with complex, chronic conditions that are expensive to treat will get the care they need. Some studies have found that patients with chronic conditions fared worse under managed care than under fee-for-service (Miller and Luft 1997).[38] Moreover, quality is notoriously difficult to measure in health care, and efforts to develop scientifically based clinical guidelines are still in their infancy (Bindman 1997). While employers and health plans have made gains in developing quality measures, their data often do not link medical interventions to medical outcomes.[39] Finally, financial bonuses that reward doctors for providing less care remain controversial; other remuneration arrangements that could lessen the temptation to over- or undertreat are often ignored.[40]

Furthermore, with consumer protections weakly developed or varying greatly across states and plan types, many patients have little recourse to prevent managed-care plans from inappropriately denying care or to punish them if they do. To be sure, many states require managed-care plans to have an internal appeals process in place. But internal grievance procedures raise questions of impartiality and whether patients will get a fair hearing from a plan that is investigating itself or its providers. Some states have gone further by mandating outside appeals mechanisms or permitting patients to seek redress through the legal system. But ERISA imposes strict limits on the use of lawsuits as a weapon of accountability and leaves the bulk of employer-provided health plans beyond the reach of tort or contract law. Thus, only state employees may sue insurers for punitive or compensatory damages for denied care; but for all other employer-provided plans, ERISA limits remedies to the amount of benefits in question and bars suits for damages or lost wages (GAO 1995, 7). In other words, because ERISA puts the bulk of employer-provided health plans beyond the reach of tort or contract law, their level of liability is far less than that of private companies in other fields of activity, which are subject to product liability suits, or that of doctors, who may face malpractice suits (Kilcullen 1996; see also Weinstein 1998).[41]

The public anxiety over managed care has generated political repercussions. Sensing the public's unease, President Clinton appointed a commission in 1996 to study the issue of regulating managed care. However, the commission failed to fulfill the president's hopes that it would devise broad consumer protections at the national level that would apply to all employer-provided and private health plans. Instead, reflecting differences of opinion among the various health care interests on the panel, the commission could only agree to a limited number of consumer protections in a "patient's bill of rights." The most basic rights would require insurers to cover hospital emergency room visits that a "prudent layperson" would deem an emergency, grant insured persons the right to appeal a health plan's denial of care to an outside panel of experts, and allow patients easier access to medical specialists. Conspicuous in their absence, however, were a patient's right to sue insurers for damages or malpractice arising from treatment denials and a call for government to enact universal coverage. The commission also called for a national Advisory Council to specify goals for improvement and for measurement of quality. But bowing to its business and insurance representatives and the requirement for unanimous decision, the commission declined to recommend federal legislation to enforce consumer protections and instead called for self-regulation by the private sector (President's Advisory Commission 1998, 3–4).[42]

Disappointed with the commission's modest recommendations, Clinton and some members of Congress continued to push for broader consumer protections enforceable under federal law. Democrats and (belatedly) Republicans have recognized that managed-care regulation is an issue that resonates with voters. In response, they haave proposed their own versions of a patient bill of rights. Though Republican bills have been more favorable to the managed-care industry and employers, these groups have not been uniformly opposed to regulation. Employers have continued to fight legal regulation of their health plans, but the managed-care industry has followed a less intransigent path on strategic grounds.[43]

Still, the two parties failed to bridge their differences on critical points to enact legislation ahead of the 2000 elections.[44] The partisan wrangling continued into the first year of George W. Bush's term. By late summer 2001, both houses of Congress had passed their own versions of a "patient's bill of rights," but President Bush had yet to take action (*Economist* 2001b; Mitchell and Pear 2001; Pear 2001a, 2001b).Thus, it remains to be seen whether Congress and the president will enact such a law and, if so, how strong its regulatory provisions will be. One thing is clear, however, and that is that the debacle of the Clinton plan has counseled reformers to scale back their ambition. Government action has generally focused on electorally popular measures to extend protection to those already insured. The problems of the uninsured have met with less visible incremental measures, and ambitious aspirations for a national insurance solution have all but disappeared from the political agenda.

Assessment: Implications of Market Reform Led by Private Actors

The particular kind of market reform that has unfolded in the United States has implications for the health sector itself and for politics more generally. I explore these themes by answering the following questions. First, what effects has unmanaged competition had on sectoral governance, especially with regard to the role of the medical profession? Second, has the market strategy delivered the expected cost savings, and if so, what effect has it had on access, the other major problem in the American health care system? Finally, what have been the implications of the market path for politics?

The Waning of the Professional Model of Governance

National health insurance had always been the American medical profession's greatest nightmare. Most doctors feared that it would have meant the destruction of the autonomy of the solo practitioner by an overweening state. Throughout the twentieth century, the AMA had vociferously and successfully beat back the challenge of national insurance, and the major government insurance programs, Medicare and Medicaid, accommodated the professional autonomy of the solo practitioner via fee-for-service reimbursement, administration by private insurers, and weak or nonexistent review of physician practice patterns.

The great irony, however, is that the private health care system and minimal government intervention that doctors fought so hard for have turned against them. Private employers and insurers, not government, have attacked the autonomy of the solo practitioner with the greatest effect.

As chapter 5 showed, the medical profession brought much of this on itself by its steadfast refusal to police its own members. The AMA waged fierce and often successful campaigns against any deviations from solo practice and fee-for-service reimbursement in both public and private insurance programs. The association also fought to protect the clinical freedom of individual practitioners by resisting, then colonizing, and finally applauding the demise of peer-review arrangements in Medicare. The defeat of the Clinton health plan (primarily by forces other than the medical profession) meant that doctors had once again dodged the bullet of government regulation of their autonomy under national health insurance. Even so, employers and insurers have taken the task upon themselves through the rough-and-tumble approach of unmanaged competition.

Employer-led market reform that relies on price competition among managed-care organizations is a unilateral attempt to rewrite the terms of the political bargain with the medical profession. It has had major consequences for medical practice, professional autonomy, and the role of doctors in health care governance. First, the "managed-care revolution" has constricted the economic freedom of physicians. Open-ended fee-for-service arrangements have given way to capitation or steeply discounted fee schedules of managed-care plans. Physician income has also become explicitly tied to performance criteria that reward doctors for doing less, such as through year-end bonus payments contingent upon individual physicians or medical groups achieving a surplus in their budgets for patient care. Managed care's reimbursement arrangements and monitoring of physician treatments and hospital stays helped slow the growth of physician incomes and spending on their services in the mid-1990s, as table 11 (column 2) shows.

Managed care has also altered the social setting of medicine in a variety of ways. Doctors are now more than ever employees of health plans.[45] Managed care has also accelerated an earlier trend toward the formation of larger practices among self-employed doctors. Managed-care plans also appear to have affected the pace of doctors' workday. According to surveys of physicians in HMO settings, respondents said that such health plans force them to see more patients and spend less time with them than under fee-for-service arrangements (Donelan et al. 1997; Muh 1997; Waitzkin and Fishman 1997). In addition, managed care has shaped physicians' choice of specialty. Because many HMOs rely on primary care gatekeepers to ration access to specialists, and HMO administrators believe there is a surplus of specialists (Donelan et al. 1997, 143), medical students have increasingly chosen primary care. Indeed, in areas like California where HMOs dominate the market, many specialists have found themselves unemployed or have had such health plans terminate their contracts.

But the most significant changes to the political bargain with doctors have been in the area of clinical freedom. Many doctors have had to experience for the first time the constraint imposed by prospective budgeting on their treatment decisions. In addition, many have felt the strictures of utilization review. Under the most intrusive procedures, health plan person-

TABLE 11. Real Per Capita National Health Expenditures and Expenditures on Physicians' Services in the United States, 1970–2007 (average annual growth rate in percentages from prior year shown)

Year	National Health Expenditures, Average Annual Growth Rate	Spending on Physicians' Services, Average Annual Growth Rate
1970–80	4.5	4.4
1930–90	5.1	6.5
1990–93	4.2	3.5
1993–96	1.5	−0.1
1996–98*	2.6	2.1
1998–2001*	3.1	3.8
2001–7*	3.4	3.8

Source: Health Care Financing Administration, cited in Smith et al. 1998, 132.
*Projected.

nel approve—or deny—individual doctors' discrete treatment and referral decisions. However, there is considerable range in what constitutes utilization review and in the severity of constraints on clinical freedom. It matters who is doing the reviews, how intrusive they are, and what criteria are used. Utilization review practices can range from requiring doctors to obtain the advance approval of the health plan for referrals to specialists and elective hospital stays, to health plans monitoring hospital stays while in progress to ensure that treatment is medically warranted, or retrospectively denying payment to doctors for care that the plan later deems inappropriate. With preauthorization, allied health professionals such as nurses are often the ones who scrutinize physician practice patterns, though problem cases are then referred to the medical director who is a doctor. Physicians themselves may also monitor their colleagues' treatment decisions through formal peer-review committees within medical groups or health plans. Some review organizations are more or less willing to accommodate the views of physicians in question or to incorporate medical advances developed in scientific journals into their review criteria (Schlesinger, Gray, and Perreira 1997). All of these techniques challenge the notion of absolute clinical freedom of the solo practitioner model. Doctors are more likely to regard preauthorization, reviews of discrete treatment decisions, and encounters with nurse reviewers as an affront to their clinical freedom, but more likely to accept peer-review committees.[46]

Not only are such review procedures unpopular with physicians and patients, they may not produce the hoped-for cost savings. Preauthorization procedures require an army of reviewers and entail high administrative costs that may negate the potential savings from refusing to pay for medically questionable treatments. Recognizing this, some managed-care plans have abandoned preauthorization and ongoing reviews and instead provide doctors with year-end summaries that compare them with their peers in an effort to goad them to align their practice patterns to those of their colleagues. Aside from the administrative savings, retrospective summaries have the potential to improve relations between health plans and doctors, and they also offer some protection of HMOs from lawsuits since they are no longer reviewing and denying individual treatment decisions. Yet managed-care plans that have moved toward retrospective summaries still wield the weapons of capitation, discounted fee schedules, or termination of physician contracts to enforce cost discipline on physicians (Freudenheim 1999b, 1999c).

The great irony, then, is that physicians have seen a more precipitous decline in their power in the private market than they would have under national health insurance. To be sure, the Clinton plan relied heavily on managed-care plans and global budgeting to contain costs, both of which had implications for the autonomy of individual physicians. But Health Security also granted the medical profession a legally institutionalized role in governance through provider advisory boards, as well as recognized new forms of collective organizations of doctors in the health care marketplace. In the current environment, however, physicians have none of these legally backed roles in health care governance. Rather, their influence depends on their efforts to shape developments in the political arena and to organize as economic actors in the health care system itself. Physicians have pursued both routes in a belated counteroffensive to regain lost ground.

Medical associations have furiously lobbied state and federal governments to impose a range of controls on the capacity of managed-care plans to regulate physicians. They have fought for legal bans on gag rules and selective contracting, greater patient access to specialists, guaranteed outside appeals for denied claims, and expanded rights for patients to sue health plans. In these battles they have become strange bedfellows with consumer groups that in the past had challenged physician dominance and paternalism in their quest for "patients' rights" but now feared that quality of care was under threat by managed care. Though some of these measures may find common ground with consumer groups, there is also an element of self-interest at work, as doctors seek to recapture their professional autonomy and prerogatives and safeguard their incomes. The medical profession has scored some successes with its political strategy.[47] But success not only depends on overcoming HMOs, which complain that such regulations rob them of their cost-containment weapons, but also the ambivalence of many doctors about assuming an explicitly political role.[48]

Increasingly, physicians are organizing collectively to increase their power in the market. More doctors are choosing to practice in larger group settings, while others have joined forces with hospitals to form integrated delivery systems to face down insurers. Some physicians have bypassed HMOs entirely by forming their own physician-sponsored organizations (PSOs). Under this kind of arrangement, doctors own their own health plan, assume financial risk for providing care, and bargain directly with employers to insure their work force (Kuttner 1997).[49] Finally, more physicians in the private sector are joining unions. Indeed, in a remarkable reversal of its long-standing opposition to unionization, the AMA in 1999 pledged to create a union for salaried doctors and medical residents and to seek changes in antitrust law to permit it to organize self-employed physicians.[50]

Doctors' efforts to organize, along with the AMA's support, mark a sea change in medical politics. They are a striking reversal of the AMA's long-standing notion of professionalism that derided unions and of its decades-long battle against organizational forms that threatened solo practice. The embrace of these new organizations also suggests how far the medical profession has fallen from its promontory atop the health care system and its desperate effort to recapture its former dominance. Still, the AMA's decision to endorse private-sector unionization was controversial, passing the House of Delegates only by a narrow margin and over the opposition of the association's Executive. The decision pitted younger, more radical members against older, more conservative doctors. To reassure the latter, the AMA pledged that its union would not strike and would focus on improving patient care rather than economic issues (Greenhouse 1999b).

The future survival of both types of organization is uncertain. The government's recognition of PSOs marks a partial shift in antitrust policy, which has long prohibited physicians from collectively setting fees (Kuttner 1997). But the obstacles to their survival are more economic than legal. The number of PSOs remains small, largely because they require substantial time and monetary commitments from physicians; because of their late entry into the market and the huge start-up costs involved, their chances of survival are slim. The prognosis for unionization of self-employed doctors is also uncertain, especially if such efforts run afoul of federal antitrust law or encounter physician resistance.[51] Still, doctors have belatedly realized that they must organize economically and politically if they hope to recapture some of the autonomy and power lost to insurers and employers.

Costs Saved and Incurred

Managed care has posted impressive cost-containment gains. Between 1993 and 1996, the period of rapid managed-care growth, the real per capita health care spending growth rate averaged only 1.5 percent per year, compared with a 5 percent annual rate between 1970 and 1993 (Smith et al. 1998, 128–29). The spread of managed care in the private, employment-based health care system revolutionized modes of delivery, remuneration, and power relations in ways that brought cost discipline to bear on health care actors. With its tools of capitation or discounted fee-for-service and restricted access to hospitals and specialists, managed care has wrung out much of the excess capacity in the health care system. A strong economy with low general and health care inflation also helped such impressive figures (Levit et al. 1997; Smith et al. 1998).

But the cost-containment victory may prove ephemeral. Experts estimate that real per capita health spending will grow at a clip of 3.4 percent each year from 1997 to 2007, and that the percentage of GDP devoted to health care spending will rise from 13.6 percent in 1996 to 16.6 percent in 2007 (Smith et al. 1998, 128–29; see also table 11, column 1, in the present volume). Likewise, employers have seen their premiums spike in recent years. The premium hikes, however, as well as the projected increases in health spending more generally, are well below the torrid rate of the inflation-ravaged 1980s, when fee-for-service ruled supreme.[52]

The reasons for the expected cost increases are varied. With mergers and acquisitions among plans and providers reaching a saturation point, the days of easy savings for HMOs have probably come to an end. Managed-care plans can no longer count on enrolling healthier, less expensive patients. If they want to grow in the future, they will increasingly have to accept those who are sicker and more expensive to treat, such as the uninsured or those in Medicare or Medicaid. In addition, after years of belt-tightening to expand market share or to accommodate employer demands for lower costs, HMOs have hiked premiums in order to restore profitability. Another reason lies in the growing dissatisfaction with HMOs, as patients have demanded greater choices and access to specialists. Many employers have accommodated their demands by offering plans with fewer controls and looser physician networks, allowing patients greater freedom of access to physicians of their choice. But as looser networks with weaker utilization controls have become more common in recent years, the cost of choice has translated into higher premiums. Doctors and hospitals, too, are behind the cost push, organizing themselves into larger networks to combat employers and health plans. In some markets, these integrated networks of providers have outmuscled employers and health plans.[53] State and federal laws mandating new benefits and loosening controls over doctors have also added to insurers' costs.[54] Finally, some secular pressures may be too difficult even for managed care to contain, such as an aging population with costly chronic or acute illnesses to treat, and continuing advances in expensive medical technologies.[55]

Political Consequences of Market Reform and the Broader Debate over Public and Private Social Protection

Clinton hoped to harness the market toward public ends by embedding it in a newly created branch of social insurance. But what the United States got instead was unmanaged competition led by private actors. This kind of market reform has had both immediate and long-term political ramifications that extend beyond the borders of the health care arena.

Aside from wanting to repair the creaking health care system, Clinton's Health Security plan was part of a broader electoral strategy designed to construct a realignment based on Democratic hegemony. National health insurance would guarantee universal access and a substantial role for the state in health care governance, thus appealing to traditional Democratic constituents. But managed competition was a hallmark of New Democrat thinking, which proposed cooperation between the public and private sectors and the harnessing of market forces to social ends. Thus, the new approach to the market and government was intended to appeal to middle-class voters as well. The Clinton plan's cross-class appeal would overcome "wedge issues" that had divided the party in the past and would deliver a new and enduring Democratic majority (Weir 1998, chap. 1).

However, the Clinton plan also figured into the quite different electoral designs of the Republican party. For Republicans, defeating the president's plan was central to their ambition to wrest Congress from the hands of the Democrats in 1994 and eventually to capture the White House. For both parties, health care reform was also part of a broader crusade to redefine the role of the state and market in social protection. New Democrats saw the state as guaranteeing basic social protections, even if not directly providing them. Republicans hoped to reduce the role of government in social provision and in the economy (Johnson and Broder 1997, xiii–xiv; Skocpol 1996, chap. 5, esp. 143–46; Weir 1998, chap. 1).

The 1994 elections, which returned Republican majorities to both houses of Congress, dashed Clinton's hopes for a new realignment. It also signaled a rightward shift in the center of political gravity. The clearest indication of this was the 1996 abolition of AFDC, the federal cash welfare program. The law was the handiwork of a bipartisan effort. But this piece of legislation was not simply the fruit of a neoliberal surge within the Republican party and its allies that pushed Clinton to the right. Rather, the Democrats themselves also shared responsibility for the rightward shift in ideas and policies. Such a process had been taking place within the Democratic party in the decades before Clinton entered the White House, with the waning of progressive forces, the growing prominence of the New Democrat wing, and augmented influence of conservative forces in the South and West in the party.[56] As we have seen, Clinton and his New Democrat compatriots articulated and pursued a more conservative, market-friendly agenda: seeking to forge a new partnership between public and private, harnessing market forces toward social ends, and promoting individual responsibility as a condition for government assistance to help the poor and disadvantaged do better in the market (Weir 1998, 27–28). In health care, managed competition embedded in social insurance was consistent with that vision.

Yet, subsequent events showed that neither party could claim victory for its broader vision of the respective roles for the state and market in health care and social protection more generally. Clinton and Congress became embroiled in a bitter standoff over Medicare reform and budget cuts in 1995 and 1996 that prompted two government shutdowns and eventually a grudging compromise. Divided government continued for the next four years following the 1996 elections. Clinton's reelection and reduced majorities in Congress made it difficult for either party or branch to advance its social and health policy agenda. The standoff has continued under Clinton's successor, George W. Bush, whose Republican party lost control of the Senate and has a bare majority in the House of Representatives. Not surprisingly, questions concerning the federal government's role in regulating managed care and private insurance and the position of the medical profession in health care governance have thus far remained a stalemate.

These questions of health care governance are part of a broader debate about redefining the role of the state and private actors in social provision, from health care and pensions to assistance and employment of the poor. That debate is far from settled and is likely to engage both parties and the public for some time to come.

Conclusion

The Limits of Markets in Health Care

This book has explored health care cost-containment reforms in Britain, Germany, and the United States through the analytical lens of sectoral governance. I investigated the extent to which such reforms relied on markets or other instruments to tame medical power and to conform it to the goal of cost containment.

This concluding chapter brings the three cases together to answer the following questions. First, how has an analytical framework linking the political and sectoral arenas helped us understand the connection between politics and policy-making to explain reform outcomes and the different ways of using markets in the health care sector in each nation? Second, how do the health care reform experiences of the three countries illuminate issues of sectoral governance? What do they suggest about the limits to and reach of medical power, markets, and the state for this particular area of social protection? Finally, what lessons do the three cases provide for the reform of systems of social protection more generally?

The Politics of Market Reform: Linking the Political and Sectoral Arenas

Britain, Germany, and the United States sought to curb physician power through distinctive uses of markets and other governance instruments. Moreover, their markets varied in terms of who constructed them, what the targets were, and the scope and degree of competition permitted. In Britain, the Thatcher government sought to shatter the corporatist-statist edifice in the National Health Service with the hammer of the market. Competition would undermine the collective bases of medical power and transform the profession into a multitude of atomized purchasers and providers. Along with new tools of oversight, competition would also make for more assertive managers who would demand more cost-effective behavior from the medical profession. But as it unfolded under John Major, the internal market involved a parallel enhancement of central state control, with government ministers and central bureaucrats imposing the market in the NHS from above and taking great care to constrain its scope and pace. Moreover, while setting new limits to the exercise of medical power, the Conservative government stopped short of destroying corporatism. Under Tony Blair's stewardship, the NHS has seen a further retreat from competition and a restoration of the corporatist-statist hybrid that Thatcher had sought to destroy. In short, the emergent governance regime in the NHS is a new hybrid that combines stronger state hierarchy, circumscribed corporatism, and a limited market that emphasizes collaborative exchange rather than cutthroat competition.

In Germany, Helmut Kohl's reform recipe called for a particular mixture of corporatism, state intervention, and market incentives. But rather than seeking to destroy corporatism and replace it with a market, Kohl continued to work through it to curb physician power and to strengthen insurers—and thereby to correct its imbalances. At the same time, the government embarked upon a cautious market experiment whose primary goal was to rectify glaring inequities of the health care system. But the market was also supposed to encourage insurers to seek cost-effective treatments from doctors and to substitute for repeated and enduring state entanglement in the day-to-day tasks of sectoral administration. In the end the government sharply delineated the scope of permissible competition and allowed it to operate only at the margins of corporatist governance. Moreover, since it was targeted at insurers and largely sidestepped the issue of selective contracting with doctors, the market stopped well short of destroying the monopoly position of the medical profession.

The United States displayed yet another type of market reform that differed starkly from British and German restraint. Like his British and German colleagues, Bill Clinton proposed that the government take a leading role in constructing and regulating the market and embedding it in a statutory guarantee of universal access. But with the failure to enact his proposals, the United States got a kind of market reform that departed significantly from Clinton's vision and the state-created, state-controlled market experiments of Britain and Germany. Instead, U.S. market reform has been a chaotic, largely unregulated process led by private employers pushing insurers, with government actors playing a mostly reactive and peripheral role. The brute force of the market has challenged medical power and autonomy to a degree unparalleled in Britain or Germany.

Each of these distinct reform outcomes was the product of a particular nation's health care politics. These politics, in turn, arose from actors and institutions in the political and health care systems, and the interplay among them. The institutions and balance of forces in the political arena determined whether reform legislation was enacted or not. But the particular configuration of actors and institutions in the health sector in no small part influenced how policymakers and health care stakeholders defined the problems in health care and the appropriate solutions. Existing governance arrangements in the health care system also provided or denied state actors the means to intervene in the health sector and to control the pace and scope of market reform in its implementation.

Institutions and actors in the political arena affected the ability of government actors to formulate and enact a radical reform program for the health sector. Political systems that centralized decision making gave the executive the capacity to unilaterally decide the terms of reform legislation. But systems that dispersed decision-making authority among different branches or levels of government or that gave sectoral interests avenues to influence the legislative process needed negotiation and compromise for reform legislation to pass. Compared to Helmut Kohl or Bill Clinton, Margaret Thatcher enjoyed enormous advantages in formulating and enacting a radical program. She could and did exclude most health care interest groups and the opposition parties from the review process that devised the internal market reforms. Moreover, the benefits of single-party government, party discipline, and an overwhelming legislative majority made it relatively easy to enact her reform agenda.

In Germany, the political system dispersed authority through coalition governments, federalism, and consultation with interest groups (Katzenstein 1987). These conditions made it difficult for the Kohl government to invoke its authority to set the parameters of the health care system. Nevertheless, health minister Seehofer achieved this rare success in 1992 through a masterful strategy of selective exclusion and inclusion, which shut out doctors from meaningful negotiations and which produced a compromise with the CDU, the opposition SPD, and the state governments against the wishes of the FDP and its health care clients.

In the United States, separation of powers, independent congressional parties, and fragmented interest groups with entry to a porous legislative process placed formidable obstacles in the path of Clinton's bid to magnify the role of the state in the private, employment-based health care system. Successful enactment of his plan required a strategy of negotiation and compromise with key stakeholders. But Clinton's closed process of policy formulation was ill-suited to these institutional and political realities. Moreover, potential allies, unable to bridge their own indecision and dissension, failed to deliver their support to the president or did so when it was far too late. This was not only true of the president's party in Congress and traditional Democratic constituencies like labor and seniors, but also of key health care stakeholders like large employers sympathetic to the Clinton plan. Unable or unwilling to support the president, these actors ceded the field to well-organized opponents of reform.

This analysis thus leads to two general conclusions about the effects of political institutions on policy outcomes. First, policymakers must work with the institutional and political terrain at hand—even an apparently hostile terrain—if they are to achieve their policy goals. Seehofer did that, turning conditions of divided government and federalism to his advantage to enact the GSG. Clinton, on the other hand, failed to enact his reform plan not least because his reform strategy disregarded the political and institutional environment he faced. In short, institutions can be strategic instruments that policymakers can use to their advantage.

Second, while political institutions can provide sectoral interests avenues to block policy initiatives, these institutions are not the sole determinant of the influence of these actors in the policy process. Rather, the organizational characteristics of interest groups themselves and their capacity to take purposive collective action also matter. In the United States, for example, key stakeholders like large employers and the medical profession were largely impotent in the battle over the Clinton plan not because they were denied access to the legislative process but because of their organizational disarray and hesitant policy stance. In their reluctance to support the Clinton plan, they ceded the political battle to other interests who were better organized and more adept in mobilizing opposition to reform at the legislative stage.

But the story of health care reform did not end at the legislative stage. Rather, major reform of systems of social protection can occur even when state efforts fail. Private market actors in the United States have radically transformed the health care delivery system and its underlying governance arrangements through the market after Clinton's initiative failed to get off the ground. State and federal authorities have played a game of regulatory catch-up with rapidly moving market developments. Alternatively, sectoral actors may brake or thwart the implementation of legislation that has been enacted, as the KVs did with the 1989 health care reform legislation in Germany. Such intransigence then prompted a more vigorous reform effort with the GSG.

Existing institutions, policies, and governance arrangements in the health sector also constrained or permitted policymakers to take an active role in molding and regulating the market. In other words, the health sector provided or denied state actors the capacity to set the terms of the market and control the behavior of sectoral actors. That capacity operated as the *legitimacy* of state intervention as well as *institutional linkages* allowing state actors to intervene in the health care system and set the terms of the market. Let us take each point in turn.

First each nation's health care system institutionalized particular understandings and expectations regarding the appropriate role of the state and the market in the sector. The statutory, universal health care systems of Britain and Germany reflected and reinforced broad solidarities that defined equity as equality, as universal access to the same level of quality care regardless of ability to pay, and justified these as social rights of citizenship. Their universalism and broad risk-pooling bound the middle class, the working class, and the poor to a common interest in ensuring access to quality care and generated expectations among voters (and most political parties) that the state should act as the guarantor of universal access.[1] These expectations held not only for the British NHS, where the central government played a dominant role in financing and providing health care and in administering the system, and where parliamentary accountability centralized responsibility in the political arena. Such expectations also held for Germany's national insurance system: even though the federal government did not directly finance or provide care, it still bore the responsibility and the authority to set the system's overall parameters to ensure universal access to care. Policymakers in both countries could ill afford to ignore such expectations; therefore, they carefully controlled the play of market forces in health care to avoid serious inequities.

Health care systems based on voluntary fringe benefits and private insurance, by contrast, erected formidable legitimacy barriers to public intervention. As we saw in the United States, employers, who were critical players in the reform debate by virtue of their role in financing health insurance, viewed Clinton's national health insurance proposal as illegitimate government intrusion in their managerial prerogative to decide the terms of fringe benefits. Their fears, as well as those of many private insurers, influenced public opinion and fed public doubts over "big government." On similar grounds, employers and insurers have resisted subsequent federal efforts to erect a uniform regulatory framework for the private market.

In short, different health care systems posed the question of the proper reach of the state and the market in opposite terms. In Britain and Germany, the question centered on "how much market." Compulsory, universal health care granted governments not only the statutory authority but also the legitimacy to set the parameters of the health care system and to safeguard its solidarity. In the United States, however, the question was "how much state." Under the private, voluntary system of fringe benefits, many stakeholders viewed an expansion of government authority in sectoral governance as illegitimate.

Second, existing governance arrangements accorded or denied state actors the institutional capacity to intervene in the health sector, to control the behavior of its constituent actors, and to shape the contours of their markets. In Britain, the hierarchical administrative tiers in the NHS linked the central government officials to the health service, allowing them to impose and control the pace and scope of marketization from above. The NHS hierarchy paralleled the unitary government structures that culminated in parliamentary accountability for NHS performance in the political arena. In Germany, corporatist public-law associations gave the federal government leverage to control the behavior of sectoral actors. State actors could mandate new policy tasks on them, such as competition for patients by insurers, as well as set limits to their competitive behavior, for example, through the risk-adjustment scheme. In the United States, by contrast, regulatory federalism erected institutional barriers to effective regulation of private, employment-based insurance. Federal and state actors often worked at cross-purposes, leaving a regulatory vacuum in their wake.

The British and German markets thus approximated "quasi-markets" (Bartlett and Le Grand 1993; Le Grand and Bartlett 1993a) or "planned markets" (Saltman and Otter 1992). State actors introduced market mechanisms into public or quasi-public service delivery systems (Bartlett and Le Grand 1993; Le Grand and Bartlett 1993a, 1993b). They took the lead in constructing the market and deployed market instruments selectively in order to realize their public policy goals (Saltman and Otter 1992, 16–18). The conscious and careful use of markets by state actors as an instrument of governance stands in stark contrast to what Saltman and Otter have termed "regulated markets" (ibid.). In the latter, the stance of state actors is reactive, seeking to curb the behavior of powerful private actors in an existing market. State efforts at regulation are difficult, subject to capture by these interests (ibid.). The experience of the United States with unmanaged competition vividly demonstrates the barriers that government actors face in controlling actors and events in a "regulated market."

The terminology used by Saltman and Otter probably overstates the degree of state control in both types of markets. As we have seen, even the planned markets in Britain and Germany have involved trial and error, uncertainty about outcomes, and sometimes heavy-handed intervention by state actors in response to immediate political pressures rather than dispassionate, long-term planning. Likewise, their term *regulated market* suggests that the state can and does regulate the behavior of market actors, which may not be the case in actual practice.

In sum, the interaction of political and sectoral actors and institutions produced different kinds of markets in health care. In the United States, a political system that dispersed decision making through independent (and sometimes undisciplined) congressional parties and gave fragmented interest groups access to the policy process required compromise and negotiation with an array of stakeholders for the enactment of major policy reforms. In addition, the liberal health care system's voluntarism and private financing of health care meant an array of private actors opposed to reform. The political system gave them the entry to resist state efforts to create a market in health care, and the private health care system left government with very limited means to control the pace of market developments subsequently unleashed by private actors. In Germany, the political and health care arenas afforded key stakeholders opportunities to influence the kind of market reform, but also granted the state the authority and institutional capacity to set the parameters of competition. Coalition governments, federalism, electoral outcomes, and interest group consultation gave different stakeholders entry to the legislative process and required negotiation and compromise for the passage of reform legislation. Thus, the design of the market satisfied advocates of solidarity as well as protected the medical profession's monopoly, reflecting the different strength of a variety of stakeholders over time. Corporatist governance of national health insurance required state actors to work with entrenched sectoral interests at the stage of implementation but also gave policymakers some leverage to set limits to their market behavior. In Britain, centralized decision making in the political arena made enactment of radical legislation relatively easy, at least compared with Germany and the United States, and hierarchical administration of health care granted the state the wherewithal to introduce its market reforms. Still, the prominence of the central government in health care financing, administration, and provision, along with a highly visible mechanism of political accountability in the parliamentary arena, meant that central government actors could not escape responsibility for NHS performance. As a result, policymakers sought to contain the market to prevent outcomes that violated solidarity.

The Place and Boundaries of Medical Influence

The health care cost-containment projects in all three countries sought to alter existing governance arrangements with physicians. But in recasting those bargains, governments and payers had to address a difficult dilemma. They believed it necessary to curb medical autonomy and influence if they hoped to control health care costs. But a certain amount of professional autonomy was needed to assure quality of care and public confidence in the health care system. The task was to strike an acceptable balance between cost control and medical autonomy.

In this section I first describe how far the political settlements with physicians have changed in the three countries. I then argue that there are good reasons to accord a place to doctors in health care policy-making and governance, though limits to that power are also necessary. Drawing on the reform experiences of our three countries, I suggest that certain kinds of governance may resolve this dilemma better than others.

New Political Settlements with Physicians

In all three countries, health care cost-containment reforms altered the political settlements with physicians. Doctors experienced new limits to their influence over policy and to their professional freedom. But in Britain and Germany, there were also continuities with prior corporatist settlements that preserved medical power and autonomy. By contrast, doctors in the United States, who had enjoyed much greater professional freedom than their British and German colleagues, saw a much more precipitous decline in their autonomy and policy influence. Having never had to assume responsibility for public policy under corporatism, U.S. doctors lacked a legal anchor in health care governance and sufficiently strong organizational resources to withstand the market onslaught against the autonomy of solo practice. Let us examine the changes to these settlements, starting first with a discussion of corporatist arrangements and then the professional model.

British and German doctors learned a hard lesson about the limits of their power in determining health policy. Neither clinical expertise nor an official, corporatist role in sectoral governance translated into an automatic right to determine the fundamental parameters of the health care system. When pressed, Thatcher and Kohl declared certain matters nonnegotiable. Britain's internal market reforms, and Germany's GSG (which ushered in a market experiment and vigorous state intervention in sectoral administration) involved only perfunctory consultations with medical associations. These were a far cry from genuine negotiations that granted the medical profession a right of veto. Furthermore, even though Major and Kohl resumed talks with doctors on questions of implementation, neither the BMA nor the KBV were able to dissuade them from their decision to press ahead with their reform programs.

The reforms also challenged physician dominance of health care administration in both countries. The Conservatives banished the BMA and its associated bodies from representation on health authorities and the boards of hospital trusts, and Blair has continued with this policy. British governments also sought to strengthen managers by granting them new authority to monitor doctors' performance. Though Kohl expanded the scope of corporatist bargaining to new areas of the health care system, he, too, pursued a countervailing power strategy by requiring that the KVs share power with the sickness funds in an expanding list of joint tasks. But policymakers in Britain and Germany stopped well short of abandoning corporatism, instead resuming negotiations with medical associations on the details of implementation and continuing to accord them a role in carrying out policies and administering the health sector.

Unlike their colleagues in Britain or Germany, however, doctors in the United States never had either an official insider position in policy formation or the public duty to act as an agent of the state implementing policies on its behalf. To be sure, the Clinton plan would have given doctors legally recognized rights of consultation on health policy. But its legislative demise put to rest this change in physician status. The AMA's influence over policy has instead rested on its ability to act as a pressure group from the outside, lobbying lawmakers and forging alliances with other interests—often with business groups—to defeat government proposals that threatened its interests and those of its members. But its power as a pressure group had significantly eroded by the 1990s. Precipitous membership losses over previous decades undermined its claim to be the exclusive voice of the profession. Moreover, its business allies had now become its foes, as employers seeking to control their health outlays embraced managed care and its techniques to rein in medical autonomy. The policy victories that the AMA and its state and local counterparts have achieved more recently have required them to build new coalitions with consumer groups against managed care.

In all three countries, the reforms have altered power relations within the medical profession to varying degrees, largely to the benefit of primary care doctors. In Britain, general practitioners recovered a voice over hospital care that they had lost with the creation of the NHS in 1948. Though fundholders were initially the beneficiaries of this newfound influence, Blair has promised to extend it to all GPs who are willing to get involved in purchasing hospital and community care services for patients in their locality. In Germany, the power of primary care remains a potential to be tapped. But primary care doctors could see greater influence once the revalued fee schedule takes hold and if experiments with gatekeeper family practitioners (*Hausärzte*) permitted by the 1977 legislation are expanded. In the United States, managed care has placed new emphasis on primary care, and in the more restrictive HMOs, primary care doctors have a pivotal role as gatekeepers to specialists and hospital care.

But the shifts among different subgroups within the medical profession are by no means settled. In fact, there are indications that specialists may be regaining some of their influence. Blair's new NHS accords them a greater voice in commissioning care, and the trend in the United States is toward less restrictive managed-care networks and legislation making it easier for patients to see the specialists of their choice.

The new bargains with doctors have also curbed their economic and social autonomy, but in different ways. As before, British doctors continue to accept salary or capitation and government-determined limits on their number and location. Likewise, German doctors must still observe regional fee schedules that their KVs negotiate on their behalf, and their fees still remain within a cap, though this has oscillated between budgets determined by state decree and the result of free collective bargaining. In addition, the Kohl government empowered KVs and insurers to limit where physicians can locate their practices. Relative to their British and German colleagues, American doctors have retained their edge in their income levels even under managed care. Even so, their incomes have risen more slowly than in the past as a result of the spread of capitation or steeply discounted fee-for-service. Most doctors in the United States also depend on managed-care contracts for their livelihood, and a growing number of them have forgone self-employment to become employees of such health plans. In addition, to a much greater degree than their European colleagues, American doctors have ceded to laypersons the determination of the scientific and technical content of their work which lies at the core of professional autonomy.

Indeed, the most striking change to the settlements with doctors in these countries has been the effect on clinical freedom. In all three countries, governments and payers put doctors on notice that they would now have to consider both the cost and clinical effectiveness of their treatment decisions and that such decisions would increasingly be held up to standardized guidelines and protocols. This has entailed the greater scrutiny of the clinical decisions of individual practitioners. Starting with the Conservatives' reforms and continuing with Blair, British policymakers have required all doctors to be subject to peer review. In Germany, for example, physicians must submit to more frequent economic monitoring by KVs and insurers; and the more restrictive U.S. managed-care plans prospectively review and authorize the treatment decisions and referrals of many physicians. Governments and payers have also relied on various budgeting schemes to shape clinical decisions in a less direct and intrusive fashion than detailed reviews. In Germany, the health ministry set prescribing budgets at the level of the KV and held doctors collectively liable for overruns, which had limited effect on prescribing behavior. Policymakers in Britain and Germany have also begun to develop target budgets to contain individual physician prescribing or remuneration. Similarly, many managed-care plans in the United States have put medical groups or individual doctors at financial risk for their treatment decisions.

A more significant redefinition of clinical autonomy has occurred at the collective level, as British and German governments have insisted that doctors share authority with laypersons in devising guidelines to be used in reviewing individual physician treatment decisions. No longer are such standards for the medical profession alone to determine. In Britain, Blair has gone where Thatcher refused to tread with his creation of two new national bodies, consisting of lay and medical representatives, to develop clinical guidelines and ensure that peer-review machinery is in place locally. In Germany, Kohl mandated that KVs and sickness funds negotiate guidelines and apply them to efficiency reviews of individual physicians. In both countries, such guidelines are supposed to contain criteria of cost as well as clinical effectiveness.

Still, American doctors have fared far worse in the battle to protect clinical freedom. The more restrictive managed-care plans rely on highly intrusive forms of utilization review, which entail nonphysician personnel, such as nurses, monitoring discrete medical decisions and possessing the authority to authorize or deny coverage of such treatments in advance. This is much greater micromanagement of medical practice than in Britain or Germany. Economic monitoring in Germany involves retrospective review of aggregate patterns of physician prescribing or practice, and doctors, along with sickness funds, conduct the reviews. In Britain, doctors alone scrutinize the clinical decisions of their peers, even if they are to use guidelines developed by the medical profession and laypersons. Moreover, governments in both countries are seeking uniformity in standards by mandating that clinical guidelines be developed at the national or regional level through negotiations between doctors and insurers or other lay authorities. And both countries's governments have assured the medical profession that it will continue to have a say in determining the content of its work, even if it is no longer the exclusive voice. In the United States, by contrast, medical organizations do not have a legally assured place to determine clinical guidelines, nor are managed-care plans and their reviewers legally bound to adhere to a set of uniform national or regional standards or procedures in their reviews. However, it appears that some American insurers are moving toward European practice by seeking to control physicians in less intrusive ways. Thus, some managed-care plans are relying on retrospective year-end reviews of clinical decisions along the lines of Germany's economic monitoring, and many use capitation schemes that require doctors to shoulder the financial risk of their treatment decisions. Such arrangements may be cheaper to administer and may retain the goodwill of doctors and patients better than detailed utilization reviews.

The Case for Medical Inclusion

Governments and payers therefore can approach the question of how to contain medical power in very different ways. They can simply try to vanquish doctors. Or they can attempt to forge a partnership with them in the quest for cost containment, which could imply a role in sectoral governance and some measure of professional autonomy. The latter approach carries with it benefits and risks, not only for doctors, but also for governments and patients; however, on balance, it will probably increase the chances that cost-containment efforts will succeed.

This point at first seems contradictory. After all, politicians, employers, or insurers in Britain, Germany, and the United States concluded that high health care costs were precisely due to the medical profession wielding too much autonomy—particularly in clinical matters—and excessive influence over policy. They expended considerable energy to rewrite the settlements with physicians in order to curb their power.

Even so, a strategy of inclusion may do better to assure the successful realization of cost containment than a strategy of imposition and exclusion. Whereas the latter is certain to invite the resentment and opposition of doctors, the former may win their acquiescence if not enthusiastic support. Giving doctors a say in negotiating and carrying out the details of implementation also gives them a stake in seeing that the reforms succeed. Making doctors responsible for reviewing the treatment decisions of their peers, rather than leaving the task to laypersons, can enhance the legitimacy of such curbs on clinical freedom in the eyes of doctors and the public.

Indeed, such inclusion can also serve as a form of "quality assurance" to offset the interests of payers or governments in reining in health care expenditures. Even if the variations in medical practice cannot be justified on scientific grounds, and even if there is a demonstrable need to base medical treatments on scientific data, most laypersons still lack the medical expertise of physicians which the latter have gained from years of training and practice. The need for medical expertise is warranted in decisions on the course of treatment for individual patients. But medical judgment may also be appropriate at higher levels of decision making and sectoral administration on broad clinical matters, such as in developing clinical guidelines against which to evaluate discrete treatment decisions or in deciding which services are medically necessary and should comprise the benefits package in statutory or private insurance plans.[2] However, this does not imply that the medical profession or its members be accountable only to themselves, as discussed below.

Granting physicians a voice in these broad areas of clinical decision making can also help sustain public trust in the health care system and in the project of cost containment itself. The need for medical inclusion is greater now in the era of austerity, as difficult rationing decisions will become more pressing and frequent. The question all countries will face is not whether to ration but how. It has long been recognized that patients' chances of recovering from illness are much better when they believe that their doctors are acting on their behalf. It is safe to say that most people will have more confidence in their doctor deciding what is medically necessary rather than in letting payers with a stake in lower health care costs exclusively make such a determination. Likewise, granting doctors the primary responsibility to monitor the treatment decisions of their members—even if they are required to do so and must justify their findings to lay authorities—can reinforce public trust in the system as a whole down to the level of the doctor-patient relationship.

Delegating the task of rationing to the medical profession may also benefit governments by deflecting some of the blame for austerity.[3] If doctors rather than state administrators or insurers review the treatment decisions of practitioners, and they base that review on guidelines developed with medical input as well as independently gleaned scientific evidence based on clinical trials, then rationing might appear fairer and legitimate in the eyes of the public. But this is not to argue that doctors will be able or willing to provide politicians political cover on fundamental questions of equity that may arise with rationing or that such questions should not be discussed openly in the political arena.[4] Moreover, the medical profession's reluctance to monitor and punish individual physicians for their treatment decisions suggests that such reviews may need to also involve insurers or state administrators.

Thus, the strategy of inclusion carries risks as well as benefits. Doctors may block reforms in the political arena or refuse to implement them in the health sector. Policymakers in all three countries have already concluded that medical autonomy cannot be exercised in the absolute, or else it will run up against fiscal limits. At the same time, however, there is a need to preserve some measure of professional autonomy, especially in the area of clinical questions, while not allowing physician influence to spill over into other areas in which their claims to expertise are not valid (Freidson 1970). But how can policymakers resolve this dilemma? Do some forms of governance hold out better possibilities for this than others?

Striking a New Balance? The Promise and Limits of Corporatism

Based on the three cases presented here, I suggest that corporatism—or at least some form of negotiation with the medical profession within limits—is the best way to resolve this dilemma. Corporatism is an inclusive approach to dealing with doctors. Through it, the state recognizes that the medical profession has a legitimate voice in negotiating the terms and conditions of service for doctors. Corporatism also accepts that doctors can have a legitimate role in deciding how to implement government policy and that they should have considerable freedom to do so in running the health care system.

However, corporatist governance also sets limits to medical power. In Britain and Germany, corporatism does not extend to the medical profession an automatic veto over what state actors consider fundamental questions of health care system organization and governance. It also permits the state the authority and means to mandate public policy obligations on doctors in exchange for their privileged position in policy-making. Furthermore, if doctors fail to fulfill their policy obligations, corporatism allows the state to overrule the profession, to suspend negotiations and self-administration, and instead to rule the sector directly, albeit on an emergency basis. Corporatist arrangements can also be redefined by state actors. Under the new bargains emerging in Britain and Germany, for example, state actors have narrowed the scope of professional autonomy, even in areas long considered the exclusive domain of doctors. The clearest example of this is in clinical matters, with governments in both countries mandating that medical associations work with managers or insurers to devise treatment guidelines.

At the same time, however, corporatism sets limits to state encroachment and recognizes the value of including the organized medical profession in health care governance. Including doctors at an early stage of policy development may increase the chances that they will comply with the policies that emerge because they have had a say in devising them. This would imply that corporatism is better able to adapt to new policy requirements than is commonly assumed and is not simply a recipe for rigidity, deadlock, and veto by entrenched interests as some of its critics suggest. Though it is too early to say how the issue of clinical guidelines will play out, it may serve as an example of corporatism's adaptability to new cost-containment tasks. Although governments in Britain and Germany have required doctors to negotiate with lay authorities these treatment guidelines, medical associations still play a major part in this task. By requiring doctors and laypersons to negotiate these protocols, governments there recognize that clinical guidelines are not solely based in science but are also a political exercise that needs medical inclusion and bargained consent from both sides if they are to be accepted. Similarly, granting the medical profession a leading if not exclusive role in reviewing medical decisions may make its members more willing to comply with such decisions.

A further advantage of corporatism, at least from the standpoint of government policymakers, is that it may be an effective way to delegate politically explosive rationing decisions to doctors and other sectoral actors and to increase public acceptance of these decisions. The exchange of clinical freedom for rationing has long been at the heart of the "implicit concordat" in the NHS. Doctors and the public have tolerated the waiting lists so long as they are seen as based on medical need rather than ability to pay, inefficiencies, or underinvestment in the health service. In Germany, too, mandates on physicians and insurers to devise guidelines and apply them in reviewing physician practice patterns serve a similar function.

The counterexample is the recent history of managed care in the United States. The medical profession's role in devising clinical guidelines and in reviewing treatment decisions of individual doctors has been at the heart of the battle over managed care and legislative efforts to rein in insurers through mandatory outside appeals mechanisms for decisions to deny care. Doctors are aggrieved at their loss of control over clinical decisions, and there is widespread public unease that rationing by insurers, who have an interest in lowering their health care outlays, will compromise quality of care. Creating formal structures that would include doctors and payers in devising clinical standards and in reviewing practitioners might not only appease the medical profession. It might also reassure the public that quality of care—at least as measured by medical expertise—has not been sacrificed and thereby make rationing more acceptable.

Still, like any other form of governance, corporatism is prone to failure unless certain prerequisites are met. As health care has shown, medical associations must be willing and able to police their members and deliver their compliance to agreements negotiated with the state or insurers. But the danger is that doctors (or even insurers) will use their privileged position in governance to block reforms in the political arena or in the health care system. Germany's variant of corporatism provides the KVs with the means to discipline their members through compulsory membership, through their exclusive agency in negotiating and disbursing physician remuneration, and through efficiency reviews of clinical practice. Even so, these weapons do not always assure that they have the will to do so, as the ongoing struggle over clinical guidelines and prescribing budgets indicates. British governments, too, have had a difficult relationship with the BMA, but not because the medical profession was too strong but because it was too weak. As a voluntary membership association whose rank and file have had a substantial voice in determining policy, the BMA has sometimes been unable to deliver its membership to agreements reached with the state. Governments in the two countries have responded to corporatism's shortcomings by granting new authority in governance to NHS managers or sickness funds in order to act as countervailing power to physicians.

Ultimately, corporatism requires that state actors use their authority to set and enforce the rules of sectoral governance on its constituent actors. Thus governments in Britain and Germany have invoked their legal authority to enact new tasks of policy implementation for doctors. And state actors in both countries have made use of their institutional capacity to bypass recalcitrant physicians and directly administer the health sector, at least until doctors decided to take up their obligations. In Britain, this has meant imposing reforms on the profession through the cadre of NHS managers, and in Germany it has taken the form of budgeting by decree.

Even when these conditions are met, corporatism still may not be able to solve all the problems of a sector. Governments may delegate tasks that overwhelm sectoral associations. British and German austerity policies, for example, have opened up distributional conflicts within the BMA and KVs that have in turn undermined their ability to represent the medical profession with one voice and deliver their members to agreements reached with the state or insurers. Should these distributional conflicts worsen, they could lead to major changes in the roles of medical associations in sectoral governance. For example, German doctors unhappy with the straitjacket of sectoral budgets might succeed in persuading policymakers or KV leaders to allow greater room for direct contracting between insurers and subgroups of doctors. If devolved forms of bargaining became widespread, the KVs would lose some of their authority to exclusively negotiate physician conditions of service, though the loss of power might be offset by the acquisition of new tasks, such as devising clinical guidelines for the health sector. Such a change in KV status would nevertheless signal a redefinition—though not necessarily the absolute demise—of corporatism.

Alternatively, government policies may strain relations between state actors and sectoral associations to the breaking point. In Britain, for example, the settlement between the state and physicians came under serious strain as doctors maintained that Thatcher's funding policies had made their job of rationing unbearable. Under Blair, there appears to have been a rapprochement, with the profession declaring its willingness to take up this task as long as its position in policy-making and governance is assured and the government commits adequate resources. In Germany, too, requiring KVs to assume collective financial liability for aggregate physician prescribing has placed them under enormous strain. Though the government has expanded the reach of corporatist negotiations to new areas of the health care system, it is far from certain that doctors have been happy with these new responsibilities.

Corporatist governance is also more precarious in liberal political economies like Britain and the United States, where voluntary membership organizations enjoy a greater degree of autonomy from the state than do associations bound by public law as in Germany. As we have seen, the BMA has sometimes been an inconstant corporatist partner with the state because it has not had the same controls over its membership as the German KVs. In the United States, corporatist governance would be an anomaly and would face significant obstacles to its introduction.[5] It would require changes to antitrust and labor law to permit private doctors to bargain collectively. For it to enjoy legitimacy, public suspicions of "special interests" would have to be overcome. State actors would have to secure more effective ways to mandate and enforce policy tasks on autonomous sectoral actors than they currently have in the private health care system. Any formal inclusion of American doctors in sectoral governance would also have to be consistent with American political traditions if it were to succeed. The model of public utility regulation, which would involve citizens and other stakeholders as well as the medical profession, is one possibility (Aaron 1996, 11); so is physician representation on independent panels that would review managed-care decisions. Or if national insurance ever came to pass, doctors might secure a legally recognized place in policymaking and administration. Were state sponsorship strategies to fail, then U.S. doctors might influence policy-making and administration in other ways, through traditional lobbying in the political arena or through novel efforts to organize and amass economic power in the marketplace.

These cautions highlight the danger of simply importing one nation's governance arrangements into another country's health care system and suggest instead that foreign models must be adapted to fit the host country.[6] Bearing this caveat in mind, it still appears that some form of negotiation and inclusion, whether through corporatism or some other arrangement, still appears to be a better way to assure yet restrict medical influence in policy and administration than either state hierarchy or market competition. Detailed directives emanating from the central government are likely to be too rigid and inflexible to adapt to local conditions or the needs of patients on the ground and may entail detailed micromanagement of clinical practice. Nor do markets relieve the state or private payers from intrusive monitoring of clinical practice, as the experiences of Britain and the United States have shown. Moreover, when such monitoring is done exclusively by lay authorities in a climate of intense price competition or severe budgetary austerity, it threatens to erode public trust in the health care system as a whole. Corporatism, by contrast, gives the state the possibility of limiting its interventions to the broad outlines of policy without getting enmeshed in detailed management of medical practice, yet still according a place to medical expertise in policy, health system governance, and clinical decisions.

Markets and Health Care: A Cautionary Tale

Did Markets Meet Health Policy Goals?

Market prescriptions became fashionable in the debates over social policy reform in the 1980s and 1990s. Market experiments also figured in the health care reform projects in our three countries. But how well did markets do? We can judge these experiments on whether they met the goals of their proponents and whether they met the goals of health policy. Market advocates argue that their approach gives consumers more choices, thus forcing service providers to be more responsive or else lose business. Competition on price also prods producers and purchasers of services to seek greater efficiencies and cost savings. But health care systems are judged against these and other goals, which may vary over time and among countries, with different nations settling for different balances among them. Cost containment and quality have become more prominent criteria in all three countries in recent decades. Though quality can be measured and defined in different ways, in recent decades, it has come to mean whether the inputs to health care (the money spent and treatments provided) yield effective outcomes (that is, health improvements). In some countries, greater responsiveness of their health care systems to patients has become prominent. Finally, equitable access to care has been a basic criterion of health care system performance. Indeed, because the issue of the market's effect on equity has been the most contentious aspect of such reforms, I discuss it at length in a separate section.

We begin our assessment by considering whether markets have helped contain health care expenditures. Market proponents argue that one of the main benefits of competition is that it will produce efficiencies that ultimately will lower costs. But markets can entail high start-up and maintenance costs. One of the hallmarks of the British NHS prior to the internal market was its lean management. But the introduction of the internal market brought with it high management costs. The market required an army of managers to develop prices and negotiate contracts, and the government made generous financial payments to GPs to help defray the start-up costs associated with fundholding.[7] The situation was similar in the United States, except that the bureaucracy was private rather than public. Indeed, one of the chief features of American managed care has been its reliance on a bevy of administrators and clerical personnel to monitor the treatment and referral decisions of doctors. Physicians, too, have complained that the myriad referral rules and different claims forms from competing health plans have required them to hire additional administrative and clerical staff to deal with the managed-care bureaucracy.

Of course, one could argue that the NHS prior to the Thatcher government reforms had been undermanaged and that better management has improved information on NHS performance. Similarly, one could argue that competition has produced more efficient health care provision that has offset the high transaction costs of the market. The evidence from the United States suggests that managed care contributed to slower rates of growth in health care spending in the mid-1990s. But as chapter 6 suggested, these savings have not been evenly shared. Much of the savings have accrued to larger market players able to negotiate lower premiums. But their cost-containment success is eroding the cross-subsidy for the uninsured, which threatens the financial survival of last-resort providers and thus the health care access for the most vulnerable members of society. Moreover, there are signs that the cost discipline of the mid-1990s was temporary, with health spending set to rise at an accelerating rate again as managed care has exhausted the easy savings from enrolling healthier patients and squeezing out excess capacity, and as patients demand fewer health plan restrictions on their choice of providers.[8]

In the quasi markets in Britain and Germany, moreover, the sharply restricted scope of competition makes it difficult to conclude that the market has been responsible for lower costs. The policy legacy of the restricted supply of hospitals and specialists in Britain meant that a competitive market could not emerge in many areas of the country. Even where there was a surplus of hospitals, as in London, policymakers sometimes preempted competition, as John Major did in deciding that an appointed commission should decide which hospitals should close or merge.

In both Britain and Germany, policymakers continued to rely on other policy instruments to contain health care expenditures. Britain's central governments have held down overall costs through global budgeting of health care under the watchful eye of the Treasury. Germany has limited aggregate health spending by linking it to the development of wages and salaries in the larger economy. But because free collective bargaining between sickness funds and providers does not always observe these limits, policymakers have also resorted to stronger cost-control mechanisms like budgets imposed by decree. Until the latest Blair reforms, Britain also kept a tight lid on the supply of hospitals and consultants, and it continues to limit access to both through gatekeeper GPs and waiting lists. Both countries have also limited physician incomes through capitation or salary (Britain) or binding fee agreements within a cap (Germany).

Still, these cost-control mechanisms were not without problems and encouraged policymakers to look to the market. Thatcher concluded that global budgets might effectively contain overall costs but were too blunt an instrument to guarantee microlevel efficiencies. National budget discipline and burgeoning waiting lists also imposed high political costs in terms of the government's popularity.[9] Kohl saw legally imposed budgets as no more than an emergency measure and disliked their intrusion on self-administration by doctors and insurers in the area of collective bargaining.

Policymakers in both nations saw markets as a promising way to enhance microlevel efficiencies and limit government involvement in detailed administration. But when all was said and done, they could not put their faith in the market alone to deliver cost containment.

Clinton shared their doubts about the ability of market competition to control costs and inserted the safeguard of a national budget cap in his version of managed competition. With the rejection of his proposal, however, the task of cost containment has fallen to the individual health plan. As we have seen, managed care has held down costs by putting providers at financial risk through capitation, or by bargaining steep discounts in fees, and by monitoring physician treatment decisions. But competition among health plans provides no guarantee that they will hold down costs; indeed, their recent market behavior suggests that they are raising premiums to recover lost profits.

Have markets preserved or improved quality of care? All three countries have moved to develop clinical guidelines that are grounded in science and that link treatment regimens to improved health outcomes and efficient use of resources. The United States has advanced furthest in this area, in large part because payers have not been able to rely on national budgeting mechanisms to hold down costs. Health plans and employers have thus had to search for other ways to control costs and have done so through various controls on utilization by providers and patients and by seeking to devise guidelines based in science and promising cost-effective outcomes. But the drive toward scientifically grounded outcomes is not exclusive to market arrangements. Demands for evidence-based medicine may emanate from the central government as part of a drive to improve hierarchical oversight of the health care system, as with Tony Blair. Likewise, Kohl's effort to introduce clinical guidelines began as an effort to improve corporatist performance under the GRG and predated his market experiment.

On other measures of quality, such as improved coordination of services, market competition may work in the opposite direction. Indeed, a major concern over Britain's internal market was that the sheer number and small size of fundholding practices would fragment the health service and undermine strategic purchasing and planning for a district's larger population. In response to these concerns, the Blair government abolished fundholding and created larger purchasers. And though the best managed-care plans emphasize preventive care and coordinated services, selective contracting in a competitive market can abruptly sever long-standing relationships between doctors and patients by limiting services to contractual providers. Some of the biggest complaints with American managed care have centered on this point, particularly when employers drop health plan choices, or health insurers sever contracts with providers. Moreover, quality measures in all countries remain underdeveloped, and many do not adequately measure health outcomes. The commonly used proxies to assess the quality of health plans, such as patient satisfaction surveys and report cards, may be good indicators of customer service but often do not measure whether the treatment a patient received produced a cure.

Have markets improved choice and responsiveness to patients? Again, the evidence is mixed. For blue-collar Germans, the market has given them greater freedom to choose their insurer. But in Britain's internal market, purchasers continued to make most choices about providers, even though many fundholders used their purchasing power to obtain prompter specialist services for them. In the United States, unmanaged competition actually reduced the choice of providers for many Americans as employers narrowed the range of health plans they offered to their workers and managed care plans restricted access to doctors. It has been the backlash to this kind of competition that has produced looser networks and greater choices.

But responsiveness can also mean broader accountability to the public or the community rather than to the individual patient or consumer.[10] In Britain's internal market, hospital Trusts resisted demands to open their board meetings or records on the grounds that these were proprietary information that should not be available to competitors. The Blair government has reversed these trends and strengthened consumer representation in NHS administration. In the United States, some of the disillusionment with managed care centers on the widespread sense that for-profit health plans are more accountable to their shareholders than to their patients or the broader communities they serve.

Markets and Equity

But it is the market's effect on equity that poses the greatest challenge to its legitimacy in health care. Markets provide powerful incentives for insurers and providers to avoid sicker and poorer individuals who are costly to cover or treat (see Enthoven 1993; Evans 1984). Insurers may respond to bad health risks in two ways. They may take a solidaristic path and spread the health care costs of such persons across a broad risk-pool through community rating or social insurance. Or they may seek to avoid such persons through underwriting practices that exclude costly medical conditions from coverage or that price insurance beyond their reach, or engage in subtle risk selection practices to skim off healthier and wealthier patients and leave behind the sicker and poorer. These practices of avoidance segment the market into good and bad risks and undermine risk-pooling that undergirds insurance. Facing similar market dictates of profit and loss as insurers, for-profit and nonprofit providers may seek out those patients with the means to pay and leave the uninsured to rely on charity institutions.

In other words, inequities in health insurance coverage and access to care are a natural byproduct of the market, the result of rational calculations of actors following dictates of profit and loss. They are commonplace in private insurance and voluntary fringe-benefit systems, as the United States has amply demonstrated. But these inequities may be socially unacceptable in universal health care systems where health care is viewed as a basic right of citizenship. The British and German health care systems have generated widely shared notions of equal access to the same level of care (even if they fall short in attaining such a standard) and have imposed strong political constraints on the workings of the market.

If solidarity requires a market bounded by rules and institutional constraints, what specific ones are needed? Our three countries suggest some minimum criteria. The first and most basic is that the market must be anchored in a statutory guarantee of universal access. In Britain and Germany, providers and payers—whether insurers or other statutory entities—by law must accept all patients and cannot deny access to care based on a person's medical condition or income. Universal access can come through a single government health care system, as in Britain's NHS, or through a system of multiple insurers, as in Germany. However, if health insurance is based in employment, firms cannot be permitted to contain their labor costs by opting out, but must offer coverage to their workers. These legal provisions to take all comers have helped minimize cream-skimming.

A second requirement is that insurers and providers must offer all patients access to a similar and comprehensive range of services. This similarity not only reflects political pressures for equal access, it is also intended to give patients as consumers information that is comparable and comprehensible in order to help them exercise their choice of insurer or provider. Thus, the German government prohibited insurers from offering less than the statutory comprehensive benefits package for fear that they would use such freedom to skim healthier patients who were not likely to require much care and wealthier individuals who could afford to pay for noncovered services on their own. But government officials decided that insurers could offer marginal extras at a higher cost without serious violation of solidarity, as long as the basic package still contained medically necessary services. The challenge, however, lies in deciding what services should be included in a defined benefit package and keeping it comprehensive enough to prevent a two- or multitiered health care system from emerging, in which the poor are condemned to an inadequate, residual package of care while the rest of the population enjoys comprehensive coverage or can afford to purchase supplemental policies. Both British and German governments have avoided these politically explosive issues by keeping the statutory benefits package comprehensive.

A third prerequisite is risk-adjusted payments to providers or insurers to discourage cream-skimming or to compensate those who may still attract a disproportionate share of bad health risks even under a statutory guarantee of universal coverage. Indeed, this was a major problem in Germany's national insurance system. Serious disparities in contributions arose from the mandatory assignment of blue-collar workers to certain funds and risk-pooling confined to a fund's membership. The risk-adjustment scheme among insurers is intended to even out the disparities in contribution rates and permit all insured members to have similar rights to choose their insurer, thereby enhancing solidarity and equity of national insurance. Risk adjustment is also supposed to ensure that funds engage in fair competition for members rather than enjoy a competitive advantage and lower contribution rates because of a healthier membership. In practice, disparities in contribution rates have continued to plague the system because the risk-adjustment formula does not adequately compensate funds with a disproportionate share of sicker members. But the Schröder government is moving to fine-tune the scheme so that it will account for morbidity of individual patients. If the changes are successful, then contribution rate differences in the future will no longer be an artifact of health risks, and price competition among funds should be based on more efficient administration or better reimbursement contracts with providers. In a similar vein, the British health ministry has been developing risk-adjusted capitation for purchasers of health services in the market to even out disparities and compensate those whose patient populations are less healthy and more costly to treat.

Fourth, the financial liability of smaller purchasers and providers needs to be limited so that they do not have to make the unenviable choice between shunning the sick or going bankrupt. In Britain, a reinsurance scheme for GP fundholders set a ceiling for each patient's costs of care, above which the health authority picked up the balance. In addition, health authorities assumed financial responsibility for complex, expensive treatments or cases from fundholders. Practices applying to become fundholders also had to meet a minimum size sufficient to spread the costs of a few sicker patients across a broader range of healthier patients.[11] The NHS Executive provided the ultimate reinsurance policy through its careful monitoring of fundholders and hospitals and its authority to take over financially ailing entities if necessary. Lastly, if government officials deemed that competition would entail unacceptable social and political repercussions, they suspended the market altogether, as with the rationalization of London hospitals through the deliberations of a special commission rather than through market forces.

The alternative to such caution is the United States, where market forces have operated without the safeguards of a statutory and universal guarantee to health care and without adequate rules to set limits to the competitive behavior of sectoral actors. Instead of the security of universal coverage, most working Americans must live with the uncertainty of being uninsured due to unemployment, a job change, or the decision of their employer to not offer insurance in the voluntary fringe-benefit system. Indeed, the voluntarism of that system permits employers to use health insurance decisions as a weapon of competitiveness. They are free to decide whether to offer insurance or what benefits to include in their insurance packages to attract workers or to clamp down on labor costs. The result is substantial variation in coverage and, to the extent that firms ratchet down benefits in an attempt to cut costs, the possibility of growing numbers of underinsured Americans. Insurers, too, have considerable leeway to cut costs or assure profits through underwriting practices that exclude or make prohibitively costly premiums for certain medical conditions or for policies in the individual and small business markets. As a result, the private insurance and voluntary fringe-benefit system is plagued by market segmentation, rampant cost-shifting, and substantial numbers of uninsured concentrated among the working poor. Competitive managed care has also restricted the choices of the insured middle class.

Markets and the State

These contrasting experiences provide general lessons about the character, possibilities, and limits of markets in health care. First, markets are political and social creations that institutionalize particular balances of power and ideas about the proper roles of the state, private actors, and interest groups in the social and economic life in each country. Institutional legacies, governance arrangements, and constellations of political and sectoral actors surrounding these nations' existing health care settlements helped shape the character of their market projects. As a result, health care markets varied cross-nationally in terms of who constructed them and how, and in the extent of competition permitted.

Second, different health care systems granted governments varying capacities to lead the way in constructing and restraining the market so as to safeguard solidarity. In both Britain and Germany, the statutory, universal health care systems granted their governments the legitimacy and legal authority to set the parameters of the health care systems to protect universal access from the ravages of the market. More important, the governance arrangements underpinning their health care systems provided them with the institutional leverage over sectoral actors to limit their market behavior. British policymakers could work through the hierarchical administrative tiers of the NHS to impose and control the pace of marketization. Corporatism permitted German officials to mandate and proscribe certain kinds of market action on the public-law bodies, and it granted policymakers emergency powers to directly administer the sector if need be.

In the United States, by contrast, the voluntary, private nature of employer-based fringe benefits put governments at arm's length from health care actors. Clinton's efforts to expand the presence of the state in the private health care system was viewed among many businesses as an illegitimate intrusion into corporate autonomy, and it fed into public fears of big government. In addition, the regulatory division of labor under federalism thwarted coherent government oversight over a substantial share of the employer-based insurance market. As a result, government actors were unable to bring order and curb the excesses of employer-led unmanaged competition. Private market actors have resisted taking responsibility to self-regulate on matters of consumer protections.

Third, all three countries demonstrate that markets in health care require the presence of the state. Economists point out that health care markets are particularly prone to failure because of the uncertainty inherent in medical care and the information asymmetries it engenders between doctors and patients, and patients and insurers (Arrow 1963; Enthoven 1993).[12] Such failures may warrant government intervention to correct them, such as requirements that insurers disclose standard information on benefits, costs, and procedures so that consumers can make informed choices among health plans. State actors may also engage in ongoing monitoring of health care markets to prevent concentrations of providers or insurers, as in the United States. And as Britain and Germany discovered, creating a market from scratch entails formidable technical problems that may prompt state assistance for their solution.

But aside from these more familiar market failures, vigorous state action is needed to prevent or mitigate serious market inequities. It matters greatly whether public or private actors lead the way in constructing and regulating the market. Safeguarding solidarity requires that state actors set the rules of the market, including the permissible scope of competition. Even if they permit sectoral actors substantial self-regulation, public authorities must ultimately be able to enforce the rules of the market. Where state actors have assumed these tasks, as in Britain and Germany, they have balanced cost and equity concerns. But where private actors have deployed market forces in the health sector, as in the United States, equity has suffered.

The State and Sectoral Governance

The foregoing discussion suggests conclusions about the role of the state in sectoral governance more generally. First, the state is not only an obvious presence in state hierarchy but is also critical to the effective working of corporatism and the market. The state validates the privileged status of associations in corporatist policy-making and implementation and delineates and enforces property rights in the market. Beyond that, the state must also promulgate and enforce rules of behavior to prevent stronger actors from exploiting their position to pursue their individual or collective self-interest at the expense of broader public policy concerns. Though corporatism is especially prone to this type of failure, given the privileged position of a small number of organized interests in policy-making and administration, so is the market if providers or insurers refuse to provide care or coverage to weaker members of society. Policymakers may deem the social and political costs of such failures to be so high as to warrant intervention to prohibit or minimize their occurrence.

However, there is no guarantee that state actors can or will intervene to set the terms of sectoral governance even when there are good reasons to do so. As we have seen in Germany and the United States, the political system may grant sectoral actors various points of entry to the policy process and make it difficult for governments to assert their authority to set the parameters of a sector. Sectoral institutions and governance arrangements may allow stakeholders to thwart policy at the stage of implementation. Or the predilections or preferences of policymakers toward the proper reach of the state in society may make them disinclined to intervene in sectoral arrangements.[13]

In addition, determining the appropriate extent of state involvement in either corporatism or the market is much harder in practice than the ideal types would suggest. As alternatives to state hierarchy, both corporatism and markets are supposed to relieve public officials from detailed and enduring entanglement in sectoral administration and from direct provision of goods and services. But Britain's internal market was accompanied by a blizzard of detailed directives from the NHS Executive. Government actors in the United States have resorted to numerous ad hoc, microlevel interventions in the market, such as laws regulating the care of discrete diagnoses. In Germany, state actors have tried to limit their involvement under corporatism to setting out broad goals and system parameters through framework legislation and allowing sectoral associations to determine how to implement the laws through their collective bargaining. But state actors have mandated tight implementation timetables for corporatist actors to observe and have also resorted to setting specific budgets by decree when these associations have failed to implement the law. Clearly, both types of governance need the state to set the rules of behavior. But state action must not be so detailed or enduring as to suffocate the independent action of sectoral actors, though exactly how much state regulation of the market or corporatism is needed is difficult to determine in practice.

Finally, it is clear that a sector may contain mixed systems of governance that are quite durable over long periods, as in the NHS prior to the internal market reforms. Still, such hybrids are likely to be more stable where there is a clear division of labor and the two elements do not encroach on one another (as in the "implicit concordat" between doctors and the state and in the deference of managers to physicians prior to Thatcher's reforms in Britain) or where one mode is dominant and the other operates in circumscribed areas (such as Germany's market experiment operating on the margins of corporatism). Modes of governance—mixed or not—are likely to experience severe strain when policymakers or other sectoral actors challenge the dominant regime and its main actors and norms with those of another regime.[14] This appears especially the case with attempts to insert markets, with their emphasis on profit and commodification of relationships, goods, and services, into social policy domains that have socialized the costs of care, have institutionalized norms of solidarity, and view benefits as a social right of citizenship.

The Nature of Change in Systems of Social Protection

The discussion thus far has focused largely on questions of policy change and sectoral governance in health care. But the health care reform experiences of our three countries raise broader issues and provide lessons for the reform of systems of social protection more generally and the changes in state-society relations they imply.

First, how should we interpret market reforms in systems of social protection? Do they signal the beginning of much greater transformations of social provision? In other words, are markets in social protection a slippery slope to privatization? Those who fear that they are argue that markets create new distinctions based on ability to pay that will undermine solidarity and public support for broader public programs, constituting a hidden and gradual path to privatization. But the question is hard to answer definitively because it assumes that we can discern from policy actions intentions that may be hidden or denied. It also requires us to extrapolate future policy developments from current policies and to make connections between policies targeted at changing sectoral governance arrangements and those dealing with financing and benefits.

Still, we can draw some conclusions from our three cases. So far, the British and German health care market experiments do not bear out these fears precisely because competition has been so limited. Policymakers in both countries have faced political and institutional pressures to constrain markets so that they did not damage solidarity. In neither country, moreover, has the market entailed an abandonment of universal access or deep cuts in spending or benefits. Instead, their markets appear more to involve efforts to restructure delivery and governance arrangements to make them more efficient and thereby obviate the need for major retrenchment.

However, critics of markets in health care can find ample confirmation of the harm to solidarity in the United States. There, actors and institutions in the private health care system have undercut government efforts to restrict the scope of competition. The result has been continued market segmentation and a further erosion of risk-pooling, a more precarious existence for the uninsured, and narrower access for many in the insured middle class. In short, the market's effects depend on the kind of health care system in which it is placed, and the capacity that governments have to control the competitive behavior of sectoral actors.

A second issue is whether we can generalize the findings about markets in health care to reform of other social policy domains. I believe we can. Take education, a domain that shares many similarities with health care.

Policymakers must deal with political opposition to change from a well-organized profession that provides services and that enjoys substantial autonomy (from teachers, most of whom are unionized). As with health care, market solutions have been touted as a cure to unresponsive service providers and bureaucracies that are blamed for poor student and school performance (Chubb and Moe 1990; Greene, Peterson, and Du 1996). Efforts to give parents greater choice of schools, through voucher programs or other choice mechanisms, have become policy in some U.S. cities and in the United Kingdom. Voucher programs permit families to select private (secular or sectarian) schools and use public money to pay for tuition. The findings from these nascent experiments suggest caution and conclusions broadly similar to the experience of markets in health care. Witte (2000) shows that a voucher program can indeed increase choices of schools available to parents. But like health insurers and providers, schools will face strong temptations to skim off higher-achieving students from wealthier families unless the government inserts and enforces safeguards, such as requirements that schools randomly select students and that the program be limited to lower-income families. In short, the government must structure the voucher market and limit the kind of competition permitted if it wants to protect equity.

Some of the lessons of quasi markets and private markets in health care are also relevant to social policy domains that involve transfer payments rather than services and that do not contend with entrenched providers. For example, a number of countries are considering or have embarked upon partial privatization of state pension schemes by encouraging private supplemental pensions or defined-contribution schemes that have no guarantee other than their market returns. But as the American experience of health care reform has shown, relying on private providers and market forces will create winners and losers, with the latter concentrated at the low end of the labor market. Those in low-paying jobs or with interruptions in paid employment (such as those in contingent work or women who have borne the responsibility of caring for children or elders) will see their reduced market earnings mirrored in lower pension benefits, unless governments provide safeguards or other forms of compensation to these groups (Myles and Pierson 2001).[15]

These examples in health care and other areas of social policy make clear that there are important differences between statutory welfare states and private forms of social protection, differences that have considerable implications for equity. A critical difference between private and public systems lies in the character of their social rights.[16] In statutory welfare states, rights to benefits have the backing of law. But in private fringe-benefit systems, such rights are far more precarious, as workers' access to pensions or health insurance rests largely on the willingness of employers to offer such benefits.[17] As the United States has shown, there has been a secular erosion of private fringe benefits for the middle and working classes, as firms drop or curb coverage in the name of competitiveness and cost control. In addition, because private fringe-benefit systems give employers and private insurers wide latitude to determine the scope and level of coverage, the distribution of benefits and burdens is highly inequitable.[18] In the United States, the uninsured are concentrated among individuals who are bad health risks or employees at the low end of the labor market. Furthermore, state actors may not have the same legal or institutional leverage in the private market that they do in statutory systems run on state-administered or corporatist lines. In the former, state and market actors may operate at a more arm's-length relationship, making it harder for governments to control the cream-skimming behavior of sectoral actors. Statist and corporatist systems, by contrast, provide state actors with the institutional and legal mechanisms to limit such behavior. Such differences in state leverage over sectoral actors have been a primary reason behind the variations in health care markets in terms of their scope of competition and their effects on equity.

Contemporary discussions about welfare state reform contemplate a transformation of the role of the state in the domain of social protection from one of "government" to "governance." Such proposals and actual policy experiments from both the left and the right seek to move away from direct state financing or provision of benefits or services to partnerships with private for-profit or nonprofit sectors.[19] But the differences between public and private arrangements for social protection raise questions about strategies of welfare state reform that envision a greater reliance on the private sector. If policymakers hope to use private markets to realize social policy objectives, they will have to decide whether social rights will have the force of law that private actors must honor or whether private providers will be allowed to decide the terms of entitlement. If they decide the former, then governments will require the institutional wherewithal to monitor the compliance of private market actors. If policymakers fail to build this capacity, then inequities are sure to follow (not to mention the possibility of high transaction costs or higher prices charged by private providers in the market). Market forms of social protection need safeguards against inequities, and social rights need legal backing and enforcement, or else private markets will be an inferior substitute for statutory welfare states.

This book has focused on the battles to reshape sectoral governance arrangements in health care. But these struggles are part of a larger attempt to redefine the terms of the capitalist settlements in advanced industrial societies in the twenty-first century. Systems of social protection, whether statutory or private and voluntary, are critical components of the capitalist bargain. They have helped to cushion the pain of economic adjustment, compensated losers in the market system, and helped capitalism to adapt by serving as a gateway for labor force entry or exit.

Contemporary efforts to alter the terms of the capitalist settlements revisit the old questions about the proper responsibilities of and boundaries between the state, the market, organized interests, and individuals in social provision. Reform also entails fundamental decisions about how to distribute the costs and benefits of economic adjustment. The choices in the future will either reinforce or redefine long-standing ideas about equity and solidarity in each country.[20]

Nations thus far have shown considerable diversity in their answers to these questions. Their settlements have reflected different balances of social and political forces and institutional configurations surrounding social provision. The outcomes of contemporary efforts to adapt systems of social protection are thus unlikely to be dictated by some inexorable economic determinism. At the same time, systems of social protection are not immutable monuments of a bygone age, impervious to adaptation. Rather, the terms of the new social bargains underpinning capitalism in the twenty-first century will ultimately be settled by politics, by conflicts or negotiations among state and societal actors.

Appendix

Information on Interviews and Methodology

This book drew its evidence from written sources and interviews. The primary written sources consisted of government documents, position papers and publications of interest groups, and articles in newspapers, periodicals, and journals. I also consulted secondary literature. The bibliography lists the written sources. This appendix provides information on interviews, all of which were conducted by the author. In the interviews, I posed open-ended questions in a semistructured format.

The initial field research spanned the autumn of 1991 through June 1992. The bulk of the time was spent in Germany, except for a research trip to Britain in March and April 1992. I conducted fifty interviews with major health care actors in the two countries. Interviews in Germany took place in Frankfurt, Bonn, and Cologne. I conducted interviews with civil servants in the federal and Land Ministries of Health; a former Bundestag deputy; representatives of the main associations of doctors, hospitals, and the pharmaceutical industry; and a physician who does economic monitoring.

Most of the British interviews in 1992 took place in London. I interviewed civil servants in the Department of Health; a government minister in the department; the clerk and members of Parliament of the Health Committee of the House of Commons; representatives of major research institutes; higher officials in the British Medical Association and the Royal Colleges; and NHS managers in the field and representatives of their official organizations.

My second research visit was to both Germany and Britain in June and July 1995. I conducted twenty-four interviews (sixteen in Britain and eight in Germany). Most of the German interviews took place in Bonn and Cologne, though some were conducted at cities in which the sickness funds' offices were located. In addition to interviewing officials of the sickness funds, I also interviewed officials in the federal health ministry, a health policy expert with the Free Democratic Party, and officials of the medical association KBV. The British interviews took place in London and at the headquarters of the NHS Executive in Leeds. I interviewed DoH officials, BMA representatives, and a GP fundholder.

I made my third follow-up field visit to Germany in January 1998 to obtain information on the 1997 health care reform laws. I conducted nine interviews in Bonn, Cologne, and Berlin. Those interviewed were officials in the federal health ministry, health policy experts with the Christian Democratic Union and the Free Democratic Party, an official of the federal association of the local funds, and the manager of the KBV. I also had informational discussions with health policy researchers in the Department of Economics at the University of Hanover and with a researcher at the Technical University in Berlin.

In deciding whom to interview, I contacted the main health policy interest groups, politicians, and relevant government ministries with jurisdiction over health policy and requested interviews with their representatives and officials. The *Civil Service Yearbook* listed civil servants in the U.K. Department of Health. In addition, many of those whom I interviewed then referred me to other persons to contact for interviews (as well as to documents useful to my research). For the 1991–92 research, I also received assistance and advice on whom to contact from my dissertation committee members and from persons affiliated with the Steuben-Schurz-Gesellschaft, particularly Klaus Scheunemann and Dr. Albrecht Magen. For the 1995 and 1998 interviews, I again contacted the relevant representatives in the health ministries and interest associations. For my 1995 field research, Philip Manow suggested key contacts for interviews in Germany, and Donald Light did so for Britain. Ulrike Schneider recommended interview contacts and arranged discussions with researchers—mostly in the Institute of Economics—at the University of Hanover in 1998.

I took precautions to protect the confidentiality of interview subjects in accordance with their wishes. The British case posed special problems of attribution of interview sources. Due to the proximity of the 1992 general election and the political sensitivity surrounding the NHS reforms at that time, the British state's perennial concern with secrecy, and the view of many civil servants that they serve the government of the day, nearly all of the civil servants I interviewed wished to remain anonymous. Many wanted their comments unattributed and treated as background information only. A few of the persons interviewed outside of the civil service also requested anonymity. Most of the British civil servants I interviewed in 1995 likewise requested anonymity, as did some of the persons interviewed outside of the civil service.

Similar problems of attribution occurred far less frequently in Germany, with a few persons requesting anonymity. I have safeguarded the confidentiality of all who requested it. Below is a selected list of those interviewed.

Georg Baum. Head of the Subdivision, Division of Health Care, German Federal Ministry for Health. Interview on July 5, 1995.

Dr. med. Karl Becker. Former CDU deputy in the German Bundestag. Interview on December 10, 1991.

Sir Douglas Black. Royal College of Physicians of London. Interview on July 19, 1995.

Günther Bölke. Director, Hospital Society of Hesse (Hessische Krankenhausgesellschaft, e. V.). Interview on November 22, 1991.

Merte Bosch. Managing Director, Hartmannbund. Interviews on December 4, 1991, and June 1, 1992.

Dr. Gerhard Brenner, Dipl.-Kaufmann. Managing Director, Central Institute of Ambulatory Health Care in Germany, Federal Association of Sickness Fund Physicians (Kassenärztliche Bundesvereinigung). Interviews on December 5, 1991, June 1, 1992, July 13, 1995, and January 14, 1998.

British Medical Association official. Interview on July 18, 1995. Referred to in the text as BMA official.

Bundesministerium für Gesundheit (German Federal Ministry for Health) official. Interviews on December 6, 1991, and June 5, 1992. Referred to in the text as BMG official.

Dr. Eamonn Butler. Director, Adam Smith Institute. Interview on March 19, 1992.

Dr. Cyril Chantler. Interview on April 14, 1992.

Pamela Charlwood, BA, MHSM, dipHSM. Director, Institute of Health Services Management. Interview on March 12, 1992; follow-up written responses to additional questions, March 18, 1992.

Clerk of the Health Committee, House of Commons (U.K.). Interview on March 10, 1992.

Peter Coe. General Manager of Tower Hamlets Health Authority. Interview on April 15, 1992.

Department of Health (U.K.) former official. Interview on April 7, 1992.

Department of Health (U.K.) official. Interview on July 19, 1995. Referred to in the text as DoH official.

Department of Health (U.K.) official. Interview on July 20, 1995. Referred to in the text as senior official in the DoH.

Maureen Dixon, Ph.D. Director, IHSM Consultants. Interview on March 25, 1992.

Milada Djekić. Press and Communication Adviser, Kassenärztliche Vereinigung-Hessen. Joint interview with Renata Naumann on November 21, 1991.

General practitioner fundholder, west London. Interview on July 17, 1995.

Dr. rer. Pol. Werner Gerdelmann. Head of Main Department of Benefits and Contracts, Association of Sickness Funds for Salaried Employees (Verband der Angestellten-Krankenkassen e. V.). Interview on July 12, 1995.

Neal Goodwin. Chief Executive of Hospital and Trust Board, St. Mary's Hospital, London. Interview on April 15, 1992.

Dr. Gunnar Griesewell. Head of Health Economics, German Federal Ministry for Health. Interviews on July 5, 1995, and January 19, 1998.

Roger Harris. Associate General Manager, Guy's Hospital, London. Interview on April 21, 1992.

Jerry Hayes. Conservative Party MP and member of Health Committee, House of Commons (U.K.). Interview on March 11, 1992.

Health policy expert for the Free Democratic Party. Interviews on July 13, 1995, and January 23, 1998.

Health services manager, Guy's Hospital. Interview on April 21, 1992.

Prof. Dr. Klaus-Dirk Henke. Chairman of the Advisory Council for the Concerted Action in Health Care (Sachverständigenrat für die Konzertierte Aktion im Gesundheitswesen); Institute for Economics, Chair for Public Finance and Health Economics, Technical University of Berlin. Interviews on January 20 and 23, 1998.

Gerald Hetherington. Department of Health (U.K.). NHS Executive. Interview on July 19, 1995.

Magdalena Heuwing. Managing Director, Federal Marburger Bund. Interview on June 4, 1992.

David Hinchliffe. Labour Party MP for Wakefield and member of Health Committee, House of Commons (U.K.). Interview on March 5, 1992.

Baroness Hooper. Parliamentary Undersecretary of State for Health, House of Lords (U.K.). Interview on March 16, 1992.

Guy Howland. Policy Manager, Institute of Health Services Management. Interview on July 17, 1995.

Dr. Otmar Kloiber. External Service Consultant, Bundesärztekammer. Interview on June 4, 1992.

Franz Knieps. Head of Association Policy Planning, AOK-Bundesverband (Federal Association of Local Sickness Funds). Interviews on July 4, 1995, and January 13, 1998.

David Knowles. Director of Purchasing Development, North West Thames Regional Health Authority. Interview on April 15, 1992.

Dr. Gordon Macpherson. Former deputy editor of the *British Medical Journal.* Interview on April 8, 1992.

Manager, Guy's Hospital, London. Interview on April 21, 1992.

Lord McColl. Interview on April 14, 1992.

Medical journalist. Interview on 21 July 1995.

Professor Elaine Murphy. Section on Psychogeriatrics, Division of Psychiatry, United Medical and Dental Schools of Guy's and St. Thomas's Hospitals, University of London. Former general manager. Interview on April 14, 1992.

Renata Naumann. Head of Press and Communications, Kassenärztliche Vereinigung-Hessen. Joint interview with Milada Djekić on November 21, 1991.

Official with the Royal College of Surgeons of England. Interview on March 4, 1992.

Sir David Price, D.L. Conservative Party MP and chairman of Health Committee, House of Commons (U.K.). Interview on March 12, 1992.

Wilfried Reischl. Assistant Head of the Working Group on Health, CDU-CSU Bundestag Fraction. Interview on January 19, 1998.

Dr. Sabine Richard, Dipl.-Volkswirtin. Contracts Division, Department of Principles and Products, Federal Association of Company Sickness Funds (Bundesverband der Betriebskrankenkassen). Interview on July 11, 1995.

Andrew Rowe. Conservative Party MP and member of Health Committee, House of Commons (U.K.). Interview on March 5, 1992.

Adrian Roxan. Deputy Head of Public Affairs, British Medical Association. Interview on July 18, 1995.

Dr. Jochen Schwalbe. Economic monitoring doctor (*Prüfarzt*). Interview on December 13, 1991.

Senior Conservative Party MP, U.K. Parliament. Interview on July 18, 1995.

Senior lecturer in public health, London. Interview on July 21, 1995.

Roger Sims, J.P. Conservative Party MP and member of Health Committee, House of Commons (U.K.). Interview on March 10, 1992.

Martin Sturges. Official in the U.K. Department of Health, NHS Executive, Personnel Directorate, review body on doctors' and dentists' remuneration. Interview on July 19, 1995.

Dr. Andrew J. Vallance-Owen, FRCSEd. Undersecretary, British Medical Association. Interview on March 13, 1992.

Prof. Dr. med. Hans Rüdiger Vogel. Managing Director, Federal Association of Pharmaceutical Industries. (Bundesverband der Pharmazeutischen Industrie, e. V.). Joint interview with Ulrich Vorderwülbecke on December 16, 1991.

Dr. jur. Ulrich Vorderwülbecke. Member of Management. Federal Association of Pharmaceutical Industries (Bundesverband der Pharmazeutischen Industrie, e. V.). Joint interview with Hans Rüdiger Vogel on December 16, 1991.

Dr. Colin Waine, OBE, FRCGP. Chairman of Council of Royal College of General Practitioners. Interview on March 13, 1992.

Univ. Prof. Dr. rer. Pol. Jürgen Wasem. Professor of Public Health, University of Munich. Interview on January 10, 1998; e-mail correspondence on January 20, 1998, and August 12, 1998.

Hans Welsch. Managing Director, Marburger Bund, Hesse. Interview on November 25, 1991.

Dr. Roger Williams, M.D., FRCP, FRCS, FRCPE, FRACP. Director, Institute of Liver Studies, King's College School of Medicine and Dentistry of King's College London. Interview on April 22, 1992.

Dr. jur. Manfred Zipperer. Director-General, Head of Directorate-General for Public Health Care and Health Insurance (retired), German Federal Ministry for Health. Interviews on July 5, 1995, and January 23, 1998.

Notes

Introduction

1. In 1993, the health care sector provided 4.5 percent of total employment in the United Kingdom. For Germany and the United States, the figures were 6.4 and 7 percent, respectively (OECD 1998).

2. For contrasting examples, Howard (1997) treats tax expenditure as a private or hidden part of the welfare state, while Clayton and Pontusson (1998) consider public sector employment as part of the welfare state. However, if the term *welfare state* grows to encompass everything from tax policies, labor markets, and industrial relations systems to macroeconomic policy, it becomes analytically meaningless. Such a broad concept is unable to distinguish statutory welfare programs from other policy domains or to investigate the interactions between them. Moreover, the differences between statutory welfare states and private arrangements are considerable and have important consequences for public policy. To equate both with a welfare state could miss those distinctions.

3. However, the social democratic welfare state socializes and remunerates caring work through state-provided day-care, even though it still relies on women to provide such services. Many welfare states compensate women and men for caregiving through child allowances or pension credits, as in Germany and Sweden.

4. The term they use is *models of social order.*

5. My definition of corporatism draws primarily on Schmitter 1979; Streeck and Schmitter 1985, 1991; and Cawson 1982, 1986.

6. This assumes, of course, that the state embodies the public interest and stands above the narrower interests of groups in society. While this may not always hold in reality, this view of the state has a long history in Germany (see Dyson 1980).

7. Wolfgang Streeck pointed out to me the difference between procedural and substantive regulation under corporatism.

8. On state autonomy, see Nordlinger 1981 and Evans, Rueschemeyer, and Skocpol 1985.

9. This strong variant exists in the German welfare state but not in industrial relations. In the former, the state has the authority and the means to intervene in sectoral administration and rule by decree if necessary. In the latter, the doctrine of free collective bargaining (*Tarifautonomie*) bars the state from interfering in negotiations between unions and employers or from dictating a settlement. The most the government can do is admonish labor and capital to negotiate responsibly, grease the wheels of exchange by offering concessions, or rely on the central bank to persuade employers and unions to act "responsibly" by punishing inflationary wage settlements with a deflationary

response (Hall 1994). In addition, the range of controls that associations possess over their membership may vary between strong and weak variants of corporatism.

10. *Corporatism* normally refers to tripartite bargaining among peak associations of business and labor and state actors over economic and social policy issues, though it also exists at the sectoral level of the economy or the welfare state (Cawson 1982, 1986; Lehmbruch 1984; Schmitter 1989; Streeck and Schmitter 1985, 1991). It may confine itself to a bipartite relationship between a state agency and a professional association (Cawson 1982, 1986) or entail the concertation of a number of antagonistic interests (Lehmbruch 1984). It may also come in authoritarian, state-coerced forms or in democratic, societal variants (Schmitter 1979).

11. There is also a rich academic literature on the question of physicians' professional autonomy. For example, see Freddi and Björkman 1989; Freidson 1970; Harrison and Schulz 1989; Navarro 1988; Owen 1976; Schulz and Harrison 1986; Tolliday 1978; Wolinsky 1988.

12. Freidson does not specifically use the term *clinical autonomy,* but he essentially defines it.

13. Not all countries have been equally affected by population aging, and its full effects will not be felt until a few decades later.

14. Anderson (1985, 36) estimated that American physicians were responsible for 80 percent of health care expenditures as a result of their fees, prescribing decisions, and hospital use.

15. This was true even in Germany, where peer review dated from the 1930s (Döhler 1987; Stone 1980).

16. For concise overviews of the New Right in Britain and the United States, see Gamble 1994; Kavanagh 1990, esp. chaps. 3 and 4; and Weaver 1998. The most prominent New Right research institutes in the United States during this period were the Cato Institute and the Heritage Foundation, and in Britain, the Adam Smith Institute and the Institute of Economic Affairs.

17. Zysman (1983) shows how different financial systems link the state to economic actors. But his notion of institutional linkages is a useful way to conceive of state capacity in the health sector. In my analysis, however, governance arrangements in the health care system serve as the linkage.

Chapter I

1. For excellent accounts of the medical profession's part in the creation and operation of the national health insurance system and the National Health Service, see Day and Klein 1992; Eckstein 1958, 1960; Grey-Turner and Sutherland 1982; and Little 1932. The historical summary provided here relies primarily on these sources.

2. In general, doctors fought the friendly societies on matters of professional autonomy. In particular, the BMA and general practitioners resented the societies' use of closed panel practice and the bidding down of fees that it entailed.

3. Lloyd George initially drafted and passed the 1911 National Health Insurance Act without consulting the medical profession. When doctors threatened to boycott NHI because it denied them a role in administration and made no provision for the free

choice of physician, the prime minister altered course and entered into negotiations between 1911 and 1913, the fruits of which were the concessions noted above.

4. The NHS Act was enacted in 1946, but the new health service was not introduced until 1948.

5. Workers' dependents, self-employed persons, sicker persons considered poor insurance risks, and most members of the middle class (since their incomes were too high to qualify) were excluded.

6. For descriptions of NHS administrative structures, see Ham 1985, 1988, and Harrison 1988.

7. In contrast to the situation in 1911, the wartime coalition government and the profession engaged in a long period of private discussions prior to the 1946 NHS Act. But as in 1911, the government secretly drafted the 1946 law without negotiating the contents with the medical profession and passed it over doctors' opposition. With the 1948 amending legislation, Bevan sought to mollify the BMA.

8. Aaron and Schwartz (1984, esp. chap. 7 and p. 101) found that doctors sometimes based their rationing decisions on social criteria rather than strict medical need, even as they sought to justify such decisions on medical grounds.

9. Eckstein makes a distinction between consultation, whereby policymakers solicit and take into account the opinions of an interest group but are free to disregard its views, and negotiation, which involves bargaining with an interest group and implies that the government's decision depends upon the approval of the latter. In short, the interest group exerts a veto over the decision (Eckstein 1960, 23–25). From 1948 until the 1980s, the state did not merely consult the BMA for its opinion on policy, it negotiated with it, but this was because such negotiations did not involve fundamental questions of constitutional design.

10. I follow here Schmitter's (1979) definition of *liberal corporatism*.

11. Membership figures are from the BMA for 1991 and February 1992.

12. Bevan secured the Colleges' support for the NHS with the concessions of the distinction awards system and private practice for consultants. In doing so, he drove a wedge between specialists and GPs (see Day and Klein 1992; Grey-Turner and Sutherland 1982, 60–74).

A number of other medical organizations represent subgroups of the profession, but their small size and the lack of state recognition as legitimate negotiating bodies for the medical profession pose little threat to the BMA. Moreover, the BMA has worked hard to neutralize these organizations by undertaking joint action with them or by coopting them through representation on important BMA committees (Garpenby 1989, 120–21).

13. The BMA commissioned an investigation of its internal structures, which issued the Chambers Report in 1972. This report was critical of the autonomy of the GMSC and the CCSC and recommended that they be abolished and replaced by committees consisting of only BMA members as officers.

14. The Chambers Report criticized what it saw as the assembly's excessive control over the Council. It recommended that the Council become a genuine executive and that the Representative Body delegate adequate authority to it for that purpose (Chambers 1972).

15. The BMA permitted nonmembers to vote in elections to the medical advisory

machinery (the Local Medical Committees [LMCs] and the Regional Committees for Hospital Medical Services [RCHMSs]). Likewise, since the GMSC and the CCSC were elected by the LMCs and RCHMSs, non-BMA doctors had equal rights to vote for or serve as representatives of these craft committees. The Chambers Report criticized these practices allowing nonmembers to have voting rights and a voice in BMA policy. Chambers argued that the practice of giving nonmembers such a large say in policy, coupled with the autonomy of the craft committees, undermined the BMA's authority and position as the voice of the medical profession.

16. For instance, many doctors broke with official BMA policy of noncooperation and joined the NHS, afraid that if they refused, they would lose patients to those who cooperated (Grey-Turner and Sutherland 1982, 69–70). Similarly, with the introduction of NHI, many physicians grudgingly chose to participate because they believed that the government would employ strikebreakers (Little 1932, 329).

17. This was known as the cross-boundary flow problem and is discussed in greater detail in chapter 2.

18. Griffiths was deputy chairman and managing director of the Sainsbury's supermarket chain. He eschewed the time-consuming and consensus-oriented method of inquiry of royal commissions for an investigative committee consisting of only himself and four others with a business background. The committee issued a twenty-four-page letter to the head of the department of health after only nine months. Griffiths also expanded the scope of his investigation from an assessment of personnel levels in the NHS to one covering all matters related to management (Harrison 1988, chap. 4; Klein 1989, chap. 7). In addition to its view that consensus management blurred the lines of accountability, the Griffiths report concluded that management teams did not adequately take into account the views of the community, and that NHS managers labored under excessive political interference from DoH intervention in their daily administrative decisions (Griffiths 1983).

19. Griffiths proposed that the supervisory board be composed of top politicians and civil servants in the DoH, the chair of the management board, and a few nonexecutive members with managerial experience. The management board would have members with a business or managerial background and a chair drawn from outside the civil service and NHS so as to bring in new thinking from the outside and reduce the influence of traditional civil servants (Griffiths 1983). Some hospitals, like Guy's in London, were early pioneers in departmental budgets (see Chantler 1988).

Chapter 2

1. On the distinction between hard versus soft budgets, see Kornai 1990, chaps. 2 and 5. Cash-limited budgets, which replaced open-ended funding, began under the previous Labour government as part of the public spending cuts that the International Monetary Fund required in its bailout of Britain in 1975. The Thatcher government continued the hard budget regime in the 1980s (Chantler 1991, 1; Harrison 1988, 78–79). Thatcher's austerity regimen for the NHS was part of its broader program of budget deficit reduction designed to free up resources for private sector investment and thus engineer national economic regeneration (Hall 1986, chap. 5; Harrison, op. cit., chap. 5).

2. The Cabinet Office's Central Policy Review Staff in 1982 considered replacing the NHS with private insurance and user charges. But because of the political uproar it caused, Thatcher distanced herself from the proposal. Thereafter Thatcher denied charges of a hidden agenda to privatize the NHS, as did Nigel Lawson, her finance minister during the formation of the internal market reforms. Thatcher insisted that she merely wanted the private sector to coexist alongside the NHS (Lawson 1993, 612–19; Thatcher 1993, 606–17; Timmins 1995, 392–94; 453–65).

3. In allocating budgets to health authorities, the central NHS administration awarded poorer districts greater sums to compensate for their historical deprivation in resources. Districts that treated large numbers of out-of-area cases did not receive payment until years later, if at all, hence the cross-boundary flow problem. Particularly hard hit were the major teaching hospitals in London, which treated complex cases referred to them from other districts and which at the same time saw reduced budgets under the equalization formula.

4. The NHS also rationed certain procedures involving expensive technology on broader social grounds, though doctors disguised these decisions in clinical terms (Aaron and Schwartz 1984).

5. From its inception, the NHS relied on rationing by waiting lists to contain demand, although this was not something its architects had anticipated. On the contrary, the Attlee government assumed that universal access would mean more patients cured of their illnesses and thus lower health care costs. Though this assumption proved false, the government's response was not to devote more money to the NHS but rather to ration nonemergency care through waiting lists (Grey-Turner and Sutherland 1982).

Klein argues that the British population accepted rationing via waiting lists as fair, because they were based on medical need rather than ability to pay, and the public was already accustomed to rationing during the war. But by the 1980s, Klein speculated that public tolerance of rationing was wearing thin as technological advances made new lifesaving medical interventions possible, as the growth of private hospitals and private insurance as a perquisite for employees in prosperous companies made queue-jumping more common, and as the transition to a service-based economy created more assertive consumers (Klein 1989, chap. 7 and 196–97).

6. The BMA eventually made such concerns explicit at its Special Representative Meeting and Annual Representative Meeting in 1992 (see Beecham 1992a, 920–21; Beecham et al. 1992, 190–91; Smith 1992). A motion passed at the annual meeting stated that rationing was "an unfortunate fact of life" that "should be done openly." Furthermore, "while doctors should be involved in deciding priorities they cannot be held responsible for the consequences of political decisions about rationing"; rationing should not be doctors' task alone but should involve "full consultation among health care professionals, the government, and the public" (Beecham et al. 1992, 191).

7. There is a vast literature on Thatcherism. This section draws especially on Bulpitt 1986, Kavanagh 1987, 1990, and Crewe and Searing 1988. Though I emphasize its neoliberal strands, Thatcherism also contained a traditional Tory blend that emphasized discipline, authority, and strong government (see Crewe and Searing 1988; Kavanagh 1987, 106–10). For additional sources on Thatcherism, see Gamble 1994; Jenkins 1987; Richardson 1994; Riddell 1991.

8. The Beveridge welfare state was a blend of solidarity (universal, state-provided programs) and liberalism. Hence, pension and unemployment benefits were low in

order to encourage people to seek private supplements or income through employment (Baldwin 1994).

9. On the postwar consensus, see especially Beer 1982b. This is not to argue that strong corporatism was prevalent in Britain. In fact, Britain's industrial relations institutions and political traditions reflected an uneasy coexistence of liberalism and corporatism. Still, both major parties justified state intervention in the economy along with corporatist policy-making and governance for much of the postwar period. Labour's vision of a socialist commonwealth required an active state and a partnership with the trade unions. Conservative political traditions of Toryism justified state intervention in the economy, and the party's communitarian strands legitimized a role for functional interests in policy-making. Both parties also justified the mixed economy and corporatism on pragmatic grounds as a way to attract votes and increase the odds of compliance of powerful interests to their economic programs (Beer 1982b; Crewe and Searing 1988; Eckstein 1960).

10. The literature on ungovernability mushroomed in the 1970s and focused mostly on Britain and the United States, reflecting the economic and political turbulence in both countries and the disillusionment of former progressives (later turned neoconservatives) with government intervention. For examples, see Birch 1984, King 1976, Offe 1984, and Beer 1982a. Most of these writers recommended a scaling-back of expectations on government but presumed such a course was politically impossible.

11. The committees are only as effective as the government wants them to be, since the latter can choose to heed or ignore their advice (Ham 1985, 84–87; interview with Clerk of the Health Committee of the House of Commons).

12. During the review, the Department of Health (DoH) was created as a separate department from the Department of Health and Social Security (DHSS). The new secretary of state for health was Kenneth Clarke, who took over from John Moore in the summer of 1988. For a list of the members of the review team, see Lawson 1993, 614–15; Thatcher 1993, 609; Warden 1989a.

Though the review team did not include health care stakeholders in the tradition of royal commissions, it did consult with certain interests. But their influence was difficult to gauge. For example, the Institute of Health Services Management (IHSM) was consulted by the review team and attended meetings with ministers and DoH officials (interviews with Pamela Charlwood, March 12, 1992, and Maureen Dixon, March 25, 1992). The IHSM probably helped persuade the government that its more radical proposals, such as vouchers and health maintenance organizations, were infeasible (Dixon interview, March 25, 1992). But the institute supported some proposals, such as health authorities as purchasers of services (letter from Charlwood, March 18, 1992). Perhaps because the reformers saw managers as catalysts for change and as leading the way in developing the internal market, the review team may have calculated it to be necessary to bring managers on board. As further examples of limited consultation, Thatcher also held two seminars at Chequers, one in March 1988 with doctors and one in April 1988 with NHS administrators, in order to inform herself more fully (Thatcher 1993, 611–12). But the physicians present were those whom she trusted to be amenable to her views rather than official representatives of the profession (Timmins 1995, 462).

13. Of the three institutes, the CPS was the most influential since its director of studies, David Willetts, had served in the prime minister's Policy Unit before coming to the CPS (Timmins 1995, 459–60). The CPS also was Thatcher's creation and therefore

had her ear. It was learned that the IEA was close to John Moore and shared his penchant for private insurance. But with his departure from the DoH, the IEA's influence on the reform debate waned. Kenneth Clarke, in contrast to Moore, wanted to preserve the NHS and its guarantee of free and universal access, even if he was amenable to inserting a market into a tax-financed public health service (Warden 1989b; 1989c, 223).

14. The review team considered proposals for privatization of the NHS, but a compromise provision for a tax deduction for private insurance held by retirees over the age of 60 was all that became law. For additional accounts of the NHS review, see Timmins 1995, chap. 19; Lawson 1993; Thatcher 1993.

15. The IEA also advocated a purchaser-provider split but did so in the context of its proposal for private insurance and vouchers (Green 1988). The ASI and CPS, by contrast, proposed an internal market within the publicly owned and financed NHS. For details of the various proposals, see Butler and Pirie 1988; Goldsmith and Willetts 1988; Peet 1991; Pirie and Butler 1988.

16. In Enthoven's internal market, DHAs would purchase care from general practitioners and consultants within the district and from other DHAs if they could offer services more quickly or cheaply. Enthoven also advocated measures to push hospital doctors to practice more efficiently, including fixed renewable contracts (rather than the tenure system), an appointment system rather than waiting lists to schedule elective surgeries, and merit pay for consultants that included criteria of efficiency (Enthoven 1985). His article received ample media coverage (see *Economist* 1985) and influenced the CPS's John Peet, while the IEA looked to his other writings on competition in health care.

17. The idea of giving GPs the ability to purchase services was first floated by economist Alan Maynard in 1984. Thatcher's Think Tank at No. 10 Downing Street picked up Maynard's idea and included it in the government's review of primary care in the mid-1980s. A draft consultative green paper on primary care in 1985 called for GP purchasers, but the idea was removed before publication and did not appear in the subsequent 1987 white paper, *Promoting Better Health*. Still, Clarke took up the general notion of granting GPs the ability to purchase a range of services once he became secretary of state of the DoH in 1988. At his initiative, GP fundholding became a key proposal in *Working for Patients* (Glennerster, Matsaganis, and Owens 1992, 8–10).

18. As *Working for Patients* stated, "The running of the hospital service cannot however be administered in detail from Whitehall by Ministers or by civil servants. The government's main task must be to set a national framework of objectives and priorities. Local management must then be allowed to get on with the task of managing, while remaining accountable to the centre for its delivery of the Government's objectives" (DoH et al. 1989b, 12).

19. This section draws on the *British Medical Journal,* particularly its accounts of official meetings of the BMA and its craft committees between 1989 and 1992. Specific references are cited in the text and notes. In addition, the section draws on official policy documents of the British Medical Association (especially BMA 1989, 1991b, 1995) and the General Medical Services Committee (1991).

20. The Thatcher and Major governments pushed for the development of primary care, preventive care, and community care as alternatives to expensive inpatient hospital care. See DHSS 1987; DHSS 1986; DoH 1991a; DoH et al. 1989a; Griffiths 1988.

21. Thus, one member of the CCHMS/CCSC, Dr. John Chawner, warned that the

reforms would move the NHS toward the U.S. system "where the accountants ruled with a consequent loss of freedom for clinicians" (Scrutator 1989, 1719). The BMA shared the GPs' fear that audits could simply become an exercise in cost control (*British Medical Journal* 1989, 1457).

22. Fundholders could reinvest their profits into patient care or use them to make improvements in their practice premises. Practices also received generous infusions of technical and financial support from government in their transition to fundholding, further widening the gap between them and non-fundholders. The BMA cited evidence that patients of fundholders received quicker access to elective hospital services than those in non-fundholding practices (see Delamothe 1992; Kingman 1993).

23. These recommendations were found in resolutions passed at meetings of the BMA and its craft committees between 1989 and 1992 and in official policy documents. The major policy documents are BMA 1989 and 1991b. The resolutions are contained in BMA 1990 and 1992b. The *British Medical Journal* also covered the meetings and resolutions passed; specific references from this journal are cited in the text and notes.

24. Antagonism between Clarke and the BMA had been building on a number of issues besides those surrounding the *Working for Patients* reforms. These included negotiations on the terms of a new GP contract as well as a drug formulary for the NHS. The bad blood was due partly to Clarke's acerbic style. See DoH 1989b; Ford and Matthews 1989; Rayner 1992.

25. See Beecham 1989a, 676–77; Delamothe 1989b; Sherman 1989a.

26. BMA 1991a, 3, 32; 1992a, 5, 32; *British Medical Journal* 1990, 1727.

27. Waldegrave gradually reduced the minimum practice size from 11, 000 to 9,000 to 7,000 patients.

28. The election campaign initially focused on the highly charged issues of waiting lists and queue-jumping by those with private insurance, but soon degenerated into recriminations over the leaked identity of a child depicted in a Labour party political commercial. Little serious debate of health care issues occurred after this point in the campaign. For press accounts surrounding the advertisement, see Buckley 1992; Hencke 1992; Timmins, Davies, and Goodwin 1992; Warden 1992a; White 1992. Waldegrave was widely seen as mishandling the defense of the government's health policy record and was replaced shortly after the election. Virginia Bottomley, the new secretary of state, had a medical background as a psychiatric social worker and had demonstrated a willingness and ability to negotiate with doctors on certain issues in her previous position as minister of health. The medical profession hoped her appointment heralded better relations ahead (Hart 1992a; Warden 1992b, 1992c).

29. According to a survey of GPs conducted for the GMSC, only 10 percent of GP respondents supported fundholding when it was first introduced, and 76 percent opposed it. By 1992, the numbers were not much better: 62 percent of respondents remained opposed, and 20 percent favored the scheme. Still, a sizable minority of GPs (36 percent of respondents) worked in practices that already were fundholding or were applying or considering applying for fundholder status. But even among these practices, nearly one-third of their general practitioners expressed opposition to fundholding (General Medical Services Committee 1992, 5).

30. Beecham, Smith, and Mayor 1993, 131–32; Laurance 1993a; J. Smith 1993.

31. The BMA's annual and special representative meetings and GPs' meetings between 1991 and 1993 amply document the BMA's internal disarray over policy. See

Beecham 1991; 1992a, 920; 1992b, 1315; Beecham et al. 1991, 127–28; 1992, 190; BMA 1992a, 5; 1992b; Hart 1992c; Smith 1991.

32. Interviews with BMA personnel in July 1995 confirmed the BMA's continuing disarray toward the reforms. According to its deputy head of public affairs, Adrian Roxan, the BMA's position was that the NHS should be primary-care led and that all GPs should be involved in health care purchasing. Hence, fundholding should be abolished because it privileged only those GPs and their patients involved in the scheme while disadvantaging non-fundholders and their patients. Roxan stated that the BMA's "official position is that we've accepted fundholders, but not fundholding" (Roxan interview, July 18, 1995). This fudging of the BMA's position seemed designed to appease both opponents and proponents of fundholding and to avoid losing fundholders as members. Another BMA official noted that while the Association officially opposed the market and competition, there were unofficial moves toward accepting the purchaser-provider split. The same official went on to note that the BMA officially accepted fundholding as long as it was one of several choices among purchasing models (interview with BMA official, July 18, 1995).

33. A special representative meeting (SRM) in 1992 likewise directed the Council to seek dialogue rather than confrontation with the government. But the SRM in 1992, called to consider the options in the BMA policy document *Leading for Health,* spent most of its time debating the NHS reforms rather than the document and declined to adopt a particular model as policy until after wider consultation of the profession and the public. On the 1992 meeting, see BMA 1992a, 5; 1992b; Beecham 1992a.

34. Indeed, a former chairman of the BMA council, Sir Anthony Grabham, and the chairman of the Joint Consultants Committee, Alexander Ross, chided Lee-Potter for giving the impression that either he or the Council was free to make policy independent of the rank and file, and reminded him that the Representative Body was the real policy-making entity (Beecham 1992c).

35. As a BMJ editorial noted, "The BMA and the royal colleges must speak with one voice, for any seeming division will be exploited to the full. The proliferation of colleges and faculties since 1948 makes this even more difficult, and so far their voice has not been heard. . . . Though normally both the BMA and the colleges and faculties have separate roles, on this occasion they must stand together" (Lock 1989, 620).

36. Like the BMA, the Royal Colleges were cool to competition. Competition between hospitals might undermine the comprehensiveness of the NHS, distort the types of care provided in hospitals, and reduce quality of care and patient choice. They also shared the BMA's fear that setting pay locally would produce a maldistribution of consultants. But unlike the BMA, the colleges supported contracts for some elective surgeries and some devolution of management to hospital level, though arguing that planning and regulating capacity at higher regional levels, especially for costly and complex technologies, were still warranted (Conference of Medical Royal Colleges 1989).

37. An outspoken critic of the NHS reforms, Macara was unhappy with Lee-Potter's low-key strategy (Hart 1993a; R. Smith 1993). Initially, the media and the government interpreted Macara's election as signaling a harder line by the BMA (Laurance 1993b; Webster 1993). But Macara's differences with Lee-Potter turned out to be, as the new chair himself asserted, more a question of style than substance.

38. Roxan also gave his impression of successive BMA chairmen and their approaches toward the government: "I think Jeremy Lee-Potter's time as chairman of

the council was a period of where there was an attempt to say, well, if we haven't managed to achieve our aims by banging on the front door, perhaps if we go around the back and knock quietly, we might be able to achieve the changes. Rather a reaction against [Marks's public] campaign from many quarters. What I think we have now under Sandy Macara, and again, the message hasn't changed, it's a sort of halfway between the two. It's perhaps banging on the front door when we need to, but also recognizing the back door is open as well" (Roxan interview, July 18, 1995).

39. British law distinguishes between negotiation and consultation, as the separate battle over the 1990 contract for general practitioners illustrated. In that dispute, Kenneth Clarke imposed the contract on GPs after they refused to endorse the agreement negotiated by DoH and the GMSC (Prentice 1989; Sherman 1989b, 1989c, 1989d). Legal counsel for the GMSC at the time recognized the distinction: "Although it has been customary since 1948 for negotiations to take place on changes to general practitioners' contracts, the only requirement placed on the secretary of state is for him to consult the profession" (Beecham 1989c, 59). The GMSC's solicitor elaborated further on what consultation meant: "Provided the secretary of state undertook proper consultations with representatives of the profession he could unilaterally alter general practitioners' contracts. The secretary of state had to tell the profession what he was planning to do and to give it an opportunity to tender helpful advice. The profession had no legal right to negotiations" (Beecham 1989e, 330).

40. Some Trusts initially seized on this opportunity in hiring new consultants. The hospitals used fixed-term contracts and enhanced pay as compensation for the impermanence or else drew up rolling contracts with renewal based on clinicians' performance (Beecham 1992d; Hart 1992b).

41. A physician still occupied a seat on the board, but was to be chosen for his or her potential individual contribution to the management of the NHS rather than as a representative of the medical profession as a whole. Health authorities continued to consult Local Medical Committees, the statutory bodies that advise the NHS on terms of service for GPs.

42. The working party, which involved the profession as well as the DoH, maintained that the distinction awards system served as a de facto performance-related pay mechanism. It appeased the profession by suggesting only minor changes to the procedures for the more lucrative, higher-level awards and by allowing the medical profession to retain its majority representation on the awards committees at all levels (NHS Management Executive, 1994c).

43. Reflecting their newfound leverage, many fundholders specified in their contracts a certain number of operations to be performed at a hospital and maximum waiting times, or else the patients would be sent elsewhere for treatment. Some fundholder contracts stipulated that consultants provide minor surgical procedures and see their patients in the general practitioners' offices rather than in the hospital (Glennerster, Matsaganis, and Owens 1992). Social policy scholar Richard Titmuss had once joked that prior to the introduction of the NHS, consultants sent Christmas cards to GPs, but afterward, the opposite occurred (ibid., 9). But with the advent of fundholding, it was said that consultants were now sending cards to general practitioners again.

44. Fundholding's potential to reorient the NHS toward primary care and to encourage consultants to become more responsive to GPs and their patients prompted the Major government to expand the scheme further. Fundholders could purchase a

broader range of services, and the minimum practice size was reduced even further to 3,000 patients. Smaller practices could purchase a more limited scope of services. The government also piloted a scheme ("total fundholding") in which fundholders would purchase the total array of health and community services for patients (NHS Management Executive 1995a, 1995c, 1995d).

45. *Working for Patients* maintained that parliamentary accountability for how resources were spent on the NHS need not imply political interference with management: "Such accountability does not mean that Ministers should be involved in operational decisions. On the contrary, these decisions must be taken locally by operational units with Ministers being responsible for policy and strategy" (DoH et al. 1989b, 12). Similarly, the NHS Executive pronounced, "Managers at all levels will be given a job to do, with clarity about what is expected and how success will be judged, and then allowed to get on with delivery, with the maximum possible freedom. . . . The ME's [Executive's] stance with the NHS will be similar—rigorous on outcomes but not usually about how they are achieved and avoiding second guessing and interference" (NHS Management Executive 1991, 7). But as we shall see, politicians and administrators of the center found it difficult to maintain their hands-off stance in practice.

46. The press and parties paid close attention to waiting lists, especially in the run-up to the 1992 general election. The Major government cited a drop in the number of patients waiting over two years for operations as an indication that the NHS reforms were working, but the Labour party charged that the government was fudging the numbers. See Brindle 1992; Fletcher 1992; Mihill 1992b; O'Sullivan and Jones 1992.

47. Private insurance nearly doubled from 1980, when 6.4 percent of the population had private coverage (Klein 1995, 155). But private insurance is highly contingent on the state of the economy because it either is provided as a fringe benefit or is affordable to those in jobs paying sufficiently high salaries (ibid., 155–57; Timmins 1995, 507). In the recession of the early 1990s, private coverage stagnated (Timmins 1995, 507).

Private sector providers also increased their numbers in the 1980s but at a moderate pace. The number of private, for-profit hospitals increased from 154 hospitals and 7,000 beds in 1980 to 216 facilities and 11,000 beds at decade's end (Klein 1995, 155). Spending on private institutional care also rose from less than 10 percent of the total in 1986 to 19 percent in 1993 (Timmins 1995, 507). But most of this went to nursing home care, which was out of the purview of the NHS (ibid.; Klein 1995, 158–60).

48. Nichol went on to admonish NHS managers against adopting the aggressive style of private-sector management, the so-called macho management in which staff are told "they have an hour to clean out their desks" (Pike 1992b). However, Eric Caines, former personnel director for the NHS, criticized the "steady state" and government control over the process of marketization (Caines 1993).

49. These political constraints only exacerbated the tensions inherent in the Griffiths approach to management adopted by the NHS earlier (see chap. 1). Griffiths had intended that the periphery achieve operational independence from the center, but his requirement of upward accountability meant that the Executive found itself enmeshed in the day-to-day administrative decisions of the health service. Centralized financing and parliamentary accountability made it politically impossible for government officials to let go of the market and let it run on its own.

50. On Major's cautious introduction of the market reforms (or "steady state" policy), see Brindle 1991a, 1991b.

51. The Major government feared that market-driven rationalization would have produced enormous disruptions in patient care, since many hospitals in question were located in the inner city, where primary care was lacking, and thus served as primary care providers of last resort.

52. Standard fundholders had a financial ceiling of £6,000 per patient, above which the costs would be borne by the health authority. Nor were fundholders financially liable for emergency services.

53. Private insurance tends to be concentrated among the better off. In 1990, 11.5 percent of the population had private policies; 23 percent of employers and managers and 27 percent of professionals did (Klein 1995, 155; Timmins 1995, 507).

54. Different contracts used by health authorities and fundholders accounted for some of the differential access to hospitals (Delamothe 1992; Kingman 1993; Whitehead 1993). Some observers countered that fundholding had positive spillover effects to the benefit of all patients, because the scheme prompted many health authorities to consult non-fundholding GPs in their purchasing decisions or to devolve purchasing responsibilities to groups of local GPs (Klein 1995, 241–42).

55. The number of managers soared from 700 in 1987 to over 13,000 in 1991. Between 1991 and 1992, management personnel increased by nearly 25 percent while hospital medical staff expanded by only 1 percent (Pike 1992a, 1992c). Fundholders also received generous start-up support for computers and additional staff (U.K. National Audit Office 1994; Sherman 1989e).

56. NHS spending was projected to rise by only 0.3 percent from 1996 to 1999 (*Economist* 1997).

57. Unless noted in the text, the source for this section is DoH 1997.

58. Margaret Beckett, Labour's shadow secretary of state for health, consulted the BMA in developing the party's health policy document, *Renewing the NHS*, published in 1995 (interview with medical journalist, July 21, 1995). The 1995 document was more radical than the 1997 white paper, since it called for an end to the purchaser-provider split altogether. But both documents took up the BMA's demand to abolish GP fundholding, and the 1997 white paper agreed with the BMA's earlier demands (BMA 1992b, 1995) to involve all GPs in purchasing services for the local population.

59. Klein (1998) is more skeptical than I am of the challenge that these two bodies pose to clinical freedom. He speculates that the government might back down and leave it to doctors to decide clinical guidelines if it decides to continue to rely on them to ration scarce resources on its behalf.

60. This source for this section is DoH 2000.

61. The new money would bring British health spending to 7.6 percent of GDP. The European Union average was 8 to 9 percent (*Economist* 2000a, 2000b).

62. For example, the white paper promised 2,000 additional GPs, 7,500 new consultants, 20,000 additional nurses, 7,000 more hospital beds, and 100 new hospitals (DoH 2000, 11).

Chapter 3

1. In 1997, the income threshold was DM 6,150 per month in the old Länder and DM 5,325 in the new (OECD 1997, 148). Of the 10 percent of the population

outside the statutory system, 9 percent had private coverage (ibid., 82, 149), while only 0.3 percent of the population had no insurance at all (BMAS 1991, 72). Civil servants are covered by a separate health insurance scheme, while the self-employed may be voluntarily insured under the statutory system or be privately insured. In contrast to Britain, migrating between the two systems is infrequent since it is nearly impossible for a person who has exited the public system to return to it later on (ibid., 83).

2. However, contribution rates levied by the substitute funds account for family size.

3. The Federal Chamber is a voluntary rather than a public-law organization. However, its members, the Land-level chambers, are compulsory membership, public-law bodies with important educational and regulatory functions over the profession. Governments regard the Federal Chamber as an official representative of the medical profession and consult it regularly on health policy matters (see Stone 1980, 30–31). Thus, it differs from the Hartmannbund, whose mission is to represent the private economic interests of individual doctors.

4. The substitute funds are also exceptional for having had only employee representatives on their decision-making bodies.

5. This section on historical development draws on Katzenstein 1987, chaps. 1 and 4; Kirkman-Liff 1990; Leibfried and Tennstedt 1986; Leichter 1979, chap. 5; Rosenberg 1986; and Stone 1980.

6. The National Socialist regime also centralized the organizations of physicians and insurers (Kirkman-Liff 1990, 76) and also suspended democratic self-governance.

7. By making physician employment in clinics owned by the funds subject to approval of the medical associations, the ban on direct provision of medical care by the funds effectively remained (Leibfried and Tennstedt 1986, 160).

8. Webber (1991, 52) echoes Stone's (1980) analysis in listing such powers: compulsory membership, monopoly over ambulatory care, and the sole authority to negotiate and distribute fees.

9. An interview with a *Prüfarzt* confirmed that the monitoring process was ineffective in controlling doctors whose prescribing and practice profiles exceeded those of their peers (Schwalbe interview, December 13, 1991).

10. During investigations of fraudulent billings in the 1980s, the KBV tended to take a cooperative line on matters of data exchange in the hope of preventing the funds from getting even more information on their own. Many doctors, however, viewed such investigations and data exchanges as threats to their economic livelihood and their self-employed status (Webber 1992a, 227–28).

11. On the tension between state and party interests in the parliament, see Conradt 1996, 190–95; and Smith 1986, 165–70. This tension has also been apparent in health policy (see Döhler and Manow 1996).

12. Manow (1997a) provides evidence of this in pensions policy, but it also occurs in health policy.

13. The KBV's manager, Gerhard Brenner, characterized the relationship more as a rivalry rather than cooperation (Brenner interview, June 1, 1992). He noted that the voluntary associations also try to influence the corporatist bodies by winning elective office in the latter (ibid.).

14. The divergence between substitute and local funds became quite pronounced

after 1979, with deindustrialization and the transition to a postindustrial economy. As the proportion of white-collar employees increased relative to blue-collar workers, the former chose substitute rather than local funds, thereby worsening the risk and income profiles of the latter. Deindustrialization also meant fewer employed members of local funds shouldering the health insurance costs of their unemployed colleagues (Files and Murray 1995, 302–3).

15. Hospital prices have risen two and a half times faster than general inflation since 1970, and even faster in the 1990s. Following declines in the 1980s drug prices rose sharply in the 1990s (OECD 1997, 74–75).

16. For discussions of corporatist concertation in health care as well as in other sectors of the German economy, see also Lehmbruch 1984; Streeck and Schmitter 1985.

17. The Council has often been headed by a health economist.

18. However, funds were free to negotiate their own monetary conversion factors and therefore could still reimburse the KVs at different levels. Thus, a common relative value scale did not amount to the creation of a unified all-payer system.

19. This description of calculating physician reimbursement draws on Brenner and Rublee 1991, 149; Henke, Ade, and Murray 1994, 256–57; Kirkman-Liff 1990, 78–81; Schneider 1991; Schulenburg 1992, 727–28; and Stone 1980, esp. 151–53.

20. The regional budgets were based on the prior use of medical services incurred by the members of a fund, the fund's current number of members, and the development of general wages and salaries. In earlier years they also included demographic and other medical factors. The budgets were initially calculated by targets, but starting in 1987 they were capped. Caps contained overall physician reimbursement more effectively than targets, but also introduced more uncertainty in individual physician earnings. Under a cap, the conversion factor was calculated retrospectively for each quarter, so that physicians could not be sure of their earnings throughout the year. Under a target, the conversion factor was set prospectively for the year, giving individual physicians greater certainty over their own income. In 1992, the conversion factor was prospectively calculated during the first two quarters and retrospectively set in the last two as needed (see Henke, Ade, and Murray 1994, 256–57; Kirkman-Liff 1990, 78–81; Schulenburg 1992, 727–28).

21. If the Concerted Action failed to make a recommendation, the federal associations of doctors and insurers were to negotiate a spending ceiling. If they failed, binding arbitration would follow (Stone 1980, 154).

Chapter 4

1. However, for dental care and eyeglasses, the law curbed NHI coverage and shifted much of the cost to patients.

2. Still, the FDP's intercession on behalf of its pharmaceutical clientele averted a government-imposed price freeze (Webber 1991, 65–70).

3. The SPD, also a champion of employees and sickness funds, exerted no influence since it did not have a majority in either the Bundestag or Bundesrat at this time. Nor was it part of the coalition commission that drafted the GRG.

4. See *Frankfurter Rundschau* 1991a, 1991b, 1992a, 1992b; *Der Spiegel* 1992a; and Ziller 1991a, 1991b, 1992.

5. During the GRG's policy process, Kohl considered structural reforms to the sickness funds to address disparities in contribution rates and choice. Facing significant opposition, he postponed action except to grant choice to wage earners above a certain income, so that few workers were eligible in practice (Webber 1989, 293–94; 1991, 80–84).

6. For prescribing costs incurred in 1993, the law set a nationwide budget for the KVs. It also limited their liability and that of pharmaceutical firms to DM 280 million each, with sickness funds slated to absorb any additional costs. From 1994 on, each KV was assigned its own prescribing budget for its member doctors' prescriptions. Physicians would be fully liable for cost overruns, unless the KVs had negotiated prescribing guidelines with insurers to be used in monitoring reviews of individual doctors (KBV 1993, 38).

7. The prescribing guidelines were to be based on physician specialty, patient mix, geographical location, and use of technology. They would serve as the basis for negotiating KV-wide drug budgets to replace state-set budgets and would also be a tool with which to monitor doctors and to levy financial penalties on offenders whose prescribing exceeded a specified norm (KBV 1993, 38–39). As it turned out, doctors and payers proved unable to agree on guidelines with which to negotiate the budgets so that the health ministry continued to set KV budgets by law.

8. The BMG developed a list of procedures and conditions to serve as the basis of the new hospital payment system and required the sickness funds and the hospitals to negotiate in their Land-level contracts the monetary conversion values for the new payment system. Hospitals could begin to introduce the system as early as 1993. If hospitals developed these payment mechanisms by 1995, the state would then lift the cap on their budgets (GAO 1993, 11, 45; KBV 1993, 49–50).

9. The risk-adjustment scheme calculated an average spending amount based on age, sex, number of dependents, income of a firm's membership (Files and Murray 1995), members' reduced work capacity (disability), and claims for sickness benefits (Deutscher Bundestag 2001, 5; Schulz, Kifmann, and Breyer 2001, 2, 6).

10. The GSG also required that funds reform their internal administrative structures along the lines of professional boards of directors that existed in the private sector. The idea was that payers would adopt more "businesslike" and cost-conscious practices as a result (*Der Spiegel* 1993c, 69).

11. The law extended copayments to all prescription drugs, even those which had fixed reference prices. Copayments for medications ranged from 3 to 7 marks, and for hospital stays amounted to DM 12 per day for a maximum of fourteen days per year. Those exempt from copayments include persons receiving social assistance, unemployment benefits, education assistance, or welfare for war victims. In addition, the GSG set income-related ceilings for single persons, married couples, and families, below which persons were exempted from copayments (BMG 1993b).

12. According to the Chamber's spokesman, the government had already decided on its policy before meeting with the Chamber (Kloiber interview, June 4, 1992).

13. The Hartmannbund's public campaign consisted of posters and handbills to doctors' offices. In addition, a Berlin doctors' association paid for sensational newspaper advertisements that charged that the health care reforms were nothing but "disguised euthanasia" and exhorted patients to "die early, cost less." This ad campaign prompted Seehofer to withdraw his acceptance of invitations for special meetings with the major medical associations (Parkes 1992b).

14. The publication was KBV 1993.

15. From 1992 to 1995, sickness funds' income from contributions rose by 7.3 percent, but health spending increased by 10.3 percent. Insurers covered their deficits in 1995 and 1996 from their limited reserves (OECD 1997, 86–87).

16. The GSG had permitted blue-collar workers to change funds only once a year, while white-collar workers could do so after a three-month waiting period (Manow 1997b).

17. Hardship clauses exempted eight million low-income adults and twelve million children. For persons with chronic illnesses, copayments were limited to 1 percent of their incomes (OECD 1997, 103–4).

18. According to the CDU's Reischl, the influence of the CDU's trade union wing was not what it had been ten years before because economic difficulties in recent years made its program of distribution harder to carry out (interview with Reischl, January 19, 1998). The BMG's Zipperer also offered the following reasons for the CDU labor wing's limited influence over the NOGs as compared to previous health care reforms:

> Partly it has to do with a waning of the unions' influence in our country, and partly because. . . . I have the impression that inside the CDU the forces which the CDA [Christlich Demokratischen Arbeitnehmerschaft, or Christian Democratic Labor Group, the trade union wing of the CDU] embodies are no longer so strong—no, that the forces which the CDA embodies do not exert much influence in the health care field. It also reflects that up to now, the CDA has not concerned itself very much with health policy questions. Its interests are more in the areas of pensions, unions, industrial relations and labor law. (Zipperer interview, January 23, 1998). (my translation of CDA)

19. Reischl noted that the FDP's clout within the coalition was especially marked after its successes in state elections in 1996. From then on, the coalition turned its energies to reducing labor costs and boosting growth and employment. This new policy direction also went against many of the positions of the trade union wing of the CDU (Reischl interview, January 19, 1998). On Seehofer's difficulties with the FDP in negotiating the NOGs, see *Frankfurter Rundschau* 1996a.

20. According to Zipperer, "Minister [Seehofer] made it clear from the beginning that the third stage of the health care reform would not be directed against the doctors and would not be implemented against them. And for this reason, the doctors' associations for the most part helped carry the government's [reform] concept." (Zipperer interview, January 23, 1998). The biggest concessions to the KVs were the lifting of legal budgets for physician reimbursement and their freedom to either negotiate target "budgets," or volumes, for individual physician prescribing or to continue with KV-wide drug budgets (Wasem interview, January 10, 1998).

21. As the KBV's Brenner noted, "with the 1993 law [the GSG], the intervention of this bureaucracy was very excessive because they [sic] not only prescribed by law what the two parties have to negotiate, . . . but they said exactly what is the result of the negotiation." He went on to give the example of how the health ministry specified the exact number for a budget and noted that "there was nothing to negotiate" (Brenner interview, July 13, 1995).

22. The NOG requires that in developing such guidelines, the Federal Committee must consult with the organizations representing the allied health professions. However, the last word on guidelines rests with the committee. Likewise, the KBV has the right to comment on contract agreements reached between sickness funds and allied

health professions in the areas of physical therapy, home care, spa treatments, and rehabilitation (*Dienst* 1997a).

23. German law makes it difficult for funds to gain access to such data. The Social
Law Book that governs health insurance bars funds from obtaining individual patients'
diagnostic information (Jost 1998, 707, and n. 13).

24. The KBV's Brenner suggested that the internal distributional battles within the
medical profession were the greatest threat to the long-term viability of the KVs (Brenner interviews, July 13, 1995, and January 14, 1998).

25. The phrase *socially bounded market* comes from Henke 1997b.

26. The government refused to allow funds to offer less than the statutory amount
for fear that they would use the restricted benefits packages to prod sicker patients to
enroll with other funds while attracting only healthier patients (Wasem interview, January 10, 1998). Policymakers also worried that funds would drop medically necessary
benefits if they were not required to provide them (Jost 1998, 703).

As another emergency intrusion in self-governance, the Kohl government in 1996
enacted the Contribution Relief Act (Beitragsentlastungsgesetz), which mandated an
across-the-board cut in contribution rates in 1997 and specified the exact amount of
permissible copayment increases. The law also struck from the NHI catalog certain
benefits of questionable medical necessity.

27. On problems with the risk-adjustment scheme, see Deutscher Bundestag 2001;
Dolle-Helms 2001; *Economist* 2001a; Lauterbach and Wille 2001; Niejahr 2001a, 2001b;
OECD 1999, 75; Osterkamp 2001; Schulz, Kifmann, and Breyer 2001. From January
1996 to July 2000, local funds lost 2.2 million members (10 percent of memberships)
(Schulz, Kifmann, and Breyer 2001, 3).

Van de Ven and Schut (1995) detected similar problems with risk-adjusted capitation payments to sickness funds in the Dutch health care system. The Netherlands
scheme only used the criteria of gender and age, which were insufficient to capture differences in individual health risks so that insurers found it easy to woo the better risks.
The authors were optimistic that the technical capability to fine-tune the risk-adjustment scheme was possible, but they expressed uncertainty whether policymakers had
the wherewithal to win the political battle to convince higher-income and healthier segments of the population to acquiesce to the overall reform effort, especially to the introduction of income-related contributions to finance compulsory health insurance,
which would entail substantial redistribution.

In Germany, company funds posted large membership gains starting in 1998
(Lauterbach and Wille 2001, 27–30). Their contribution rates also tend to be lower than
those of the local funds (ibid.). The lower rates partly reflect the arrival of new company
funds on the Internet that have attracted younger and healthier persons and that have
lower administrative costs (since they are websites without large office staff) than other
funds (Schulz, Kifmann, and Breyer 2001, 3). But the lower contribution rates also
partly reflect the initial advantage accruing to most company funds, which primarily
insure working people, who tend to be the healthiest portion of the population, while
local funds have been last-resort insurers for the unemployed, disabled, and chronically
ill. It is unclear why younger and healthier persons appear to be exercising their choice
options while many older and sicker members remain with the local funds. Possibly the
latter groups lack educational background, experience with the Internet, correct information about choices available, or experience with or interest in choosing their funds
that would permit them to act as "smart consumers" in the market.

28. Manow has found a pattern to equalize differences among various funds in pensions as well as health care (see Giaimo and Manow 1999, 980–81).

29. Still, some worry that the German public's sense of solidarity may be waning under pressure from scare-mongering by political and economic elites (Hinrichs 1995, 679–83). But others find evidence that solidaristic notions remain durable and widespread (Stone 1995, 692–94).

30. First developed in the interwar period and later resurrected in its democratic form in the postwar era, the social market economy sought to forge a third way between laissez-faire capitalism and socialism, and to rehabilitate German conservatism, which had been tainted by its National Socialist associations. The SME achieved this reconciliation by wedding conservatism to political liberalism and to the recognition of the rights of social groups (Manow 1999). See also Rimlinger 1971, 137–48.

31. But the Advisory Council is composed of noneconomists as well, including physicians and public health professionals—and it is by no means of one mind on the value of competition and other neoliberal solutions to the problems of the health care system. Still, the influence of the health economists is apparent in the tone of the Council's reports in recent years, which have increasingly framed the arguments and set the terms of debate in the language of welfare economics (see, for example, KAG 1997, preface).

32. If the health sector was to have more competition in the future, Henke argued, the state would have to assume a stronger role in monitoring health care actors' behavior to protect solidarity. Henke suggested state monitoring agencies along the lines of the Insurance Office (Versicherungsamt) in the Finance Ministry, the Insurance Supervisory Board (Versicherungsaufsicht) in the Labor Ministry, or the Cartel Office (Kartelamt), as well as two public agencies that monitored social and medical insurance in Berlin (Henke interview, January 20, 1998).

33. For examples of these bleak assessments, see Esping-Andersen (ed.) 1996, chap. 3; Manow 1997a. I do not mean to imply that this scenario is inevitable. Policymakers, for example, could expand the labor force participation of women or could create a low-wage service sector that could inject much needed revenues into the social insurance system, even if it remained financed by wages and salaries. Such proposals have been made for Germany (Scharpf 1997). The Netherlands provides a concrete case where such action has been taken (Visser and Hemerijck 1997). Policymakers could also look to other revenue sources beyond payroll taxes.

34. For analysis of the political aspects of this debate, see Giaimo 1998, 2001, and Hinrichs 1995. For discussion of the specific proposals, see also KAG 1995, 1997.

35. Henke (1997a) has also considered this proposal.

36. The Advisory Council of the Concerted Action proposed for discussion a plan for compulsory insurance for core services (KAG 1997, chap. 4). Henke (1997a, 12–14) considers compulsory basic insurance and voluntary supplemental coverage a necessary solution in the long term. But new forms of financing or benefits remain controversial, as the Concerted Action's debate on the full 1997 report of the Advisory Council made clear (Henke interview, January 23, 1998). For an enumeration of the Advisory Council's financing proposals, see KAG 1997, vol. 2, chap. 4. The Advisory Council itself was divided on the question of financing; as a result, it was forced to produce a compromise document that all of its members could agree on.

37. Zipperer explained why proposals to change the financing of health insur-

ance—for example, expanding the financial basis of statutory health insurance or eliminating employers' share of health insurance contributions—were not enacted:

> These suggestions did not find a consensus because first, they were very revolutionary suggestions that were, in my opinion, not yet sufficiently discussed; they were too new. The main reason, though, was that the social policymakers inside the CDU/CSU, particularly the acting party head, Dr. Geissler, Heiner Geissler . . . fought against such a regulation [to eliminate employer contributions], because they were of the opinion that this regulation not only would destroy the parity between the employer and employees in the social insurance, but also that it would have negative effects on our system of social security. And of course there are also very strong differences between the [CDU/CSU] social policymakers and the FDP.

Still, Zipperer acknowledged that the problems associated with payroll-based financing of health insurance and social security—which he noted included high labor costs and corresponding unemployment; fewer people working to finance social insurance; the inequitable burden of contribution-based financing for labor-intensive firms with lower productivity; new financial pressures on social insurance arising from medical-technical advances and demographic and morbidity developments but with wages rising more slowly than in the past—would not go away: "These are questions, I think, that will be dealt with in the next 5 to 10 years. This question will come up in the USA as well, I'm convinced, because the premiums are also drawn from the wages. And you have Social Security whose financing is based on premiums [from payroll taxes]" (Zipperer interview, January 23, 1998).

Chapter 5

1. In 1998, 22.1 percent of federal spending went to health care, while 14.2 percent of state and local government expenditures were devoted to health care (U.S. Department of Health and Human Services 2000, 322).

2. This historical account of failed national insurance initiatives draws on Anderson 1985, chaps. 6 and 7; Starr 1982, 235–89, 379–419; and Steinmo and Watts 1995, 336–61.

3. Both organizations are voluntary membership bodies, have a high degree of internal democracy, lack effective sanctions over the rank and file, and have memberships ambivalent toward assuming a trade union role. That said, the BMA has power advantages that the AMA lacks. With approximately 70 percent of physicians as members and a corporatist role in policy-making and administration, the BMA's claim to represent the profession is stronger than the AMA's.

4. This account of the development of private insurance draws from Starr 1980, 291–334, and Bodenheimer and Grumbach 1994.

5. Blue Cross plans were nonprofit insurance for hospital care.

6. For detailed treatment of the role of the AMA in the development of Medicare legislation, see Campion 1984; Marmor 2000; Ruggie 1996; Starr 1982. Marmor, however, argues that the AMA's influence lay more in its shaping the parameters of the reform debate than in developing the actual details of the law (Marmor 2000, esp. 77, 97–99).

Medicare payments were based on the prevailing charges in a local area, known as "usual, customary, and reasonable" fees, or UCR. But in many areas, physicians could also bill Medicare patients for the amounts that the government did not pay, which effectively precluded any hard limits on their fees. Though Medicaid also paid doctors on a fee-for-service basis, it did so at a much lower percentage of what physicians billed than either Medicare or private insurers. Moreover, doctors could not bill Medicaid patients for the remaining balance and either had to write such sums off as a loss or try to recoup the amounts by charging private insurers even higher rates.

7. Though the U.S. Supreme Court ruled that the AMA could not ostracize doctors who participated in these rival forms of practice, the AMA found it could work through the states, many of which accommodated medical officialdom by enacting legislation outlawing such health plans. These plans were also subject to local physician boycotts. As a result, they grew very slowly and did not pose a serious threat to the solo practitioner. Only a handful of states (California, Oregon, New York, and Washington) recognized and protected prepaid group practice and consumer cooperatives (Starr 1982, 305–9, 320–27). Prepaid health plans also challenged the economic autonomy of the medical profession, understood as fee-for-service medicine, to the extent that they paid doctors on a salaried or capitation basis.

8. Quoted in Starr 1982, 178.

9. This section draws on Anderson 1985, chaps. 14–17, 19; Ruggie 1996, chap. 4; and Starr 1982.

10. For an overview of the PSRO program and the other regulatory efforts by federal and state governments in the 1970s, see Campion 1984, chap. 18, esp. 325–39; Ruggie 1996, chap. 4; Starr 1982.

11. One problem was "DRG-creep," in which attending physicians assigned a more complex diagnosis than warranted so that the hospital would be paid more. See Ellis and McGuire 1986, esp. 130.

12. For an excellent account of early HMO policy and politics, see Brown 1983.

13. The federal government required HMOs to observe community rating (discussed on p. 161) and offer additional benefits, hindering their ability to compete with commercial insurers. The Reagan administration also decided to not reauthorize the HMO grant program (Brown 1983, chap. 6; Ruggie 1996, 209, 211, 230 n. 29).

14. For a discussion of these early developments, see Martin 1995a; Starr 1982, esp. 428–49.

15. Access also depends on availability of health care providers, which in turn reflects geographical, racial, and class factors. Rural areas and poor neighborhoods in urban areas tend to have too few providers, especially in primary care.

16. For example, insurers often depict younger, healthier individuals or families in their advertising. Or they will promote preventive services like health club memberships but seldom publicize that they cover expensive treatments like heart surgery.

Chapter 6

1. Medicaid would have been folded into the new national insurance system. Medicare fee-for-service would have remained a separate program, but seniors would have had the option to obtain coverage under the new national insurance program.

2. The Clinton plan required employers and health alliances to offer workers and individuals at least three types of health plan: a low-cost HMO with the most restricted choice of doctors and hospitals, a fee-for-service plan offering greatest choice of providers but also highest cost-sharing, and an intermediate-option preferred provider organization, or PPO, in which patients could see outside providers but had to pay the balance over and above the PPO's fee schedule. Employers would have shouldered 80 percent of the premium of the cheapest plan, with employees paying 20 percent plus any additional premium costs if they chose more expensive plans. Patient cost-sharing had a ceiling of $3,000 per year for each household, but with a lower amount for low-income patients (WHDPC 1993, xiii, and chap. 30).

3. However, Health Security would not have run roughshod over federalism. States would have gained substantial powers to regulate alliances and to implement federal law, and they would have had the freedom to create a single-payer system and to mandate additional benefits above the national minimum.

4. According to Hacker (1997), Clinton viewed his proposal for managed competition within a budget cap as a compromise that would appeal to both left and right. The HMO industry, many large employers, and conservative Democrats in Congress found Enthoven's version of managed competition attractive because it relied on market forces and HMOs rather than single-payer or government price controls to contain costs. Paul Starr's "liberal synthesis," which Clinton drew upon, also called for managed competition but added a budget cap to placate left-wing Democrats and labor unions who supported a Canadian-style single-payer system but feared that it and price controls were politically infeasible.

5. For comprehensive accounts of the policy-making process surrounding the Clinton plan's rise and fall, see Skocpol 1996 and Johnson and Broder 1997, and Peterson 1998 for a concise treatment. For earlier, albeit fragmentary analyses, see Aaron 1996; *Health Affairs* 1995; *Journal of Health Politics, Policy and Law* 1995; Mann and Ornstein 1995 (esp. Schick in that volume); and Manow and Giaimo 1995.

6. Steinmo and Watts (1995) contend that American political institutions make it impossible to enact national health insurance. But their definition of institutions is too broad so that it includes parties and interests. In addition, they downplay the possibility that the balance of political forces can change over time and can override institutions, and they view American political institutions simply as obstacles to rather than as opportunities for policy change.

7. The decline of political parties began with Progressive-era reforms in the early twentieth century, but the 1970s reforms only weakened them further (Epstein 1986).

8. For example, leaders of the Chamber of Commerce initially favored the Clinton plan, but could not deliver their badly divided membership to this policy line. Facing defections of members to the NFIB, the Chamber reversed its earlier support for the Clinton plan. The Business Roundtable, which represents the largest American firms, also refused to endorse the Clinton plan. See Judis 1995; Clymer, Pear, and Toner 1994; Martin 1994; Toner 1994; and Skocpol 1996. For an excellent analysis of internal decision-rules and membership of American business groups, see Martin 1997.

9. To limit input of health care stakeholders in devising health care reform, Clinton administration officials stated that interest groups could "express their views but would not be allowed to participate directly in the process of sifting proposals" (Pear 1993a). Clinton's task force not only kept interest groups at arm's length, but also alien-

ated key health care experts in Congress. According to Congressman Pete Stark, "They came over and saw us all the time, but ignored what we said" (Clymer, Pear, and Toner 1994). This was not the first or last time that the president treated congressional Democrats in a cavalier fashion or distanced himself from the liberal wing of his party. He also did so with the budget bill in 1993 and the welfare reform law of 1996.

10. Hillary Clinton initially met with a respectful audience in Congress, but her legitimacy gradually came under attack from the media and opponents of Health Security, as did the secrecy of the task force (Pear 1993b).

11. The American Association of Retired Persons (AARP) and the AFL-CIO representing labor belatedly endorsed a proposal akin to the Clinton plan without ever mentioning it explicitly by name. Many seniors feared that the administration's proposal to finance Health Security (including new benefits for elders) from cuts in Medicare spending would gut their insurance program. Organized labor's lukewarm support of the Clinton plan resulted from its feeling that the president had betrayed unions on the North American Free Trade Agreement (Skocpol 1996, 91–96, 205 n. 47; Schick 1995).

12. Union membership peaked in the 1950s at 40 percent of the private sector work force and had skidded to 11 percent by the 1980s. Organizing in the public sector did not compensate for these losses (Freeman 1994, 16–17).

13. Opinion polls registered public support for key provisions of Health Security—such as employer mandates and higher taxes to finance universal coverage—from the president's September 1993 speech until February 1994 (Skocpol 1996, 74–75).

14. Clymer, Pear, and Toner 1994; Schick 1995; Skocpol 1996, 53, 198 n. 13, 142, 158–62.

15. In 1965, approximately 65 percent of doctors were AMA members (Skocpol 1996, 198, n. 13). That figure had fallen to 45 percent in 1989 and 34 percent a decade later (Greenhouse 1999b).

16. The AMA filed suit to open up the meetings of the task force. The subsequent ruling required the task force to announce its meetings in advance and open information-gathering meetings to the public. However, meetings to devise recommendations to the president could remain closed (Pear 1993a, 1993b).

17. *New York Times* 1995; Georges 1995; Pear 1995a, 1995b.

18. Alliances could have been nonprofit organizations, independent state agencies, or part of the state bureaucracy itself (WHDPC 1993, 60). The first two possibilities would have been quasi-public bodies somewhere between state and society, akin to the public-law sickness funds in Germany. But the Congressional Budget Office's (CBO) analysis of the Clinton plan illustrated how unfamiliar this model of governance was to American political traditions. The CBO considered regional alliances as extensions of the federal government rather than government regulation of private transactions and also viewed corporate alliances as part of the federal government since they would be "standing in" for regional alliances (see CBO 1994, 46).

19. Much of this section draws on Giaimo 1996 and Giaimo and Manow 1999.

20. For an excellent survey of managed care developments in the 1990s, see Wilkerson, Devers, and Given (eds.) 1997b.

21. Federal legislation in 1995 allowed Medicare patients to enroll in private HMOs (Wilkerson 1997), and the Balanced Budget Act of 1997 allowed Medicare to pursue limited experiments with medical savings accounts (MSAs) (Moon, Gage, and Evans 1997). MSAs permit individuals to opt out of the Medicare pool, purchase a high-

deductible policy for catastrophic illness, and set aside money into a savings account to pay for medical care below the deductible. Any balance remaining in the MSA at year's end may be withdrawn for any purpose, medical care or otherwise. For an excellent analysis and critique of MSAs, see White 1995.

MSAs and managed care in public insurance programs are controversial. Since both programs cover the sicker, poorer, and more costly segments of society, HMOs may not be suitable for these patients, given their financial arrangements that encourage less care. Alternatively, HMOs and MSAs might try to survive by designing their benefits packages to attract healthier and wealthier seniors but could then undermine risk-pooling in and the financial health of fee-for-service Medicare (Moon, Gage, and Evens 1997). Thus far, managed care's record in public insurance programs has been discouraging. Arguing that the government's capitation rate is too low, many HMOs have reduced benefits or withdrawn from the Medicare and Medicaid markets (see Kilborn 1998).

22. An example of piecemeal regulation is the 1996 federal law requiring all insurers to provide a forty-eight-hour minimum hospital stay for women who give birth (U.S. Department of Labor n.d., 17–18). However, the federal government has had some success in issuing broad consumer protections for Medicare and Medicaid through administrative decrees (Pear 1996b, 1998c, 1998j).

23. Access to insurance remains especially difficult for employees seeking individual policies, with insurers charging premiums as high as 140 to 600 percent of the standard rate (GAO 1998, 6) and withholding or sharply reducing commissions to agents who sell them (Pear 1998f). On the contents of the Kassebaum-Kennedy law, see Clymer 1996a, 1996b; Fuchs et al. 1997; Purdum 1996.

24. The percentage of near-poor children without health insurance between 1998 and 1999 fell from 27.2 percent to 19.7 percent. Coverage of these children by Medicaid and the new State Children's Health Insurance Program (S-CHIP) only rose from 39.3 percent to 40.5 percent. (It should be noted that government data do not separate S-CHIP from Medicaid.) The big gains in coverage thus came mainly from expanded employment-based coverage (which covered 34.5 percent of children above the poverty level in 1999, compared to 30.5 percent in 1998) and individually purchased policies (covering 10.3 of near-poor children in 1999, up from 7.8 percent in the previous year). These developments reflected the late 1990s economic boom (Fronstin 2001, 9–10).

25. Potential barriers include threatened tax revolts or businesses relocating to lower-tax states (see Grogan 1995). Partisan changes in state legislatures and governorships also dampened the reform momentum in some states.

26. Self-insured plans, in which employers assume the risk of health care coverage of their workers, covered 17 percent of the U.S. population, or forty-four million individuals, in 1993, up from thirty-nine million in 1989 (GAO 1995, 2–3, 9, 47–50).

27. ERISA considers private insurers and managed care plans that contract with employers to provide care or benefits to their employees to be engaged in "the business of insurance" and therefore subject to state regulation. However, self-insured plans are exempt from state regulation because ERISA does not consider them insurance since the employer assumes the financial risk of health care coverage. Federal regulation of self-insured plans is limited to reporting requirements to the Department of Labor, disclosure requirements to plan beneficiaries, and an appeals process that permits only the recovery of the amount of benefits in question, and not damages or lost wages (GAO

1995; *Mealey's Litigation Reports* 1997; Pear 1998g). On ERISA and its consequences for health insurance regulation, see Chirba-Martin and Brennan 1994; GAO 1995; O'Keefe 1995; and Polzer and Butler 1997.

28. To the extent that fee-for-service plans attracted sicker patients unwilling to surrender their choice of provider, they might have faced extinction in a competitive environment. But the Clinton plan's requirement for risk-adjusted payments among health plans would have gone some way to compensate for such outcomes and might have helped them survive.

29. In 1996, 80 percent of those employed by small firms had only one health plan offered to them. Among large firms, most employees were limited to a choice of two plans; only 30 percent of workers enjoyed a choice of three or more plans (Gabel, Ginsburg, and Hunt 1997, 105).

30. Freudenheim 1999a. Aetna, for example, has nearly 60 percent of the Houston market.

31. Wilkerson, Devers, and Given (1997a, 1997b) coined the phrase *competitive managed care* to describe this state of affairs. They note that while managed care plans have a long history in some states, intense price competition among them, or "competitive managed care," is of recent vintage (see esp. chap. 1).

32. Coverage decisions may involve employees of managed care plans determining whether a treatment in question is medically necessary or appropriate for the diagnosis.

33. For-profit HMOs grew from 12 to 62 percent of total HMO enrollees and from 18 to 75 percent of health plans between 1981 and 1997. Stocks comprised 69 percent of the external capital of HMOs between 1991 and 1997, up from 20 percent between 1988 and 1990 (Srinivasan, Levitt, and Lundy 1998, esp. 126–27).

34. A study by the California Medical Association (CMA) in the early 1990s found that among the top ten plans that devoted the most to patient care seven were nonprofits, while among the ten plans that devoted the least amount of the premium to patient care, eight were for-profits. Some of the larger for-profits spent only 70 to 80 percent of their premium on patient care and had administrative costs ranging from 11 to 16 percent (California Medical Association n.d.) However, organizational form rather than nonprofit status may account for the difference in performance. Kaiser, a nonprofit, scored best in terms of share of premium devoted to patient care (96.5 percent) and low administrative costs (2 percent) (ibid.). But because it is a highly integrated HMO that has owned its own hospitals and clinics, it may have had lower transaction costs than looser managed care networks. Though the CMA might be expected to be an opponent of managed care, it drew on outside sources such as reports from the state Department of Corporations (which regulated HMOs in California), the Securities and Exchange Commission 10-K forms, and the California Association of HMOs.

35. For an overview of the varied issues surrounding for-profits, community benefits, and nonprofit conversions, see *Health Affairs* 1997a.

36. The 1997 Kaiser survey mirrored results of other surveys conducted between 1995 and 1997. The Kaiser survey found that 48 percent of respondents had themselves experienced problems with their health plans or else knew someone who had. It also registered substantial majorities favoring regulation of health plans along the lines proposed by Clinton's quality commission (see text below) and 64 percent supporting the option of malpractice suits against insurers (*Kaiser/Harvard National Survey* 1998).

37. Examples are Kaiser in Northern California and Harvard Pilgrim Health Plan in Massachusetts (whose medical groups eventually spun off as autonomous providers contracting with the Harvard insurance entity as well as other insurers).

38. Studies showed that low-income Medicare patients with chronic medical conditions enrolled in HMOs had substantially worse health outcomes than those patients with the same characteristics who were in fee-for-service plans (Miller and Luft 1997).

39. The data that employers use to compare health plans on quality provide useful indicators on throughputs, such as the number of immunizations a health plan achieves. They also rely on consumer satisfaction surveys that measure patients' experiences of waiting times for appointments or courtesy of doctors and staff. But none of this data measures whether a given treatment yields a cure or an improvement in health.

40. British GPs, for example, receive bonus payments in addition to capitation, if they meet targets to provide more preventive services. Salaried remuneration avoids the incentives to overtreat as well as the incentives to undertreat, since it decouples physician income from the volume of services provided to patients.

41. Some judicial decisions have also extended ERISA's exemption from state regulation to managed care plans on the grounds that they are not insurance (Polzer and Butler 1997, 98).

Arguments against granting patients broad rights to sue their health plans center on their added costs to employers, which could encourage them to withdraw coverage. Yet CBO estimates of additional costs of lawsuits were a rather modest $85 per year for an individual policy and $200 for a family policy. Opponents also cite the lengthy process of lawsuits and the small number of patients that would likely benefit, and have suggested an alternative similar to no-fault worker's compensation insurance (Weinstein 1998).

42. President's Advisory Commission 1998; Pear 1997a, 1997b, 1997c, 1998a. The CBO estimated that compliance with the commission's bill of rights would be small, raising premiums by 0.75 percent (Pear 1998a).

43. The American Association of Health Plans (AAHP), the political representative for managed care, initially favored self-regulation. But judging legislation to be likely and hoping that a more conciliatory stance would allow it some influence on the contents, the AAHP later signaled its willingness to consider legislation (Pear 1997c, 1998d, 1999). Earlier, a number of prominent nonprofit HMOs publicly supported government-set national standards in the hope of restoring the sagging public image of the managed care industry (Pear 1998h; Zatkin 1997).

44. Both parties in Congress accepted most of the recommendations of Clinton's quality commission, as well as requiring better disclosure of plan information to patients and banning gag rules. But they remained divided over whether patients should be able to sue health plans and whether federal regulations should extend to all employment-based plans or only to some private plans. Republican proposals tended to be less generous on both questions than Democratic bills. See Alvarez 1998a, 1998b; Mitchell and Pear 2001; Pear 1998b, 1998d, 1998e, 2001a, 2001b.

45. In 1983, 41 percent of doctors were self-employed in solo practice, 35 percent were self-employed in group practices, and 24 percent were employees of a larger company. By 1997, however, the figures were 26 percent, 31 percent, and 43 percent, respectively. Data on the sources of physician income tell a similar story. In 1988, 61 percent of doctors were in practices with at least one managed care contract; in 1997, 92 percent

were. In 1988, the percentage of physicians' revenues derived from managed care was 23 percent; in 1997, that figure had risen to 44 percent (Henry J. Kaiser Family Foundation, cited in Stolberg 1998).

46. Another constraint on clinical freedom is posed by gag rules, contractual provisions that prohibit physicians from discussing treatment options not covered by the health plan or financial arrangements—including bonuses to reduce medically unnecessary care—between doctors and the health plan. The prevalence of such clauses is disputed, but bans on gag rules have featured in federal and state efforts to regulate managed care. See Pear 1995c, 1996.

47. Thirty-one states enacted anti–gag rule laws in 1997 (*American Health Line 50 State Report* 1997, 1–2), and twenty-seven states passed legislation banning selective contracting in 1996 (Jaklevic 1996). But devising consumer—and physician—protections is a work in progress: The Supreme Court ruled that HMOs cannot be sued in federal court for financial arrangements that reward doctors for providing less care, but left the door open to Congress to legislate patient rights (see Greenhouse 2000; Pear 2000).

48. As an example of the profession's ambivalence toward political activities, in 1996 the California Medical Association remained neutral on two statewide referenda that would have mandated a host of regulations on HMOs (Olmos 1996). Both referenda were defeated, largely because they split the votes of supporters.

49. Provider-owned HMOs comprised at least 25 percent of all HMOs in eighteen states, with even higher proportions in some western states (American Association of Health Plans 1997).

50. Adelson 1997; Greenhouse 1999a, 1999b; Klein 1999. Five percent of U.S. doctors, or 35,000 practitioners, belong to unions, up from 25,000 in 1996, and labor experts estimate that unionization among the profession will grow by 15 percent or more each year (Greenhouse 1999a). Up to this point, doctors have been organized by other unions. But the AMA's 1999 decision marks a commitment to assume this task itself.

51. Federal labor law allows employees to unionize, but not self-employed professionals such as private-sector doctors. However, citing their powerlessness in the face of HMOs, many physicians counter that unionization is warranted. See Greenhouse 1999b; Yellin 1999.

52. Employers' insurance premiums rose sharply in the late 1980s, slowed significantly in the 1990s, and reached record lows in 1996. In 1988, employers' health benefits costs rose 19 percent, up from a 7 percent rate a year earlier, and continued to increase at 17 percent per year through 1990. Health benefits costs actually declined by 1 percent in 1994 and barely rose until 1998. By 2000, costs had risen by 8 percent, still well below the blistering pace of the late 1980s (Fronstin 2001, 15–16). The average annual premium for family coverage rose 111 percent between 1988 and 1996 (from $2,530 to $5,349), while the CPI rose only 33 percent. Single coverage during this period rose 79 percent (from $1,153 to $2,059 per year) (GAO 1997, 27).

53. In 2000, for example, Partners, a consortium of leading teaching hospitals and medical groups in the Boston area, threatened to sever its relationship with Tufts Health Plan unless its members received more money. Tufts yielded.

54. For discussions of the different reasons behind the renewed increase in health care spending, see Freudenheim 1997, 1998; Fronstin 2001, 16–17; GAO 1997, 3; Smith et al. 1998.

55. Even with health care costs on the rise starting in 1998, however, firms of all sizes continued to offer workers insurance, with the biggest expansions among small employers. Nor did employers shift the rising cost of health care onto their employees. Employer generosity was likely due to the labor shortage in the strong economy and the use of fringe benefits to attract and retain workers (Fronstin 2001).

Still, the good news contained a mixed message. Despite the economic expansion in the 1990s, the proportion of working adults with job-based insurance was stagnant at 72.3 percent between 1994 and 1997 and only nudged up to 73.3 percent between 1997 and 1999. The proportion of Americans under age sixty-five with employment-based insurance had also recovered somewhat since the recession of the early 1990s and stood at 65.8 percent in 1999, but this figure remained below the 1987 peak of 69.2 percent (ibid., esp. 4–5). Moreover, since fringe benefits are contingent on the costs of health care as well as the state of the economy, the prognosis is that employment-based coverage will contract and employee cost sharing will increase in the next recession (ibid., 19). Finally, the American "jobs miracle" of the 1990s depended in no small part on employers not having to offer fringe benefits to their workers, particularly at the low end of the labor market, in order to remain competitive. Thus, the existence of fringe benefits may be more independent of the business cycle than Fronstin suggests.

56. On the growing influence of conservative forces and the rise of the New Democrats in the Democratic party, see Ferguson and Rogers 1986; Weir 1998, chap. 1.

Conclusion

1. To be sure, German sickness funds segmented the population into smaller risk communities, whereas Britain's NHS had only one national risk pool. But public policy in Germany has also worked in a solidaristic direction by mandating similar benefits among funds and requiring financial transfers among them to eliminate different contribution levels based on historic inequities. Also health insurance contributions within a fund involve redistribution from healthier and wealthier and single persons to sicker, poorer, and families.

2. However, the concept of medical necessity changes over time, not only because of advances in medical technology. Those who must determine which services should be considered medically necessary may also be subject to political pressures from governments or interest groups representing patients or other constituencies. For example, Charles et al. (1997) demonstrated how medical necessity has been redefined to meet evolving policy goals in Canadian national health insurance. Still, acknowledging that the task of defining medical necessity has political aspects does not mean that the organized medical profession cannot play a key role in defining it for national health policy. In Germany, for example, national health insurance laws require that the population have access to medically necessary services and that KV doctors provide these. But it is the task of the Federal Committee of Physicians and Sickness Funds to determine which new procedures should be considered medically necessary and to update the schedule of services covered by national health insurance.

3. On strategies of blame avoidance, see Weaver 1988 and Pierson 1994.

4. These issues require a broader public debate on the scope of national insurance coverage and also need to involve patients in decisions about their own care. Still,

rationing is not going to go away and already occurs in most if not all health care systems. In the United States, rationing has long been based on ability to pay, with the uninsured—and, increasingly, those in restrictive managed care plans—having more limited choices and access to care. In Britain, doctors have rationed elective treatments largely on the basis of clinical need (though at times social and political criteria have crept in, as government waiting-list directives have suggested). Germany has only begun to address the question and has rationed mainly by eliminating medically questionable services from the national insurance catalog.

Yet, rationing raises explosive ethical and political problems involving questions of who should decide what for whom, and on what grounds people should receive less care. These involve fundamental questions—and possible redefinitions—of equity and solidarity. And there may be limits to how far doctors can cover for politicians. Even in Britain, where doctors have long rationed for governments, waiting lists have been a potent political issue, and physicians have tired of this responsibility in times of austerity and political exclusion.

5. In the United States, associational governance has generally been limited to the interwar years or to certain sectors like agriculture (Wilson 1982).

6. For a similar conclusion, see Klein 1997.

7. Chapter 2 provides detailed information on such transaction costs.

8. For actual and estimated health care costs in the United States, see chapter 6.

9. Klein (1995) notes that Thatcher's success in cost control exacted high political costs.

10. On the different types of accountability, see Day and Klein 1987.

11. The Major government repeatedly lowered the minimum practice size and thus increased the possibility of bankruptcies. But the other limits on financial liability might have offset some of this danger.

12. One of the requirements of a well-functioning market is perfect and free information. But Arrow (1963) has pointed out that information asymmetries and uncertainty are rampant in health care and health insurance. For example, insurers may not know if subscribers have costly medical conditions when they enroll. If their insured pool is too small and they enroll too many sick persons, the insurer will experience adverse selection. To prevent this, insurers may engage in medical underwriting practices that seek to uncover health status and to include these costs in experience-rated premiums. Information asymmetries are also present in the doctor-patient relationship. Lacking medical expertise, patients must rely on their doctors to prescribe the appropriate course of treatment. There is also uncertainty in predicting whether one will become sick or knowing whether a treatment was responsible for a cure (or whether one got better for some other reason).

13. These conclusions call into question the assumption of some of the governance literature that the state occupies a privileged position in sectoral governance (see, e.g., Lindberg and Campbell 1991).

14. Streeck and Schmitter (1985, 123) conclude that conflicts among actors within a given governance mode are likely to be less destabilizing than clashes between two different governance modes.

15. These could include pension credits for interruptions in paid employment to care for family members, some redistribution, or government subsidies to the pension contributions of low-paid workers.

16. Esping-Andersen (1990) classifies welfare state regimes by the different character of their social rights of citizenship. His primary focus is the degree of decommodification, or freedom from the labor market, in securing welfare, which differs from my distinction developed here.

17. Of course, workers may pursue legal remedies if an employer reneges on a contractual commitment it has made to provide fringe benefits. But employers are under no legal compulsion to enter into such arrangements to provide benefits in the first place.

18. For a similar finding, see Howard 1997.

19. For example, Germany has enacted legislation to permit private pensions to supplement public pensions. This has been British policy since the 1980s. In health care, Blair has encouraged NHS purchasers to make greater use of private providers and facilities.

20. Future reform choices, their effects on solidarity, and public perceptions of the changes will depend on the particular problems in existing social protection arrangements and the specific politics of reform in each country. For instance, countries with universal health care provision might decide to adopt a defined-benefits package that is mandatory, universal, and comprehensive for their national program, while permitting individuals with the means to do so to purchase extra benefits at an additional charge. Such a policy change would officially sanction some differences in access based on ability to pay and would narrow the concept of solidarity from a recognition that everyone is entitled to the same benefits to one that ensures that the most vulnerable have a right to fairly comprehensive coverage. It is unclear whether citizens in these countries would view such action as a violation of solidarity or as an attempt to preserve equity in the face of austerity. Conversely, if nations that relied largely on private and voluntary provision against social risks were to adopt a defined-benefits package under national insurance, such action would imply a broadening of solidarity.

Bibliography

100 Begriffe aus dem Gesundheitswesen. 1991. Cologne: Madaus AG.

Aaron, Henry J., ed. 1996. *The Problem That Won't Go Away.* Washington, D.C.: Brookings Institution.

Aaron, Henry, and William B. Schwartz. 1984. *The Painful Prescription: Rationing Hospital Care.* Washington, D.C.: Brookings.

Acs, Gregory, Stephen H. Long, M. Susan Marquis, and Pamela Farley Short. 1996. "Self-Insured Employer Health Plans: Prevalence, Profile, Provisions, and Premiums." *Health Affairs* 15 (2) (summer): 266–78.

Adelson, Andrea. 1997. "Physician, Unionize Thyself." *New York Times,* April 15, p. 27.

Alber, Jens. 1989. "Structural Reforms in the West German Health Care System." Paper for the Conference on Structural Reforms of National Health Care Systems, University of Maastricht, December 8–9.

Altenstetter, Christa. 1987. "An End to Consensus on Health Care in the Federal Republic of Germany?" *Journal of Health Politics, Policy and Law* 12 (3): 505–36.

Alvarez, Lizette. 1998a. "After Polling, GOP Offers a Patients' Bill." *New York Times,* July 16, pp. A1, A22.

———. 1998b. "GOP Prescription." *New York Times,* July 27, p. A9.

American Association of Health Plans. 1997. "AAHP Survey Finds That Many State-Licensed Health Plans Are Provider-Owned: 37% of HMOs Licenses in 42 States over the Past Two Years Are Provider-Owned." (Downloaded from AAHP website.)

American Health Line 50-State Report, Fall 1997. 1997. Washington, D.C.: National Journal Group.

Anderson, Odin W. 1985. *Health Services in the United States: A Growth Enterprise since 1875.* Ann Arbor: Health Administration Press.

———. 1989. Chap. 3, "The United Kingdom." In *The Health Services Continuum in Democratic States: An Inquiry into Solvable Problems,* 25–45. Ann Arbor: Health Administration Press.

Appleby, John, Paula Smith, Wendy Ranade, Val Little, and Ray Robinson. 1993. "Monitoring Managed Competition." In Ray Robinson and Julian Le Grand, eds., *Evaluating the NHS Reforms,* 24–53. London: King's Fund Institute.

Arrow, Kenneth J. 1963. "Uncertainty and the Welfare Economics of Medical Care." *American Economic Review* 53 (December): 941–73.

Baldwin, Peter. 1990. *The Politics of Social Solidarity.* Cambridge: Cambridge University Press.

———. 1994. "Beveridge in the Long Durée." In John Hills, John Ditch, and Howard Glennerster, eds., *Beveridge and Social Security,* 37–55. Oxford: Clarendon.

Banks, Dwayne, Kimberly Kunz, and Tracy Macdonald. 1994. "The Uninsured." In Dwayne Banks, Kimberly Kunz, and Tracy Macdonald, eds., *Health Care Reform*, 17–26. Berkeley: Institute of Governmental Studies.

Bartlett, Will, and Julian Le Grand. 1993. "The Theory of Quasi-Markets." In Julian Le Grand and Will Bartlett, eds., *Quasi-Markets and Social Policy*, 13–34. Basingstoke: Macmillan.

Beecham, Linda. 1989a. BMA Affairs. From the Council. *British Medical Journal* 298 (March 11): 676–79.

———. 1989b. BMA Affairs. From the GMSC. *British Medical Journal* 298 (May 27): 1457–59.

———. 1989c. BMA Affairs. From the LMC Conference. *British Medical Journal* 299 (July 1): 57–60.

———. 1989d. BMA Affairs. From the JCC. *British Medical Journal* 299 (July 29): 327–29.

———. 1989e. BMA Affairs. From the GMSC. "Negotiators Re-elected to Reopen Contract Discussions." *British Medical Journal* 299 (July 29): 329–30.

———. 1990a. BMA Affairs. From the Senior Staffs Conference. *British Medical Journal* 300 (June 16): 1593–95.

———. 1990b. BMA Affairs. From the LMC Conference. *British Medical Journal* 300 (June 23): 1657–60.

———. 1990c. BMA Affairs. From the GMSC. "Dangerous Effects of Indicative Prescribing." *British Medical Journal* 300 (June 30): 1729.

———. 1991. "BMA Council Chairman Criticised." *British Medical Journal* 303 (July 13): 76–77.

———. 1992a. Medicopolitical Digest. "SRM Calls for Continued Opposition to NHS Reforms." *British Medical Journal* 304 (April 4): 920–22.

———. 1992b. Medicopolitical Digest. *British Medical Journal.* 304 (May 16): 1315–16.

———. 1992c. Medicopolitical Digest. "Chairman Criticised for Press Interview." *British Medical Journal* 304 (May 16): 1315.

———. 1992d. Medicopolitical Digest. "Sharing Experience of Trusts." *British Medical Journal* 304 (June 20): 1637.

———. 1992e. "Opening up Merit Awards." *British Medical Journal* 304 (June 27): 1653.

———. 1992f. Medicopolitical Digest. From the LMC Conference. *British Medical Journal* 305 (July 4): 57–59.

———. 1992g. Medicopolitical Digest. "Encouraging All GPs to Commission Care." *British Medical Journal* 305 (October 24): 1024.

Beecham, Linda, Jane Smith, and John Mayor. 1993. Medicopolitical Digest. The Week in Torquay. *British Medical Journal* 307 (July 10): 131–36.

Beecham, Linda, Jane Smith, Richard Smith, and Andrew Woodward. 1991. Medicopolitical Digest. The Week in Inverness. *British Medical Journal* 303 (July 13): 127–36.

———. 1992. Medicopolitical Digest. The Week in Nottingham. *British Medical Journal* 305 (July 18): 189–97.

Beer, Samuel H. 1982a. *Britain against Itself: The Political Contradictions of Collectivism.* New York and London: Norton.

———. 1982b. *Modern British Politics: Parties and Pressure Groups in the Collectivist*

Age. New York and London: Norton. Previously published under the title *British Politics in the Collectivist Age.*

Bernardi-Schenkluhn, Brigitte. 1992. "Politischer Problemdruck und actuelle Reformstrategien im Vergleich." In *Westeuropäische Gesundheitssystems im Vergleich: Bundesrepublik Deutschland, Schweiz, Frankreich, Italien, Großbritannien,* Jens Alber and Brigitte Bernardi-Schenkluhn, eds. Frankfurt am Main: Campus.

Bindman, Andy B. 1997. "The Challenge of Measuring and Monitoring Quality." In John D. Wilkerson, Kelly J. Devers, and Ruth S. Given, eds., *Competitive Managed Care,* 100–112. San Francisco: Jossey-Bass.

Birch, Anthony H. 1984. "Overload, Ungovernability and Delegitimation: The Theories and the British Case." *British Journal of Political Science* 14 (Part 2, April): 135–60.

Blair, Tony. 1996. *New Britain: My Vision of a Young Country.* London: Fourth Estate.

Blendon, Robert J., Mollyann Brodie, John M. Benson, Drew E. Altman, Larry Levitt, Tina Hoff, and Larry Hugick. 1998. "Understanding the Managed Care Backlash." *Health Affairs* 17 (4): 80–94.

Blendon, Robert J., and Karen Donelan. 1989. British Public Opinion on National Health Service Reform." *Health Affairs* 8 (4): 52–62.

BMA (British Medical Association). 1989. *Special Report on the Government's White Paper: Working for Patients.* SRM2. London: British Medical Association.

———. 1990. "Resolutions Passed by the Annual Representative Meeting 1990." Typescript.

———. 1991a. *Annual Report of the Council, 1991.* London: British Medical Association.

———. 1991b. *Leading for Health: A BMA Agenda for Health.* London: British Medical Association.

———. 1992a. *Annual Report of the Council, 1992.* London: British Medical Association.

———. 1992b. "Resolutions Passed by the Special Representative Meeting, 26 March 1992." Typescript.

———. 1995. *Future Models for the NHS: A Discussion Paper.* Health Policy and Economic Research Unit, Discussion Paper no. 3. April 1995. London: British Medical Association.

———. n.d. "Forum 22, 1991–92." London, British Medical Association. Typescript.

BMA, General Medical Council, Joint Consultants Committee, Committee of Postgraduate Medical Deans, Council of Deans of UK Medical Schools and Faculties, Conference of Medical Royal Colleges and Their Faculties in the UK. 1994. *Core Values for the Medical Profession.* Report of conference held on November 3/4, 1994. London: British Medical Association.

BMAS (Federal Republic of Germany. Bundesministerium für Arbeit und Sozialordnung). 1991. *Übersicht über die Soziale Sicherheit.* 2. Auflage. (Esp. chap. 4, "Sozialgesetzbuch: 5. Buch—Krankenversicherung," 65–144, and chap. 22, "Organisation und Selbstverwaltung," 489–99.) Bonn: Der Bundesminister für Arbeit und Sozialordnung. Referat Öffentlichkeitsarbeit.

BMG (Federal Republic of Germany. Bundesministerium für Gesundheit). 1993a. *Die Gesetzliche Krankenversicherung.* Bonn: Bundesministerium für Gesundheit. Referat Öffentlichkeitsarbeit, April.

———. 1993b. "The Statutory Health Insurance Reform Law: Because We Feel

Responsible for Your Health." Bonn. Bundesministerium für Gesundheit. Typescript.

———. 1997. "Bundestag bestätigt Richtungsentscheidung im Gesundheitswesen." Pressemitteilung. Bundesministerium für Gesundheit. June 12.

———. 2001a. "Eckpunkte zur Reform des Risikostrukturausgleichs." *BMG-Pressemitteilungen 2001.* March 28, no. 28. http://www.bmgesundheit.de/presse/2001/2001/28.htm. (Downloaded October 23, 2001.)

———. 2001b. Pressemitteilungen 2001. December 21, no. 141. http://www.bmgesundheiet.de/presse/2001/2001/141.htm. (Downloaded April 1, 2002.)

Bodenheimer, Thomas, and Kevin Grumbach. 1994. "Paying for Health Care." *Journal of the American Medical Association* 272 (8) (August 24/31): 634–39.

Brenner, Gerhard, and Dale A. Rublee. 1991. "The 1987 Revision of Physician Fees in Germany." *Health Affairs* 10 (3): 147–56.

Brindle, David. 1991a. "Soft-Shoe Shuffle to the NHS Shake-up." *Guardian* (London; international ed.) March 27, p. 25.

———. 1991b. "'Brakes off' Market System, but Change Will Start Slowly." *Guardian* (London; international ed.) July 25, p. 7.

———. 1992. "NHS Fails to Clear 2-Year Waiting List." *Guardian* (London; international ed.) April 3.

British Medical Journal. 1988. "Supplementary Annual Report of Council. Appendix VI: Evidence to the Government Internal Review of the National Health Service." *British Medical Journal* 296 (May 14): 1410–18.

———. 1989. BMA Affairs. From the Special Representative Meeting. *British Medical Journal* 298 (May 27): 1455–57.

———. 1990. BMA Affairs. From the ARM. "From National Health to No Hope Service." *British Medical Journal* 300 (June 30): 1727–28.

Brown, Lawrence D. 1983. *Politics and Health Care Organization: HMOs as Federal Policy.* Washington, D.C.: Brookings.

Buckley, Neil. 1992. "Temperatures Soar in Health Quarrel." *Financial Times,* March 27, p. 8.

Bulpitt, Jim. 1986. "The Discipline of the New Democracy: Mrs. Thatcher's Domestic Statecraft." *Political Studies* 34 (March): 19–39.

Butler, Eamonn, and Madsen Pirie. 1988. *The Health of Nations.* London: Adam Smith Institute.

Caines, Eric. 1993. "No Way to Run a Health Service." *Financial Times,* April 27, p. 17.

California Medical Association. n.d. *Knox-Keane Plan Expenditure Summary, FY 1993/94. Public Information Package.*

Campbell, John L., and Leon N. Lindberg. 1991. "The Evolution of Governance Regimes." In *Governance of the American Economy,* ed. John L. Campbell, J. Rogers Hollingsworth, and Leon N. Lindberg, 319–55. Cambridge and New York: Cambridge University Press.

Campion, Frank D. 1984. *The AMA and US Health Policy since 1940.* Chicago: Chicago Review Press.

Cassel, Dieter, and Klaus-Dirk Henke. n.d. "Reform of the Statutory Medical Insurance System in the Federal Republic of Germany. Between Utopia and Pragmatism: Cost Cutting as a Structural Reform?" University of Duisburg, Department of Economics, Discussion Paper 112. Typescript.

Cawson, Alan. 1982. *Corporatism and Welfare: Social Policy and State Intervention in Britain.* London: Heinemann.

———. 1986. *Corporatism and Political Theory.* Oxford and New York: Basil Blackwell.

CBO (U.S. Congressional Budget Office). 1994. *An Analysis of the Administration's Health Proposal.* Congress of the United States, Congressional Budget Office. February. Washington, D.C.: U.S. Government Printing Office.

CCHMS (Central Committee for Hospital Medical Services). 1988. *NHS Funding: The Crisis in the Acute Hospital Sector.* London: British Medical Association.

Chambers, Sir Paul. 1972. "British Medical Association: Report of an Inquiry into the Association's Constitution and Organization." *British Medical Journal Supplement* (2): 45–67.

Chantler, Cyril. 1988. "Guy's Hospital 1985–1988, A Case Study." London: King's Fund College International Fellowship, March 16. Typescript.

Chapman, Carleton B. 1978. "Doctors and Their Autonomy: Past Events and Future Prospects." *Science* 200 (May 26): 851–56.

Charles, Cathy, Jonathan Lomas, Mita Giacomini, Vandna Bhatia, and Victoria A. Vincent. 1997. "Medical Necessity in Canadian Health Policy: Four Meanings and . . . a Funeral." *Milbank Quarterly* 75 (3): 365–94.

Chirba-Martin, Mary Ann, and Troyen A. Brennan. 1994. "The Critical Role of ERISA in State Health Reform." *Health Affairs* 13 (spring II): 142–56.

Chubb, John E., and Terry M. Moe. 1990. *Politics, Markets, and America's Schools.* Washington, D.C.: Brookings.

Clayton, Richard, and Jonas Pontusson. 1998. "Welfare State Retrenchment Revisited: Entitlement Cuts, Public Sector Restructuring, and Inegalitarian Trends in Advanced Capitalist Societies." *World Politics* 51 (1): 67–98.

Clymer, Adam. 1996a. "Accord Reached on Expanding Workers' Health Benefits." *New York Times,* August 1, p. D22.

———. 1996b. "House Backs Bill Granting Workers Portable Benefits." *New York Times,* August 2, p. A1.

Clymer, Adam, Robert Pear, and Robin Toner. 1994. "For Health Care, Time Was a Killer." *New York Times,* August 29, pp. A1, A8–9.

Conference of Medical Royal Colleges and Their Faculties in the U.K. 1989. *Building on the White Paper: Some Suggestions and Safeguards. Proposals for Discussion from the Conference of Colleges.* July.

Conradt, David P. 1996. *The German Polity.* 6th ed. White Plains, N.Y.: Longman.

Cooper, Philip F., and Barbara Steinberg Schone. 1997. "More Offers, Fewer Takers for Employment-Based Health Insurance: 1987 and 1996." *Health Affairs* 16 (6) (November/December): 142–49.

Crewe, Ivor, and Donald D. Searing. 1988. "Ideological Change in the British Conservative Party." *American Political Science Review* 82 (2): 361–84.

Cromwell, Jerry, and Janet B. Mitchell. 1986. "Physician-Induced Demand for Surgery." *Journal of Health Economics* 5 (December): 293–313.

Day, Patricia, and Rudolf Klein. 1987. *Accountabilities: Five Public Services.* London and New York: Tavistock.

———. 1989. "The Politics of Modernization: Britain's National Health Service in the 1980s." *Milbank Quarterly* 67 (1): 1–34.

———. 1992. "Constitutional and Distributional Conflict in British Medical Politics: The Case of General Practice, 1911–1991." *Political Studies* 40 (3): 462–78.

Deering, Christopher J., and Steven S. Smith. 1985. "Subcommittees in Congress." In *Congress Reconsidered*, 3d ed., Lawrence C. Dodd and Bruce I. Oppenheimer, eds. Washington, D.C.: Congressional Quarterly.

Delamothe, Tony. 1989a. "Review Review." *British Medical Journal* 298 (February 11): 394.

———. 1989b. "Battling for Their Hearts and Minds." *British Medical Journal* 298 (April 8): 911.

———. 1989c. "GPs Vote Three to One against New Contract." *British Medical Journal* 299 (July 29): 285.

———. 1989d. "Poster Mortem." *British Medical Journal* 299 (September 16): 745.

———. 1990. "New Chairman of Council for BMA: Life after Marks." *British Medical Journal* 301 (July 7): 6.

———. 1992. "Hospitals Cut Elective Surgery in Attempt to Stay Solvent." *British Medical Journal* 305 (December 12): 1451.

Deutscher Bundestage. 2001. *Unterrichtung durch die Bundesregierung. Bericht der Bundesregierung über die Untersuchung zu den Wirkungen des Risikostrukturausgleichs in der gesetzlichen krankenversicherung*. Drucksache 14/5681, March 28.

Devers, Kelly J. 1997. "The Challenges of Implementing Market-Based Reform for Public Clients." In John D. Wilkerson, Kelly J. Devers, and Ruth S. Given, eds., *Competitive Managed Care*, 259–96. San Francisco: Jossey-Bass.

DHHS (U.S. Department of Health and Human Services). 2000. *Health United States*. Washington, D.C.

DHSS (Department of Health and Social Security, Welsh Office, Northern Ireland Office, and Scottish Office). 1986. *Primary Health Care: An Agenda for Discussion*. Cmnd. 9117. London: HMSO.

DHSS. 1987. *Promoting Better Health: The Government's Programme for Improving Primary Health Care*. Cm 249. London: HMSO.

Dienst für Gesellschaftspolitik. 1997a. February 20, no. 7–97.

———. 1997b. March 27, no. 12–97.

Dodd, Lawrence C., and Bruce I. Oppenheimer, eds. 1985. *Congress Reconsidered*. 3d ed. Washington D.C.: Congressional Quarterly.

DoH (U.K. Department of Health). 1989a. *Funding General Practice: The Programme for the Introduction of General Practice Budgets*. n.p. Department of Health.

———. 1989b. *General Practice in the National Health Service: The 1990 Contract*. London: HMSO. August 1989.

———. 1989c. *The Government's Plans for the Future of the National Health Service*. Government's Reply to the Eighth Report from the Social Services Committee, Session 1988–89. Cm 851. London: HMSO.

———. 1989d. *Self-Governing Hospitals: An Initial Guide: A Paper for a National Conference on 20 June 1989*. London: HMSO.

———. 1989e. Working Papers on *Working for Patients* (working papers 1–11):

Self-Governing Hospitals (Working Paper 1)

Funding and Contracts for Hospital Services (Working Paper 2)

Practice Budgets for General Medical Practitioners (Working Paper 3)

Indicative Prescribing Budgets for General Medical Practitioners (Working Paper 4)

Capital Charges (Working Paper 5)
Medical Audit (Working Paper 6)
NHS Consultants: Appointments, Contracts and Distinction Awards (Working Paper 7)
Implications for Family Practitioner Committees (Working Paper 8)
Capital Charges: Funding Issues (Working Paper 9)
Education and Training (Working Paper 10)
Framework for Information Systems: Overview (Working Paper 11)
————. 1990a. *Developing Districts.* London: HMSO.
————. 1990b. *Improving Prescribing: The Implementation of the GP Indicative Prescribing Scheme.* n.p. Department of Health.
————. 1991a. *The Health of the Nation: A Consultative Document for Health in England.* Cm 1523. London: HMSO.
————. 1991b. *The Patient's Charter.* HPC1. London: HMSO.
————. 1993. *Managing the New NHS. A Background Document.* Leeds: NHS Management Executive.
————. 1997. *The New NHS: Modern—Dependable.* Cm 3807. London: HMSO.
————. 2000. *The NHS Plan: A Plan for Investment, A Plan for Reform.* Cm. 4818-I. From NHS website (www.nhs.uk/nhsplan). (Downloaded September 2000.)
————. n.d. *Managing the New NHS: Information and Briefing for NHSME and RHA Staff.* Leeds: NHS Management Executive.
DoH and Office of Population Censuses and Surveys. 1992. *The Government's Expenditure Plans, 1992–93 to 1994–95. Departmental Report.* Cm 1913. London: HMSO.
DoH, Department of Social Security, Welsh Office, Scottish Office. 1989a. *Caring for People: Community Care in the Next Decade and Beyond.* Cm 849. London: HMSO.
DoH, Welsh Office, Northern Ireland Office, Scottish Office. 1989b. *Working for Patients.* CM 555. London: HMSO.
Döhler, Marian. 1987. "Regulating the Medical Profession in Germany: The Politics of Efficiency Review." Berlin: Social Science Research Center, Research Unit Market Processes and Corporate Development, May 1987. Typescript.
————. 1989. "Physicians' Professional Autonomy in the Welfare State: Endangered or Preserved?" In *Controlling Medical Professionals: The Comparative Politics of Health Governance,* ed. Giorgio Freddi and James Warner Björkman. London: Sage.
————. 1991. "Policy Networks, Opportunity Structures and Neo-Conservative Reform Strategies in Health Policy." In *Policy Networks: Empirical Evidence and Theoretical Consideration,* ed. Bernd Marin and Renate Mayntz. Frankfurt am Main: Campus.
————. 1995. "The State as Architect of Political Order: Policy Dynamics in German Health Care." *Governance* 8 (3): 380–404.
Döhler, Marian, and Philip Manow. 1996. "Gesundheitspolitik von Blank bis Seehofer" (Formation and Change of a Policy Domain: Health Policy from Blank to Seehofer). Typescript.
Döhler, Marian, and Philip Manow-Borgwardt. 1991. "Korporatisierung als gesundheitspolitische Strategie." MPIFG Discussion Paper 91/9. Cologne: Max-Planck-Institut für Gesellschaftsforschung, October.
————. 1992. "Korporatisierung als gesundheitspolitische Strategie." *Staatswissenschaften und Staatspraxis* 3 (1): 64–106.
Dolle-Helms, Elke. 2001. "Der Wechsel zur privaten Krankenversicherung steckt voller

Tücken." *Die Zeit* (5). http://www.zeit.de/2001/05/Wirtschaft/200105_solidus
.html (Downloaded October 4, 2001.)

Donelan, Karen, Robert J. Blendon, George D. Lundberg, David R. Calkins, Joseph P. Newhouse, Lucian L. Leape, Dahlia K. Remler, and Humphrey Taylor. 1997. "The New Medical Marketplace: Physicians' Views." *Health Affairs* 16 (5): 139–48.

Dyson, Kenneth H. F. 1980. *The State Tradition in Western Europe: A Study of an Idea and Institution.* New York: Oxford University Press.

———, ed. 1992a. *The Politics of German Regulation.* Aldershot, England.

———. 1992b. "Theories of Regulation and the Case of Germany: A Model of Regulatory Change." In *The Politics of German Regulation,* 1–28. Aldershot, England: Dartmouth.

———. 1992c. "Regulatory Culture and Regulatory Change: Some Conclusions." In *The Politics of German Regulation,* 257–72. Aldershot, England: Dartmouth.

EBRI (Employee Benefits Research Institute). 1997. "Trends in Health Insurance Coverage." *EBRI Issue Brief,* no. 185.

Eckstein, Harry. 1958. *The English Health Service: Its Origins, Structure, and Achievements.* Cambridge: Harvard University Press.

———. 1960. *Pressure Group Politics: The Case of the British Medical Association.* Stanford: Stanford University Press.

The Economist. 1985. "Some Reforms That Might Be Politically Feasible." June 22, pp. 61–64.

———. 1997. "An Unhealthy Silence." March 15, p. 57.

———. 1998. "Bevan's Baby Hits Middle Age." July 4, p. 56.

———. 2000a. "A New Prescription." March 25, p. 55.

———. 2000b. "Luck and Judgment." March 25, p. 56.

———. 2001a. "Misprescribing for Health Care." April 16, p. 49.

———. 2001b. "Hillary, You Won the War." June 23, p. 33.

Ellis, Randall P., and Thomas G. McGuire. 1986. "Provider Behavior under Prospective Reimbursement: Cost Sharing and Supply." *Journal of Health Economics* 5 (1986): 129–51.

Enthoven, Alain C. 1985. *Reflections on the Management of the National Health Service: An American Looks at Incentives to Efficiency in Health Services Management in the UK.* London: Nuffield Provincial Hospitals Trust.

———. 1988. "Managed Competition: An Agenda for Action." *Health Affairs* 7 (3): 25–47.

———. 1993. "The History and Principles of Managed Competition." *Health Affairs* (Supplement) 24–48.

Epstein, Leon D. 1986. *Political Parties in the American Mold.* Madison and London: University of Wisconsin Press.

Esping-Andersen, Gøsta. 1985. *Politics against Markets: The Social Democratic Road to Power.* Princeton: Princeton University Press.

———. 1990. *The Three Worlds of Welfare Capitalism.* Princeton: Princeton University Press.

———. 1994. "Welfare States in the Economy." In Neil J. Smelser and Richard Swedberg, eds., *The Handbook of Economic Sociology,* 711–32. Princeton: Princeton University Press; New York: Russell Sage Foundation.

———. 1996a. "After the Golden Age? Welfare State Dilemmas in a Global Economy."

Chap. 1 in Gøsta Esping-Andersen, ed., *Welfare States in Transition: National Adaptations in Global Economies*, 1–31. London, Thousand Oaks, and New Delhi: Sage.

———. 1996b. "Welfare States without Work: The Impasse of Labour Shedding and Familialism in Continental European Social Policy." Chap. 3 in Gøsta Esping-Andersen, ed., *Welfare States in Transition: National Adaptations in Global Economies*, 66–87. London, Thousand Oaks, and New Delhi: Sage.

———. 1999. *Social Foundations of Postindustrial Economies*. Oxford and New York: Oxford University Press.

Estes, Carroll L., Steven P. Wallace, and Elizabeth A. Binney. 1989. "Health, Aging, and Medical Sociology." In *Handbook of Medical Sociology*, 4th ed., Howard E. Freeman and Sol Levine, eds., 400–418. Englewood Cliffs: Prentice Hall.

Evans, Peter B., Dietrich Rueschemeyer, and Theda Skocpol., eds. 1985. *Bringing the State Back In*. Cambridge: Cambridge University Press.

Evans, Robert G. 1984. "Risk, Uncertainty, and the Limits of Insurability." In *Strained Mercy: The Economics of Canadian Health Care*, 27–52. Toronto: Butterworth.

Federal Minister of Labour and Social Affairs. 1980. *Co-determination in the Federal Republic of Germany*. Bonn: Federal Minister of Labour and Social Affairs.

Ferguson, Thomas, and Joel Rogers. 1986. *Right Turn: The Decline of the Democrats and the Future of American Politics*. New York: Hill and Wang.

Files, Ashley, and Margaret Murray. 1995. "German Risk Structure Compensation: Enhancing Equity and Effectiveness." *Inquiry* 32 (fall) 300–309.

Fletcher, David. 1992. "Hospitals' Two-Year Waiting List Slashed from 50,000 to 1,600." *Daily Telegraph*, April 3.

Ford, Richard, and Robert Matthews. 1989. "Clarke Accuses GPs of Feeling for Their Wallets." *Times* (London) March 10, p. 2.

Frankfurter Rundschau. 1991a. "Kranke Vorschläge." Editorial. November 28, p. 3.

———. 1991b. "Hasselfeldt will notfalls Sparzwang verordnen." December 4.

———. 1992a. "Ärzte machen gegen Ministerin Hasselfeldt mobil." January 14, p. 6.

———. 1992b. "Relativitäts-Therapie." Editorial. January 14, p. 6.

———. 1996a. "Da passt kein Krankenschein mehr dazwischen." September 25, p. 3.

———. 1996b. "Schlag gegen Kranke." Editorial. September 25, p. 3.

Freddi, Giorgio, and James Warner Björkman, eds. 1989. *Controlling Medical Professionals: The Comparative Politics of Health Governance*. London: Sage.

Freeman, Richard B. 1994. "How Labor Fares in Advanced Economies." In *Working under Different Rules*, 1–28. New York: Russell Sage Foundation.

Freidson, Eliot. 1970. *Profession of Medicine: A Study of the Sociology of Applied Knowledge*. New York: Dodd, Mead.

Freudenheim, Milt. 1994. "To Economists, Managed Care Is No Cure-All. *New York Times*, September 6, pp. A1, A10.

———. 1997. "Health Care Costs Edging up and a Bigger Surge Is Feared." *New York Times*, January 21, pp. A1, D20.

———. 1998. "Health Insurers Seek Big Increases in Their Premiums." *New York Times*, April 24, pp. A1, C4.

———. 1999a. "Concern Rising about Mergers in Health Plans." *New York Times*, January 13.

————. 1999b. "Big H.M.O. to Give Decisions on Care Back to Doctors." *New York Times*, November 9, p. A1.

————. 1999c. "Medical Insurers Revise Cost-Control Efforts." *New York Times*, December 3, p. A1ff.

Fronstin, Paul. 1997. "Sources of Health Insurance and Characteristics of the Uninsured." *EBRI Issue Brief*, no. 192 (December). Employee Benefits Research Institute.

————. 2000. "Testimony before the Health, Education, Labor, and Pensions Committee, United States Senate. Hearing on Health Insurance Coverage and Uninsured Americans." October 4. (Downloaded from Employee Benefits Research Institute website, www.ebri.org.)

————. 2001. "Employment-Based Health Benefits: Trends and Outlook." *EBRI Issue Brief*, no. 233 (May). Employee Benefits Research Institute.

Fuchs, Beth C., Bob Lyke, Richard Price, and Madeleine Smith. 1997. *The Health Insurance Portability and Accountability Act of 1996: Guidance on Frequently Asked Questions.* CRS Report for Congress. 96–805 EPW. Washginton, D.C.: Congressional Research Service, Library of Congress. (Updated April 10, 1997.)

Gabel, Jon R., Paul B. Ginsburg, and Kelly A. Hunt. 1997. "Small Employers and Their Health Benefits, 1988–1996: An Awkward Adolescence." *Health Affairs* 16 (5): 103–10.

Gamble, Andrew. 1994. *The Free Economy and the Strong State: The Politics of Thatcherism.* Durham: Duke University Press.

GAO (U.S. General Accounting Office). 1993. *German Health Reforms: New Cost Control Initiatives.* Report to the Chairman, Committee on Governmental Affairs, U.S. Senate, Washington, D.C.: GAO, July.

————. 1995. *Employer-Based Health Plans: Issues, Trends, and Challenges Posed by ERISA.* GAO/HEHS-95–167. July. Washington, D.C.: GAO.

————. 1997. *Private Health Insurance: Continued Erosion of Coverage Linked to Cost Pressures.* GAO/HEHS-97–122. July. Washington, D.C.: GAO.

————. 1998. *Health Insurance Standards: New Federal Law Creates Challenges for Consumers, Insurers, Regulators.* GAO/HEHS-98–67. February. Washington, D.C.: GAO.

Garpenby, Peter. 1989. *The State and the Medical Profession: A Cross-National Comparison of the Health Policy Arena in the United Kingdom and Sweden, 1945–1985.* Linkoping, Sweden: University of Linkoping.

Der Gelbe Dienst. 1992. "Gesetzesvorhaben 'Sicherung und Strukturverbeserung [*sic*] der gesetzlichen Krankenversicherung' auf den Weg gebracht." 12 (June 2): 2–14.

Georges, Christopher. 1995. "House GOP Medicare Bill Wins over Doctors with Hidden Enticements, Promise of Profits." *Wall Street Journal*, October 12, p. A24.

Giaimo, Susan M. 1995. "Health Care Reform in Britain and Germany: Recasting the Political Bargain with the Medical Profession." *Governance* 8 (3) (July): 354–79.

————. 1996. "Health Care Reform in Britain and Germany: Lessons for the United States." Paper presented at the Robert Wood Johnson Foundation Scholars in Health Policy Research Program Meeting, Aspen, Colo., May 29–June 2.

————. 1998. *Cost Containment vs. Solidarity in the Welfare State: The Case of German and American Health Care Reform.* AICGS Policy Papers no. 6. Washington, D.C.: American Institute for Contemporary German Studies.

————. 2001. "Who Pays for Health Care Reform?" In Paul Pierson, ed., *The New Politics of the Welfare State*, 334–67. Oxford: Oxford University Press.

Giaimo, Susan, and Philip Manow. 1997. "Institutions and Ideas into Politics: Health Care Reform in Britain and Germany." In Christa Altenstetter and James Warner Björkman, eds., *Health Policy Reform, National Variations and Globalization*, 175–202. London: Macmillan; New York: St. Martin's.

————. 1999. "Welfare State Adaptation or Erosion? The Case of Health Care Reform in Britain, Germany, and the United States." *Comparative Political Studies* 32 (8) (December): 967–1000.

Giddens, Anthony. 1998. *The Third Way: The Renewal of Social Democracy.* Cambridge, Oxford, and Malden: Polity.

Given, Ruth S. 1997. "Ensuring Competition in the Market for HMO Services." In John D. Wilkerson, Kelly J. Devers, and Ruth S. Given, eds., *Competitive Managed Care*, 167–97. San Francisco: Jossey-Bass.

Glennerster, Howard, Manos Matsaganis, and Pat Owens. 1992. *A Foothold for Fundholding: A Preliminary Report on the Introduction of GP Fundholding.* London: King's Fund Institute.

GMSC (General Medical Services Committee). 1991. *Building Your Own Future: An Agenda for General Practice.* London: British Medical Association.

————. 1992. *Your Choices: Report to a Special Conference of Representatives of LMCs on 23/24 June 1992.* SC2 1991/92. London: British Medical Association.

Goldsmith, Michael, and David Willetts. 1988. *Managed Health Care: A New System for a Better Health Service.* London: Centre for Policy Studies, February.

Göpffarth, Dirk. 1997. "Auswirkungen der aktuellen Gesetzesvorhaben auf das Krankenhauswesen." June 2. Typescript.

Gordon, Linda, ed. 1990. *Women, the State, and Welfare.* Madison and London: University of Wisconsin Press.

Gourevitch, Peter. 1986. *Politics in Hard Times: Comparative Responses to International Economic Crises.* Ithaca and London: Cornell University Press.

Green, David G. 1988. *Everyone a Private Patient: An Analysis of the Structural Flaws in the NHS and How They Could Be Remedied.* London: Institute of Economic Affairs.

Greene, Jay P., Paul E. Peterson, and Jiangtao Du. 1996. "The Effectiveness of School Choice In Milwaukee: A Secondary Analysis of Data from the Program's Evaluation." PEPG96–3. Typescript.

Greenhouse, Linda. 2000. "H.M.O.s Win Crucial Ruling on Liability for Doctors' Acts." *New York Times,* June 13, pp. A1, A20.

Greenhouse, Steven. 1999a. "Angered by H.M.O.s' Treatment, More Doctors Are Joining Unions." *New York Times,* February 4, pp. A1, A25.

————. 1999b. "A.M.A.'s Delegates Decide to Create Union of Doctors." *New York Times,* June 24, p. A1.

Grey-Turner, Elston, and F. M. Sutherland. 1982. *History of the British Medical Association,* vol. 2, 1932–81. London: British Medical Association.

Griffiths, E. R. (Sir Roy). 1983. *NHS Management Inquiry.* London: Department of Health and Social Security.

————. 1988. *Community Care: Agenda for Action.* London: HMSO.

Grogan, Colleen. 1995. "Hope in Federalism: What Can the States Do and What Are They Likely to Do?" *Journal of Health Politics, Policy and Law* 20 (2): 477–84.

Hacker, Jacob S. 1997. *The Road to Nowhere: The Genesis of President Clinton's Plan for Health Security*. Princeton: Princeton University Press.

Hafferty, Frederic W. 1988. "Theories at the Crossroads: A Discussion of Evolving Views on Medicine as a Profession." *Milbank Quarterly* 66 (Supplement 2): 202–25.

Hall, Peter A. 1986. *Governing the Economy: The Politics of State Intervention in Britain and France*. Cambridge: Polity.

———, ed. 1989. *The Political Power of Economic Ideas: Keynesianism across Nations*. Princeton: Princeton University Press.

———. 1994. "Central Bank Independence and Coordinated Wage Bargaining: Their Interaction in Germany and Europe." *German Politics and Society* 31 (spring): 1–23.

Ham, Chris. 1985. *Health Policy in Britain: The Politics and Organisation of the National Health Service*. 2d ed. Basingstoke and London: Macmillan.

———. 1988. "Governing the Health Sector: Power and Policy Making in the English and Swedish Health Services." *Milbank Quarterly* 66 (2): 389–414.

Ham, Chris, Ray Robinson, and Michaela Benzeval. 1990. *Health Check: Health Care Reforms in an International Context*. London: King's Fund Institute.

Harrison, Stephen. 1988. *Managing the National Health Service: Shifting the Frontier?* London: Chapman and Hall.

Harrison, Stephen, David J. Hunter, and Christopher Pollitt. 1990. *The Dynamics of British Health Policy*. London: Unwin Hyman.

Harrison, Stephen, and Rockwell I. Schulz. 1989. Clinical Autonomy in the United Kingdom and the United States: Contrasts and Convergence." In *Controlling Medical Professionals: The Comparative Politics of Health Governance*, Giorgio Freddi and James Warner Björkman, eds. New York: Sage.

Hart. [pseud.] 1992a. The Week. "Snuggling up Together." *British Medical Journal* 304 (April 25): 1074.

———. 1992b. The Week. "Vigilance in the Face of Bullishness." *British Medical Journal* 304 (June 13): 1530.

———. 1992c. The Week. "Dithering Doctors?" *British Medical Journal* 305 (July 11): 78.

———. 1993a. The Week. "All a Matter of Style." *British Medical Journal* 307 (July 3): 12.

———. 1993b. The Week. "Fundholding: Sending the Right Message." *British Medical Journal* 307 (July 24): 224.

Hartmannbund. 1989. *Das "Gesundheits-Reformgesetz": Inhalt, Folgen, Anwendung für den niedergelassenen Arzt*. Bonn: Hartmannbund—Verband der Ärzte Deutschlands e.V.

———. n.d. *Die Konzertierte Aktion im Gesundheitswesen*. Bonn: Hartmannbund—Verband der Ärzte Deutschlands e. V.

Health Affairs. 1995. Special Issue. Health Reform: Past and Future. *Health Affairs* 14 (1) (spring).

———. 1997a. Special Issue. Hospital and Health Plan Conversions. *Health Affairs* 16 (2) March/April.

———. 1997b. Special Issue. The Safety Net vs. the Market. *Health Affairs* 16 (4) July/August.

Health Security. The President's Report to the American People. 1993. White House Domestic Policy Council.

Heidenheimer, Arnold J., Hugh Heclo, and Carolyn Teich Adams. 1990. Chap. 3 in *Comparative Public Policy: The Politics of Social Choice in America, Europe, and Japan,* 57–96, 3d ed. New York: St. Martin's.

Heilemann, Ulrich, and Hermann Rappen 1997. *The Seven Year Itch? German Unity from a Fiscal Viewpoint.* AICGS Research Report No. 6, Economic Studies Program. Washington, D.C.: American Institute for Contemporary German Studies.

Hemerijck, Anton, and Philip Manow. 1998. "The Experience of Negotiated Reform in the German and Dutch Welfare State." Paper prepared for the conference "Varieties of Welfare Capitalism," Max Planck Institute for the Study of Societies, Cologne, June 11–13.

Hencke, David. 1992. "Consultant Blamed Lack of Money for Operation Delay." *Guardian* (London; international ed.), March 26, pp. 1, 22.

Henke, Klaus-Dirk. 1997a. *Quo Vadis, Health Care?* Discussion Paper 1997/13. Technische Universität Berlin, Wirtschaftswissenschaftlichen Dokumentation, Fachbereich 14.

———. 1997b. "Sozial gebundener Wettbewerb als neuer Ordnungsrahmen im Gesundheitswesen." In Arbeitskreis Evangelischer Unternehmer in Deutschland e.V., ed. *Die Soziale Marktwirtschaft als Wirtschafts- und Werteordnung,* 171–94. Cologne: Institut der deutschen Wirtschaft Köln, Deutscher Instituts-Verlag.

———. n.d. "The Allocation of National Resources in Health Care: Between Competition and Solidarity." Typescript.

Henke, Klaus-Dirk, Claudia Ade, and Margaret Murray. 1994. "The German Health Care System: Structure and Changes." *Journal of Clinical Anesthesiology* 6 (May/June): 252–62.

Henke, Klaus-Dirk, and Ursula Raschold. 1997. "Solidarity and Competition in the Health Service." In *Social Protection in Europe.* Evangelische Akedemic Bad Boll, 161–71.

Himmelstein, David U., Steffie Woolhandler, and the Writing Committee of the Working Group on Program Design. 1989. "A National Health Program for the United States: A Physicians' Proposal." *New England Journal of Medicine* 320 (January 12): 102–8.

Hinrichs, Karl. 1995. "The Impact of German Health Insurance Reforms on Redistribution and the Culture of Solidarity." *Journal of Health Politics, Policy and Law* 20 (3) (fall): 653–88.

Hoffenberg, Sir Raymond, Ian P. Todd, and Sir George Pinker. 1987. "Crisis in the National Health Service." *British Medical Journal* 295 (December 12): 1505.

Hoffmann, Wolfgang. 1991. "Gegen die Verfassung." *Die Zeit* (42): 12.

House of Commons (U.K.). Health Committee. 1991. *Public Expenditure on Health and Personal Social Services.* Vol. 3: Appendices to the Minutes of Evidence. Third Report. Session 1990–91. HC 614-III. London: HMSO.

———. Social Services Committee. 1988. *The Future of the National Health Service.* Fifth Report, Session 1987–88. HC 613. London: HMSO.

———. 1989a. *Resourcing the National Health Service: The Government's Plans for the Future of the National Health Service.* Eighth Report, Session 1988–89. HC 214-III. London: HMSO.

———. 1989b. *Resourcing the National Health Service: The Government's White Paper; Working for Patients.* Memoranda Laid before the Committee. Session 1988–89. HC 214-IV. London: HMSO.

Howard, Christopher. 1997. *The Hidden Welfare State: Tax Expenditures and Social Policy in the United States.* Princeton: Princeton University Press.

Huber, Evelyne, and John D. Stephens. 1997. "The Politics of the Welfare State after the Golden Age: Quantitative Evidence." Paper prepared for delivery at the Annual Meeting of the American Political Science Association, Washington, D.C., August 28–31.

Iglehart, John K. 1991. "Health Policy Report: Germany's Health Care System. Part Two." *New England Journal of Medicine* 324 (June 13): 1750–56.

Immergut, Ellen M. 1992. *Health Politics: Interests and Institutions in Western Europe.* Cambridge: Cambridge University Press.

Institute of Health Services Management. 1988. *Working Party on Alternative Delivery and Funding of Health Services: Final Report.* London: Institute of Health Services Management.

Iversen, Torben. 2001. "The Dynamics of Welfare State Expansion: Trade Openness, Deindustrialization and Partisan Politics." In Paul Pierson, ed., *The New Politics of the Welfare State,* 45–79. Oxford: Oxford University Press.

Iversen, Torben, and Thomas R. Cusack. 1998. "The Causes of Welfare State Expansion: Deindustrialization or Globalization?" Paper presented at the American Political Science Association Annual Meeting, Boston, September 3–6.

Iversen, Torben, and Anne Wren. 1998. "Equality, Employment, and Budgetary Restraint: The Trilemma of the Service Economy." *World Politics* 50 (4): 507–46.

Jaklevic, Chris. 1996. "A Good Year for 'Patient Protection' Laws." *Modern Healthcare,* October 28, 22.

James, John H. 1995. "Reforming the British National Health Service: Implementation Problems in London." *Journal of Health Politics, Policy and Law* 20 (1) (spring): 191–210.

Jenkins, Peter. 1987. *Mrs. Thatcher's Revolution: The Ending of the Socialist Era.* London: Jonathan Cape.

Johnson, Haynes, and David S. Broder. 1997. *The System: The American Way of Politics at the Breaking Point.* Boston, New York, Toronto, and London: Back Bay Books/Little, Brown.

Jones, Judy. 1991. "Fears Grow over Delay in Hospital Trust Plans." *Independent* (London), October 17, p. 5.

Jost, Timothy. 1998. "German Health Care Reform: The Next Steps." *Journal of Health Politics, Policy and Law* 23 (4): 697–711.

Journal of Health Politics, Policy and Law. 1995. Special Section on the Failure of Health Care Reform. *Journal of Health Politics, Policy and Law* 20 (2) (summer).

Judis, John B. 1995. "Abandoned Surgery: Business and the Failure of Health Care Reform." *American Prospect* 2 (spring): 65–73.

KAG (Sachverständigenrat für die Konzertierte Aktion im Gesundheitswesen [Advisory Council for Concerted Action in Health Care]). 1992. *Jahresgutachten 1992: Ausbau in Deutschland und Aufbruch nach Europa.* Baden-Baden: Nomos.

———. 1995. *Health Care and Health Insurance 2000: A Closer Orientation towards*

Results, Higher Quality Services and Greater Economic Efficiency. Summary and Recommendations of the Special Expert Report, 1995. Bonn.

———. 1996. *The Health Care System in Germany: Cost Factor and Branch of the Future.* Vol. 1: *Demographics, Morbidity, Efficiency Reserves and Employment. Special Report 1996. Summary.* Bonn.

———. 1997. *The Health Care System in Germany: Cost Factor and Branch of the Future.* Vol. 2: *Progress and Growth Markets, Finance and Remuneration. Special Report 1997, Summary.* Bonn.

Kaiser/Harvard National Survey of Americans' Views on Consumer Protection in Managed Care. 1998. Kaiser Family Foundation, January 21. (Chart pack and press releases downloaded from Kaiser Family Foundation website, www.kff.org, July 11).

Katzenstein, Peter J. 1987. *Policy and Politics in West Germany: The Growth of a Semisovereign State.* Philadelphia: Temple University Press.

Kavanagh, Denis. 1987. *Thatcherism and British Politics: The End of Consensus?* Oxford: Oxford University Press.

———. 1990. *Thatcherism and British Politics: The End of Consensus?* 2d ed. Oxford: Oxford University Press.

KBV (Kassenärztliche Bundesvereinigung). 1993. *Gesundheits-Strukturgesetz 1993: Informationen und Handlungsempfehlungen für den Kassenarzt.* Cologne: Special supplement of *Deutsches Ärzteblatt* (1/2), January 11.

———. 1994. *Grunddaten zur kassenärztlichen Versorgung in der Bundesrepublik Deutschland, 1994.* Cologne: Kassenärztliche Bundesvereinigung, Fachbereich für Volkswirtschaft und Statistik. Deutscher-Ärzte Verlag, GmbH.

Kilborn, Peter T. 1998. "Largest HMOs Cutting the Poor and the Elderly." *New York Times,* July 6, pp. A1, A9.

Kilcullen, Jack K. 1996. "Groping for the Reins: ERISA, HMO Malpractice, and Enterprise Liability." *American Journal of Law and Medicine* 22 (1): 7–50.

King, Anthony, ed. 1976. *Why Is Britain Becoming Harder to Govern?* London: British Broadcasting Co.

Kingman, Sharon. 1993. "Hospitals Slow down as Money Runs Out." *British Medical Journal* 306 (January 23): 227–28.

Kirchberger, Stefan. 1986. "Public-Health Policy in Germany, 1945–1949: Continuity and a New Beginning." In *Political Values and Health Care: The German Experience,* Donald W. Light and Alexander Schuller, eds. Cambridge and London: MIT Press.

Kirchheimer, Otto. 1966. "Germany: The Vanishing Opposition." In Robert A. Dahl, ed., *Political Oppositions in Western Democracies,* 237–59. New Haven: Yale University Press.

Kirkman-Liff, Bradford L. 1990. "Physician Payment and Cost-Containment Strategies in West Germany: Suggestions for Medicare Reform." *Journal of Health Politics, Policy and Law* 15 (1): 69–99.

Klein, Rudolf. 1989. *The Politics of the National Health Service.* 2d ed. London: Longman.

———. 1995. *The New Politics of the NHS.* 3d ed. London: Longman.

———. 1997. "Learning from Others: Shall the Last Be the First?" *Journal of Health Politics, Policy and Law* 22 (5) (October): 1267–78.

———. 1998. "Why Britain Is Reforming Its National Health Service—Yet Again." *Health Affairs* 17 (4): 111–25.

Klein, Sara A. 1999. "AMA to Establish National Collective Bargaining Unit." *American Medical News*, 5 July, 33–35.

Kornai, Janos. 1990. *Vision and Reality, Market and State: Contradictions and Dilemmas Revisited.* New York: Routledge.

Korpi, Walter. 1983. *The Democratic Class Struggle.* London: Routledge and Kegan Paul.

Kurbjuweit, Dirk. 1992. "Allein gegen die Lobby." *Die Zeit* (19): 27.

Kuttner, Robert. 1997. "Physician-Operated Networks and the New Antitrust Guidelines." *New England Journal of Medicine* 336 (5) (January 30): 386–91.

Labour Party. 1995. *Renewing the NHS: Labour's Agenda for a Healthier Britain.* London: Labour Party, John Smith House.

Larkin, G. V. 1988. Medical Dominance in Britain: Image and Historical Reality." *Milbank Quarterly* 66 (Supplement 2): 117–32.

Laurance, Jeremy. 1993a. "BMA Backs down on Fundholding to Avoid Split." *Times* (London), June 29, p. 2.

———. 1993b. "BMA Elects Vocal Critic of Reforms." *Times* (London), July 2, p. 5.

Lauterbach, Karl W., and Eberhard Wille. 2001. "Modell eines fairen Wettbewerbs durch den Risikostrukturausgleich. Sofortprogramm 'Wechslerkomponente und solidarische Rückversicherung' unter Berücksichtigung der Morbidität." Abschlussbericht. Gutachten im Auftrag des Verbandes der Angestellten-Krankenkassen e. V. (VdAk), des Arbeiter-Ersatzkassen-Verbandes e. V. (AEV), des AOK-Bundesverbandes (AOK-Bv) und des IKK-Bundesverbandes (IKK-BV).

Lawson, Nigel. 1993. *The View from Number 11: Britain's Longest-Serving Cabinet Minister Recalls the Triumphs and Disappointments of the Thatcher Era.* New York: Doubleday.

Le Grand, Julian. 1997. "Knights, Knaves, or Pawns? Human Behaviour and Social Policy." *Journal of Social Policy* 26 (2): 149–69.

Le Grand, Julian, and Will Bartlett. 1993a. "Introduction." In Julian Le Grand and Will Bartlett, eds., *Quasi-Markets and Social Policy,* 1–12. Basingstoke: Macmillan.

———, eds. 1993b. *Quasi-Markets and Social Policy.* Basingstoke: Macmillan.

Lehmbruch, Gerhard. 1984. "Concertation and the Structure of Corporatist Networks." In *Order and Conflict in Contemporary Capitalism,* ed. John H. Goldthorpe. Oxford: Clarendon.

———. 1992. "The Institutional Framework of German Regulation." In Kenneth Dyson, ed., *The Politics of German Regulation,* 29–52. Aldershot, England: Dartmouth.

Leibfried, Stephan, and Florian Tennstedt. 1986. "Health-Insurance Policy and Berufsverbote in the Nazi Takeover." In Donald W. Light and Alexander Schuller, eds., *Political Values and Health Care: The German Experience,* 127–84. Cambridge and London: MIT Press.

Leichter, Howard M. 1979. "Germany: The Pioneer in National Health Care." Chap. 5 in *A Comparative Approach to Policy Analysis: Health Care Policy in Four Nations,* 110–56. Cambridge and New York: Cambridge University Press.

Levit, Katharine R., Helen C. Lazenby, Bradley R. Braden, and the National Health

Accounts Team. 1998. "National Health Spending Trends in 1996." *Health Affairs* 17 (1): 35–51.

Light, Donald W. 1997. "Lessons for the United States: Britain's Experience with Managed Competition." In John D. Wilkerson, Kelly J. Devers, and Ruth S. Given, eds., *Competitive Managed Care.* San Francisco: Jossey-Bass.

———. n.d. *Strategic Challenges in Joint Commissioning: Challenges and Strategic Issues in Comparative Perspective.* London: North West Thames Regional Health Authority.

Lindberg, Leon N., and John L. Campbell. 1991. "The State and the Organization of Economic Activity." In *Governance of the American Economy,* John L. Campbell, J. Rogers Hollingsworth, and Leon N. Lindberg, eds., 356–95. Cambridge and New York: Cambridge University Press.

Lindberg, Leon N., John L. Campbell, and J. Rogers Hollingsworth. 1991. "Economic Governance and the Analysis of Structural Change in the American Economy." In *Governance of the American Economy,* John L. Campbell, J. Rogers Hollingsworth, and Leon N. Lindberg, eds., 3–34. Cambridge and New York: Cambridge University Press.

Little, Ernest Muirhead. 1932. *History of the British Medical Association, 1832–1932.* London: British Medical Association.

Lock, Stephen. 1989. "Steaming through the NHS." *British Medical Journal* 298 (March 11): 619–20.

Lowry, Stella. 1989. "BMA—Working for Patients, with a Mandate." *British Medical Journal* 298 (May 27): 1411–12.

Macpherson, Gordon. 1989. "BMA Meets Ministers on NHS Review." *British Medical Journal* 298 (June 24): 1665.

Maioni, Antonia. 1998. *Parting at the Crossroads: The Emergence of Health Insurance in the United States and Canada.* Princeton: Princeton University Press.

Mann, Thomas E., and Norman J. Ornstein, eds. 1995. *Intensive Care: How Congress Shapes Health Policy.* Washington, D.C.: American Enterprise Institute/Brookings.

Manow, Philip. 1997a. "Social Insurance and the German Political Economy." MPIfG Discussion Paper 97-2. Max Planck Institute for the Study of Societies, Cologne.

———. 1997b. "Structural Characteristics and Potential Effects of Current Reforms in the German Health Care System." July. Typescript.

———. 1999. " 'Liberalism by Default': The Uneasy Compromise between Liberal and Corporatist Ideas in the Postwar German Welfare State." Paper prepared for the conference "Liberalism and Change: Political Rights and Economic Capacities in Germany and the United States," Center for German and European Studies, University of California, Berkeley, January 22–24.

Manow, Philip, and Susan Giaimo. 1995. "Welfare State Regimes, Globalization, and Health Care Reform: The Cases of Britain, Germany, and the United States." Paper presented at the American Political Science Association Annual Meeting, Chicago, August 31–September 3.

Marmor, Theodore R. 2000. *The Politics of Medicare.* 2d ed. Hawthorne, N.Y.: Aldine de Gruyter.

Marmor, Theodore R., Amy Bridges, and Wayne L. Hoffman. 1983. "Comparative Politics and Health Policies: Notes on Benefits, Costs, Limits." In *Political Analysis and*

American Medical Care: Essays, Theodore R. Marmor, ed., 45–57. Cambridge: Cambridge University Press.

Marshall, T. H. 1963. "Citizenship and Social Class." In *Sociology at the Crossroads, and Other Essays*. London: Heinemann.

Martin, Andrew. 1997. *What Does Globalization Have to Do with the Erosion of Welfare States: Sorting out the Issues*. Working Paper, Center for European Studies, Harvard University.

Martin, Cathie Jo. 1995a. "Nature or Nurture? Sources of Firm Preference for National Health Reform." *American Political Science Review* 89 (4) (December): 898–913.

———. 1995b. "Stuck in Neutral: Big Business and the Politics of National Health Reform." *Journal of Health Politics, Policy and Law* 20 (2) (summer): 431–36.

———. 1997. "Mandating Social Change: The Business Struggle over National Health Reform." *Governance* 10 (4): 397–428.

———. 2000. *Stuck in Neutral: Business and the Politics of Human Capital Investment Policy*. Princeton: Princeton University Press.

Martin, Jurek. 1994. "Business Snubs Clinton Health Bill." *Financial Times*, February 4, p. 5.

Mayhew, David. 1974. *Congress: The Electoral Connection*. New Haven and London: Yale University Press.

Maynard, Alan. 1991. "Developing the Health Care Market." *Economic Journal* 101 (September): 1277–86.

Mead, Lawrence. 1986. *Beyond Entitlement: The Social Obligations of Citizenship*. New York: Free Press.

Mealey's Litigation Reports: Managed Care. 1997. "U.S. Judge in Massachusetts Criticizes ERISA while Holding Statute Bars Claims." November 20. (Downloaded December 4, 1997).

Mihill, Chris. 1992a. "Fundholding Offered to 5,000 GPs." *Guardian* (London; international ed.) January 22, p. 8.

———. 1992b. "Patients 'Culled from Waiting List.'" *Guardian* (London; international ed.) February 13, p. 8.

Miller, Robert, and Harold S. Luft. 1994. "Managed Care Plan Performance since 1980: A Literature Analysis." *Journal of the American Medical Association* 271 (19) (May 18): 1512–19.

———. 1997. "Does Managed Care Lead to Better or Worse Quality of Care?" *Health Affairs* 16 (5): 7–25.

Ministry of Health and Central Office of Information (U.K.). n.d. *The National Health Service*. London: HMSO.

Mitchell, Alison, and Robert Pear. 2001. "Senate Considers Patients' Rights in Test with Bush." *New York Times*, June 18, pp. A1, A12.

Moon, Marilyn, Barbara Gage, and Alison Evans. 1997. *An Examination of Key Medicare Provisions in the Balanced Budget Act of 1997*. September. New York: Commonwealth Fund.

Muh, Carrie Rebecca. 1997. "Managed Care, Physicians and Public Policy: Boston as Case Study." Master's of Science thesis, Department of Political Science, Massachusetts Institute of Technology, Cambridge, September.

Murray, Charles. 1984. *Losing Ground: American Social Policy, 1950–1980*. New York: Basic Books.

Myles, John, and Paul Pierson. 2001. "The Comparative Political Economy of Pension Reform." In Paul Pierson, ed., *The New Politics of the Welfare State*, 305–33. Oxford: Oxford University Press.

National Audit Office. 1994. *General Practitioner Fundholding in England.* National Audit Office. Report by the Comptroller and Auditor General. London: HMSO. (Published December 9.)

Navarro, Vicente. 1988. "Professional Dominance or Proletarianization: Neither." *Milbank Quarterly* 66 (Supplement 2): 57–75.

New York Times. 1995. "Bribes for the Doctors." Editorial, October 15.

NHS (National Health Service) Management Executive. 1990. *NHS Trusts: A Working Guide.* London: HMSO.

———. 1991. *A Review of the Functions and Organisation of the Management Executive.* February. London: NHS Management Executive.

———. 1994a. *Managing the New NHS: Functions and Responsibilities in the New NHS.* July. Leeds: NHS Management Executive.

———. 1994b. *Developing NHS Purchasing and GP Fundholding.* EL(94)79. October 20. Leeds: NHS Executive Headquarters.

———. 1994c. *Report of the Working Party on the Review of the Consultants' Distinction Awards Scheme.* EL(94)99. December 30. Leeds: NHS Executive Headquarters.

———. 1995a. *Developing NHS Purchasing and GP Fundholding: Towards a Primary Care–Led NHS.* January. Heywood, Lancashire: Department of Health, Health Publications Unit.

———. 1995b. *Annual Report of the Advisory Committee on Distinction Awards.* January. EL(95)20, February 23. Leeds: NHS Executive Headquarters.

———. 1995c. *An Accountability Framework for GP Fundholding: Towards a Primary Care–Led NHS.* April. Leeds: NHS Executive.

———. 1995d. *General Practice Fundholding: A Primary Care–Led NHS.* May. N.p. Department of Health.

———. 1995e. *Priorities and Planning Guidance for the NHS: 1996/97.* EL(95)68. June 9. Leeds: NHS Executive Headquarters.

———. 1995f. *Revised Arrangements for B, A and A+ Distinction Awards.* EL(95). August 1995. Leeds: NHS Executive.

Niejahr, Elisabeth. 2001a. "Die Bundesregierung muss sich entscheiden, wieviel Wettbewerb es im Gesundheitswesen geben soll." *Die Zeit* (8). http://www.zeit.de/2001/ 08/Wirtschaft/200108_argument.html. (Downloaded October 4, 2001.)

———. 2001b. "Deutschlands kranke Kassen." *Die Zeit* (31), July 26. http://www.zeit.de. (Downloaded October 4, 2001.)

———. 2001b. "Deutschlands kranke Kassen: *Die Zeit* (31), July 26. http://www.zeit.de. (Downloaded October 4, 2001.)

Nordlinger, Eric. 1981. *On the Autonomy of the Democratic State.* Cambridge: Harvard University Press.

Norton, Philip. 1984. *The British Polity.* New York and London: Longman.

OECD (Organisation for Economic Cooperation and Development). 1992. *The Reform of Health Care: A Comparative Analysis of Seven OECD Countries.* Paris: OECD.

———. 1993. *OECD Health Systems: Facts and Trends, 1960–1991.* Vol. 1. Paris: OECD.

———. 1994a. *The OECD Jobs Study: Facts, Analysis, Strategies.* Paris: OECD.

―――. 1994b. *The Reform of Health Care Systems: A Review of Seventeen OECD Countries.* Paris: OECD.

―――. 1996a. *Aging in OECD Countries: A Critical Policy Challenge.* Social Policy Studies No. 20. Paris: OECD.

―――. 1996b. *OECD Economic Surveys: Germany 1995–1996.* Paris: OECD. (Esp. chap. 3, "The Tax and Transfer System.")

―――. 1997. *OECD Economic Surveys: Germany 1996–1997.* "Reforming the Health Sector: Efficiency through Incentives," 67–117. Paris: OECD.

―――. 1998. *OECD Health Data 98: A Comparative Analysis of 29 Countries.* Paris: OECD. (CD-ROM version).

―――. 1999. *OECD Economic Surveys: Germany 1998–1999.* Paris: OECD.

Offe, Claus. 1984. "Ungovernability: The Renaissance of Conservative Theories of Crisis." In *Contradictions of the Welfare State,* ed. John Keane. London: Hutchinson.

O'Keefe, Anne Marie (1995). "Will ERISA's Wall Come Tumbling Down?" *Business and Health* (February): 35–40.

Olmos, David R. 1996. "Doctors Lying Low Regarding Props. 214, 216." *Los Angeles Times,* November 1, pp. D1, D10.

Orloff, Ann Shola. 1993. "Gender and the Social Rights of Citizenship: The Comparative Analysis of State Policies and Gender Relations." *American Sociological Review* 58 (3): 303–28.

Ornstein, Norman J., Robert L. Peabody, and David W. Rohde. 1985. "The Senate through the 1980s: Cycles of Change." In *Congress Reconsidered,* 3d ed., Lawrence C. Dodd and Bruce I. Oppenheimer, eds. Washington, D.C.: Congressional Quarterly.

Osterkamp, Rigmar. 2001. "Das deutsche Gesundheitssystem im internationalen Vergleich: Bewertung und Reformalternativen." *Ifo Schnelldienst* 54 (10): 9–16.

O'Sullivan, Jack, and Judy Jones. 1992. "NHS Waiting List Figures Show Tories Near Target." *Independent* (London), April 3.

Owen, David. 1976. "Clinical Freedom and Professional Freedom." *Lancet* (May 8): 1006–9.

Parkes, Christopher. 1992a. "German Cabinet Approves Curbs on Health Spending." *Financial Times,* August 13, pp. 1, 10.

―――. 1992b. "Campaigning Doctors Outrage Bonn." *Financial Times,* September 4, p. 2.

Pear, Robert. 1993a. "White House Shuns Bigger A.M.A. Voice in Health Changes." *New York Times,* March 5, p. A1.

―――. 1993b. "Judge Puts Limits on Secret Sessions for Health Policy." *New York Times,* March 11, pp. A1, A11.

―――. 1995a. "Doctors' Group Backs Plan of Republicans on Medicare." *New York Times,* October 11, pp. A1, A10.

―――. 1995b. "Doctors' Group Says GOP Agreed to Deal on Medicare." *New York Times,* October 12, pp. A1, A10.

―――. 1995c. "Doctors Say H.M.O.'s Limit What They Can Tell Patients." *New York Times,* December 21, p. A1.

―――. 1996a. "Laws Won't Let H.M.O.'s Tell Doctors What to Say." *New York Times,* September 17, p. A12.

―――. 1996b. "U.S. Bans Limits on H.M.O. Advice in Medicare Plan." *New York*

Times, December 7, p. A1.

———. 1997a. "Clinton Names Panel to Draft Health Consumer Bill of Rights." *New York Times,* March 27, p. A29.

———. 1997b. "Panel of Experts Urges Broadening of Patient Rights." *New York Times,* October 23, pp. A1, A24.

———. 1997c. "Clinton Plans New Health Care Fight." *New York Times,* November 24.

———. 1998a. "Health Panel Declines to Endorse Laws for Patients' Bill of Rights." *New York Times,* March 13, p. A1.

———. 1998b. "Bipartisan Support Grows for Managed Care Patients." *New York Times,* May 11, p. A12.

———. 1998c. "White House Adds Broad Protection in Medicare Rules." *New York Times,* June 23, pp. A1, A17.

———. 1998d. "GOP Unveils a Bill to Define Patients' Rights." *New York Times,* June 25, pp. A1, A20.

———. 1998e. "Two Patients' Rights Bills Take Divergent Roads." *New York Times,* July 4, p. A1.

———. 1998f. "Clinton to Punish Insurers Who Deny Health Coverage." *New York Times,* July 7, pp. A1, A13.

———. 1998g. "Hands Tied, Judges Rue Law That Limits H.M.O. Liability." *New York Times,* July 10, pp. A1, A7.

———. 1998h. "H.M.O. Group Backs Controls GOP Rejects." *New York Times,* July 14, pp. A1, A12.

———. 1998i. "Clinton to Expand Medicaid for Some of the Working Poor." *New York Times,* August 4, p. A11.

———. 1998j. "Administration to Set down New Protections for H.M.O. Medicaid Patients." *New York Times,* September 17, p. A25.

———. 1999. "Unlikely Lobbyist Will Lead H.M.O.s into Battle." *New York Times,* July 12, p. A12.

———. 2000. "Ruling Sends Call for Action to Congress and the States." *New York Times,* June 13, p. A20.

Pear, Robert. 2001a. "Patients' Rights: Key Agreement over Liability." *New York Times,* June 28, pp. A1, A21.

———. 2001b. "Bill Establishing Patients' Rights Passes in Senate." *New York Times,* June 30, pp. A1, A10.

Peel, Quentin. 1992a. "Germans Warned of Health Spending Cuts." *Financial Times,* September 12–13, p. 2.

———. 1992b. "Germans Agree on Plan on Health Reforms." *Financial Times,* October 6, p. 2.

———. 1992c. "German Health Bill Raises Temperature." *Financial Times,* November 6, p. 2.

Peet, John. 1991. "Healthy Competition: How to Improve the NHS." In *Policies of Thatcherism: Thoughts from a London Think Tank,* Richard Haas and Oliver Knox, eds. London: Centre for Policy Studies; Lanham: University Press of America.

Peterson, Mark A. 1998. "The Politics of Health Care Policy: Overreaching in an Age of Polarization." In Margaret Weir, ed., *The Social Divide: Political Parties and the Future of Activist Government,* 181–229. Washington, D.C.: Brookings Institution Press; New York: Russell Sage Foundation.

Pfaller, Alfred, Ian Gough, and Göran Therborn, eds. 1991. *Can the Welfare State Compete? A Comparative Study of Five Advanced Capitalist Countries.* Esp. introduction, "The Issue," 1–14. London: Macmillan.

Pierson, Paul. 1993. "When Effect Becomes Cause: Policy Feedback and Political Change." *World Politics* 45:595–628.

———. 1994. *Dismantling the Welfare State? Reagan, Thatcher, and the Politics of Retrenchment.* Cambridge: Cambridge University Press.

———. 1995. *The New Politics of the Welfare State.* ZeS Arbeitspapier Nr. 3/95. Zentrum für Sozialpolitik (Center for Social Policy), University of Bremen.

———. 2001. "Post-industrial Pressures on Mature Welfare States." In Paul Pierson, ed., *The New Politics of the Welfare State,* 80–104. Oxford: Oxford University Press.

Pike, Alan. 1992a. "NHS Managers' Wage Bill Soars." *Financial Times,* September 5–6, p. 4.

———. 1992b. "NHS Reform Is a Tricky Operation." *Financial Times,* December 9, p. 9.

———. 1993. "Rise of 25% in NHS Managers." *Financial Times,* December 11, p. 6.

Pirie, Madsen, and Eamonn Butler. 1988. *Health Management Units: The Operation of an Internal Market within National Health Service.* London: Adam Smith Institute.

Pochet, Philippe, and Bart Vanhercke, eds. 1998. *Social Challenges of Economic and Monetary Union.* Brussels: European Interuniversity Press.

Polanyi, Karl. [1944] 1957. *The Great Transformation: The Political and Economic Origins of Our Time.* Boston: Beacon Press.

Pollitt, Christopher. 1993. "The Politics of Medical Quality: Auditing Doctors in the UK and the USA." Lengthened and updated version of a paper published in *Health Services Management Research* 6 (1). Typescript.

Polzer, Karl, and Patricia A. Butler. 1997. "Employee Health Plan Protection under ERISA." *Health Affairs* 16 (5) (September/October): 93–102.

Pontusson, Jonas, and Peter Swenson. 1996. "Labor Markets, Production Strategies, and Wage Bargaining Institutions: The Swedish Employer Offensive in Comparative Perspective." *Comparative Political Studies* 29 (2): 223–50.

Prentice, Thomson. 1989. "Doctors Threaten to Resign." *Times* (London), October 16, pp. 1, 24.

President's Advisory Commission on Consumer Protection and Quality in the Health Care Industry. 1998. *Quality First: Better Health Care for All Americans.* Final Report. Washington, D.C.: U.S. Government Printing Office.

Purdum, Todd S. 1996. "Clinton Signs Bill to Give Portability in Insurance." *New York Times,* August 22, p. B12.

Rabin, et al. 1995. "How Public Health Care Got So Sick." *Los Angeles Times.* October 29.

Rath, Thomas. 1996. "Krankenhausreform—Chronik einer. Reise ins Ungewisse." In *Krankenhaus-Report '96: Aktuelle Beiträge, Trends und Statistiken.* Michael Arnold and Dieter Paffrath, eds., 25–38. Stuttgart, Jena, Lübeck, Ulm: Gustav Fischer.

Rayner, Bryan. 1992. "The Development of Primary Health Care Policy in the 1980s: A View from the Centre." In *Managing Change: Implementing Primary Health Care Policy,* Patricia Day, ed. Bath: Centre for the Analysis of Social Policy, School of Social Sciences, University of Bath.

Rein, Martin. 1996. "Is America Exceptional? The Role of Occupational Welfare in the

United States and the European Community." In Michael Shalev, ed., *The Privati-zation of Social Policy: Occupational Welfare and the Welfare State in America, Scan-dinavia and Japan,* 27–43, Basingstoke: Macmillan; New York: St. Martin's Press.

Reinhardt, Uwe E. 1990. "West Germany's Health-Care and Health-Insurance System: Combining Universal Access with Cost Control." Report prepared for the United States Bipartisan Commission on Comprehensive Health Care, August 30, 1989. Revised June 25, 1990. Typescript.

———. 1992. "The United States: Breakthroughs and Waste." *Journal of Health Politics, Policy and Law* (winter): 637–66.

———. 1995. "Turning Our Gaze from Bread and Circus Games." *Health Affairs* 14 (1) (spring): 33–36.

Rhodes, Martin. 1995. " 'Subversive Liberalism': Market Integration, Globalization and the European Welfare State." *Journal of European Public Policy* 2 (3): 384–406.

Richardson, Jeremy. 1994. "Doing Less by Doing More: British Government 1979–1993." *West European Politics* 17 (July): 178–97.

Riddell, Peter. 1991. *The Thatcher Era and Its Legacy.* 2d ed. Oxford and Cambridge: Basil Blackwell.

Rimlinger, Gaston V. 1971. *Welfare Policy and Industrialization in Europe, America, and Russia.* New York: John Wiley and Sons.

Robinson, Ray, and Julian Le Grand, eds. 1993. *Evaluating the NHS Reforms.* London: King's Fund Institute.

Rosenberg, Peter. 1986. "The Origin and Development of Compulsory Health Insur-ance in Germany." In Donald W. Light and Alexander Schuller, eds., *Political Val-ues and Health Care: The German Experience,* 105–26. Cambridge and London: MIT Press.

Ruggie, Mary. 1996. *Realignments in the Welfare State: Health Policy in the United States, Britain, and Canada.* New York: Columbia University Press.

Russell, Louise. 1979. *Technology in Hospitals: Medical Advances and Their Diffusion.* Washington, D.C.: Brookings.

Ryll, Andreas. 1990. "Power and Income Distribution among Physicians." Paper pre-sented for the Second World Congress on Health Economics, Zurich, September 10–14.

Safran, William. 1967. *Veto-Group Politics: The Case of Health-Insurance Reform in West Germany.* San Francisco: Chandler.

Sainsbury, Diane, ed. 1994. *Gendering Welfare States.* London, Thousand Oaks, and New Delhi: Sage.

Salamon, Lester. 1992. *America's Nonprofit Sector: A Primer.* New York: Foundation Center.

Saltman, Richard B., and Casten von Otter. 1992. "The Emergence of Planned Mar-kets." In *Planned Markets and Public Competition: Strategic Reform in Northern European Health Systems,* 12–21. Buckingham, U.K., and Philadelphia: Open Uni-versity Press.

Scharpf, Fritz. 1997. "Employment and the Welfare State: A Continental Dilemma." MPIFG Working Paper 97/7. Cologne: Max-Planck-Institut für Gesellschafts-forschung/Max Planck Institute for the Study of Societies. July.

———. 1999. *Governing in Europe: Effective and Democratic.* Oxford: Oxford University Press.

Schick, Allen. 1995. "How a Bill Did Not Become a Law." In Thomas E. Mann and Norman J. Ornstein, eds., *Intensive Care: How Congress Shapes Health Policy*, 227–72. Washington, D.C.: American Enterprise Institute and Brookings Institution.

Schlesinger, Mark J., Bradford H. Gray, and Krista M. Perreira. 1997. "Medical Professionalism under Managed Care: The Pros and Cons of Utilization Review." *Health Affairs* 16 (1): 106–24.

Schlozman, Kay Lehman, and John T. Tierney. 1986. *Organized Interests and American Democracy*. New York: Harper and Row.

Schmitter, Philippe C. 1979. "Still the Century of Corporatism?" In *Trends toward Corporatist Intermediation*, Philippe C. Schmitter and Gerhard Lehmbruch, eds. Beverly Hills: Sage.

———. 1985. "Neo-corporatism and the State." In Wyn Grant, ed., *The Political Economy of Corporatism*. Basingstoke and London: Macmillan.

———. 1989. "Corporatism Is Dead! Long Live Corporatism!" *Government and Opposition* 24 (1): 54–73.

Schneider, Markus. 1991. "Health Care Cost Containment in the Federal Republic of Germany." *Health Care Financing Review* 12 (3): 87–101.

Schneider, Ulrike. 1998. "What Goes around Comes Around: Prospects for German Health Policy after the Change of Government." Typescript. November 11.

Schulenburg, J.-Matthias Graf v. d. 1983. "Report from Germany: Current Conditions and Controversies in the Health Care System." *Journal of Health Politics, Policy and Law* 8 (2): 320–51.

———. 1992. "Germany: Solidarity at a Price." *Journal of Health Politics, Policy and Law* 17 (4): 715–38.

Schulz, Rockwell, and Stephen Harrison. 1986. "Physician Autonomy in the Federal Republic of Germany, Great Britain and the United States." *International Journal of Health Planning and Management* 2:335–55.

Scrutator. [pseud.] 1987. The Week. *British Medical Journal* 295 (December 12): 1575.

———. 1989. BMA Affairs. The Week among the Crafts. *British Medical Journal* 298 (June 24): 1714–20.

Schulz, Erika, Mathias Kifmann, and Friedrich Breyer. 2001. "Risikostruk turausgleich am Scheideweg—Senkung der Wirtschaftlichkeitsanreize für die Krankenkassen sollte vermieden werden." *DIW-Wochenbericht 14/01*.

Shalev, Michael, ed. 1996. *The Privatization of Social Policy? Occupational Welfare and the Welfare State in America, Scandinavia and Japan*. Basingstoke and New York: Macmillan and St. Martin's Press.

Sherman, Jill. 1989a. "BMA Wages War 'to Protect Patients.'" *Times* (London), March 3, p. 3.

———. 1989b. "Outcry as Clarke Imposes Contracts on GPs." *Times* (London), October 17, pp. 1, 2.

———. 1989c. "Clarke Asks Doctors to Avoid Disruption." *Times* (London), October 19, p. 5.

———. 1989d. "GPs End Threat of Sanctions over New Contract." *Times* (London), October 20, pp. 1, 2.

———. 1989e. "16,000 Pounds for Budget-Holding GPs." *Times* (London), December 14, p. 22.

Shonfield, Andrew. 1965. *Modern Capitalism: The Changing Balance of Public and Private Power.* London, Oxford, and New York: Oxford University Press.

Skocpol, Theda. 1996. *Boomerang: Clinton's Health Security Effort and the Turn against Government in U.S. Politics.* New York: Norton.

Smith, Gordon. 1986. *Democracy in Western Germany.* 3d ed. Aldershot, England: Gower.

Smith, Jane. 1993. "GPs in Britain Withdraw Opposition to Fundholding." *British Medical Journal* 306 (June 26): 1713.

Smith, Richard. 1991. "The BMA in Agony." *British Medical Journal* 303 (July 13): 74.

———. 1992. "BMA Says No to Purchaser-Provider Split but Yes to Rationing." *British Medical Journal* 304 (April 4): 862.

———. 1993. "New BMA Chairman Asks Government to Stop and Think." *British Medical Journal* 307 (July 10): 83.

Smith, Sheila, Mark Freeland, Stephen Heffler, David McKusick, and the Health Expenditures Projection Team. 1998. "The Next Ten Years of Health Spending: What Does the Future Hold?" *Health Affairs* 17 (5): 128–40.

Smith, Steven Rathgeb, and Michael Lipsky. 1993. *Nonprofits for Hire: The Welfare State in the Age of Contracting.* Cambridge and London: Harvard University Press.

Speller, S. R. 1948. *The National Health Service Act, 1946.* Annotated. London: H. K. Lewis.

Der Spiegel. 1992a. "Kampf gegen die Haie." June 8, pp. 112–19.

———. 1992b. "Ausgebufft, mit allen Wassern gewaschen." October 5, pp. 158–61.

———. 1993a. "Ärzte haben überreagiert." February 1, pp. 203–6.

———. 1993b. "Sparen mit dem Fallbeil?" February 1, pp. 200–203.

———. 1993c. "Ärzte im Würgegriff." September 13, pp. 54–72.

———. 1993d. "Fürchtet sich nicht." December 27, pp. 180–81.

———. 1993e. "Mal ausgepfiffen, dann wieder Lichtgestalt." December 27, pp. 181–83.

Srinivasan, Srija, Larry Levitt, and Janet Lundy. 1998. "Wall Street's Love Affair with Health Care." *Health Affairs* 17 (4): 126–31.

Starr, Paul. 1982. *The Social Transformation of American Medicine.* New York: Basic Books.

———. 1994. *The Logic of Health Care Reform: Why and How the President's Plan Will Work.* New York: Penguin/Whittle Books.

Steinmo, Sven, Kathleen Thelen, and Frank Longstreth, eds. 1992. *Structuring Politics: Historical Institutionalism in Comparative Analysis.* Cambridge: Cambridge University Press.

Steinmo, Sven, and Jon Watts. 1995. "It's the Institutions, Stupid! Why Comprehensive National Health Insurance Always Fails in America." *Journal of Health Politics, Policy and Law* 20 (2): 329–72.

Stephens, John D. 1979. *The Transition from Capitalism to Socialism.* London: Macmillan.

———. 1996. "The Scandinavian Welfare States: Achievements, Crisis, and Prospects." In Gøsta Esping-Andersen, ed., *Welfare States in Transition,* 32–65. London, Thousand Oaks, and New Delhi: Sage.

Stephens, John D., Evelyne Huber, and Leonard Ray. 1999. "The Welfare State in Hard Times." In Herbert Kitschelt, Peter Lange, Gary Marks, and John D. Stephens, eds.,

Continuity and Change in Contemporary Capitalism, 164–93. Cambridge: Cambridge University Press.

Stevens, Beth. 1988. "Blurring the Boundaries: How the Federal Government Has Influenced Welfare Benefits in the Private Sector." In Margaret Weir, Ann Shola Orloff, and Theda Skocpol, eds., *The Politics of Social Policy in the United States,* 123–48. Princeton: Princeton University Press.

Stolberg, Sheryl Gay. 1998. "As Doctors Trade Shingle for Marquee, Cries of Woe." *New York Times,* August 3, p. A14.

Stone, Deborah A. 1980. *The Limits of Professional Power: National Health Care in the Federal Republic of Germany.* Chicago: University of Chicago Press.

———. 1993. "The Struggle for the Soul of Health Insurance." *Journal of Health Politics, Policy and Law* 18 (2) (summer): 287–317.

———. 1995. "The Durability of Social Capital." *Journal of Health Politics, Policy and Law* 20 (3) (fall): 689–94.

Streeck, Wolfgang. 1997. "German Capitalism: Does It Exist? Can It Survive?" In Colin Crouch and Wolfgang Streeck, eds., *Political Economy of Modern Capitalism: Mapping Convergence and Diversity.* London, Thousand Oaks, and New Delhi: Sage.

Streeck, Wolfgang, and Philippe C. Schmitter. 1985. "Community, Market, State—and Associations? The Prospective Contribution of Interest Governance to Social Order." *European Sociological Review* 1 (2): 119–38.

———. 1991. "From National Corporatism to Transnational Pluralism: Organized Interests in the Single European Market." *Politics and Society* 19 (2): 33–164.

Die Tageszeitung. 1992. "Ärztelobby im Boot der Pharmakonzerne." September 7.

Taylor-Gooby, Peter. 1991. "Social Cohesion and Support for Welfare Citizenship." Chap. 5 in *Social Change, Social Welfare and Social Science,* 106–36. Toronto and Buffalo: University of Toronto Press.

Teeling-Smith, George. 1985. "Should GPs Hold the Purse Strings?" *Health and Social Service Journal* 95 (October 24): 1338.

Thatcher, Margaret. 1993. *The Downing Street Years.* New York: HarperCollins.

Thelen, Kathleen A. 1991. *Union of Parts: Labor Politics in Postwar Germany.* Ithaca and London: Cornell University Press.

Lord Thomas of Swynnerton. 1991. "Introduction." In *Policies of Thatcherism: Thoughts from a London Think Tank,* Richard Haas and Oliver Knox, eds. London and Lanham: Centre for Policy Studies and University Press of America.

Thorpe, Kenneth E. 1997. "Incremental Approaches to Covering Uninsured Children: Design and Policy Issues." *Health Affairs* 16 (4): 64–78.

Timmins, Nicholas. 1995. *The Five Giants: A Biography of the Welfare State.* London: HarperCollins.

Timmins, Nicholas, Patricia Wynn Davies, and Stephen Goodwin. 1992. "Broadcast Row Rages On." *Independent* (London), March 27, p. 1.

Timmins, Nicholas, and Judy Jones. 1991. "Waldegrave Stands Firm on NHS Changes." *Independent* (London), October 17, p. 1.

Titmuss, Richard M. 1974. *Social Policy: An Introduction.* Brian Abel-Smith and Kay Titmuss, eds. New York: Pantheon Books (George Allen and Unwin).

———. 1987a. "Developing Social Policy in Conditions of Rapid Change: The Role of Social Welfare." In Brian Abel-Smith and Kay Titmuss, eds., *The Philosophy of*

Welfare: Selected Writings of Richard M. Titmuss, 254–68. London: George Allen and Unwin.

———. 1987b. "The Role of Redistribution in Social Policy." In Brian Abel-Smith and Kay Titmuss, eds., *The Philosophy of Welfare: Selected Writings of Richard M. Titmuss,* 207–19. London: George Allen and Unwin.

Tolliday, Heather. 1978. "Clinical Autonomy." In *Health Services: Their Nature and Organization and the Role of Patients, Doctors, and the Health Professions,* ed. Elliot Jacques. London: Heinemann.

Toner, Robin. 1994. "Autopsy on Health Care." *New York Times,* September 27, pp. A1ff.

Tuohy, Carolyn Hughes. 1999. *Accidental Logics: The Dynamics of Change in the Health Care Arena in the United States, Britain, and Canada.* Oxford and New York: Oxford University Press.

U.S. Department of Labor. Pension and Welfare Benefits Administration. n.d. *Questions and Answers: Recent Changes in Health Care Law.* Washington, D.C. Reproduced by the Library of Congress, Congressional Research Service. http://gatekeeper.dol .gov/dol/pwba/public/pubs/q&aguide.htm. (Downloaded July 7, 1997.)

Van de Ven, Wynand P. M. M., and Frederik T. Schut. 1995. "The Dutch Experience with Internal Markets." In *Health Care Reform through Internal Markets: Experience and Proposals,* 95–117. Montreal: The Institute for Research on Public Policy; Washington, D.C.: Brookings Institution.

Van Kersbergen, Kees. 1995. *Social Capitalism: A Study of Christian Democracy and the Welfare State.* London and New York: Routledge.

Visser, Jelle, and Anton Hemerijck. 1997. *'A Dutch Miracle': Job Growth, Welfare Reform and Corporatism in the Netherlands.* Amsterdam: Amsterdam University Press.

Vogel, David. 1978. "Why Businessmen Distrust Their State: The Political Consciousness of American Corporate Executives." *British Journal of Political Science* 8 (January): 45–78.

Vogel, Steven. 1996. *Freer Markets, More Rules.* Ithaca and London: Cornell University Press.

Waitzkin, Howard, and Jennifer Fishman. "Inside the System: The Patient-Physician Relationship in the Era of Managed Care." In John D. Wilkerson, Kelly J. Devers, and Ruth S. Given, eds., *Competitive Managed Care,* 136–62. San Francisco: Jossey-Bass.

Warden, John. 1989a. "NHS Review." *British Medical Journal* 298 (4 February): 275.

———. 1989b. Letter from Westminster. "Clarke's Radical Caution." *British Medical Journal* 298 (February 11): 351–52.

———. 1989c. Letter from Westminster. "Mr. Clarke Changes Tactics." *British Medical Journal* 299 (July 22): 223.

———. 1992a. Letter from Westminster. "The War of Jennifer's Ear." *British Medical Journal* 304 (April 4): 866.

———. 1992b. Letter from Westminster. "From Bevan to Bottomley." *British Medical Journal* 304 (April 18): 1004.

———. 1992c. Letter from Westminster. "New Ministers." *British Medical Journal* 304 (May 2): 1136.

Weaver, R. Kent. 1988. *Automatic Government: The Politics of Indexation.* Washington, D.C.: Brookings Institution.

———. 1998. "Ending Welfare as We Know It." In Margaret Weir, ed., *The Social Divide: Political Parties and the Future of Activist Government*, 361–416. Washington, D.C.: Brookings Institution Press; New York: Russell Sage Foundation.

Webber, Douglas. 1989. "Zur Geschichte der Gesundheitsreformen in Deutschland—II. Teil: Norbert Blüms Gesundheitsreform und die Lobby." *Leviathan* 2:262–300.

———. 1991. "Health Policy and the Christian-Liberal Coalition in West Germany: The Conflicts over the Health Insurance Reform, 1987–8." In *Comparative Health Policy and the New Right: From Rhetoric to Reality*, Christa Altenstetter and Stuart C. Haywood, eds. Basingstoke and London: Macmillan.

———. 1992a. "Die Kassenärztlichen Vereinigungen zwischen Mitgliederinteressen und Gemeinwohl." In *Verbände zwischen Mitgliederinteressen und Gemeinwohl*, Renate Mayntz, ed.. Gütersloh: Verlag Bertelsmann Stiftung.

———. 1992b. "Kohl's Wendepolitik after a Decade." *German Politics* 1 (2): 149–80.

Webster, Philip. 1993. "Mawhinney Rejects BMA Criticism of Health Reforms." *Times* (London) July 5, p. 7.

Weinstein, Michael. 1998. "Getting Litigious with H.M.O.s." *New York Times*, July 19, sect. 4, p. 5.

Weir, Margaret. 1998. "Political Parties and Social Policymaking." In Margaret Weir, ed., *The Social Divide: Political Parties and the Future of Activist Government*, 1–45. Washington, D.C.: Brookings Institution Press; New York: Russell Sage Foundation.

Weir, Margaret, Ann Shola Orloff, and Theda Skocpol. 1988. "Introduction: Understanding American Social Politics." In Margaret Weir, Ann Shola Orloff, and Theda Skocpol, eds., *The Politics of Social Policy in the United States*, 3–27. Princeton: Princeton University Press.

Weir, Margaret, and Theda Skocpol. 1985. "State Structures and the Possibilities for 'Keynesian' Responses to the Great Depression in Sweden, Britain, and the United States." In Peter B. Evans, Dietrich Rueschemeyer, and Theda Skocpol, eds., *Bringing the State Back In*, 107–63. Cambridge: Cambridge University Press.

Weisbrod, Burton A. 1985. "America's Health Care Dilemma." *Challenge* 28 (4): 30–34.

Wennberg, John E. 1984. "Dealing with Medical Practice Variations: A Proposal for Action." *Health Affairs* (summer): 6–32.

WHDPC (White House Domestic Policy Council). 1993. *The President's Health Security Plan: The Clinton Blueprint*. New York: Times Books.

White, Joseph. 1995. *Medical Savings Accounts: Fact versus Fiction*. Brookings Occasional Paper. Washington, D.C.: Brookings Institution.

White, Michael. 1992. "Tory 'Big Lie' Charge Falters." *Guardian* (London; international ed.), March 26, p. 1.

White, Stuart. 1998. "Interpreting the 'Third Way': Not One Road, but Many." *Renewal* 6 (2): 17–30.

Whitehead, Margaret. 1993. "Is It Fair? Evaluating the Equity Implications of the NHS Reforms." In Ray Robinson and Julian Le Grand, eds., *Evaluating the NHS Reforms*, 208–42. London: King's Fund Institute.

Wilensky, Harold. 1975. *The Welfare State and Equality*. Berkeley: University of California Press.

Wilkerson, John D. 1997. "Messing with Medicare: Markets and Politics in the 104th

Congress." In John D. Wilkerson, Kelly J. Devers, and Ruth S. Given, eds., *Competitive Managed Care*, 297–321. San Francisco: Jossey-Bass.

Wilkerson, John D., Kelly J. Devers, and Ruth S. Given. 1997a. "The Emerging Competitive Managed Care Marketplace." In *Competitive Managed Care*, 3–29. San Francisco: Jossey-Bass.

———, eds. 1997b. *Competitive Managed Care: The Emerging Health Care System*. San Francisco: Jossey-Bass.

Willetts, David, and Michael Goldsmith. 1988. *A Mixed Economy for Health Care: More Spending, Same Taxes*. London: Centre for Policy Studies, March.

Wilsford, David. 1991. *Doctors and the State: The Politics of Health Care in France and the United States*. Durham and London: Duke University Press.

Wilson, Graham K. 1982. "Why Is There No Corporatism in the United States?" In Gerhard Lehmbruch and Philippe C. Schmitter, eds., *Patterns of Corporatist Policy-Making*, 219–36. London and Beverly Hills: Sage.

———. 1985. *Business and Politics: A Comparative Introduction*. Chatham, N.J.: Chatham House.

———. 1990. "No More Mandarins? Recasting the Culture of Whitehall in a Different Image." Paper for the Annual Convention of the American Political Science Association, San Francisco.

———. 1992. "The View from Downing Street: Presidents and Prime Ministers Revisited." Paper for the Annual Convention of the American Political Science Association, Chicago, September 3–6.

———. n.d. "And with One Bound? Reagan, Thatcher and the Governance of the Right." Typescript.

Witte, John F. 2000. *The Market Approach to Education: An Analysis of America's First Voucher Program*. Princeton: Princeton University Press.

Wolinsky, Frederic D. 1988. The Professional Dominance Perspective, Revisited." *Milbank Quarterly* 66 (Supplement 2): 33–47.

Yates, John. 1987. *Why Are We Waiting? An Analysis of Hospital Waiting Lists*. Oxford: Oxford University Press.

Yellin, Emily. 1999. "Some Doctors See Relief in Plan for A.M.A. Union." *New York Times,* June 25, p. A18.

Zelman, Walter A., and Robert A. Berenson. 1998. *The Managed Care Blues and How to Cure Them*. Washington, D.C.: Georgetown University Press.

Ziller, Peter. 1991a. "Den Krankenkassen droht neues Milliardendefizit." *Frankfurter Rundschau,* October 21, pp. 1, 2.

———. 1991b. "Drastische Kürzungen bei Kassen verlangt." *Frankfurter Rundschau,* November 28, pp. 1, 2.

———. 1992. "Ersatzkassen fordern Vollbremsung." *Frankfurter Rundschau,* May 26, p. 1.

Zysman, John. 1983. *Governments, Markets, and Growth: Financial Systems and the Politics of Industrial Change*. Ithaca and London: Cornell University Press.

Index

Aaron, Henry J., 235n. 8, 237n. 4
Adam Smith Institute (ASI), 50, 51, 52, 234n. 16, 239n. 15
AFL-CIO, 254n. 11
   See also *Inland Steel* case; labor unions (U.S.)
Aid to Families with Dependent Children (AFDC), 191
American Association of Health Plans (AAHP), 257n. 43
American Association of Labor Legislation (AALL), 149–50
American Association of Retired Persons (AARP), 175, 254n. 11
American Federation of Labor (AFL), 150
   See also AFL-CIO; *Inland Steel* case; labor unions (U.S.)
American Medical Association (AMA)
   and Clinton plan, 175–76, 254n. 16
   contrast to BMA, 154, 201, 251n. 5
   contrast to KVs, 201
   and Medicare, 251n. 6
   and national health insurance, 150–51, 153, 156, 163, 169
   organizational characteristics, 154–57, 254n. 15
   political influence, 153–54, 175
   and professional autonomy, 156–57
   relations with other medical groups, 155–56
   responses to managed care, 188–89, 252n. 7
   role in professional model of governance, 15, 185, 201
   and unionization, 188–89, 258n. 50
Anderson, Odin W., 234n. 14

antitrust law (U.S.), and doctors, 155, 168, 188–89, 209
Arrow, Kenneth J., 260n. 12
associationalism. *See* corporatism
Associations of Sickness Fund Physicians (Kassenärztliche Vereinigungen).
   See KVs
Attlee, Clement, 32, 33–34, 237n. 5
autonomy, clinical. *See* autonomy, professional
   See also economic monitoring (Germany); implicit concordat; medical audit (Britain); professional model of governance; solo practitioner, autonomy of (U.S.); utilization review
autonomy, medical. *See* autonomy, professional
autonomy, professional, 3
   components of, 12–15, 18
   in corporatism, 207–8, 210
   defined, 12–13, 234nn. 11, 12
   and governance of doctors, 14–15, 200–204, 204–6
   levels of, 12–13
   See also corporatism; governance; guidelines, clinical
autonomy, professional (Britain)
   Blair reforms, 82, 84
   and national health insurance, 234n. 2
   in NHS, 32–34, 38
   and Thatcher and Major reforms, 55–57, 67–72
   See also BMA; implicit concordat
autonomy, professional (Germany), 92–93
   and economic monitoring, 95–96

293